CONTENTS

P9-AFR-406

KEY

▬	**Sights described**
★★★	**Highly recommended**
★★	**Recommended**
★	**Interesting**
	See if possible
▒	**Other landmarks**

NATIONAL GALLERY

ROYAL HOSPITAL

REGENT STREET

ST. GEORGE'S BLOOMSBURY

ROYAL ACADEMY OF MUSIC

Conventional signs

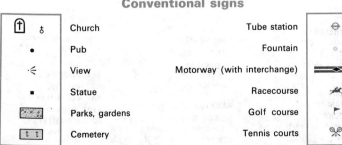

✝ ⚲	Church	Tube station	⊖
•	Pub	Fountain	⊙
⋖	View	Motorway (with interchange)	▬◆▬
▪	Statue	Racecourse	🐎
▦	Parks, gardens	Golf course	⚑
⌇ ⌇	Cemetery	Tennis courts	⚔

The maps and town plans in this guide are based upon the Ordnance Survey of Great Britain with the permission of the Controller of Her Majesty's Stationery Office. Crown Copyright reserved.

SIGHTS AND MAPS IN THE GUIDE

PRACTICAL INFORMATION

SIGHTSEEING

London Transport run a circular sightseeing tour of London which, if it is your first visit or you are not familiar with the capital, is an excellent way to get your bearings and see at least the exterior of famous buildings to which you may then return at your leisure. Tours, which take 2 hours and run every hour from 10am, start from Grosvenor Gardens, Victoria, Piccadilly Circus and Marble Arch (Park Lane) : fare £1.15.

Pendants and corollaries to assorted sights visited on your own

When visiting:

- **St Paul's,** don't forget to walk round the precinct and spot the steeples of nearby City Churches. Enquire from the City of London Information Centre, St Paul's Churchyard, Tel. 01-606 3030, extensions 236, 237, if there are any special events taking place.
- The **Guildhall,** don't forget the Clock Museum.
- The Tower, take time also to visit (i) All Hallows to see the model ships, the Grinling Gibbons font cover, the brasses (on request) ; (ii) St Olave's Church. Relax afterwards in St Katharine Dock.
- **Greenwich,** in addition to the Maritime Museum (including paintings) and RN College (chapel and refectory), allow time for the Queen's House, Flamsteed House and the Old Observatory, (even if not astronomically minded!) ; continue to the Ranger's (or Chesterfield) House and allow time to explore Blackheath and/or Greenwich town and riverside.
- **Southwark Cathedral,** visit also Guy's Hospital and St Thomas's Operating Theatre, then the pubs down Borough High St and Trinity Church Sq or Clink St and Bankside.
- **Westminster Abbey,** don't forget to look into Dean's Yard and St Margaret's.
- The **Silver Vaults,** allow time to see Lincoln's Inn and at least look into the Public Record Office.
- **Westminster Cathedral,** cross the road and explore Queen Anne's Gate.
- The **City** don't forget Dr Johnson's House and the Temple Church, the hall and gardens.
- The **Nash Terraces,** go afterwards to sit in Queen Mary's Garden.
- **Sadler's Wells Theatre** (even after dark), make sure you see Myddelton Sq.
- The **British Museum,** approach by different routes, in time to take in Bedford and all the surrounding squares and St George's Church.

Children's half-term outing or a day in town

- The Tower; St Katharine Dock; the *Belfast.*
- Museum of London (not Mondays) ; St Paul's dome (view). At Christmas go first to Leadenhall Market to see the poultry.
- Boat down river to Greenwich – Maritime Museum; Old Observatory; the Park.
- Mme Tussaud's; the Science and/or Natural History and/or Geological Museum; Battersea Park or the Children's Zoo or St James's Park – pelicans and wildfowl on the lake.
- Changing the guard at Buckingham Palace or mounting the guard at Horse Guards Parade; Westminster Abbey (older children) or Palace of Westminster (tour – older children) ; Westminster Cathedral campanile (view).
- British Museum (Roman Galleries and/or coins and/or stamps and/or Egyptian mummies) ; open air theatre performance in Regent's Park.
- Brass rubbing (St James's Piccadilly) ; up the Burlington Arcade; Museum of Mankind; Trafalgar Square to see Nelson, the pigeons, Standard Measures, King Charles and/or see the Christmas Tree and sing carols.
- Mermaid Theatre: science performances – at Christmas: pantomime or children's play ; decorations and shop windows in Oxford St; Bethnal Green Museum – dolls, dolls' houses, costume or Bear Gardens Museum, Southwark and St Thomas's Operating Theatre.
- The Zoo (picnic areas).
- RAF Museum, Hendon.
- Imperial War Museum.
- National Army Museum and Chelsea Hospital.
- Royal Artillery Museum, Woolwich and Woolwich ferry.
- The National, National Portrait, Tate Galleries – special holiday arrangements for children; ICA special films.
  A London Calendar on p 30 lists a selection of annual attractions.

Off the cuff suggestions for simple outings at different seasons

A wet **winter's day**: the British Museum – the Nereid Monument against its blue sky! (Greek wing), the rooms of treasure and riches or the manuscripts and illuminations (British Library). The National Portrait Gallery.

An early **spring day**: crocuses in Hyde Park (Marble Arch and Knightsbridge) ; daffodils in Green Park, Hyde Park (Knightsbridge), Hampton Court, Kew.

Mid and **late spring**: bluebells at Kew; rhododendrons and azaleas in Battersea Park, at Kenwood, Kew, in the Woodland Garden, Bushy Park, and Isabella Plantation, Richmond Park; chestnut avenue, Bushy Park; cherry blossom in Battersea Park and at Kew.

A **summer's day**: roses in Queen Mary's Garden, Regent's Park, at Kew and Hampton Court; the houses to London's west – Osterley, Ham House, Syon Park, Strawberry Hill, Marble Hill, Orleans House (and Montpelier Row).

An **autumn day**: Kensington Palace followed by a walk to see the autumn tints in the park.

A grey autumn or winter's day: the Tower.

For page references (with visiting hours) turn to final index.

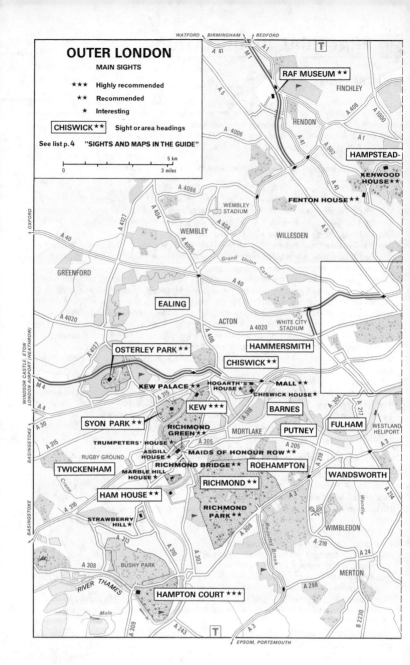

OUTER LONDON

MAIN SIGHTS

★★★ Highly recommended

★★ Recommended

★ Interesting

CHISWICK ★★ Sight or area headings

See list p. 4 "SIGHTS AND MAPS IN THE GUIDE"

0   5 km
0   3 miles

FACILITIES

Information. – To obtain details on **special events**:

– look in the press (daily and weekly) and the weekly *What's On*
– visit or phone – London Tourist Board, 26 Grosvenor Gardens SW1, Tel. 01-730 0791
     British Tourist Authority, 64 St James's St SW1, Tel. 01-629 9191
     City of London Information Centre, St Paul's Churchyard, EC4
     Tel. 01-606 3030, extensions 236, 237
– phone the venue or organiser
– enquire at the local public library or town hall for a local event.

Exhibitions, theatrical performances, concerts: the press, the organiser or venue (including commercial galleries), apply to a ticket agency.

Accommodation. – See *Michelin Greater London,* hotels and restaurants Red Guide; published annually and available from bookshops (an excerpt from the *Michelin Great Britain and Ireland* annual Red Guide).

     For the stranded there are commercial hotel accommodation agencies at Heathrow and Gatwick and at Victoria Station where there is also a London Tourist Board office.

Youth Hostels: there are four hostels in central London:

– Holland House, Holland Park, Kensington W8
– 84 Highgate West Hill, N6
– 38 Bolton Gardens, Old Brompton Rd, SW5
– 36 Carter Lane, St Paul's, EC4.

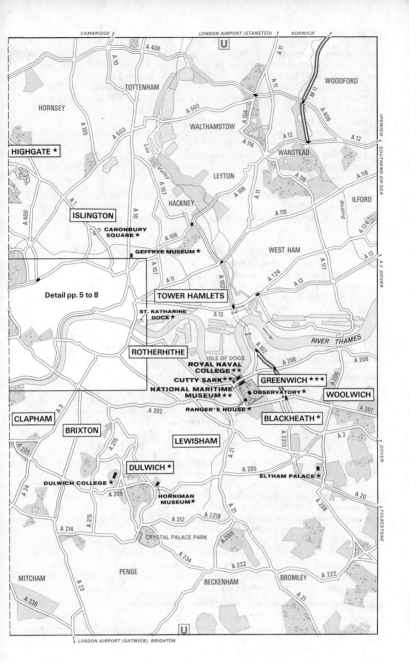

The Disabled. – Facilities are gradually being provided for those in wheelchairs (toilets, lifts in museums, theatres and public buildings). For full details see two booklets published by Ward Lock and Access for the Disabled both entitled *London for the Disabled.*

Information by telephone. – Teletourist – 01-246 8041 (a selection of the main events of the day in and around London).
– Children's London – 01-246 8007.
– The Weather – 01-246 8091.
– Motoring Information – 01-246 8021 (within a radius of 50 miles).

Lost property. – In the street – enquire at the local police station,
– on trains – enquire at the local station,
– in taxis – The Police Station, 15 Penton St N1 (01-278 1744),
– on London Transport – report within hours at the nearest underground station or bus garage or after 2 or 3 days call or write (with full details of article and journey) at 200 Baker St, NW1 5 RZ. Monday to Friday 10 am to 6 pm (no phone calls).

The Travellers' Friends
Great Britain and Ireland:

Michelin Red Guide for hotels and restaurants.
Michelin Map 986, 14 miles to 1 inch.

TRANSPORT

Bus and Underground. – London Transport Offices which supply information and sell the special tickets listed below are situated in underground stations at: Victoria, St James's Park, King's Cross, Oxford Circus, Piccadilly Circus, Euston.

Enquiries by phone: 01-222 1234 (line very crowded in summer).

There are short term bus and underground passes which, if you concentrate your travelling in the capital into a few days, are highly advantageous:

Buses – **Red Rovers:** unlimited travel on the red buses for the day.

Underground – **Central Tube Rover:** travel for one day on the tube anywhere in central London.

Buses and Underground – **Go as you Please Tickets** for 4 or 7 days travel (except to the furthest limits of the underground) on either or both underground and bus services (discount on the Round London Sightseeing Tour p 13).

Taxis. – Available principally at railway termini, airports and on a few ranks (see Taxi-cabs in phone directory). Taxis are not obliged to go beyond the limits of the Metropolitan Police District (an area broadly corresponding but slightly less extensive than Greater London) and within that area, beyond 6 miles from where the customer has picked up the cab.

Any journey outside the MPD is subject to negotiation. Special rates obtain after midnight, at weekends on public holidays – always find out before hiring. Although when you are in a hurry, it's raining or you need one urgently, it doesn't seem as if any exist, there are, in fact, just under 11 500 licensed cabs in the capital. If you are entertaining a schoolboy from abroad, get a driver to show off the lock on his cab by turning round within the road width!

Mini-cabs – see telephone directories.

Car parks. – There are street meters, daytime and 24 hour car parks *(see Michelin Greater London annual Red Guide)*. Arrangements providing additional space for special occasions are announced by the police in the press; information also from LTB.

Steamers, Thames Passenger Services. – Daily throughout the year from Westminster to Charing Cross, Tower Bridge and Greenwich and daily throughout the summer upstream from Westminster to Battersea, Putney, Kew, Richmond and Hampton Ct.

Information from the piers: Westminster downstream 01-930 4097

Westminster upstream	01-930 2074
Charing Cross	01-839 5320
Tower	01-709 9855

Railway terminals. – The six terminals are interconnected by the underground and in some cases by special inter-station single decker buses.

The stations and their relevant destinations and telephone numbers *(for timetable information* not *seat reservations)* are:

Liverpool St	East Anglia, Essex	01-283 7171
King's Cross	East and northeast England; Scotland via the east coast	01-837 3355
Euston	East and west Midlands; northeast England; Scotland via the west coast; north Wales	01-387 7070
Paddington	South Midlands, west of England; south Wales	01-262 6767
Victoria	Southern England	01-928 5100
Waterloo	Southern England	01-928 5100

Airports. – London Airport, Heathrow, Middlesex.

Access by car by M4 or Great West Rd (A4; car parks at airport); by underground (Piccadilly Line) to Hounslow West and express (A1) bus; by airport coach (every 15 minutes approximately – time 45-55 minutes) from West London Terminal, Cromwell Rd; and British Airways, Buckingham Palace Rd.

Reservations, travel information:

UK, Republic of Ireland, Channel Islands, Europe, N. Africa, Israel... 01-370 5411.
Intercontinental 01-828 9711.

Flight information, arrivals, departures:

UK, Republic of Ireland, Channel Islands, Europe, N. Africa, Israel... 01-759 2477.
Intercontinental 01-759 2525.

Enquiries and purchase and collection of tickets from British Airways, Dorland Hall, Lower Regent St, British Airways sales shops and accredited travel agents.

Passenger Immunisation Centres: British Airways, Terminal, Buckingham Palace Rd, Victoria, very crowded in summer, phone in advance: 01-834 2323, also at Heathrow (01-759 5511).

London Airport, Gatwick, Crawley, W Sussex.

Access by car by A23 (car parks) and by train from Victoria.

Flight enquiries: Crawley 02-9331 299.

Air Terminals:

British Caledonian-Victoria Station	01-834 9411
Reservations (193 Piccadilly)	01-437 3701
TWA, 380 Kensington High St	01-602 0141
Reservations (200 Piccadilly)	01-636 4090
Pan Am, Semley Place, Buckingham Palace Rd	01-730 4742
Reservations (193 Piccadilly)	01-734 7292

NB: *The stations, London Transport, the airports are equipped with automatic in-coming storage telephone call systems – hang on, therefore, and your turn will come!*

ENTERTAINMENT

Theatres, Concerts. – For programmes and times of performances, see Sunday, daily and evening papers and *What's On*. Notices include phone nos. *See map below for situation.*

Cinemas: for programmes and times see evening and other papers and *What's On*. Notices include phone nos and addresses.

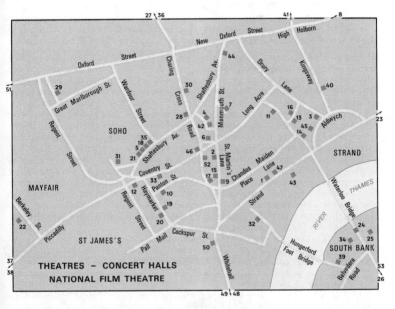

THEATRES – CONCERT HALLS
NATIONAL FILM THEATRE

Shopping. – Magnitude of turnover and competition serve the central London shopper in providing a fantastic number of small specialist shops where he or she may hunt for the exotic, the particular, the luxurious version of an everyday article, handmade still by craftsmen. At the other extreme there are big multiple stores with full ranges of a diversity of branded goods from whitewood furniture to raincoats, from tin mugs to fine glass and china and also with their own lines, made up in their own workrooms or imported especially from abroad, whether couture clothes or carved rose quartz figurines.

The big stores, with prices as disparate as their situations, are located along Oxford St, in Regent St, at Piccadilly Circus, in Bond St, Sloane Sq and King's Rd and at Knightsbridge, with furniture also at the north end of Tottenham Ct Rd.

The small shops traditionally and still radiate from Bond St. They extend north across Oxford St into Wigmore St and Marylebone High St (St Christopher's Place includes within its 50 yds, the Button Queen, a military memorabilia shop and an orientalist), east to Regent St, particularly along Brook (Halcyon Days) and Maddox Sts, and west to Park Lane across the parallel Davies, Duke, Audley and Park Sts, intersected by Mount St. Still in the same quarter are South Molton St, a pedestrian precinct with summer pavement cafés, and Burlington Arcade with glittering windows beneath rose coloured arches.

In St James's, silk shirts, bespoke hats and shoes, tobacconists, gunsmiths, are as numerous as the antique furniture and fine art shops; in Belgravia (Motcomb St and Halkin Arcade) the emphasis is more on antiques. Beyond are the outer groups, particularly of antique shops, in Hampstead, Kensington (Church St), the west end of King's Rd, in Camden Passage. Every group, whether in one of the outer villages or at the centre, is widely assorted so that antique dealers neighbour silver shops, porcelain shops, print and secondhand bookshops and the would-be purchaser may have far to travel. In other cases the shops will be within walking distance as are the four major antiquarian booksellers, Quaritch (Lower John St), Francis Edwards (Marylebone High St), Sotheran (Sackville St) and Maggs (Berkeley Sq). There is probably a shop for everything, whether one requires cooking utensils, David Mellor (Sloane Sq), Divertimenti (Marylebone Lane), Christmas presents (General Trading Co, Sloane St) an umbrella (from that perfect example of Victorian shop design, James Smith & Sons, New Oxford St), Christmas cards (at the museums and HMSO, 49 High Holborn, where there are also posters, maps and monographs), books and booklets on special areas and aspects of London (GLC bookshop, 54 Charing Cross Rd and in County Hall), a special pasta (Parmigiani, Frith St), brass fittings (Beardmore, Percy St)...

GROWTH OF THE CAPITAL

A capital grows in three ways: visibly in the increase in its population and in its physical expanse and cumulatively through the continuous activities of its inhabitants which make it the historical centre of the country.

Population. – There may have been as many as 25 – 30 000 souls by the time the king, courts of law and parliament were established at Westminster, the City a rich port and 12-13C London had become the **capital** of the kingdom.

It is from Tudor times that numbers begin to grow apace: in 1558, at the death of Mary Tudor, the London population was 100 000; at the death of Elizabeth in 1603, 200 000 out of a total for England and Wales of approximately 4 million. (The three other biggest towns of the period, York, capital of the north, Norwich, centre of the wool trade and Bristol, a flourishing mercantile and inland port, numbered 20 000 each.)

In 1700 there were 670 000 people living in London; in 1801 the first census showed there to be 1 100 000 out of a population of just under 9 million in England and Wales together. By the year of the Great Exhibition it was 2 700 000 and in the next 50 years it more than doubled to 6 600 000 (1901) due to the influx from the provinces to industry and commerce in the capital and to improved housing.

In 1939 London's population reached its maximum with 8 610 000: by 1975 it had dropped to 7 million out of a population in England and Wales of just under 50 million.

Physical expanse. – The City, as an important bridgehead and port, was encircled by a defence wall by the Romans after Boadicea's attack in 61 AD; in the dark ages assaults were chiefly by invaders sailing upriver and the wall fell into decay only to be rebuilt largely on the same base in the Middle Ages with an extension to the west (north and east sections visible at London Wall and by the Tower). In 1643, during the Civil War, earthworks were thrown up ringing the capital from Wapping to Vauxhall by way of Spitalfields, St Giles-in-the-Fields and Westminster and south of the river, circling Lambeth and Southwark to reach Rotherhithe. Never at any time did any of these barriers stop London extending: in 1598 Stow was describing "the suburbs without the walls".

Queen Elizabeth passed the first of many acts prohibiting the erection of any new houses within 3 miles of the City gates. The reason for the royal alarm was twofold: the newcomers, country people come to work in the City and docks, were not rich and it was feared that they might easily be led into rebellion and secondly it was appreciated that water supplies were inadequate (not to mention means of sewerage disposal and burial grounds). Elizabeth's and later parliamentary ordinances, however, were impracticable, were ignored and London continued to spread.

Industrial development, the growth of public transport, meant that by this century the centre was heavily fringed by long Victorian streets and an outer circle of suburbs. Only in 1930s was a visionary solution proposed and enacted (1938): a **Green Belt**, in itself 840 sq miles in area, was designated to run through the home counties encircling London at a radius of between 20 and 30 miles.

Although the belt does not completely contain the metropolitan sprawl, although some sections have disappeared completely, although exceptional buildings have been erected on it in some places, yet as no other measure has it arrested the expanse.

The historical centre. – In the second half of 20C the Port of London shifted down river; for the first time in 2 000 years cargo ships are no longer a common sight in the Pool, moored in midstream or tied up along the banks or dock quays built in 19C.

Ships began to sail out of the estuary in 5C BC, to arrive and drop anchor, when London, a Celtic derived name, was a riparian settlement congregated at the river's first ford, a place where the gravel subsoil proved suitable on which to build a bridge. They came in greater numbers under the Romans who transformed the village into a major town, erecting in it some of their largest buildings north of the Alps and traversing the river with a permanent stone bridge. Most important of all the Romans made it the hub of their road system, the place through which legionaries and merchandise alike, landed in the auxiliary Kentish and south coast ports as well as in London itself, passed on the way to Verulamium (St Albans), the capital or Camulodonum (Colchester), the later capital, and to the cities and settlements of the north.

In the Dark Ages, the time of Germanic and Danish invasions, of siege and fire, of **Alfred** briefly uniting the kingdom and constituting London a major city, of the unsuccessful attempt to establish the metropolitan see in London, of no mention for scores of pages in the *Anglo-Saxon Chronicle* – in the face of oblivion, trade went on; London in 8C was the "mart of many nations by land and sea".

The **City** was an ordered and rich community: in 1016 the gemut or assembly of London elected Edmund Ironside as king. When he died his successor, Canute, exacted tribute and the citizens rendered £10 500 – an eighth of the total paid by the whole of England. Edward the Confessor was also elected king by the people of London but once named there was no question that he should remain in the City; he went to **Westminster**, an area quite apart, upstream, to rebuild the abbey, build a royal palace and thus lay the foundation for London's double centre – a feature unique to London in all the world's capital cities.

Jealous of its independence the City obtained **charters** affording it privileged status from William I, Henry I and John. It elected its own mayor, held its own courts of law; it lent money to kings to wage war abroad but did not get involved. It traded. In the age of exploration it raised loans, it fitted out and financed merchant adventurers. The queen knighted her navigators, it was the City, however, which raised the wind for Drake, Frobisher and Hawkins to sail the Spanish Main, singe the King of Spain's beard and defeat the Armada, for Raleigh to sail to Virginia. The aim of the venturers was discovery, battle and

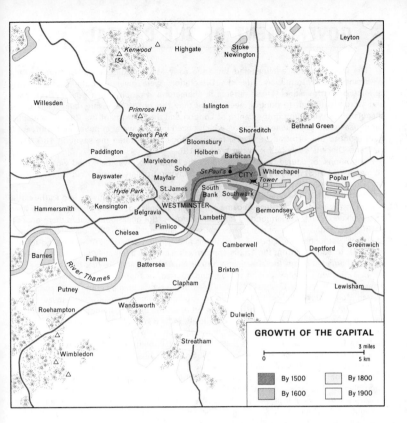

Map labels (reading across): Leyton, Kenwood 134, Highgate, Stoke Newington, Willesden, Primrose Hill, Islington, Bethnal Green, Shoreditch, Regent's Park, Paddington, Bloomsbury, Holborn, Barbican, Marylebone, Soho, St.Paul's, CITY, Whitechapel, Poplar, Bayswater, Mayfair, Tower, Hyde Park, St.James, South Bank, Southwark, Hammersmith, Kensington, Belgravia, WESTMINSTER, Bermondsey, Pimlico, Lambeth, Chelsea, Camberwell, Deptford, Greenwich, Barnes, River Thames, Fulham, Battersea, Brixton, Lewisham, Putney, Clapham, Roehampton, Wandsworth, Dulwich, Streatham, Wimbledon

GROWTH OF THE CAPITAL

3 miles
0   5 km

By 1500   By 1800
By 1600   By 1900

booty, of the City, the establishment of trading posts, of parliament, in later times, coloni-
sation. The results were quite unforeseeable: in 1600 Queen Elizabeth, under a charter of
incorporation, granted a monopoly of trade between England and India to a new undertaking, the **East India Company;** by 18C the larger part of India was being ruled by the company; in mid 19C, after the Mutiny (1858), it passed to the crown. In 1670 the Hudson
Bay Company was founded with a monopoly in the fur trade with the Red Indians (monopoly ended 1859). All company head offices were in the City.

In England the mediaeval wool trade had given way to a trade in cloth; the agricultural
life of centuries, in mid 18C, began, with ever increasing momentum, to be transformed into
the most intensely industrialised economy ever known. As the spinning wheel and loom in
the cottager's room gave place to the flying shuttle (1733), the spinning jenny, Arkwright's
spinning frame, Crompton's mule and Cartwright's power loom, the population moved into
towns to work in factories and textiles and other products poured out for home and export
markets.

The **roads,** never remade since the departure of the Romans in 4C, were improved by
the establishment of Turnpike Trusts, who by mid 19C had constructed 20 000 miles of
good turnpike roads and nearly 8 000 toll gates and bars (including one at Marble Arch,
another at Hyde Park Corner and one still remaining at Dulwich). Canals were excavated
and finally in 1825 the first **railway** was opened.

All roads (and railways), literally and metaphorically, led to London.

The City at no time encroached on Westminster and with a few notable exceptions,
citizens held no office under the crown or parliament. Many of the merchants and, as time
went on, insurance brokers and bankers who took over more and more from the actual
commodity dealers, particularly in earlier times, were related to landed families — Richard
Whittington, the younger son of a Gloucestershire squire, like many, was sent to seek his
fortune in the City. As they made their pile they built houses in the West End and further
out, to found new dynasties in their turn.

The **Industrial Revolution** produced a new type of MP after the Reform Bill of 1832,
industrial working class with no feudal manorial connection such as had existed for better
or worse with earlier landowners. The new members were far apart from the City men but
brought new blood to London.

In the second half of 20C the capital is still growing — not in the size of the population,
not in extent, but historically. The City and Westminster as ever remain distinct; the villages, coalesced in places to the outward eye, are claimed with individual pride by their
inhabitants. Fired, blasted, blitzed as never before the City remained blackened but upright
— and, as before, was rebuilt. As in previous periods new museums, concert halls, houses
have been built; new schools and new amenities in tune with the age.

But, of course, it is Londoners and adopted Londoners who make "London town" —
refugees, 14-17C Flemish and French Huguenots, 20C Chileans, kings and princes,
political theorists from Marx and Engels to the man now sitting in K12 in the British
Museum (or British Library) Reading room, philosophers such as Voltaire, painters such as
Holbein, capital citizens of genius, architects, painters, writers, musicians, doctors, scientists and lawyers and the nameless millions who, if they are true cockneys, ply their daily
trade with wit and humour.

GOVERNMENT OF THE CAPITAL

The City has been administered since the early Middle Ages by the Corporation, but Westminster and Southwark after the Dissolution, were given into the care of newly appointed parish vestries. These differed in character and probity, their powers overlapped and were insufficient to control, even where they thought it necessary, such men as the speculators jerrybuilding in the centre of London and the outskirts of the City, who erected tall houses with inadequate sanitation which oozed into the water supplies and who let off each room to one or often to several families. Hogarth illustrated the scene in 18C, Mayhew and Dickens described it in the press in 19C.

Conditions, of course, were not uniform: the "good life" was being led with considerable elegance in St James's and Whitehall, in Mayfair, St Marylebone, Knightsbridge, Kensington and further west.

By the late 17C the river was ceasing to be the capital's main highway and as the traffic increased the roads in all areas became appallingly congested: where once there had been only walkers, riders, costermongers and their barrows, the occasional coach, there appeared in 17C, sedan chairs and hackney carriages and in 18 and 19C, curricles and gigs, phaetons, barouches and landaus, broughams and hansom cabs (7020 were plying for hire in 1886). In addition, from the 1830s company horse buses alternately blocked or, in fierce rivalry, charged through the streets still further encumbered after 1870s, by trams.

In 1855, with reform long in the air, and spurred, or frightened, by considerable epidemics of cholera in 1832 and 1848, the Government established a central body, the Metropolitan Board of Works, with special responsibility for main sewerage and to act as coordinator of the now elected parish vestries left in charge of local drainage, paving, lighting, and the maintenance of streets. The board itself, in its 33 years, through its chief engineer, Joseph Bazalgette, reconstructed the drainage system for central London, removed the outflows from the Thames and, as part of the scheme, built the embankments — the (Victoria) Embankment 1864-70, the Albert 1866-9 and Chelsea, 1871-4.

In 1888 the County of London was created with an area equivalent to the present 12 inner London boroughs with the LCC as the county authority. In 1964, in the newly defined area of Greater London, the LCC was superseded by the GLC, a regional authority. Greater London comprises the former County of London and former local authority areas surrounding London, in all a total of 610 square miles, with a population of about 7 million. The annual budget amounts to £2 062 000 000 (1977/78).

The council's membership is 92 councillors, elected on the first Thursday in May every fourth year from 1977. The Chairman, elected annually, is the civic head of the council, the Leader of the GLC, the elected head of the majority party. (There are an opposition leader, whips etc as in parliament.) The council meets in open session (public galleries) in the Council Chamber at County Hall every three weeks (except in recess periods) on Tuesdays at 2.30pm. The GLC staff, including ILEA, numbers 120 000.

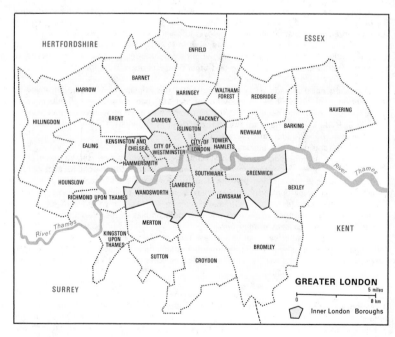

A comparison with other cities

	Area in sq miles	Population in millions
LONDON (Greater)	610	7
PARIS (agglomeration)	290	6.5
NEW YORK	300	7.6
TOKYO	827	8.8
HONG KONG	404	4.5

London's services and amenities

The origin and extent of some of the capital's major facilities are as follows:

Rates. — Rates were first exacted from householders under a statute of 1601, a measure instituted to provide a dole for vagrants and the destitute after the Dissolution of the monasteries had removed the traditional almoners! For centuries the major part of the levy was employed for the relief of the poor — in 1813 out of £8½ million raised in local taxation throughout the country, £7 million went in relief and £1½ million only on all other local necessities.

GLC finance today derives from a proportion of the rates collected locally through the municipal boroughs and City Corporation, rents and payments for services and specific government grants and subsidies. The Rate Support Grant received from the government is passed to the borough councils. Major capital expenditure is financed through loans, the issue of stock, bonds, mortgages, etc.

Water. — The Thames Water Authority, constituted in 1975 and which levies an independent water rate, is the latest in a line of ever larger enterprises supplying Londoners with water. As part of its function it is responsible for the Thames above Teddington.

The earliest supplies to householders were by water carrier from the Thames; from wells (after which some areas are still named — Clerkenwell, Sadler's Wells, Muswell Hill) and after 1285, from conduits, constructed by means of hollowed tree trunks or leather pipes from such streams as the Tyburn to lead cisterns in the City — the three in Cheapside appear on many old maps and engravings.

To augment supplies licences were granted from 16C to individuals to pump water from the Thames, the first successful project being by a Dutchman who installed tidal water-wheels beneath the north arches of London Bridge, a second being at Charing Cross where in c 1697 the first steam engine began pumping water into a tower from which pipes were laid to Hanover Sq.

Sources remained inadequate and polluted, however, until at the beginning of 17C Hugh Myddelton completed construction of the New River *(qv)*. The enterprise, supplying householders with water on tap at a rate of 5s a quarter, eventually proved highly profitable and was sold for £5 million when it was taken over with seven other companies in 1903 to form the Metropolitan Water Board.

Only since 1852 has water been compulsorily filtered and prohibited from withdrawal from the tideway.

No salmon have yet been caught in the Thames as in Izaak Walton's day but the pollution, which once caused such a stench that questions were asked in the House, is gradually being eradicated and fish are descending the stream and entering the estuary.

The Streets: paving, lighting, numbering. — The so-called Improvement Acts of 1762 were well named in that they began the transformation of every street in the capital many of which were still in a worse than mediaeval condition, while others, although fine and handsome were rough surfaced and ill-lit.

Paving became the responsibility of vestries who, though often corrupt, found it in their interests to relay the streets which previously had been in the hands of individual householders each paving his frontage, or not, with stone or rubble at a level convenient to his house without regard to the general course. The vestries abolished the kennels or deep central drains replacing them with shallow underground sewers and lateral gutters; they provided scavengers and sweepers to try and eliminate night soil and garbage still thrown out of doors, from remaining on the streets.

Houses in 17C were being built of brick and tile and were no longer advanced so bridging narrow alleys with their upper storeys; new streets were wider. Legislation called for the removal of balconies and projections, of coal shoots and lean-tos at pavement level and of house, inn and trade signs, to let in light and air. The small stagnant alleys and courts, however, were not reformed, slaughterhouses remained adjoining private dwellings, rookeries continued and the problems of the overcrowded burial yards remained with "poor's holes" or open pits, earthed over only when full in non-epidemic as well as plague years.

Progress in all but the worst areas nevertheless was marked: the streets were cleaner, the squares were cleared of accumulated refuse and were enclosed and planted.

House numbering and street lighting were instituted under the same 1762 acts. Since 1416 householders had been required to burn a candle nightly outside their doors, since 1716 those in the City had been ordered to burn lights on the 18 dark nights of each winter moon, but snuffers and lampholders outside the 18C houses of St James's and Mayfair are a reminder of how, in the circumstances, every man bore his own flaming torch, and link boys walked ahead of sedans and carriages.

Revolution began in 1738 when the vestries installed in such main thoroughfares as Oxford St, 15 000 oil fed lamps with cotton wicks which burned from sunset to sunrise. In 1807 there was a second advance when after a preliminary demonstration outside Carlton House, 13 gas lamp-posts were set up in Pall Mall. Seventy years later, in 1878, electricity had arrived and the first major street lighting project was inaugurated with the illumination of the Embankment.

Today, the GLC is responsible for 870 miles of metropolitan thoroughfares and the outer boroughs for 6 800 miles of local roads. The GLC is also directly responsible for naming streets and numbering buildings in Inner London — the latter although not necessarily with odd and even numbers on alternate sides, always with no 1 at the street end nearest to Charing Cross.

The corollary to the 1762 Improvement Acts has come within the last 25 years with the passage of the Clean Air Acts (1956, 1962) controlling the burning of coal in furnaces and open grates, so banishing for ever the notorious London pea-soup fogs.

Housing. – Out of a total of about 3 million houses and flats in the Greater London area, rather more than 2 million are privately owned, some 670 000 belong to the boroughs and 210 000 to GLC. The GLC has also embarked on new overspill areas in Hertfordshire and on a different scale, the construction of the new town of Thamesmead *(qv)*.

Historical note. – Municipal housing is a modern phenomenon: from the late Middle Ages the City Companies and a few, endowed, charities provided almshouses for a small number of old employees but working citizens lodged in their own houses or rented what they could – in the case of the very poor a room or part of a room; many lived on the streets, orphan children especially, sleeping and finding shelter where they could.

The first major housing scheme was financed by the American philanthropist, George Peabody who in 1864 had constructed in Commercial St, Spitalfields, a massive 5 storey building of 3 room flats with running water, sanitation and laundry facilities available at 5s a week. As twenty-nine other vast blocks were erected, charitable bodies began to follow suit. Octavia Hill, in 1845, with financial help from Ruskin and later from others, began a different type of enterprise; on a very small scale she reconstituted run down houses and let them at modest rents. The combined efforts of all, however, by the late 19C could not keep pace with the increasing population much less make inroads on the slums which were only removed by the cutting of new roads in the centre (Charing Cross Rd, Kingsway, etc.), the clearances begun by the LCC in 1920-30s, the "blitz" and the subsequent rebuilding by the boroughs and GLC.

Fire service. – Frequent fires, a "London inconvenience" as Fitzstephen termed them in 12C, raged unchecked until the Great Fire stirred invention and engines were built which forced a jet of water on burning buildings. From the same calamity fire insurance so increased that companies organised private brigades for the protection of the property which they advertised as covered by means of their own firemarks *(see opposite)*. By 1832 ten of the major companies had combined to form the London Fire Brigade but even it was powerless to prevent the total loss of the Houses of Parliament in 1834, the Royal Exchange in 1838, the burning out of the Tower armoury in 1841, and the devastation of three acres of warehouses worth £2 million in Tooley St. Finally in 1866 the government established the Metropolitan Fire Brigade.

The London Fire Brigade (under the GLC with hq on the Albert Embankment) today numbers 6 460, based on 114 stations and two river stations. It has more than 570 fire fighting appliances, 27 turntable ladders, 8 hose laying lorries (6 carrying a mile of hose), seven rivercraft, including two fireboats. The total annual cost (including fire prevention – 31 000 visits...) is £45 million; the number of calls 93 500.

Police. – Thieves, miscreants and the innocent, footpads and murderers alike were seized by paid informers, thief-takers and hired strong men until the mid 18C; malefactors were brought before so-called "trading justices" and thrown into one of the infamous jails or, if convicted, on any one of the then 156 capital offences, were hanged, often at Tyburn where there were, on average, 12 public hangings a month – some 50 000 in all between 1170 and 1783 when the gallows were removed to Newgate. Reform began in Bow Street under the honest magistracy of the Fieldings, Henry, the novelist, and his younger half-brother John, the Blind Beak, who recruited the first band of six honest men to apprehend villains – the Bow St Runners.

So great was the fear of the institution of a national police body that it was not until 1829 that Sir Robert Peel's bill was passed, founding the Metropolitan Police Force. (The River Police had been formed in 1800.) The "Peelers", when they made their appearance on the streets, to attract as little attention as possible, wore navy serge frock coats and top hats and, as now, were unarmed, except for a discreetly concealed truncheon.

Unlike the Metropolitan Police who are under the jurisdiction of the Home Secretary, the City Police, founded in the same decade, are a separate body under the Corporation. The combined forces (men and women) number 21 650.

Transport. – Commuting, which began in 1836-8 with the inauguration of the London Bridge – Deptford – Greenwich Railway, increased with every new line laid to a London terminal and took on phenomenal proportions when the connecting Metropolitan Railway (Paddington to Farringdon St) opened in 1863. On its first day the line carried 30 000 passengers and in the first year 9½ million – in open carriages behind steam engines through the tunnels.

London Transport, established in 1933 as a public corporation to co-ordinate and modernise the underground, railway and bus companies in existence, since 1970 has been under the overall policy and financial control of the GLC. To cater for some 2 000 million journeys made by Londoners and visitors each year, there are 7 000 red buses (2 700 one man operated) and 4 500 railway cars.

Education. – A century ago there were only in the capital the schools of ancient foundation such as Westminster (1371) and St Paul's (founded by the Dean, John Colet, in the cathedral churchyard – 1510), small charity schools, Sunday schools and a few groups run by the Ragged Schools' Union organised by Lord Shaftesbury in 1844. The government had the right of inspection in 258 of these institutions and in 1854 reported attendance by 57 000 or an estimated 12½ % of the child population.

Change came in 1870, 1876 with the Education Acts which provided schools and laid upon parents the duty of seeing that their children "received elementary education in reading, writing and arithmetic" – the 3Rs. Responsibility has since devolved on the LCC (1903) and subsequently the GLC for Inner London (the old LCC area) and the City from which the authority has come to be known as ILEA.

The ILEA Budget which at September 1976 provided education for 396 000 children in 1211 primary, secondary, special and nursery schools, also maintained teachers' training colleges, evening institutes, and numerous services, is about £475 million.

The Arts. – Support and patronage, as necessary today as in Handel's, Shakespeare's, Dryden's times, are supplied in 20C London by the government through the Arts Council, the BBC (Promenade Concerts) and the GLC. The latter aids the South Bank concert halls, gallery and theatre besides giving grants with the Arts Council to the four symphony orchestras – the London Symphony, London Philharmonic, New Philharmonia and Royal Philharmonic – which, with chamber orchestras, ensembles, academies, quartets and quintets, have made London the music capital of the world. Ballet, opera, museums (the London, in conjunction with the City Corporation) and galleries (Whitechapel and Dulwich) are aided, besides no less appreciated concerts and entertainments in the parks and a host of other undertakings to a total of nearly £4 million a year or a rate of 0.21p in £.

Open Spaces. – At the centre of London and on the west and east boundaries are the Royal Parks and still ringing the capital the age-old commons, some 3 500 acres in extent despite encroachment by peasants, manorial farmers, larger landowners and, in 19C, by land speculators, builders and local authorities constructing roads. Among those of considerable size north of the river are Hackney Marshes (340 acres), Hampstead Heath (208 acres), Wormwood Scrubs (200 acres; reduced by the construction of the prison) and on the south side Wimbledon and Putney Heath (1 200), Clapham (205), Wandsworth (175, again reduced by the prison), Streatham (58), Tooting Bec (218), the last four probably continuous originally and,further east, Peckham Rye (64), Plumstead (104), Woolwich (240) and historic Blackheath (271 acres), a rallying point for Wat Tyler, Jack Cade and the Kentish rebels, where James I introduced golf to England...

Parks are in another category – a countless number are tended by the 32 borough councils and some 30 with more than local interest by the GLC – Kenwood, Lesnes Abbey Woods (12C ruins, Bexley), Crystal Palace, Alexandra Park and Palace (Harringey) and, the latest addition, next to County Hall on the South Bank, Jubilee Park. These and many of the commons and gardens, besides their natural or landscaped features and flowers have sports facilities – football and cricket pitches, bowling greens, golf courses, tennis and other courts; bands; children's summer zoos and playgrounds.

The City within its square mile has no room for parks but since 1878 has acquired superb tracts of land "for the recreation and enjoyment of the public": Epping Forest (6 000 acres), Burnham Beeches (504 acres), Coulsdon Commons (430), Highgate Wood (70), Queen's Park, Kilburn (30), West Ham Park (77) and Spring Park and West Wickham, Kent (76). The Corporation has converted Bunhill Fields into a garden, maintains a bowling green at Finsbury Circus, has created gardens and courts in the blitzed and not reconstructed churches and in churchyards (Postman's Park by St Botolph's). There are "open spaces" in the City not two

Victoria Embankment bench.

yards square, pavements charged with modern statuary and, in summer, window boxes bursting with colour. All of which, parks, gardens, squares, greens and commons, we take for granted, but it nevertheless makes London the most luxuriantly green capital in the world.

Iron street furniture. – In 19C design and iron casting complemented each other highly successfully in the production of street furniture, notably the Egyptian inspired bench ends along the Embankment by Cleopatra's Needle, the cannon barrel and ball bollards marking among other places, the Clink, Southwark, the pair of George IIII lampposts in Marlborough Rd, St James's and the beautiful dolphin lamp standards of 1870 which line the Albert Embankment from Westminster Bridge.

Also to be noted although of earlier date and of wrought not cast metal are the gold crowned bracket lanterns at St James's Palace.

Pillar boxes are a subject apart. The first to be erected in London, fifteen years after the introduction of the penny post in 1840, were in Fleet St, the Strand, Pall Mall, Piccadilly, Grosvenor Place and Rutland Gate – they were rectangular with a solid round ball crowning the pyramid roof. Designs, hexagonal, circular, fluted, conical and flat roofed have followed, crowned and plain, most emblazoned with

Dolphin lamppost.

the royal cipher, Hexagonal boxes (1866-79) can still be seen in London today also some of the 1880s, "anonymous" series when the Post Office forgot to put its name on the box! They were first painted red in 1874.

Firemarks date from 18-19C when they were issued by insurance companies to policy holders – the early ones are numbered – as tokens of identification for the fire brigades, receipt and advertisement. Among the 150 companies which issued tin, copper and cast iron marks were the Sun Fire Office (f 1710), Hand-in-Hand (f 1696), Royal Exchange Assurance (f 1720).

CAPITAL CITIZENS AND THEIR PURSUITS

ARCHITECTS AND ARCHITECTURE

Only from 17C do the names of architects become known — before the only signatures to endure appear in the idiosyncratic fashioning of walls of columns, in the grace of rounded or pointed arches... highly distinctive in the case of Master William, Henry III's chief mason and builder of large areas of Westminster Abbey and of Robert Vertue, master mason to Henry VII and builder of his chapel.

The bare sequence of styles followed by the early constructors and later designers, as still exemplified in London churches dates back 1 100 years.

ECCLESIASTICAL ARCHITECTURE

Norman. – Although found in parts of Westminster Abbey as rebuilt by Edward the Confessor and therefore preceding the arrival of William, Duke of Normandy, Norman is now most beautifully extant in St Bartholomew the Great and in St John's Chapel in the White Tower.

Gothic. – Gothic arrived in England from the continent in the 12C and remained the predominant style until the 16C, the centuries being marked by three distinct phases: **Early English** in 13C, when the original style took on an English idiom; **Decorated,** in late 13-14C, notable for the richness and variety of design of the geometrical, and later, curvilinear, tracery in ever widening windows — as in Westminster Abbey but most successfully in cathedrals such as Lincoln; and **Perpendicular,** which for 50 years overlapped the previous style and inspired architects, on occasion, to abandon the quadrangular for the polygonal, so as to give greater visual play to the windows as in Westminster Abbey Chapterhouse. The style continued to evolve with increased emphasis on the vertical line, outside in ever greater height, spires, flying buttresses and finials and inside as clusters of attached columns sweeping to overhead ribbed vaulting. Surfaces were divided into tiers of panels, blind and cusp arched on walls, framed by mullions and transomes in windows; the vaulting was lierne and tierceron ribbed before being supplanted by fan vaulting, the hallmark of Late Perpendicular and of which there are three great examples in southeast England: St George's Chapel, Windsor (1474), King's College, Cambridge (1446, 1508-15) and Henry VII Chapel (1503-19).

There were, by then, in the capital, old St Paul's Cathedral, dating from its 12-14C Gothic rebuilding, Westminster Abbey, churches formerly attached to monasteries and allowed to continue after the houses had been dissolved as in the cases of St Helen's Bishopsgate and St Bartholomew the Great and, in the City particularly, hundreds of parish churches. Ecclesiastical building then came to a halt.

One hundred and fifty years later it was re-instituted on a scale never attained before or since. The Great Fire had destroyed four fifths of the City, St Paul's and nearly 180 churches. In the next 45 years Wren rebuilt the Cathedral and 51 of the churches.

Renaissance. – Although the style never came to England except in decoration, Wren might be considered a Renaissance man and took into his embrace, as architect, ideas from Italy, France and the Netherlands, combining designs inspired by the ancient Roman architect, Vitruvius, with those of his own time, to combine for example, in St Paul's, a classical dome and Baroque west towers.

Classical. – The reaction to Wren's last decorated, Baroque, period was a return to the Classical as seen in Hawksmoor's Christchurch, Spitalfields, St Anne's, Limehouse, St George's, Bloomsbury. The principles remained but by the late Georgian period had begun to be freely adapted as in John Nash's design for All Souls (1822-4).

19C. – The period was again one when hundreds of churches were to be built as the suburbs spread. A profound respect for the past, coupled with painstaking erudition, produced the neo-Gothic style — Perpendicular spires spiked the sky, every element was accurately and skillfully included in the detailed designs of Gilbert Scott and Augustus Pugin — alone inspiration was lacking as it was also in the neo-Norman, neo-Early Christian and neo-Italian Romanesque of the mid century.

20C. – Only in 1920s did Edward Maufe make the break with the neo-Gothic tradition and begin the line of thought which has produced the new cathedrals outside London (Coventry, Liverpool RC, Bristol RC) and the rebuilt or new churches in the capital such as St John's, Peckham, the churches of the Annunciation and Resurrection, Beckenham...

SECULAR ARCHITECTURE

It begins boldly with the White Tower by Norman William and continues with Westminster Hall, constructed by his son, William Rufus, and given its great hammerbeam roof by Richard II, then divides into two categories: the royal, official and public domain and that of the private house, in and out of town.

Construction materials were stone, quarried first in Kent or imported from Normandy and later brought from Portland (St Paul's in 17C was the first building to be constructed in London of Portland stone) and Yorkshire (Houses of Parliament), brick, made locally from fields (in Kensington, Islington) — and timber. Roofs until 15-16C were for the most part thatched in the City and were only uniformly tiled or slated after the Fire.

Tudor and Jacobean Gothic. – In the public domain the greatest examples (despite later additions) are St James's Palace and Hampton Court, both with archetypal gateways, and the latter with the decorative chimney stacks, the courts and great hall with a hammerbeam roof to be found also at Eltham and in the Middle Temple.

17 and 18C, Early Classicism or Palladianism, Classical Baroque and the Classical Revival. — The long period translates, in terms of architects, into Inigo Jones, Wren, his followers Hawksmoor and Vanbrugh (whose principal works, however, were respectively at Oxford and Cambridge, Blenheim and Castle Howard), George Dance Senior and finally Sir William Chambers. Their monuments include the Palladian inspired Queen's House at Greenwich and Banqueting House, Whitehall, the R N College, Greenwich by Wren, Hawksmoor and Vanbrugh, Wren's Royal Hospital, Chelsea, Hampton Court and Kensington Palace, the Mansion House by Dance, Somerset House, and, in light vein, the Pagoda at Kew by Chambers.

Late 18, early 19C or late Georgian-Regency. — The period which should have been marked by Henry Holland's Carlton House and Sir John Soane's Bank of England and other central London buildings, is now only represented by lesser buildings: Nash's Haymarket Theatre, the garden front of Buckingham Palace, Decimus Burton's screen at Hyde Park Corner, the Athenaeum, the domed building of University College by William Wilkins...

1830-1930, Victorian, Edwardian and Post World War I. — As in ecclesiastical building the period was one of imitations and influences; it was a period of prosperity and ornament could be applied with no fears as to expense, there were therefore the Classically inspired British Museum (1804-48) by Sir Robert Smirke, the Gothic Houses of Parliament (1836-1865) by Sir Charles Barry and Augustus Pugin, the neo-Quattrocento Travellers' Club and neo-Cinquecento Reform, both by Barry being built at the same time as the new government offices in Whitehall also in neo-palazzo style and the neo-Gothic St Pancras Hotel by Gilbert Scott.

As a result of the success of 1851 Exhibition museums and the Albert Hall were erected, drawing inspiration from different sources. There was no original, no native, style.

The Modern Period. — Pre-war abandonment of decoration and revelation of the outlines (BBC, British Airways) continued after the war, being carried to logical, if monotonous extremes, in all too many tower blocks in the City. In halls and galleries a new departure was made at the South Bank where each building has been designed first to fulfil a function and has then been clad, effect and character deriving from line and mass.

English houses have always had a remarkable beauty and sense of ease whether in town or country, whether mansion, terrace house or cottage. It is a category in which named and unnamed architects alike have delighted.

Tudor and Jacobean. — Staple Inn, Holborn, comprises a short range of half-timbered houses with advanced upper floors beneath pointed gables such as one sees in old prints. Although late 16C they are among the capital's oldest domestic buildings, fire having swept the City, Westminster and Southwark so often that only street courses not the houses that lined them remain. Other single houses of the period include no 17 Fleet St with the gateway to the Inner Temple below, Prince Henry's Room above and a crowning gable, the house above the much older gateway to St Bartholomew the Great in Little Britain and nearby houses in Cloth Fair and the gate to Charterhouse. Many pubs also date from Tudor-Jacobean times: the Cheshire Cheese, Old Wine Shades, The Anchor, London Apprentice...

No 7 Adam St.

16C was also the age when City financiers and great merchants, often the younger sons of landed families, in addition to their town mansions (Crosby Hall) began to build themselves country houses of such splendour that they were able to accommodate the queen on her summer tours — Sir Thomas Gresham received Elizabeth I at Osterley Park, Protector Somerset his king at Syon Park before his own execution.

A new style evolved with gables influenced by the Dutch (Kew Palace), the timber frame was displaced by brick and stone, windows enlarged after the Gothic technique, a greater symmetry designed on either side of full height, decorated, porches to afford the Jacobean style of Audley End, Charlton and Hatfield Houses. The interiors were as impressive with panelling, musicians' galleries and screens, long galleries, strapwork decorated plaster ceilings and stairs with carved balustrades and newel posts around a square well.

17-18C Classical, Queen Anne and Georgian. — Palladianism was a long standing influence, Marble Hill House, built in 1720s, was a direct descendant of Inigo Jones' Queen's House of 1616; Chiswick House in 1725-29, the manifestation of inspiration from the same source. Classicism in other hands brought the apparently effortless simplicity that comes from perfection of proportion in individual houses and terraces such as those round Richmond Green, notably Maids of Honour Row (1724), Sion and Montpelier Rows, Twickenham, and in central London, the earlier Bedford Row (1700), Queen Anne's Gate and the streets off Smith Sq.

It was also the period of the early squares of which there remain complete Bedford Sq (1774) and Fitzroy (1793-8). This last was by Robert Adam and is all that remains of his work in the centre apart from single houses in St James's Sq (no 20), in Chandos St and in what was once the Adelphi area. His conversions and decoration of large houses is splendidly displayed at Kenwood, Syon Park and Osterley Park.

Regency House,
Wilton Crescent.

1800-1837, Late Georgian, Regency. – The period is typified by two men, John Nash architect, planner and developer, and Thomas Cubitt, quality builder and developer. The interest of both was the private house which Nash realised superbly in the terraces surrounding Regent's Park, in the course, if no longer the buildings, of Regent St and in the monumental Carlton House Terrace, besides such projects as the palace, the pavilion and country houses. Cubitt, from George Basevi's designs, erected Belgrave Square, followed by Belgravia (1825), Pelham Crescent (1820-30) and squares, crescents and streets from Putney to Islington.

19C Victorian. – The appeal of classical lines vanished in 19C in admiration of High Gothic – not the scholarly Gothic of Pugin and Scott but that of a century earlier displayed by Horace Walpole at Strawberry Hill (1751). The result was an adventitious use of Gothic turrets and gables, of pointed windows and stained glass, to which were added neo-Renaissance pavilion roofs and corner turrets brought over as the century advanced as the latest fashion from France. In the hands of Norman Shaw (New Scotland Yard, the south end of St James's St) such buildings had character; in those of all too many others the result was fulsome. Even the builders erecting mile upon mile of houses along suburban streets to accommodate the rapidly growing population were affected and added bay windows, gables, decorated porches, to give a full dressed appearance.

Mid and second half of 20C. – Attractive modern houses are few and far between: Hampstead, Highgate, Blackheath, a group in Belgravia, flats in St James's...

Belgrave Square.

Victorian House, Cadogan Sq.

PAINTERS AND SCULPTORS

What has become the great tradition of portrait painting in this country began, and for several centuries was led, by artists who came here from Germany and Holland, Holbein in 16C who painted Sir Thomas More and his family in Chelsea, Henri VIII, his court and the great merchants of the day; van Dyck in 17C who portrayed Charles I, his queen, children and the nobility of the period; Sir Peter Lely, who after Commonwealth personalities, went on to paint those of the Restoration, Charles II, his queen, children, mistresses, the *Hampton Court Beauties* and the *Admirals*. Finally, Sir Godfrey Kneller who at his academy school, completed hundreds of political and other figures of the reign of William and Mary and Queen Anne among them the *Windsor Beauties* and the *Kit Cat Club*.

In 18C portraiture was reborn under Sir Joshua Reynolds, who was successfully emulated by Gainsborough and followed by Ramsay and Raeburn, so that there remain splendid likenesses of a great number of the major figures and, in the paintings of Gainsborough, also of the beautiful women. In 19C tradition competently pursued, was enlivened by the sophistication of Sir Thomas Lawrence and, at the turn of the century, by Sargent's portrayal of Edwardian High Society. The new century brought Augustus John and a new style.

Topographical painting, exemplified by the Van de Veldes in 17C with their wonderful seascapes and by Canaletto in his views of London (1746-56), was transformed, by Gainsborough into landscape painting and advanced again by Constable (18-19C).

Outside the mainstream have been the three figures of Hogarth in 18C, Blake in late 18 early 19C and, in 19C, Turner.

In sculpture the evolution from Gothic tombal effigies to modern abstract form begins with William Torel, citizen and goldsmith of London, who modelled Henry III and Eleanor of Castile (1291-2) and Torrigiano, the visiting (1511-20), early Renaissance, Florentine, who cast the gilt bronze figures of Henry VII, his queen, Elizabeth, and mother, Margaret, Duchess of Richmond. Actual portraiture appears in 17C in the works of, among others, Nicholas Stone (John Donne) and the French Huguenot, Le Sueur's bronzes of Charles I and James I, also Grinling Gibbons' statues of Charles II and James II although it is as a wood-carver of genius that he remains celebrated.

In 18C, as a Classical style began to appeal to graduates of the Grand Tour, the Flemings, Michael Rysbrack and Peter Scheemakers, the Frenchman, François Roubiliac, the Englishmen John Bacon, John Flaxman and Nollekens executed hundreds of figures, many with considerable strength of character, until the genre became stylised and empty in 19C. Vigour began to return in 20C, in portraiture with works by Jacob Epstein, in religious and human themes with Henry Moore, in abstract form with Barbara Hepworth.

WRITERS

Not all have felt with William Dunbar "London thou art the flower of cities all", nor even with Dr Johnson that "there is in London all that life can afford" but at some point in their careers the great majority of writers have lived in London.

Dramatists have come to play before the necessary audiences – Marlowe, Shakespeare, Ben Jonson, Wycherley, Congreve, Sheridan... Oscar Wilde; others were held by their daily work – Chaucer, Donne, Milton, Fielding, Lamb, Disraeli, T S Eliot; many were journalists and wrote outside the daily stint – Johnson, Addison and Steele, Dickens, Bernard Shaw, Edgar Wallace; others devoted themselves to writing and always lived in London like John Galsworthy. With lyric and other poets the attachment has been more tenuous – Keats came to study medicine, Wordsworth mused on Westminster Bridge but lived by the Lakes, Byron enjoyed high society...

For many it has been the logical next step – Arnold Bennett, J.B Priestley this century, even though now with the development first of radio, then of television and easier travel, the tendency seems now more to get away.

Despite their numbers there has been no forum down the years – groups have shifted from the pubs near Blackfriars theatre to those on Bankside and down the Borough High St close to the Globe; to Highgate, to Chelsea and for a charmed circle, to Bloomsbury; at the turn of the century a band around Oscar Wilde which included Aubrey Beardsley and Max Beerbohm and artists of the day met at the Café Royal. As many have begun or earned living as journalists, the first regular haunts were the coffeehouses around Fleet St – Addison and Steele frequented the George and Vulture, then doing greater business in tea, chocolate and coffee than in ale, and subsequently Button's, at both of which they wrote copy for the *Tatler* and *Spectator*. Dr Johnson called at many coffeehouses and taverns but nearest his own house was the Cheshire Cheese, where tradition has it, many of the great conversations took place.

Some have detested the capital, some indulged in a love-hate relationship, some known that for them it was the only place in the world to live, so that, in consequence, English literature from detective stories to diaries, from novels to biographies and histories, is permeated with London life and scenes.

MUSICIANS

Greensleaves, There was a lover and his lass (Morley) and the light airs of Merrie England, developed into rounds, cannons and finally a golden age of madrigals between 1588-1630 (Orlando Gibbons, *The Silver Swan*). In the same period Thomas Tallis and the great William Byrd, were composing religious music for the organ and voice in masses and anthems. Their successors, Henry Purcell, in the latter half of 17C embraced an even wider range with *Te Deums* and also entered the secular field with airs, songs and full length operas (*Dido and Aeneas*, 1689).

Purcell not only dominated his own age but native composers for centuries to come, the void being filled, fashionably, by Italian opera which became "all the rage" and magisterially by great visiting German composers – the Hanoverians were the ruling house although Handel actually arrived (1711-12) before George I.

Handel remained in England until his death in 1759 and in that time poured out operas (satirised by John Gay in *The Beggar's Opera*, 1728), occasional pieces such as the *Fireworks* and *Water Music* and the great succession of oratorios, *Esther, Israel in Egypt, Messiah* 1742 – ms presented to the Foundling Hospital), *Judas Maccabaeus...*

(National Portrait Gallery)

Handel.

Mozart visited England as a *protégé* of 8 in 1764, Haydn in 1790s when he was the greatest musical figure in Europe. Mendelssohn came early in 19C (the *Scottish Symphony* and *Midsummer Night's Dream* were only completed some 20 years later).

An entirely new period in English music began at the end of 19C: it started to become widely popular – through the operettas of Gilbert and Sullivan (1875-99) and through the inauguration, under the conductor, Henry Wood, of the Promenade Concerts (1895). From 1936 as radio became general and the BBC began to broadcast the Promenade Concerts, music entered people's lives as never before. The post war corollary has been the establishment of permanent centres of opera at Covent Garden and the London Coliseum, the construction of concert halls on the South Bank and the upsurge of numerous provincial festivals.

The opening of the 20C also saw the appearance of a host of new British composers: Elgar (*Enigma Variations* 1899, *Dream of Gerontius* 1900), Delius, Vaughan Williams (9 Symphonies, the ballet *Job*) and Gustav Holst (*The Planets*, 1914-16). These were joined in 1920s by Bantock, Bax, Bliss (*Checkmate* 1937) and William Walton (*Balshazzar's Feast* 1931). After the war they were reinforced by Michael Tippett (*A Child of Our Time* 1941, *The Midsummer Marriage* 1955) and Benjamin Britten who produced a magnificent series of operas – *Peter Grimes* (1945), *Albert Herring, Let's Make an Opera, Billy Budd, Turn of the Screw, Noye's Fludde, Midsummer Night's Dream, The Burning Fiery Furnace, Prodigal Son*, and the operetta *Paul Bunyan*.

CABINET MAKERS
AND FURNITURE DESIGNERS

The great transformation in English furniture making occurred in 18C when in place of oak, imported mahogany was used and later tropical satinwood, before a return to native walnut. To these new woods were added, besides carving, enrichments of brass in the form of inlays and gilded mounts, hardwood veneers and marquetry. The great English names of the period were Thomas Chippendale, the leader with a classical sureness of style which he illustrated in *The Gentleman and Cabinet Maker's Director* (1754) and who produced pieces for the great houses being designed or remodelled by Robert Adam and his contemporaries; John Linnell, executor of Adam's designs and his follower who left mirrors and chairs especially of delightful form and William Vile, cabinet maker to George III, who made superbly finished, massive library tables and bureau cabinets.

Carolean: 1680.

George Hepplewhite marked a new departure with a characteristic lightness and delicacy in every piece, achieving effect not only by slimming down but by delicate inlay and carving. Elegant simplicity attained a peak in his shield back chairs. A thorough

Chippendale: 1755.   Adam lyre back: 1770.   Hepplewhite: 1775.

bred's lightness was the hall mark of Thomas Sheraton who frequently used satin wood for richer pieces besides carving and inlay. Among favourite subjects are his small worktables, beautiful side boards, secretaires and full height bookcases. He also produced, many "harlequin" or dual purpose items such as library tables containing hidden step ladders...

DOCTORS AND LAWYERS

The population of London which in 1700s was 670 000 had doubled to 1 274 000 by 1820 due, in no small measure, to a sudden advance in medical knowledge. The 18C marked the beginning of the end of practice by apothecaries and barber-surgeons (the Royal College separated from the City guild in 1745) and the establishment, in addition to the two mediaeval foundations of Bart's and Thomas's, of five new hospitals between 1720-45: Guys Westminster, St George's, the London and Middlesex, of Thomas Coram's Foundling Hospital and the Lying-in Hospital. Anatomy schools existed in the universities but those who wished to practice came to the capital, to hospitals and private laboratory and dissecting rooms often set up in their own houses for research by men of science in the tradition of Thomas Linacre, physician to Henry VII and VIII and founder of the Royal College of Physicians in his house in 1518. William Harvey, a century later, gave his early lectures to members of the college on the circulation of the blood.

In 18C, William Hunter, after studies in Glasgow and Edinburgh where there had been advanced medical schools since 1505, came south to become the first great teacher of anatomy and later of obstetrics. He was joined in 1748 by his younger brother, the anatomist and physiologist, John Hunter, who was elected surgeon at St George's in 1758 and after who have come Englishmen and Scots (Jenner, Gray – *Gray's Anatomy* 1858) in ever widening fields.

By late 16C when *The Comedy of Errors* was staged in Gray's Inn and *Twelfth Night* beneath the hammerbeam roof of Middle Temple Hall, the four Inns of Court and dependent Inns of Chancery (no longer in existence) had been established for nearly 300 years as the country's great law societies. The courts in Westminster Hall, in the adjoining palace in the Court of Star Chamber, where, before it became a royal instrument in 17C and was abolished, were heard cases of "riot, rout and misdemeanour" and in White Hall, where there were a Court of Requests for poor equity, required a plenitude of advocates. Litigation was a serious business: there were endless disputes on land entitlement and inheritance, but bringing action for slurs and insults, real and imagined, was also a fashionable and obsessive pastime indulged in by many. It all offered a lucrative field and was, besides, a good stepping stone to high office: from 16C there were some 2 000 students dining in the halls.

Clerks or students, benchers, barristers, justices, have always formed a close-knit group with traditional attachment to plays, masques and revels, with always among their number, many of the most learned men of every age: Thomas More, Thomas Cromwell, Francis Bacon, William Cecil, Lord Burghley, H H Asquith, F E Smith, Lord Birkenhead, Lord Justice Birkett.

Francis Bacon.

LEARNED SOCIETIES

The Royal Society, founded as the Philosophical Society in 1645, granted a royal charter at the Restoration and incorporated in 1662, took as its province the whole field of human knowledge. Founder members were from all walks of life: Robert Boyle, the natural philosopher and chemist, Abraham Cowley, the poet, Dryden, John Aubrey the antiquarian and John Evelyn, the society's first secretary. Meetings were held in Gresham College, the City institution founded under the will of the Elizabethan financier, Sir Thomas Gresham, to which Christopher Wren was appointed Professor of Astronomy in 1657.

Members in the early days, and since, have been men of wide experience and interest, such as Pepys, who was president from 1684-5 and Sir Hans Sloane, president 1727-40, or who were practising in a certain field and presented original papers to members, as did Wren, Newton, and in later years, Humphry Davy, T H Huxley, Lister, Rutherford and Florey.

Unlike the continental academies and societies of the same period (the Académie Française was founded in 1635), London's learned societies were assigned no special task to perform by the government of the day, royal patrons sought no reflected glory. Other societies formed at the time or later in the same spirit, include the Society of Antiquaries (1717), the Linnean Society (1778), Geological Society (1807), Royal Geographical Society (1830) and the British Association for the Advancement of Science (1831).

The societies, therefore, in a city where the university was not founded until 19C, provided the meeting place for men in all branches of knowledge to publish and exchange ideas and by attracting not only men who were working in the capital to attend conferences, did much to make London the centre of knowledge throughout the kingdom.

FASHION

Fashions, which at their peak greatly affected London and influenced taste and architecture, include coffeehouses, clubs and the Grand Tour.

Coffeehouses, which were introduced to the capital during the Commonwealth (1652) and, serving originally as meeting place, in the City for the exchange of shipping news ('Lloyd's'), multiplied in number and spread to Covent Garden and the Strand, St James's, Mayfair and Westminster, until by 1715 there were more than 500.

Customers of like interest would foregather regularly, in many cases daily, in the same houses or call at several houses at different times to pick up messages and even mail, to auction a cargo, a ship, raise a loan in any of the lounges around the Exchange. To gossip and hold literary talk one went to Will's, to gather news and write reviews to Button's, to talk of law and art to the Grecian, to discuss Tory politics the Cocoa Tree, Pall Mall, to embroil in Whig intrigue, the St James's (no 87)... a major attraction were the news sheets which at first circulated from one house to another and later the newspapers (*Daily Courant,* 1702) which would be available to customers for the price of a single cup of hot chocolate or coffee.

At the end of 18C the City coffeehouses reverted to being pubs and the West End houses disappeared except Boodle's and White's which became clubs.

Clubs were the new fashion: they were for gaming, drinking, conviviality and display of the latest masculine attire. They became the setting for legendary wagers placed on a throw of dice, the turn of a card; others took on a literary or political character, a service atmosphere, and acquired spacious premises built by the architects of the day in Waterloo Place, Pall Mall and St James's. They were also a haven for the younger sons of large Victorian families who, not having inherited the family town house and, if in neither the army nor the church, found themselves living in rooms from which the obvious place to repair for the day was the club with its library, dining room, smoking room and famous club servants.

In Edwardian days there were more than 150 clubs — today the number decreases annually as they merge, so that there remain only a few 19C palazzos along Pall Mall and 18C houses in St James.

The London Season dates from 1705. It was the outcome indirectly of the growing intellectual and social curiosity which had always brought men to the capital and with the newly improved roads and development of carriages, brought their families also. But travel to London was only the first step: the **Grand Tour** became the thing.

Artists had long been going to Italy and by 17C were followed by individual collectors and patrons — Inigo Jones went alone on his first visit (1601) when he studied Vitruvius and Palladio; on a second visit in 1613-4, he went as adviser to the collector, Thomas Howard, Earl of Arundel.

The exile of royalist families during the Commonwealth familiarised many with the continent and continental taste including Charles II himself. From the time of the Restoration, painters began to work as part of their training and often stayed on, to study in Rome; the sons of the wealthy were sent on journeys of a year or two years to France and Italy, thus in 1714-5 in Rome, Richard Boyle, Earl of Burlington, met William Kent, painter, guide and agent for English noblemen on the Grand Tour. After a second visit in 1719, Burlington returned to influence architecture and taste in the direction of Classicism once more.

Collecting, by the knowledgeable — Soane — and the knowledgeable but eclectic — Horace Walpole — developed to such lengths that some, like Sir William Hamilton, even commissioned vessels to ship home statuary, vases and thousands of items for their country and town houses. In 1775 when Edward Gibbon was in Lausanne, he learned that it was estimated that there were 40 000 English "milords— and their servants abroad in Europe — gentlemen if they did not possess a title took them, it was said, for the occasion — all were "milords"!

(Thomas Cook organised his first grand circular tour of Europe in 1856.)

A LONDON CALENDAR

Listed below are a few of the most popular annual events; for full details, for th special and commemorative exhibitions held by all museums, commercial gallery exhibi tions and sporting and other events, consult the daily and weekly press, the **British Touris Authority** (64 St James's St, SW1; Tel. 01-629 9191) or the **London Tourist Boar** (26 Grosvenor Gardens SW1; Tel. 01-730 0791).

Floodlighting: in summer the most rewarding and important monuments in Westminster, th City and along the river especially are floodlit.

Thames Boat Services: the boats run at Easter and from the June holiday Monday to lat autumn (p 152).

JANUARY	Camping and Outdoor Holiday Exhibition	Olympia
	Boat Show	Earls Court
	Rugby: Triple Crown + France	
	England v Scotland (Calcutta Cup) and France, odd years, differing months	
	England v Wales and Ireland even years, differing months	Twickenham
	30: Wreath laid by Royal Stuart Society (11 am)	Charles I statue, Whitehall
FEBRUARY	Cruft's Dog Show	Olympia
	English Folk Dance and Song Society Festival	Royal Albert Hall
MARCH	Ideal Home Exhibition	Olympia
	Chelsea Antiques Fair	Old Town Hall, King's Rd
	Oxford and Cambridge Boat Race	Putney to Mortlake
EASTER	Service and distribution of purses (Maundy Thursday)	Westminster Abbey
	Service and distribution of Hot X buns to poor widows (Good Friday)	St Bartholomew the Gt
	Carnival Parade (Easter Sunday)	Battersea Park
	London Harness Horse Parade (morning Easter Monday)	Regent's Park
	Fairs on Hampstead Heath, Blackheath, Wanstead Flats, etc.	
APRIL	Royal Horticultural Society Spring Flower Show	RHS Westminster
	Football League Cup Final	Wembley
MAY	Chestnut Sunday — the avenue in bloom	Bushy Park, Hampton Ct
	Royal Windsor Horse Show	Gt Park, Windsor
	Chelsea Flower Show	Royal Hospital, Chelsea
	F.A. Cup Final	Wembley
	Beating the Retreat	Horse Guards Parade, Westminste
	29: Oak Apple Day Parade: Chelsea Pensioners	Royal Hospital, Chelsea
JUNE	Royal Academy Exhibition	Burlington House, Piccadilly
	Antiques Fair	Grosvenor House, Park Lane
	Trooping the Colour (second Saturday)	Horse Guards Parade
	The Derby	Epsom
	Royal Ascot	Berkshire
	Antiquarian Book Fair	Europa Hotel, Grosvenor Sq
	All England Lawn Tennis Championships (2 weeks)	Queen's Club, Wimbledon
	Test Matches — MCC play in sequence on an approxi- mately 4 year cycle: Australia; Pakistan and NZ; India; W. Indies (Australia: 1977)	Lord's
JULY	Open Air Theatre Season	Regent's Park
	Royal Tournament	Earls Court
	Royal International Horse Show	Wembley
	Royal Regatta	Henley
	Promenade Concerts (mid July for 8 weeks)	Royal Albert Hall
	Benson and Hedges Cup Final	Lord's
	National Rose Show	RHS Westminster
	Swan upping	The Thames
	Doggett's Coat and Badge Race	London Bridge to Chelsea Bridg
	(rowed by 6 men of the Watermen and Lightermen's Company) (last Friday in the month)	
AUGUST	Hampstead Heath Fair (also Blackheath, etc.) (holiday Monday weekend)	Hampstead
	Greater London Horse Show	Clapham Common
	Summer Flower Show	RHS Westminster
	Outdoor Theatre Season	Holland Park
	Test Match (see also June; late August/Sept.)	The Oval
SEPTEMBER	Gillette Cup Final (1st Saturday)	Lord's
	Chelsea Antiques Fair	Old Town Hall, King's Rd
	Farnborough Air Show (even years only; in first week)	Farnborough, Hants
OCTOBER	Horse of the Year Show	Wembley
	Opening of Michaelmas Law Term: Procession of Judges in full robes and with nosegays	Westminster Abbey
	National Brass Bands' Championship	Royal Albert Hall
NOVEMBER	Remembrance Sunday (11am service; Sunday closest to 11th)	Cenotaph, Whitehall
	London to Brighton Veteran Car Run (1st Sunday)	
	Lord Mayor's Show (Saturday closest to 9th)	The City
	London Film Festival	NFT
	State Opening of Parliament	Westminster
DECEMBER	Royal Smithfield Show	Earls Court
	Lighting of the Norwegian Christmas Tree; carols nightly (middle of the month)	Trafalgar Sq
	Carol services	

LONDON SIGHTS

Listed alphabetically

APSLEY HOUSE ★ (Westminster)

Map p 101.

Apsley House stands on the site of the old lodge of Hyde Park and an older public house. As the first house beyond the turnpike it became known in 19C as No 1, London.

The House. — Wellington bought the house, designed nearly 40 years before by Robert Adam for Baron Apsley, in 1817: views on porcelain in the Plate and China and Striped Drawing Rooms show Adam's construction as small, square and built of brick. Later the duke and his architect, Benjamin D. Wyatt, transformed it: outside they added the pedimented portico and refaced the walls entirely with Bath stone; inside, excepting the Portico and Piccadilly Drawing Rooms, all was re-arranged and, in 1829, a west extension added containing the Muniment or Plate and China Room below and the Waterloo Gallery above. In 1947 the 7th duke presented it to the nation.

The Wellington Museum★. — *Open daily 10am (Sundays 2.30pm) to 6pm; closed Good Friday, 24, 25, 26 December, 1 January.*

The exhibits, in the main, have the dual interest of association and high artistry; porcelain from Meissen, Berlin, Sèvres; gold and silver plate from London and Lisbon; jewellery, enamelwork on orders of chivalry, field marshal's batons, snuffboxes; paintings by English, Spanish, Dutch and Flemish masters including more than 100 captured in 1813 following the Battle of Vitoria from Joseph Bonaparte who had appropriated them from the Spanish royal collection — a red asterisk flags the Spanish acquisitions. The chandeliers throughout the house are 19C English.

Entrance hall. — A dominant bust and full length portrait, a Landseer painting of Waterloo, Turner's *Tapping the Furnace* in commemoration of the casting of the equestrian statue for the Wellington Arch, set the scene.

Plate and China or Muniment Room. — Among the orders and decorations, note the silver Waterloo Medal, the first ever campaign medal. There are 10 batons of seven different armies, swords and daggers, the Prussian Service (Berlin: 1819), one of the 4 porcelain and 3 silver and gilt services (most of several hundred pieces); there are rich gold, enamelled and jewelled snuffboxes, field equipment and silver and gilt plate, most notably in figured relief, the great Wellington Shield.

Basement. — The corridors are hung with a programme, printed on silk, and a panorama of the duke's remarkable funeral and a commentary on his political career by newspaper cartoonists of the day.

Staircase Vestibule. — Wellington never met Napoleon but in the hall are gathered his brother, Joseph, the Empress Josephine, his sister Pauline, Princess Borghese and the emperor himself in painted (Lefèvre) and sculpted likeness, an 11ft 4in Carrara marble statue by Canova.

Piccadilly Drawing Room and Portico Room. — *(First floor).* The rooms are beautiful examples of interior Adam decoration. The drawing room in green and white, highlighted in gold, is hung with 17C Dutch paintings (Vermeer, "Velvet" Brueghel, Pieter de Hooch), a Ribera and the duke's personal favourite, *The Agony in the Garden,* by Correggio.

The Waterloo Gallery. — The early Waterloo Day (18 June) reunion dinners, with only the generals present, were held in the dining room. By 1829, with Wellington now premier, the list had lengthened and he added the 90ft gallery, decorated in 18C French style which set a fashion favoured until the end of the Edwardian era. The ceiling decoration combines the Wellington arms and the George within the Garter collar. Down the room is the banquet table set with the 26ft silver centrepiece from the Portuguese Service. The paintings are dominated by the portraits of Charles I after van Dyck, William IV by Wilkie and the Goya portrait of the duke himself in the classic Spanish pose on horseback — so standard, in fact, that recent x-rays have revealed that it was painted somewhat prematurely and the head of Joseph Bonaparte had to be rapidly overpainted with that of the ultimate victor!

The windows are fitted with sliding mirrors which enhanced still further the already glittering gold decoration, chandelier, silver centrepiece and plate, the uniforms...

(By courtesy of the V & A)

The Wellington Boot.

Yellow and Striped Drawing Rooms. — The first, hung with yellow damask resembling that originally in the Waterloo Gallery, is rich with Spanish paintings — four by Velasquez including the *Spanish Gentleman* and *Water Seller of Seville* and a Murillo. There is also a Rubens' portrait. The maroon and white striped room displays two services: the Saxon (Meissen) and the Austrian, decorated with portrait medallions. The pictures salute Waterloo and Wellington himself (by Lawrence).

Dining Room. — The amazing portrait of George IV in Highland dress by Wilkie overlooks the silver-gilt Ambassador Service, breakfast sets and massive, two handled Waterloo Vase.

BARNES (Richmond upon Thames)

Barnes remains incredibly countrified in character: the **Green,** ringed with trees, possesses a pond, the weatherboarded early 19C Sun Inn and the former village school.

St Mary's Parish Church. — Of the church, said to have been consecrated in 1215 by Archbishop Langton after the signing of *Magna Carta,* there are considerable remains: the chancel east and south walls and the roof, lancet windows and fragments of a painted frieze. Monuments inside name Sir Richard Hoare, Lord Mayor of London in 1745 and the 9 ins high brass figures (south wall), of Edith and Elizabeth Eylde, simply dressed and with hands clasped, "which died virgins" in 1508.

On either side of the church are early 18C houses: no 113, The Homestead, to the west Strawberry House, formerly the Rectory, and the Grange with a diamond pantile decoration.

At the opening of the **High Street** is Milbourne House, where Henry Fielding lived in the 1750s. Rose House (no 70) is the oldest in Barnes.

Two adjoining riverside inns give a colourful idea of 19C pub architecture before **Barnes Terrace,** which runs upriver as a line of 18C residences, terrace houses and cottages.

BATTERSEA (Wandsworth)

Battersea's transformation into an industrial town of 151 000 inhabitants took just 100 years. In 1782, 2 160 souls were engaged in growing strawberries and asparagus, herbs (Lavender Hill) and vegetables for seed and transporting their produce over the wooden bridge, erected in 1771, to Westminster; by 1845 the railway had extended to Clapham Junction and the population explosion begun.

Battersea Old Church, St Mary's. — Since Saxon times there has been a church well forward at the river bend. The current building with a conical green copper spire dates from 1775 (portico 1823) and contains inside the pointed east window outline of a 14C predecessor, amusing epitaphs and memorial busts of the St John — Bolingbroke family, lords of the manor in 17/18C.

Vicarage Crescent. — **Old Battersea House,** a two storey brick mansion with a hipped roof and pedimented doorway, dates from 1699 when it was built by Sir Walter St John. **Devonshire House** is an early 18C, salmon orange, stucco house of three storeys with a Doric porch, small curved iron balconies and a contemporary wrought iron gate.

High Street. — **The Raven** of tawny orange stucco with top-heavy curving Dutch gables outlined in white, has dominated the crossroads since the middle of the 17C.

Sir Walter St John's School, founded in 1700, was rebuilt in 19/20C on the original site in Tudor Gothic style. Note the St John motto surmounted by helm and falcon at the entrance.

Battersea Park. — In the 16C Battersea Fields was a favourite meeting place; however by 1828 when Wellington and Lord Winchelsea exchanged shots over the Catholic Emancipation Bill it had become ill-famed. **Thomas Cubitt,** in 1843, suggested that the site be laid out as a park: a bill was passed and 360 acres purchased. 20C features include the Festival Pleasure Gardens (1951), sculptures by Henry Moore and Barbara Hepworth and a garden for the handicapped.

Battersea Dogs Home. – *4 Battersea Park Rd. Open Monday to Friday 9.30am to 5pm; claims only, Saturday, Sunday and public holidays, 2 to 4pm; 10p.*

The home, established in 1860, moved to its present site in 1871. The number of dogs and cats brought in annually numbers thousands.

BLACKHEATH ★ (Greenwich)

Blackheath★. — The high expanse of Blackheath is ringed by stately **terraces** and **houses★** mostly built of brick relieved by stone dressings or of sparkling white painted stucco. They date from the 18C and early 19C when merchants newly wealthy from the rapidly expanding docks, began to build in the vicinity.

The present calm gives the lie to the rumbustiousness and pageantry of the past. Blackheath Rd, Blackheath Hill and Shooters' Hill, which cross the heath, mark the course of the Roman Watling Street between the coast and London. In the 18C the area was notorious for highwaymen and earlier as a rallying ground for rebel forces: Wat Tyler — 1381; the Kentishmen under Jack Cade — 1450; the Cornishmen under Audley — 1497. It has also always been a fairground, meeting place and encampment: citizens greeted Henry V on the heath on his victorious return from Agincourt in 1415; Charles II was met there by the Restoration Army; James I is said to have taught the English to play golf on it when in residence at Greenwich in 1608.

Among the almost unbroken, circle of buildings overlooking the green are **Colonnade House,** South Row — a big early 19C house with a Tuscan portico decorating the front along its full length which gives it its name; **The Paragon,** a late 18C shallow crescent by Michael Searles, of seven brick villas linked by white, Tuscan columned arcades; All Saints Church — built of Kentish ragstone in neo-Gothic style — an oddity by Furley with even the tower in a peculiar position crowning the south wall. Lindsey House, on the corner, is all in brick with white trims; Grotes' Buildings, a mid 18C terrace; Heathfield House, early 19C, stucco with a Tuscan columned, paired bow window. Dartmouth Row is notable for the early 18C Spencer and Perceval Houses with eleven bays, several Georgian groups and survivals of the original 1680-90s houses.

Blackheath Village, the main street, and traffic noisy, Tranquil Vale, lead off the heath to the south; the more modern estates by Span and others lie farther back.

Morden College. – *Open by appointment.*

The college, designed by Wren in 1695, stands in 18C landscaped parkland, an attractive low, two storeyed building in mellow brick with stone dressings. An ornamented central stone gateway which rises to a double niche contains the figures of the founder, the city merchant, Sir John Morden, and his wife, and leads to an inner, collegiate style, quadrangle.

Charlton. – The parish church, the big house, the Bugle Horn Inn, a rebuilt post-house, the 18C White Swan, mark the length of the main street still characteristically rural and appropriately named The Village — except on a Saturday when Charlton Athletic are playing at home!

St Luke's. – *Charlton Lane. Open Wednesdays 1 to 2.45pm; key obtainable from rectory.*

The present brick church with its square tower and Dutch gable doorway, dates, in the main, from 1630 when it was rebuilt by Sir Adam Newton *(see below).* Inside are a memorial tablet to Master Edward Wilkinson (d 1567), Yeoman of the Mouth to Henry VIII and Edward VI and Master Cook to Queen Elizabeth, a 17C heraldic north window, the hatchment (west wall) of the Spencer Percevals and Spencer Wilsons, who in the 18C owned Charlton House, the royal arms of Queen Anne and the tablet and bust of Spencer Perceval, assassinated in the House of Commons when prime minister in 1812.

The church, a landmark from the Thames, served as a navigational aid in the early 18C and so flies the white ensign on St George's and St Luke's days.

Charlton House. – *View by appointment with the warden.*

The house, the finest extant example of Jacobean architecture in London, was built between 1607 and 1612 for Adam Newton, Dean of Durham and tutor to Prince Henry, eldest son of James I.

Characteristically, of deep red brick with stone dressings, it has a shallow H shaped plan with symmetrical bays at the end of each wing and balustrades lining the crest and terrace. At the centre is the door with a surround dated 1616, and two storey bay above in stone, exuberantly decorated in an inexplicable German style.

Features inside include the plasterwork, particularly the ceiling with pendants in the Grand Saloon over the two storey hall, the fireplaces, Long Gallery and typical staircase with square well and carved newel posts. The gateway, stranded on the front lawn, is the original Tuscan pillared entrance with an added 18C crest.

Eltham Palace★. – *Off Court Road. Open Thursdays and Sundays only, April to October 10.30am to 12.15pm and 2.15 to 6pm (4pm November to March).*

Eltham, described as a manor in *Domesday,* became a favourite with the Plantagenets and by the 14C was described by the chronicler, Froissart, as "a very magnificent palace". Edward IV added the Great Hall in 1479-80; Henry VIII resided there until a growing interest in his ships made him prefer Greenwich. During the Commonwealth, according to John Evelyn, it fell into "miserable ruins", and was finally valued only as building material (£2 754). At long last, in 1931, it was let to Mr Stephen Courtauld who restored the Great Hall.

The Great Hall. – The hall, 101ft long, 36ft wide and 55ft to the roof apex is built of brick, faced with stone along its length and decorated with grotesque heads. Inside is the hall's chief glory, in all but the technical sense since the posts are tenoned, a **hammerbeam** roof of four centred arches, with braces, open traceries, cusped spandrels, elaborate pendants, and massive main timbers, intricately moulded.

Outside the Tudor House, on the right was "My Lord Chancellor's lodging" or the occasional residence of Cardinal Wolsey.

BLOOMSBURY ★ (Camden)

The once residential area with its many squares is dominated by two major learned institutions, the British Museum *(p 36)* and the ever expanding London University.

The development of Bloomsbury Sq in 1661 brought a new concept in local planning: the 4th Earl of Southampton, descendant of the Lord Chancellor to whom Henry VIII had granted the feudal manor in 1545, erected houses for the well-to-do around three sides of a square, a mansion for himself on the fourth, northern, side and — the innovation — a network of secondary service streets all around, with a market nearby, so ordering, in Evelyn's words, "a little town". He was successful: by 1667, when he died, he had a magnificent residence, the focus of fashion had transferred to his estate and he had made a fortune. His only daughter, Lady Rachel, married the future 1st Duke of Bedford, uniting two great estates.

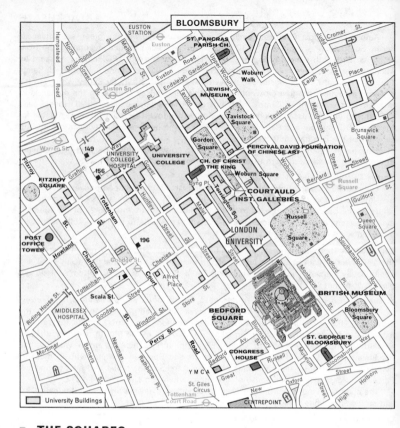

■ THE SQUARES

Development of the second and most elegant Bedford Sq was realised by Gertrude, widow of the 4th Duke with Thomas Laverton as architect in 1775. The remainder, all different and now lined in part or incorporated within the university precinct, followed in 19C: **Russell** in 1800, **Tavistock** 1806-26, **Torrington** 1825, **Woburn** 1829, **Gordon** (originally by Thomas Cubitt), 1850.

Bedford Sq★★, still complete, with three storey brick terrace houses with rounded doorways and first floor balconies, is relieved halfway along each range by a pedimented stucco centrepiece. Bloomsbury Sq contains none of the original houses but on the west side are the 18/19C Pharmaceutical Society and in the corner two mid 18C houses, one, with a cherub decorated plaque, the residence from 1818-26 of Isaac and Benjamin Disraeli.

The squares' most famous residents were the **Bloomsbury Group** of Virginia Woolf and Vanessa Bell, Roger Fry, the art critic who in 1910 organised the first Post-Impressionist Exhibition to be held in London, Leonard Woolf, who with his wife Virginia, founded the Hogarth Press, Clive Bell, E.M. Forster, Lytton Strachey, Duncan Grant, Maynard Keynes the economist, David Garnet and Wyndham Lewis. The group were joined in Gordon Sq and in houses in neighbouring streets and squares including Fitzroy where several lived, by Rupert Brooke, D.H. Lawrence, Bertrand Russell, Lady Ottoline Morrell... By the early 30s their ideas and works, literary, critical and artistic, had become widely known and accepted, their influence absorbed into the artistic tradition.

■ LONDON UNIVERSITY

London University, incorporated as an examining body by charter in 1836, as a teaching university in 1900, moved from Kensington to Bloomsbury only after the war, although the cold Portland stone building with a tall square tower (library) by Charles Holden had been under construction since 1932. Colleges, faculties and new institutes are now housed throughout the local streets and squares in the old 18/19C houses and in the ever extending, heterogeneous complex of brick, stone, concrete, steel, mosaic and glass.

The university has nearly 35 000 registered internal and 37 000 external students.

University College. – The central range of this, the oldest of the university buildings, is marked by an imposing pedimented portico, behind which rises a high dome (1827-9). Guarding either side of the courtyard are a pair of miniature, domed, observatories. The college houses the **Flaxman Sculpture Galleries**, renowned Egyptology Galleries and the figure of Jeremy Bentham (1748-1832), inspiration of the college's founders. Opposite are the 19C red brick, gabled and decorated University College Hospital, and extensive new clinics and institutes.

Courtauld Institute Galleries★★. – *Courtauld-Warburg Building, Woburn Sq. Open daily 10am to 5pm, Sundays 2 to 5pm; closed 1 January, Good Friday, 24, 25, 26 December.*

The luxurious galleries exhibit the major art bequests to London University: Primitives to Renaissance paintings; the Bloomsbury Group and Impressionist pictures of Roger Fry (1866-1934) and the unrivalled private collection assembled by Samuel Courtauld of

Impressionists with canvases by Manet *(Bar at the Folies Bergères),* Degas, Bonnard, Gauguin (Tahitian scenes), Van Gogh *(Peach Trees in Blossom, the Artist with his ear cut off),* Seurat and Cézanne, including the wondrous *Lake at Annecy.*

Percival David Foundation of Chinese Art★. – *53 Gordon Sq. Open Mondays 2 to 5pm, Tuesdays to Fridays 10.30am to 5pm, 1pm on Saturdays; closed at Christmas, Easter, holiday Mondays and preceding Saturdays.*

The porcelain – rimmed bowls, ewers, foliate edged plates, jars, vases, pillow head-rests – collected by their marks (and so precisely dated) as well as for their aesthetic beauty, was assembled between the wars by Percival David, scholar, sinologist and connoisseur. *Famille rose, famille verte,* blue and white objects, green ware, pure white, white rimmed with brown, oxblood red, brown black, grey-blue, deep yellow ware, cela-dons... have each a still, sophisticated, beauty.

Church of Christ the King. – *Gordon Sq.* The church, built in 1853 in the Early English style to cathedral proportions – the interior is 212ft long – is now the University Church.

■ ADDITIONAL SIGHTS

Jewish Museum. – *Upper Woburn Place, Tavistock Sq. Open Mondays to Thursdays 2.30 to 5pm, Fridays and Sundays 10.30am to 12.45pm; closed Saturdays, Jewish Holy Days, holiday Mondays, 1 January, Good Friday, Easter Sunday, 24, 25, 26 December.*

Crowded into a single room, overlooked by the portraits of 17/19C worthies, are ritual objects including a 16C Venetian Ark of the Law, scrolls in embroidered silk beaten silver covers, bells, lamps, Ram's Horns, historic wedding rings and 18/19C miniatures.

Tottenham Ct Rd. – The road, named after the feudal manor of Tottenhall, is known especially for the interior decoration and furnishing shops at its northern end: Maple's (new building, no 149), Habitat no 156, Heal's no 196, Ryman's Interiors no 200 and for Centrepoint, a tower office block of 34 storeys by Richard Seifert, erected in the 1960s, and the 1970s YMCA.

Pollock's Toy Museum and Shop. – *1 Scala St. Open Mondays to Saturdays 10am to 5pm; closed Sundays and holiday Mondays; 20p.*

Toy theatres, that 19C delight made from sheets described by Robert Louis Stevenson as "one penny plain and twopence coloured" can be seen amidst a mass of 19 and 20C toys: wax, porcelain, peg and spoon dolls, teddy bears, carved wooden animals, optical toys...

Post Office Tower. – *Cleveland St. Tower not open to the public; panoramic, revolving restaurant (open for main meals only).*

London's tallest building (620ft including the mast) has been a dominant, if undisting-uished, landmark since 1965 when it was erected to provide a path unimpeded by other high buildings for the capital's telecommunications system.

Fitzroy Sq★. – The square, almost at the foot of the PO Tower, is now a paved pedestrian precinct on three sides. Development began when **Robert Adam** built the east and south sides in Portland Stone in 1793 and was completed 50 years later in stucco on the other sides. Note the giant columned centrepiece on the east side repeated in miniature at either end and as the centrepiece of the south terrace.

The quarter was frequented by artists and writers from late 18 to early this century: Madox Brown, Bernard Shaw (no 29; 1887-98), in Fitzroy Square: Whistler and Sickert in Fitzroy St; Verlaine and Rimbaud in Howland St; Richard Wilson, Constable (no 76) in Charlotte St; Wyndham Lewis in Percy St...

Congress House. – *Great Russell St.* The structural mass of the T.U.C. headquarters is lightened by a glass screen at ground level, giving a view of an inner court and hall and distinguished by a war memorial before an upper green marble screen, carved on the spot from a 10 ton block of Roman stone by Jacob Epstein (1958).

St George's Bloomsbury. – **Hawksmoor's** church (1716-31) externally makes the most of a difficult site, with a grand pedimented portico at the top of a flight of steps and a stepped stone tower surmounted by a spire. Topping the steeple, to the contemporary public's derision, is a classical statue of the unpopular George I. Inside the problem of orientation on such a cramped site, resolved by Hawksmoor by hollowing out a small apse in the east wall, has since been confused by the transfer of the high gilded and inlaid reredos (1727), to the north wall. At the centre of the flat rectangular ceiling is a flower 5ft in diameter in richly gilded plaster and in the shell over the east niche, another delicate gilded relief, both by the master plasterer, Isaac Mansfield.

St Pancras Parish Church. – *Upper Woburn Place, Euston Rd.* The church was built in 1819-22 at the time of the Greek Revival and the design, selected from 30 submitted in response to an advertisement, shows the obvious inspiration of the Erechtheum in the caryatids supporting the roofs of the square vestries to north and south, the Tower of the Winds in the columned, two stage elevation of the octagonal west tower and the Classical colonnade. The interior is capacious with galleries on columns after the Elgin marbles.

The caryatids outside are a prime example of ladies who have withstood being sawn in half: they were made too tall and a middle section had to be removed from each to make her fit!

Woburn Walk, to the rear, is lined by small, antique jewellery, book and other shops behind early 19C shopfronts in colour washed, three storey houses.

Foundation. – It was the bequest in 1753 by **Sir Hans Sloane,** physician, naturalist, traveller, of his collection to the nation which finally spurred Parliament to found the BM. Already acquired (1700), but left in vaults in Westminster, was the priceless collection of mediaeval manuscripts of Sir Robert Cotton (1570-1631), and deposited with them, the old Royal Library of 12 000 volumes, assembled by monarchs since Tudor times (officially presented to the museum by George II in 1757); elsewhere were mss, charters and rolls collected by Robert Harley and his son Edward, Earls of Oxford (dd 1724, 1741) and made available in 1753. The collections were so magnificent, so extensive, that a building apart was necessary. A lottery was launched, money raised, and for £21 000 Montagu House, built in 1675 for the Duke of Montagu, ambassador to the court of Louis XIV, and rebuilt in 1686 after a fire, to designs by the French architect Puget, was purchased and altered. Although access, when the museum opened in 1759, was limited to certain weekdays and, until 1810, was by ticket only – always free – attendances soon mounted to 10 000 a year (now nearly 1 000 an hour). Arrangement in the main rooms and on the staircase landing was miscellaneous; engravings show stuffed giraffes, portraits, fossils and mss, books, dried plants, Classical marble statues and coins, pots and Buddhas, against a background of heroic frescoes and plasterwork ceilings. There were no labels – Cobbett christened the institution "the old curiosity shop".

Collections. – Within 50-75 years Montagu House was bursting. Acquisition was by presentation, bequest and special parliamentary purchase: to a great degree, it was in this period that the foundations of the present museum were laid. Chief among the acquisitions were: Thomason Tracts, pamphlets published during the Civil War and Commonwealth 1642-1660 (presented by George III, 1762): David Garrick Library (1 000 printed plays including First Folios, 1779), Sir William Hamilton collection of antique vases (£8 400; 1772): Cracherode collection of books, fine bindings, great master drawings, Greek and Roman coins (1799): Egyptian antiquities including the Rosetta Stone (under the Treaty of Alexandria, 1802, following Nelson's victory on the Nile); Greek and Roman sculptures, bronzes and terracottas, the Towneley Marbles (1804; £20 000); sculptures from the Temple of Apollo at Bassae, 1815): sculptures from the Parthenon, the Elgin Marbles (purchased 1816; £35 000)... In addition, there were purchases of mss, minerals (Greville), libraries (Hargrave, legal) music collections (Burney), natural history collections, French Revolution tracts and ephemera. In 1823, George IV presented his father's library of 65 000 volumes, 19 000 pamphlets, maps, charts; in 1824 came the Payne-Knight bequest of Classical antiquities, bronzes and drawings; in 1827 the Banks bequest of books, botanical specimens and ethnography.

(By courtesy of the BM)

Lewis Chessmen.

The building. – To house the burgeoning collections, temporary buildings were erected (1804-8) until, in 1824, **Robert Smirke,** appointed to design a permanent extension, produced plans which, beginning with a wing projecting from the northeast corner of the old house, continued wing by wing around a quadrangle to culminate in the replacement of the decayed Montagu House itself by a new, Greek inspired, colonnaded façade. It took 20 years to complete and, with three later additions, the Reading Room (1857) the Edward VII (1914) and Duveen Galleries (1938), is the building we know today.

Extensions. – In 1880-83 renewed pressure on space brought about the removal of the natural history departments to South Kensington; in 1905 of the newspapers to Colindale. In December 1970, the ethnographic collections transferred to 6 Burlington Gardens *(p 118).* In addition to building a new extension on the last remaining space on the Bloomsbury site, the museum is now engaged in re-arrangement whereby, in the main, primary collections (or key items) are on display in the galleries, secondary collections are held in reserve stores.

Bequests did much to give the museum its physical form; to an even greater degree have they influenced its immense variety; the early sequence of acquisitions increased in the later 19 and 20C by finds by archaeologists attached to the museum, brought the BM the reputation it has as the greatest centre of world antiquities.

The British Library. – The museum's library departments since 1973, have been vested in a separate authority and will eventually move into a new building at Somerstown.

The round **Reading Room** in the museum, came about through a combination of factors: rooms, at first in the basement, subsequently on the ground floor, were available to "men of letters", but Antonio Panizzi, refugee Italian revolutionary appointed Keeper of Printed Books in 1837 and Principal Librarian (Director) in 1856 was determined that the library should be open equally to "the poorest student". Robert Smirke's King's Library, splendid in appearance and size, could not provide sufficient seating; the quadrangle at the centre of the new wings had proved damp and gloomy, and, finally, in 1847, a new bequest, the Grenville Library, provided a climactic, albeit magnificent, embarrassment. Panizzi and Sydney Smirke (younger brother of Robert) combined and in 1857 the new Reading Room, beneath the 40ft wide dome was opened. It seats 400 readers with 25 miles of shelving (1 300 000 books), surrounding the circular room. Less spectacular, but equally if not more fundamental, Panizzi organised the compilation of the catalogue.

Open Mondays to Saturdays 10am to 5pm, Sundays 2.30 to 6pm; closed 1 January, Good Friday, 24, 25, 26 December. Coffee Shop, Special facilities: Readers' and Students' tickets available on application to the Keepers of Departments.

To help you find what you want to see:

Named objects — look in the right hand column; note the gallery name and colour in left column; find corresponding colour and gallery on plans p 38;

The table is divided into 5 area sections: ground and upper floors, east and west and the King Edward VII Galleries, listed in sequence and colour keyed to the plans to enable you to start a general visit in the area of most personal interest.

GALLERY		CONTENTS	SELECTED OBJECTS

Ground Floor West

GALLERY		CONTENTS	SELECTED OBJECTS
Assyrian Transept	26	Colossal human headed winged lion gates from Nimrud (9C BC); obelisks.	**Assyrian Black Obelisk** (9C).
Egyptian Sculpture Gallery	25	Obelisks, statues of the kings, sarcophagi, colossal red granite lions (1360 BC).	**Rosetta Stone**; Lions of Amenophis III; Rameses II; King Amenhotep II (1420 BC).
Northwest Staircase		Animals, birds, hunting scenes from 4-6C Carthage.	
Nineveh Gallery	21	Low reliefs of the Sack of Nineveh.	
Nimrud Gallery	19	Large low reliefs; coronation and other scenes with tall spade bearded, winged or bird headed men (Palace of Ashurnasirpal II).	
Assyrian Saloon	17	Low reliefs, chariot lion hunts.	
Assyrian Basement (downstairs)	18	Low reliefs of the wars of Ashurbanipal.	
Bronze Age Room	2	Vases, bath-tub and chest coffins (1400 BC); bronze and gold figurines.	
Early Greek Room	3	1000-500 BC; cases, statues; figurines.	
Room of the Kouroi	4	Marble figures of two youths (6C AD).	
Room of the Harpy Tomb	5	Busts, tomb monuments.	Strangford Apollo; Harpy Tomb; "Chatsworth" Head of Apollo.
Bassae Room	6	High relief frieze — warring Centaurs and Lapiths.	Temple of Apollo at Bassae.
Nereid Room	7	Nereid Monument at Xanthos: tomb temple displayed against a blue sky; statues of the Nereids — breezes; lion gate guardians.	
Duveen Gallery	8	Frieze, metopes of the battles of the Lapiths and Centaurs and pediments from the Parthenon (5C BC).	**Elgin Marbles**; the Horse of Selene.
Room of the Caryatid	9	The statue and a fluted Ionic pillar — both Pentelic marble; terracotta figurines; a recumbent bull; Greek jewellery and seal stones (480-330 BC).	**Caryatid** from the Erechtheum on the Acropolis 5C BC.
Payava Room	10	Tombs and funerary bowls, minute bronzes; warriors full of movement, terracotta figures.	Payava Tomb 350 BC.
Etruscan Art (mezzanine)	11	Sarcophagi, painted panels, pottery, bronzes, Etruscan gold.	Terracotta sarcophagi of Seianti Tlesnasa (2C BC).
Mausoleum Room	12	Statues, friezes (battle of Greeks and Amazons) from the Mausoleum or tomb of Mausolus, at Halicarnassus; column drum from the temple of Artemis at Ephesus.	Forepart of a horse (from chariot group on crest of the tomb); Cnidus lion tomb monument.
Hellenistic Room	13	Statues, bronze heads, jewellery.	Goddess **Demeter** from Cnidus; bronze head of **Sophocles** 3C BC; jewelled sceptre.
First Roman Room	14	Gilded glass bowls; figures in bronze and terracotta.	Bronze of "Hermes in his travelling hat"; **Tanagra** terracotta figurines; **Portland Vase.**
Second Roman Room	15	Mosaic underwater and statues.	Apollo with a lyre.

Ground Floor East

GALLERY	CONTENTS	SELECTED OBJECTS
Grenville Library: Manuscript Saloon	Illuminations and mss; autographs, letters; charters, orders of execution; early music mss.	Nelson *Victory* Logbook, letter; **Magna Carta;** Essex' death warrant; Shakespeare's signature; Lindisfarne Gospels; Codex Sinaiticus.
Bible Room	Bibles and psalters.	
King's Library	Fine bindings; early and recent printed books; special exhibitions.	Gutenberg Bible; incunabula; First Folio; Caxton and Wyken de Worde's books; Winchester Gospels.
Northeast Staircase	Totem pole, 88 steps high	

BRITISH MUSEUM★★★

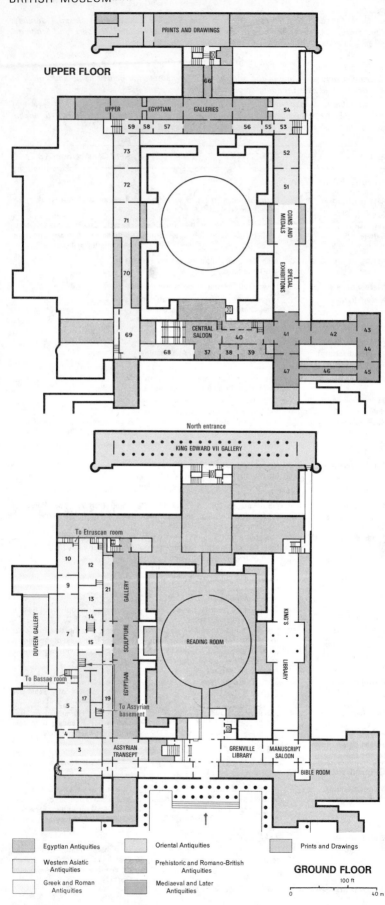

UPPER FLOOR

PRINTS AND DRAWINGS

66

UPPER   EGYPTIAN   GALLERIES   54
59 58 57   56 55 53
73   52
72   51
71   COINS AND MEDALS
70   SPECIAL EXHIBITIONS
69   CENTRAL SALOON   40   41   42   43
68   37 38 39   44
47   46   45

North entrance
KING EDWARD VII GALLERY

To Etruscan room
10   12
9   21
13   SCULPTURE GALLERY   KING'S
14   LIBRARY
7   15   READING ROOM
To Bassae room   EGYPTIAN
5   17 19
To Assyrian basement
4
3   ASSYRIAN TRANSEPT   GRENVILLE LIBRARY   MANUSCRIPT SALOON
2   1   BIBLE ROOM

DUVEEN GALLERY

Egyptian Antiquities   Oriental Antiquities   Prints and Drawings

Western Asiatic Antiquities   Prehistoric and Romano-British Antiquities

Greek and Roman Antiquities   Mediaeval and Later Antiquities

GROUND FLOOR
100 ft
0   40 m

GALLERY		CONTENTS	SELECTED OBJECTS

Upper Floor West

Terracottas, Bronzes	68	Greek; Etruscan and Roman.	
Greek and Roman Life Room	69	Farming tools, writing materials, weights and measures, games counters; jewellery; sandcore, moulded, carved, blown glass — coloured, opalescent.	$\frac{1}{4}$ of a Roman wooden waterwheel; Minoan and Mycenaean jewellery (1700-1100 BC).
Greek and Roman Vase Rooms	71-73	Vases illustrating Classical mythology; Cypriot antiquities.	The gods and heroes; the Man from Tamassos (bust, 700 BC).
Ivory Room	58	Nimrud carved ivories.	
Syrian Room	57	Stelae and antiquities from Asia Minor, Palestine and Syria.	
Room of Writing	56	From 2280 BC — Inscriptions on cylinders, tablets, seals.	Date stamps in reverse for imprinting bricks.
Prehistoric Room	55	Pottery, figurines, stone seals.	
Neo-Hittite Landing	53	Sculptured slabs, column (Persepolis).	
Sumerian and Babylonian Room	54	Headdresses with gold leaves; earrings, gold goblets, a silver lyre, a harp; animal masks; (reconstructed) shrine.	Early Sumerian jewellery; the Chaldees treasure from the city of Ur.
Anatolian Room	51	Miniature figures of Hittite Gods; coins, bronzes, arms and armour.	
Iranian Room	52	Luristan bronzes, gold objects and jewellery, sculpture from Persepolis.	
Upper Egyptian Galleries	60-65	Mummies bandaged in cases and coffins; mummified cats, a crocodile; domestic objects; mirrors, musical instruments, clothing and hairstyles, furniture; papyri; wall paintings.	The **Mummies.**
Coptic Corridor	66	Reliefs and paintings of Roman and Coptic periods in Egypt, 1-9C AD.	

Upper Floor East

Central Saloon	35	Early Christian mosaic: 4C AD, central male head before Chi-Rho monogram thought to be Christ; wrought iron burial furniture 1C BC; vessels; British goldwork of 2000-1500 BC beaten paper thin or wrought, interwoven to rope-like thickness...	**Pavement** from Hinton St Mary, Dorset; 4 legged iron frame; Celtic "Lorraine Flagons", 4C BC; discs, bracelets, fasteners.
Prehistory Rooms	37-38	Earliest human societies; advance from 2000 BC — 1 AD; pre-Roman metalwork — shields, helmets; early Celtic neck rings, jewellery.	
Roman Britain Room	40	Daily life (1-4C AD) portrayed through common objects — trade religion, the army, the home (tableware, mosaics, wall paintings).	**Mildenhall Treasure** (4C silver).
Early Mediaeval and Mediaeval Rooms	41-42	Anglo-Saxon royal ship burial deposit with all the necessities for after life; jewellery, plate, weapons, textiles, utensils.	**Sutton Hoo Treasure; Lewis Chessmen** (12C) in walrus ivory; **Gold Cup** of the Kings of England and France (c 1380).
Mediaeval Pottery and Tile Room	43	English and continental pottery and ceramics.	
Horological Room	44	Clocks before and after the introduction of the pendulum; watches.	Ilbert Collection.
Waddesdon Bequest	45	Renaissance jewellery, plate, enamels, bronzes.	**Thorn Reliquary; Lyte Jewel** (James I miniature); Limoges enamels; 1584 iron shield.
Renaissance and Later Corridor	46-47	Brilliantly arranged to compare British life at Court craftsmanship (native and refugee) with those of Western Europe; mementoes.	**Huguenot silver;** royal seals; Battersea enamels.
Coins and Medals Gallery		2000 years of coins and medals in Britain from the first coins of 580-800 to decimalisation in 1970. Displayed by reigns.	Celtic — Roman coins — London mint in Roman times; Tudor... Commonwealth, Restoration... 1972 Maundy money.

King Edward VII Galleries

| Ground Floor | | Chinese porcelain, jade, bronze, terracotta, ivory; Japanese porcelain; Central Asian bronzes; Buddhas; Persian, Syrian metalwork, enamelwork, porcelain; glass; cloisonné ware; Syrian astronomical instruments. | **T'ang horses** and camels; Judge of Hell (16C Chinese); Yuan blue and white porcelain; Sambas Treasure of Buddhist images. |
| Upper Floor | | Prints, drawings displayed in special exhibitions; portrait drawings; watercolours; modern lithographs. | Michelangelo, Rubens, Rembrandt, Turner, Blake, Dürer, Piper, Sutherland... |

BRIXTON (Lambeth)

Brixton's history is modern – apart from a mention in the *Domesday Book*, there is little in the records until the 18/19C. The population, at first one of migrants from the over-crowded City and other parts of England, come to work in the ever more numerous factories, is now, noticeably, West Indian. The substantial council estates of the 1960s and '70s, the brilliantly coloured **street markets** of Electric Avenue, Pope's and Station Rds, reflect the life of the town today, particularly on a Saturday, as the buildings at the road junction, around the small open space, a green plot grazed by sheep and grandly called **Brixton Oval**, reflect late 19/20C local prosperity.

City of London Almshouses. – *Ferndale Rd (east end)*. Retired freemen live in the brick terraces rebuilt in 1884, and the smaller, stone trimmed Gresham terrace – note the cricket above the plaque – which frame three sides of a shaded green acre.

St Matthew's Parish Church. – The church of 1822, is a massive edifice with a pedimented tower. A faded notice on the churchyard pillar recalls time past: "Carriages to enter at this gate".

Trinity Congregational Church. – *St Matthew's Rd*. An attractive small church of 1828.

Brockwell Clinic. – *Tulse Hill*. The 18C square fronted house of white stucco and stock brick is one of the few survivors of its period.

Brockwell Park. – The park includes an old walled garden with arbours, a yew arch, round goldfish pond, roses... The **Hall**, a two storey stock brick house of 1816, has a Classical columned porch in front, terrace at the side and at the back a two storey bow window and a later angular bay window with a canopied balcony on iron pillars.

Brixton Prison. – *Jebb Avenue, Brixton Hill*. The 1820 prison, of which only a high wall can be seen from the end of the avenue, is London's oldest and holds the doubtful distinction of being the first, in 1823, to introduce the treadmill.

Brixton Windmill. – *Blenheim Gardens, Brixton Hill*. This solid reminder of Brixton's rural past has brick walls 14ins thick, five storeys high, a boat shaped wooden cap, and gleaming white sails (restored: 1964).

BUCKINGHAM PALACE ★★ (Westminster)

Mulberry Garden to Royal Palace. – In 1703, John Sheffield, newly created Duke of Buckingham, received from his queen, Anne, a grant of land planted the previous century by James I as a mulberry garden at the west end of St James's Park. His Grace built himself a town residence of brick which he named Buckingham House. Little more than half a century later, in 1762, the mansion was purchased for £28 000 by **George III** and presented to his bride, Charlotte. Although renamed Queen's House, few major alterations were made except the construction in the south wing of George III's octagon library, demolished and replaced in 1854 by the Ball Room (the library was presented to the British Museum).

George IV summoned **John Nash** and their imaginations fired each other as they had for the recently completed Brighton Pavilion. The architect produced around the core of the old brick mansion, a palace clad in Bath stone. The king however, died before it was complete and

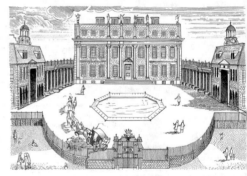

(After engraving, Pitkin Pictorials)

Buckingham House *c* 1710.

Nash, although technically exonerated, was discredited and retired, the work in hand being taken over by Edward Blore and only completed in 1837, by which time William IV had also died.

Victoria, three weeks after her accession, took up residence; the royal standard, at last, was flown on the Marble Arch designed by Nash as a state entrance to the open forecourt. Ten years later came the construction of the east face linking the advanced, north and south wings, enclosing the forecourt in a quadrangle and including what has since become the palace's focal point on public occasions, the balcony. The grand entrance remained in its original position and is approached through arches in the east front; Marble Arch was rendered superfluous and was removed. Finally, in 1912, the east front was heightened and refaced in Portland stone to harmonise with the Mall and new Victoria Memorial.

The West Front and the Gardens. – The west front of golden Bath stone, stepped from an attic frieze at the centre, descends to twin pedimented pavilions from which the eye returns along the line of the white stone terrace balustrade to the central steps and the great bow, balconied and columned at first floor level, balustraded and green saucer domed above. As achieved, the front is a reduced version of Nash's extravaganza: the stone, the strong horizontal lines, the bow, however, were his in essence.

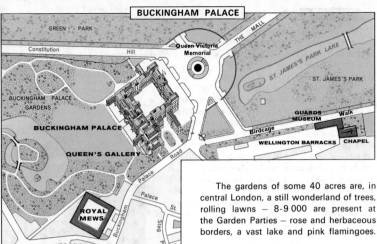

The gardens of some 40 acres are, in central London, a still wonderland of trees, rolling lawns – 8-9 000 are present at the Garden Parties – rose and herbaceous borders, a vast lake and pink flamingoes.

The interior. – The decoration of the **State Apartments** *(not open to the public)* remains much in the grand manner decreed by George IV and ably executed by Nash and his followers in columned proportion with tall windows, coved ceilings, flowing staircases, emphasised in coloured marbles, bronze, ivory, highlighted everywhere with gold and reflected in splendid mirrors and chandeliers. The areas of the palace most familiar to the public are the **Ball Room** where investitures and the larger state banquets are held and the **Bow Room** through which those invited, pass to the garden parties.

The Ball Room, with ivory coloured walls, is 123ft long by 60ft wide and has the canopied royal dais as a focal point in scarlet and gold at the west end. Beneath the canopy, domed, gold fringed and embroidered with the crown, are the thrones and royal arms. On either side gold capitalled pilasters and candelabra; above, supporting emblematic figures, recessed covings outlined in gold as are the compartmented ceiling, the corbelled and pedimented doorways, cornice, panelling wainscoting... In summer, the focus of the Bow Room, also with a decoration of ivory and gold, is the garden seen through the semicircle of tall windows framed by deep crimson curtains.

The apartments of the Royal family are in the north wing.

The Queen's Gallery★★. – *Buckingham Palace Road. Open Tuesdays to Saturdays and holiday Mondays, 11am to 5pm, Sundays 2 to 5pm; closed Mondays, Good Friday, 24, 25 December and between exhibitions; 30p.*

Selections of paintings, drawings and furniture from the superb Royal Collection are displayed as temporary exhibitions in the gallery constructed on the site of a former domestic chapel.

Changing of the Guard★★. – *Time 11.30am unless affairs of state intervene, or it is raining – ask the police on duty or telephone 01-730 0791.*

This colourful ceremony takes place in the forecourt when the sovereign is in residence (Royal Standard flying over the palace).

The guard is mounted by the five regiments of Foot of the Guards Division whose uniform of bearskin, whose scarlet tunic and dark blue trousers is distinguished by badges, buttons and insignia: the Grenadiers (f 1656), by a white plume, buttons evenly spaced, Coldstreams (f 1659), scarlet plume, buttons by twos, Scots (f 1642), no plume, buttons by threes, Irish (f 1902), blue plume, buttons by fours, Welsh (f 1915), green and white plume, buttons by fives.

Wellington Barracks, Chapel and Museum. – *Birdcage Walk. Under reconstruction.*

The Guards' Museum. – *Open daily 10am to 5pm; Sundays and holidays, Mondays 11.30am to 1.30pm, 2.30 to 5pm (4pm November to February); closed 1 January, Good Friday, 24, 25, 26 December; 5p.*

The Guards' Chapel. – The chapel arose in 1962-3 from the devastation of a direct hit by a flying bomb in June 1944 when more than 120 died.

The lofty clean lined interior is of white marble with clear glass lancet windows opposing brightly lit memorial chapels aligned in a cloister along the south wall. Above hang regimental colours. Note the dark, mosaic lined, apse – all that remained of the 19C church – the engraved chapel windows, the terracotta frieze of the Household Cavalry and the beautiful modern silverwork on the altars.

The Royal Mews★★. – *Buckingham Palace Rd. Open Wednesdays and Thursdays 2 to 4pm; closed Royal Ascot week in June; 15p.*

The mews which, apart from the earlier Riding House (1764) were built by Nash around a square courtyard, are entered through a lion and unicorn gate then a Classical archway, topped by a small clock tower.

The blocks around the tree shaded court are occupied by the stables (the horses are sometimes away on duty), saddlery (parade harness) and coach houses where the equipages vary in splendour from modest, covered two wheelers to the open state landau, the Glass Coach in which royal brides and bridegrooms return from Westminster Abbey, the Irish Coach in which the Queen rides at the State Opening of Parliament and the Gold State Coach (1762) which has been used by every monarch at their coronation since 1820.

CHELSEA ★★ (Royal Borough of Kensington and Chelsea) _____

The completion of the embankment in 1874 removed for ever the atmosphere of a riverside community with boats drawn up on the mud flats, trees shading the foreshore, people walking along a country road, so typically painted by Rowlandson in 1789 *(Chelsea Reach)*, watched in his old age as the sun was setting by Turner, painted luminously by Whistler *(Old Battersea Bridge)*.

Chelsea has a Royal Hospital but no "big houses", a few squares, terraces, attractive individual houses of all periods and 19 and 20C red brick flats.

By the late 19C, of course, the roads and bridge were constructed and the river no longer served as Chelsea's main access as it had when **Sir Thomas More** came upriver and bought a parcel of land at the water's edge west of the church (where Beaufort St is now approximately). The house he built was large enough to contain his extensive family, portrayed vividly by **Holbein** on his first visit to England (National Portrait Gallery). Another regular guest in the twelve years More lived in Chelsea before sailing down river to his execution in 1535, was **Erasmus** and another who came informally appearing unannounced at the river gate, was Henry VIII himself. Reminders of More, that "man of marvellous mirth and past-times and sometimes of as sad a gravity, (that) man for all seasons" remain in the memorial inscription he composed himself in the church *(see opposite)* and the statue, a seated, black robed figure with gilded face and hands, on the pavement outside.

(After photograph, Pitkin Pictorials)

Sir Thomas More.

Since those times a varied cavalcade has lived in the village: Nell Gwynn, Ellen Terry (215 King's Rd), Sybil Thorndyke; Sir Joseph Banks (botanist, explorer and PRS); Sir John Fielding (the Blind Beak, reformer of the penal system), Sir Marc Isambard Brunel and his son, Isambard Kingdom; Mrs. Gaskell; the Pre-Raphaelites – **Dante Gabriel Rossetti**, his sister Christina, **Burne-Jones**, William and Jane Morris, Holman Hunt, Swinburne, Millais. Other artists include William de Morgan, Wilson Steer, Sargent, Augustus John, Orpen, Sickert. Mark Twain, Henry James, T S Eliot are among Chelsea Americans. Smollett lived in Lawrence St, **Oscar Wilde** at 34 Tite St. There were also Hilaire Belloc, the Sitwells, Arnold Bennett... **Thomas Carlyle** lived in Cheyne Row for 47 years.

Chelsea, in addition, has frequently been the setting for a new or revived fashion-extreme and exclusive in the case of the Pre-Raphaelites, individual in that of Oscar Wilde and his green carnation, cosmopolitan, crowded, gay and smart before it degenerated into unkempt raffishness in that of the Ranelagh and Cremorne Gardens. The latest began with the opening in 1955 of Bazaar by the designer **Mary Quant**. From one shop with brightly coloured, cleverly cut, clothes entirely managed by a handful of people, a complete change in dress style developed which influenced fashion at home and abroad and grew into a worldwide business in which the **King's Rd** became a Mecca, and Chelsea in the '60s, the "navel of swinging London".

■ CHEYNE WALK★ Downstream towards the Royal Hospital

The terraces of brick houses standing back from the river front are rich with memories of artists, writers... Turner spent his last years in near seclusion at 119 Cheyne Walk, (restored to the same tall narrow form with a rooftop studio); Brunel House, 105 Cheyne Walk, a three storey block of flats commemorates the memory of the engineers, father and son.

Lindsey House. – *96-100 Cheyne Walk, west end.* The house, from 1752 the London headquarters of the Moravian Brethren (their burial ground to the right of Milman's St can be seen from the rear of the flats), was built for the 3rd Earl of Lindsey in 1674 on the site of Sir Thomas More's farm. The 17C Lindsey mansion (since subdivided) is of brick with a pedimented and quoined centre and corner pavilion and a central door crowned by a broken pediment, ornately decorated.

Nos 92 and 91 Cheyne Walk. – The houses, built in 1771, include a remarkable number of Venetian windows – 2 on either side of a central bay in 92, 3 in 91 and a further two in blind form; other characteristics are parallel arches over the garage (formerly a passage) and front door in 92, a modestly fine entrance to 91 and a conservatory on the first floor, with a commanding view of the river. Nos 93 and 94 date from 1777.

Crosby Hall. – *Open daily 10am to noon 2.15 to 5pm; afternoons only on Sundays.*
A regrettable post-war annexe and a neo-Tudor building of 1926, the premises of the British Federation of University Women, look puny beside the great hall of the 15C wool merchant, **Sir John Crosby**, whose residence, built between 1466-75, stood in mediaeval Bishopsgate. Panelling, three tier windows in the oriel at the dais end and a splendid timber roof remain as a reminder of the once substantial mansion of which the hall was transferred to Chelsea in 1908.

Roper's Garden. – This walled garden once part of More's orchard, is named after William Roper, his son-in-law. An upstanding stone relief of a woman walking against the wind by **Jacob Epstein** commemorates the artist's years in Chelsea (1909-14).

Chelsea Old Church. – The church dates from pre-Norman, possibly Saxon times, evolving until by 20C it appeared with a nave and tower of c 1670, 13C chancel and early 14C chapels of which the south one had been remodelled by Sir Thomas More in 1528. In 1941 it was badly bombed except for the More chapel; in 1950-8 it was reconstructed on the old foundations so that it looks substantially as in old prints and paintings with a stocky square brick tower rising beside the river. Inside, the short, wide nave divides beneath three arches at the east end into the chancel, the Lawrence and More Chapels; the monuments, rescued from the rubble are old; the furnishings old supplemented by modern replacements – the altar and rails are 17C, the small marble font dates from 1673, the cover is modern, the **chained books,** presented by Sir Hans Sloane and the only ones in a London church, consist of a Vinegar Bible (1717), a prayer book (1723), *Homilies* (1683) and two volumes of Foxe's *Book of Martyrs* (1684).

Quite new are the kneelers, embroidered 1953-8, to commemorate by coats of arms or symbolically, those of all times associated with the church – among the 400 are Elizabeth I, Holman Hunt, Thomas Doggett, institutor of the race, Sir Hans Sloane, Sir Thomas More... Among the monuments are the reclining figure of Lady Jane Cheyne (1699), Sarah Colville rising in her grave clothes with aghast expression and upraised hands (1631; Lawrence Chapel), the massive Stanley monument of 1632 and, near the squint, the small alabaster group of Sir Thomas Lawrence, City goldsmith and merchant adventurer, at prayer with his wife and eight children. More's self-composed inscription stands against the south wall of the sanctuary by the arch with capitals dated 1528, designed by Holbein.

It was in Lawrence Street that the Chelsea China Works flourished in the 18C before being transferred to Derby. Among 18C houses to remain are the early Georgian, Drake's and Monmouth Houses, sharing a pedimented porch on carved brackets (nos 23-24).

Carlyle's House. – *24 Cheyne Row. Open March to October, Wednesdays to Saturdays 11am to 1pm and 2 to 6pm or sunset if earlier; closing time 3.30pm in winter; Sundays afternoons only; closed Mondays, Tuesdays and all December; 50p.*

Thomas Carlyle lived in this modest Queen Anne house, working, walking, dour and apart, though his young wife loved company. The "Sage of Chelsea" is commemorated in a statue by Boehm in Cheyne Walk gardens.

Before the new flats rounding the southwest corner of Oakley Street is a bronze of a boy poised high above a dolphin by David Wynne.

Henry VIII's Chelsea Palace. – Nos 19-26 Cheyne Walk, dating from c 1765, mark the site of the palace built by Henry beside the river in 1537 but which was to endure only 250 years. Known as the New Manorhouse (the Old Manorhouse, demolished in 1704, stood where Lawrence St is), the two storey Tudor brick mansion included "three cellars, three halls, three parlours, three kitchens... a large staircase, three drawing rooms, seventeen chambers" and had water brought by conduit from Kensington. It was the residence of the young Prince Edward, Princess Elizabeth and their cousin Lady Jane Grey until, on the death of the king, it became the dower house of, first, Catherine Parr (d 1548) and then Anne of Cleves (d 1557). In 17C it was owned by the Cheynes; in 1712 it was purchased by **Sir Hans Sloane,** who retired to Chelsea from Bloomsbury with his two daughters and his collection. On his death in 1753, his collection returned to Bloomsbury to form the nucleus of the BM and the house was demolished.

No 18 was the popular Don Saltero's coffeehouse and museum, no 16, named the **Queen's House** after Catherine of Braganza, although it was not built till 1717, twelve years after her death, was the home of the poet and painter DG Rossetti and where the Pre-Raphaelites used to meet. The house, the largest in the row, is, apart from the bay window (which figures graphically in John Fowler's *French Lieutenant's Woman*), unaltered with a central pediment, segment headed windows, brick corner pilasters and the finest among several contemporary iron gateways. A fountain in the gardens opposite includes a portrait bust of Rossetti by Seddon.

No 6 is remarkable for the Chippendale-Chinese gate and railings before the large plain parapet while no 5 has beautiful, conventional, railings. A Corinthian pilastered and entablatured entrance marks no 4 where the painter Maclise lived and George Eliot spent her last weeks. Old Swan House, no 17 on the Embankment, dating from 1876 is an example of one of Norman Shaw's town houses.

Chelsea Physic Garden. – *Specialists only may be considered for admission on application in writing (send sae): Clerk to the Trustees, City Parochial Foundation, 10 Fleet St, EC4.*

The garden was founded in 1673 by the Worshipful Society of Apothecaries of London on land leased from Sir Hans Sloane who in 1722 granted the Society the lease in perpetuity. The record of the garden, overlooked at the centre by a statue of Sir Hans, is remarkable: Georgia's cotton seeds came from the South Seas via the Physic Garden, India's tea from China, her quinine *(cinchona)* from S America, Malaya's rubber from S America...

National Army Museum★. – *Royal Hospital Rd. Open weekdays 10am to 5.30pm, Sundays 2 to 5.30pm; closed Good Friday, 24 to 26 December, 1 January.*

The museum tells the story of the British army from the formation of the Yeomen of the Guard by Henry VII on Bosworth Field in 1485, of the Indian army and of colonial forces. It illustrates campaigns, the evolution from armour to khaki and tin helmets, from hand weapons to firearms, pikes and pistols, swords, rifles... The Weapon Gallery exhibits today's missiles, the uniform gallery the carefully tailored, buckskin breeches, the helmets, caps, hats in which the officers once went to war. Among notable honours and decorations, are medals and insignia of the Coldstream Guards from Tangier (1680) to Ulster and orders presented to HRH Duke of Windsor, including some no longer in existence and many beautiful in their coloured enamelwork and craftsmanship. The art gallery contains principally portraits (several by Reynolds, Romney, Gainsborough and Lawrence).

43

■ THE ROYAL HOSPITAL★★

Chelsea Pensioners, some 400 in number, have been colourful members of the local community now for nearly 300 years. The idea for a veterans' hostel would appear to have come to Charles II, who had re-established a standing army in 1661, from reports of the Invalides built by Louis XIV in Paris in 1670. The next ten years are summarised in the Latin inscription in the Figure Court: "This hospital", it runs, "was founded by Charles II, expanded by James II and completed by King William and Queen Mary – 1692".

The buildings. – Wren produced a quadrangular plan after the Oxford Colleges with a main court open on the south to the grounds and the river. He expanded it by abutting courts to east and west always leaving one side open. The long, regular brick ranges are marked at the angles with stone quoins and midway by stone centre-pieces pierced at ground level, colossally pilastered and plainly pedimented.

Figure Court, Royal Hospital.

Entrance is through the lantern crowned gateway in the north range of the original **Figure Court,** so-called after the Classical statue of Charles II by **Grinling Gibbons** at the centre.

The porch emerges beneath the portico of giant Tuscan pillars, entablature and pediment which is the principal feature of the court, ennobled by a colonnade extending above small paired Tuscan pillars, the full length of the range. Along the entablature runs the historical Latin inscription *(see above).*

Chapel and Great Hall. – *Open: daily 10am to noon, 2 to 4pm, Sundays 2 to 4pm; Council Chamber Sundays 11.45 to 12.15pm, 2 to 4pm and summer Saturdays 2 to 4pm.*

The pillared doorway leads into the Octagon Porch from which steps rise on either side to the Chapel and Great Hall, both panelled beneath tall rounded windows. The Chapel has a barrel vault, compartmented and decorated like the piers and spandrels with delicate plasterwork (Henry Margetts) and, at the end, a domed, painted, apse.

The end wall of the Hall is decorated with an 18C mural of Charles II on horseback before the hospital, with full length portraits and captured colours between the windows. Note the old leather beer jugs.

The Museum. – *Open 10am to noon, 2 to 5pm; Saturdays and Sundays 2 to 4.30pm only.*

Wellington mementoes, the hospital's history, that of its members, provide the exhibits.

Ranelagh Gardens. – These celebrated gardens opened in 1724, affording patrons *al fresco* meals, concerts and spectacles in the Rotunda, a building 150ft in diameter encircled by tiers of boxes from which the fashionable descended to promenade in the arena. On the garden's closure in 1805 the land was repurchased by the hospital.

The **Chelsea Flower Show** *(p 30)* when thousands come to gaze on thousands of flowers and plants – and everything else imaginable for a garden – has been held in the grounds under the auspices of the Royal Horticultural Society since 1913. The show covers 30 acres with the Great Marquee alone occupying 3½ acres.

In line with the entrance to the Royal Hospital, a broad walk runs directly to the river and a double avenue (planted in 1692-4), **Royal Avenue** extends north across the fields known as Burton's Court to King's Rd – it was intended that it

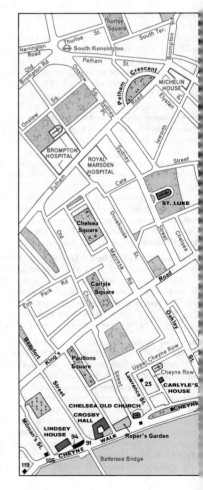

should progress to Kensington Palace but was never completed. The terrace houses on either side of Royal Avenue date from the early and mid 19C. **St Leonard's Terrace** is Chelsea's most attractive mid 18C, Georgian row (14-31), the small streets off the north side of King's Rd, lined by former artisans' cottages, its most traditional.

■ ADDITIONAL SIGHTS

Sloane Sq is notable for quite different reasons: architecturally, Peter Jones erected in 1936 on an awkward site, remains one of London's most successful shop exteriors: historically it was where William Willett invented daylight saving or **summer time** (adopted 1916), and theatrically, the **Royal Court Theatre** has twice, since it opened in 1870, been the scene of a new wave in the theatre: in 1904-07 when Harley Granville Barker put on Arthur Pinero farces, his own translations from the Russian and plays by Bernard Shaw and Somerset Maugham and in 1956-8 when the English Stage Co under George Devine presented 32 plays, among them Osborne's *Look Back in Anger*.

Of the squares Paultons is 1830-40 Georgian, Carlyle mid 19C, Chelsea mixed 18-19-20C and the graceful Pelham Crescent (South Kensington) mid 19C, probably by Basevi.

Holy Trinity. – *Sloane St.* The church was rebuilt in 1888 when the Pre-Raphaelites were at their height. **Burne-Jones** seeing it under construction proposed the design with flowing tracery of the 48 panel east window of the saints for which the glass was made by William Morris. All decoration is of the period and harmonises the architect, Sedding's, free flowing arcade arches which rise uninterrupted by capitals from the piers, the variously coloured marbles, the relief and sculptured decoration, the grilles inside and the singular railings outside on Sloane St.

King's Road. – Originally a path taken by Charles II to visit Nell Gwynn in her house at Fulham, the King's Rd remained a private route open only to those holding a royal pass until the reign of George IV. Chelsea's main street is now famous for its fashion boutiques, antiques, restaurants and pubs.

St Luke's. – *Sydney St.* The Bath stone church of 1820, an early example of the Gothic Revival, is tall and lanky both outside and in. The pinnacled and slimly buttressed 142ft west tower is pierced at the base to provide a porch which extends the full width of the west front.

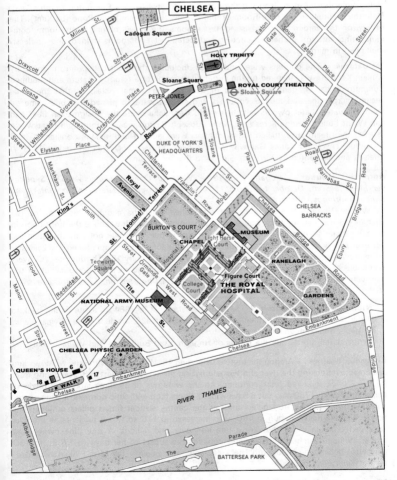

Chiswick remained a country village until the 1860s when within 20 years the population increased from 6 500 to 15 600. But whereas neighbouring Ealing, Acton, Brentford, in the same circumstances, became suburbs, Chiswick has retained its individuality. Georgian houses remain in roads leading down to the river such as Church St and most notably in the attractive riverside reach overlooking the Eyot, Chiswick Mall. Even within a stone's throw of such 20C monuments as the Gt West Rd roundabout, there are enclaves like Chiswick Sq (on Burlington Lane) where a forecourt, flanked by low, two storey houses of 1680 precedes the three floor Boston House, built in 1740 where Thackeray had Becky Sharp throw away her dictionary.

Chiswick House★. – *Burlington Lane. Open May to September daily 9.30am to 1pm and 2 to 7pm (April 4pm); October to March, Wednesdays to Sundays 9.30am to 1pm and 2 to 4pm; closed 24, 25, 26 December; 5p.*

Chiswick, a Jacobean mansion set in extensive acres, was purchased by the first Earl of Burlington in 1682 as a country place; in 1725-9 Richard Boyle, 3rd **Earl of Burlington** (1695-1753), connoisseur, and generous host patron (Kent, Pope, Swift, Gay, Thomson, Handel...), rebuilt the house to his own plans. Fashion had changed from Wren's ebullient Baroque to the Classically inspired and Burlington on his return from his second Grand Tour (1714, 1719), set about designing a Classical pavilion. **William Kent** (1686-1748) a follower of Inigo Jones and Burlington's protégé, was responsible for much of the interior decoration and the gardens. (18 and 19C additions made by Georgiana, Duchess of Devonshire and queen of society and her successors who entertained Charles James Fox, Canning, Edward VII, the tsars... have since been demolished, leaving only Burlington's villa.)

Exterior. – The villa, approached up a brief avenue of terms (busts carved in one with short base pillars) and less than 70ft square, has all the grace of Classical proportion. Paired double dog-leg staircases ascend to a portico behind whose pediment is a raised octagonal dome, guarded on either side by four roof obelisks.

Interior. – On the walls of the ground floor octagon-hall, lobbies and library on the garden front, hang Burlington's architectural drawings. On the first floor, the state apartments follow a square plan of intercommunicating rooms around a central octagon which, with four pedimented doors, itself communicates with the oblong shaped room on each of the three sides and the gallery opposite the entrance. The **Dome Saloon**, its eight walls punctuated alternately by gold highlighted doors and Classical busts, rises by way of an ochre coloured entablature to a windowed drum and diamond patterned dome. The Red, Green and Blue Velvet Rooms, so-called after their original wall hangings, are rich with gilded highlights on ceiling coffering, Venetian windows and pedimented door casings, carvings, chimneypieces (the flues lead out through the roof obelisks – a Burlington *trompe l'œil*). Note the roundels in the Blue Room of Inigo Jones (by Dobson) and Pope (by Kent). The **gallery,** on the garden front consists of three rooms: the apsed, oblong centre room, communicating through arches to circular and octagonal end rooms, gilded and endlessly multiplied in mirrors.

The Gardens. – The gardens were landscaped, including the giant cedars, in the main, by William Kent. He was inspired by the current persuasion of a return to nature and modified Burlington's earlier, geometrical, plan of avenues and formal vistas, so that the canal became serpentine and temples, obelisks and statues were so placed that one came on them unawares. Later owners left their mark: Georgiana made the design even freer and had Wyatt build a bridge across the water; Joseph Paxton was brought from Chatsworth to erect the greenhouse: Italian formal gardens were laid out and remain a brilliant pattern of colour. The Inigo Jones Gateway *(at the back on the right)* was erected in 1621 in Chelsea and presented by Sir Hans Sloane to the 3rd Earl in 1736.

Hogarth's House★. – *Hogarth Lane, Great West Rd. Open weekdays April to September 11am to 6pm; October to March 11am to 4pm; closed on Tuesdays (in winter) and Sunday mornings; 50p.*

William Hogarth was 52 and well established when he acquired his "box by the Thames", a three storey brick house, with a hanging bay window above the front door, in a small garden shaded by a still flourishing mulberry tree. He spent not only the summers, but ever longer periods at Chiswick although a Londoner born, apprenticed (in Leicester Fields now Sq) and famous as a commentator on contemporary 18C London life. "Conversation pieces", collected by contemporaries who recognised in them personalities of the day, can be seen in the house: *The Rake's Progress, the Election, London Scenes, The Harlot's Progress, Mariage à la Mode.*

St Nicholas Parish Church. – The church, last rebuilt in 1884 on a site dating back to 1181, has a buttressed and battlemented west tower of 1436. Inside, the list of vicars, with a few gaps, traces incumbents by name to 1225.

In the burial ground are the tombs of Hogarth, Lord Burlington and William Kent.

Chiswick Mall★★. – Among the more outstanding 18/19C houses with bow windows and balconies overlooking the river and wisteria hazing the walls, are **Morton House,** dating from 1730, of brick with red brick surrounds to the windows of its three storeys, **Strawberry House,** next door, 1730 also but 6 bays wide, 2 floors high with attic dormers, a wide central balcony supported on iron pillars and, at the centre, slender fluted pillars outlining the porch. **Walpole House,** begun in 16C, was increased in 17C so that it presents an irregular advanced brick face. In front are a fine iron gate and railings. A one time owner was Barbara Villiers, Duchess of Cleveland, towards the sunset of her days (d 1709). In 19C the house became a school with Thackeray among its pupils – the Miss Pinkerton's Academy of *Vanity Fair* it is said.

Map pp 9-12.

The City, fortified by the Romans and with the perimeter rebuilt in the Middle Ages, retains a unity of place, although walls, ditches, gates and bars remain in name only; urban development beginning as early as 12C in suburbs just beyond the walls, increased by the Plague and the Great Fire, when some 300 000 left the inner city, and intensified in 19 and 20C, hems the City on all sides, but does not blur its particularity. The buildings, relatively, have never been old: the fires for centuries were too frequent — in 7, 8C, in 1087 when St Paul's was burnt, and finally in 1666, too devastating. When the Act for Rebuilding the City of London in 1667 stipulated that all future structures, houses included, should be of brick and thus reduce fire damage, the demands of commerce which occupied an ever greater area, called for repeated rebuilding to expand or, as a mark of prosperity, to be in the latest approved 19 or 20C style be it Victorian, Classical, 20 s modern... Finally fire again, in the form of bombs, cleared much of the ground once more and with further demolition, provided space for tower office blocks.

Of the **Celtic fishing village** established on the north bank where twin hills rose behind the gravel strand which provided the first ford and subsequently first bridging point across the river, nothing remains outside the Museum of London; of the Roman **Londinium**, a river crossing fortified after Boadicea and her hordes had sacked the City in 61AD and it had been rebuilt as a bridgehead and hub of the road system which led from the Kentish ports to all parts of the country including the more important, capitals of Verulamium (St Albans) and Camulodunum (Colchester), there are stretches of wall and the Temple of Mithras.

William I, who received a separate submission by the citizens two months after the Battle of Hastings, built the Tower, his fellow Norman, Baynard's Castle (and another, Mountfichet), at either river extremity of the City wall, both fortified less against future invaders than as a symbol of strength should the citizens reconsider their submission! The spokesmen requested and the Conqueror granted the City a **Charter,** the first, whereby government, law and dues devolved directly upon the citizens themselves; under John, who in 1215 confirmed a second charter, government advanced towards the Corporation and Londoners were empowered to elect annually their own mayor (elsewhere a royal appointment) who had only to submit himself formally at Westminster for royal approval — "ridings" now known as the Lord Mayor's Show. The City thrived: it loaned or gave money to Edward III and Henry V for wars on the continent and apart from the risings of Wat Tyler in 1381 and Jack Cade in 1450, kept clear of strife, even the Wars of the Roses. Merchants, such as Whittington, and including the Hanseatics who had arrived by 1157, grew rich in every variety of trade particularly wool and cloth; they built great timber framed, gabled, mansions and some bought country estates. The craft and artisan guilds developed into livery companies with a powerful voice; the population teemed, increased by refugees especially Flemish, and later French, Huguenots (15-16C). Houses, tall and oversailing, lined the narrow streets.

In place of royal and ecclesiastical palaces there were monasteries with magnificent churches erected by the religious orders — the Dominicans who arrived in England in 1221 and constructed Blackfriars in 1276, the Franciscans (1224) whose Greyfriars Church was begun at Newgate in 1306, the Carmelites (1241) had a house off Fleet St and the Austin Friars (1253) by Moorgate; there were also priories, Rahere's with the attached medical school of St Bartholomew, St John's and Charterhouse. All were ripe for picking at the time of the **Dissolution** and Henry VIII plucked them all, seizing riches, destroying buildings, nominating himself as re-founder of the hospitals — St Bartholomew's and Bedlam — and all without souring his relations with the City from now on the home of the royal wardrobe. Finally St Paul's, one of the great Gothic cathedrals of Europe was stripped of its holy statues and remaining riches under Edward VI.

Elizabeth's merchant adventurers were financed more often by the City than the queen but James I subsidised the New River scheme which brought fresh water to the street standards. Charles I, always forcing loans, requiring gifts, ship money and tonnage, and applying restrictions to trade, worsened relations to a degree that the five members the king went down to the Commons to search out in 1642 were given sanctuary in the City; under Cromwell the Jews, banished in 1292, returned in strength.

The City was by now peopled not only by merchants, bankers and craftsmen but had entered on the period which persists, of being the forum of those who write and print broadsheets and newspapers and talk, of Shakespeare, Donne, Ben Jonson, Dryden, Pepys, Evelyn, Addison and Steele, Swift, Dickens, of Wren, of Reynolds, of Samuel Johnson...

One fifth of the increasingly humanly diversified City within the walls remained standing on 6 September 1666 after the **Great Fire** had died down. Wren submitted a sketch plan for its rebuilding on 11 September and Evelyn on 13 September 1666. Neither materialised. **Wren** eventually rebuilt St Paul's but not as a focal point; the streets and courts, of which 400 had been destroyed, were soon lined by new brick houses and taverns; the prisons, numerous, insanitary, corrupt and cruel were rapidly rebuilt. Only in 19C were wide roads cut through to the bridges in an endeavour to ease the persistant traffic congestion.

Today the resident population numbers less than 5 000; the workforce nearer 4 million. Traditions are maintained alongside the latest practices — transactions are still agreed on the nod as well as contracted on a worldwide electronic network, there is an annual cutting of a red rose by the Fishmongers, the occasional presentation of a fan; the PM makes a major policy speech at the Lord Mayor's Banquet, visitors of state attend a banquet or ceremony in the City, the royal carriage halts at Temple Bar when the sovereign enters the City — gestures symbolising a unique tradition, jealously guarded.

NB: *the Square Mile being so compact and the interest being particularly by subject, sights have been grouped: St Paul's and the City Churches; the Corporation and Livery Companies; the Bank and exchanges; the markets; the main thoroughfare landmarks.*

■ ST PAUL'S CATHEDRAL★★★

Where its predecessors had perished, Wren's cathedral was preserved (on specific orders from Churchill) and became, for wartime Londoners, a talisman, as the dome and cross, which had soared above the smoke and flames of the raid of 29 December 1940 when the whole City and docks were set ablaze, remained inviolate and appeared serene each morning against the pale dawn sky.

HISTORY

S.PAULES CHURCH

THAMESIS

(After Vischer's engraving, Pitkin Pictorials)

St Paul's before the Great Fire.

Our St Paul's is probably the 4th or even the 5th in line on the site. The first, of which no trace remains, was founded in 604 AD; a second was possibly built in 675-85 under the aegis of St Erkenwald, Bishop of London. It or its successor was burnt down by the Danes in 962, rebuilt and burnt again in the fire which devastated the City in 1087. The cathedral which next arose took until 1240 to construct being on a great scale with a nave of 12 bays, far flung transepts and a shallow, apsed chancel which was replaced in 1258-1314 by a longer decorated choir until finally the building measured 620ft from west to east. Above the central crossing the massive tower was beautified in 1221 by the addition of a lead covered steeple which rose to 514ft. In 1561 this spire was struck by lightning and caught fire; in spite of appearances to the contrary in some contemporary engravings, it was never replaced — a situation symptomatic of the general neglect and even desecration into which the cathedral had fallen: the west towers were used as prisons, relics and shrines had been looted, "the south aisle", wrote a Bishop of Durham of the time, was used "for popery and usury and the north for Simony, and the horse fair in the midst for all kinds of bargains, meetings, brawlings, murders, conspiracies and the font for ordinary payments of money".

Royal commissions under the first two Stuarts on the "decayed fabric" resulted in the refacing of the nave and west transept walls, repairs to the choir screen and in **Inigo, Jones** erecting an outstanding Classical portico with columns 50ft high at the cathedral's west end. Neglect in the Civil War brought, in Carlyle's words, "horses stamping in the canons' stalls" and mean shops squatting in the portico. A new commission on the fabric established in 1663, included among its members **Christopher Wren,** then 31 and untried as an architect though reputed as a geometer, astronomer, FRS. On 27 August 1666 his fellow commissioner, John Evelyn, noted in his diary "I went to St Paul's church with Dr Wren... to survey the general decays of that ancient and venerable church; ... we had a mind to build it with a noble cupola". Ten days later, after the Fire, he was writing: "St Paul's is now a sad ruin and that beautiful portico now rent in pieces...".

Wren's cathedral. — Within 6 days of the end of the Fire, Wren had submitted a plan for rebuilding the City — it was not accepted. For two years the authorities dallied with the idea, opposed by Wren, of patching up the cathedral fabric — then in 1668, they invited him to submit designs. He produced the First Model, the Great Model, the Warrant Design; each rejected by the church authorities until he resolved to submit no more plans but as Surveyor General to the King's Works (1669) to go ahead "as ordered by his Majesty". The foundation stone was laid without ceremony on 21 June 1675 and work proceeded until after thirty-three years unceasing work, Wren saw his son set the final stone, the topmost in the lantern, in place — he was 75, the date 1708. Fifteen years later, in 1723, he was buried within its walls.

Figures. — The cost of the cathedral, on record as £736 752 3s 3¼ d was met, together with that of rebuilding the City Churches, by a tax levied on all sea coal imported into the Port of London. Wren was paid £200 a year during the cathedral's construction (the font cost £350 in 1727). The dimensions are: length overall 500ft; height to the summit of the cross 365ft; of the portico columns 40ft. St Paul by Francis Bird at the pediment apex is 12ft tall. The length of the nave is 180ft, the width, including the aisles, 121ft; width across the transepts 242ft; internal diameter of the dome 110ft; height of the nave 92½ft; to the Whispering Gallery 100ft; to the internal dome apex 218ft. The total area is approximately 78 000 sq ft.

TOUR

Open 8am to 7pm (5pm from October to March); access to the Church Floor is very limited in extent during services. – **NB:** *the Dome 10.45am to 3.15pm, 4.45 to 6pm; October to March 10.45am to 3.15pm only; Crypt 10.45 to 3.30pm, 4.45 to 6pm; October to March 10.45 to 3.30pm; dome and crypt are both closed on Sundays, St Paul's Day (25 January), Good Friday, Ascension Day and 25 December.*

Exterior. – The **dome,** mounted on a balustraded drum, encircled by pillars and crowned above a stone lantern by a golden ball and cross, is not only the cathedral's dominant feature but also that of the London skyline from the river, Hampstead Heath, a plane – even today when office blocks rise all around.

The dome is, in fact, three structures *(see illustration):* the outer profile, a lead covered timber superstructure; an invisible inner brick cone which supports the weight of the lantern; and the inner brick dome with a 20ft diameter opening at the apex into the

St Paul's from the south.

space beneath the lantern and which as frescoed and circled by the Whispering Gallery, is the one seen from inside the church. The drum, outside, is in the form of two tiers, the lower encircled by columns, punctuated 8 times (for structural reasons) by a decoratively niched radiating wall and crowned by a balustrade; the upper tier is recessed behind the balustrade in such a way as to afford a circular viewing gallery, the **Stone Gallery.** Unlike Bramante's and Michelangelo's St Peter's, which so fascinated and influenced Wren, it is not a true hemisphere. The lantern, 21ft across, is also of restrained English Baroque with detached columns projecting on all four sides and a small cupola serving as plinth to the 6½ ft diameter golden ball.

The **west end** presents, at the top of two wide flights of steps, a two tier portico of coupled Corinthian and composite columns beneath a decorated pediment surmounted by the figure of St Paul. On either side rise the west towers, Wren's most Baroque spires, designed as the close foil to the dome.

The **north and south sides, and east end** are enclosed within a wall two storeys high with coupled pilasters against the rusticated stone, punctuated, at the lower level by rounded windows with segmental hoods, garlanded and cherub decorated beneath the cornice frieze. On the upper level the blind windows are designed as niches.

The **transepts,** which are shallow, end in semicircular, columned porticoes crowned by statues surmounting the triangular pediments. The upper level of the 111ft high wall, except at the east and transept ends, is an advanced screen – an enclosure of the structural buttressing, and is itself a support for the dome.

The overall design is majestic; each feature fits and adds to the effect – many only stand out, to the untutored eye, when caught by a change in the light or when the floodlights are on. Finally, and on no account to be missed, is the carving everywhere: statues, reliefs, figures by Caius Cibber, Francis Bird, garlands, swags, panels, cherub heads in the stone by Grinling Gibbons.

Interior. – The immediate impression is one of size, of almost luminescent stone all around and, in the far distance, of gold and mosaic.

Wren's church was without extraneous monuments. They were introduced in 1790 when the figures of four national benefactors (Joshua Reynolds, John Howard the penal reformer, Dr Johnson and Sir William Jones the orientalist) were placed by the dome piers; since then marble statuary has proliferated.

The nave. – Before advancing up the nave, note immediately abutting the aisles respectively to left and right the chapels of St Dunstan, and St Michael and St George each preceded by a 17/18C finely carved wooden screen rising to a crest incorporating broken pediments, coats of arms, vases. The square pillars dividing the nave and aisles are faced towards the centre with fluted, Corinthian pilasters which sweep up to the entablature, the wrought iron gallery railing, clerestory and garlanded saucer domes.

The Wellington monument, which occupies the entire space between two piers on the left and ascends from a recumbent bronze effigy at the base to a full size equestrian statue of the duke at the apex, was the lifework of Alfred Stevens and only completed in 1912 long after the sculptor's death (1875).

Note the late 19C bronze gasoliers and in the pavement the Night Watch memorial stone (cathedral guardians 1939-45), the inscription commemorating the resting of Sir Winston Churchill's coffin in the cathedral during the state funeral service on 30 January 1965 and, beneath the dome, Wren's own epitaph in Latin: Reader, if you seek his monument, look around you.

Lo. A. 5

The Dome. – *Times of opening: p 49; 30p. Entrance: south aisle transept: 588 steps.*

From the **Whispering Gallery** *(259 stairs)* there is an impressive view of the concourse far below; there are also unusual perspectives to be seen of the choir, the arches, the clerestory and close views including that of the interior of the dome itself painted by **Thornhill.**

Of the **views★★★** from outside, because one can move round to see clearly in all directions, and overrides most of the post-war tower blocks, the best is from the **Golden Gallery** at the top of the dome *(542 steps from the ground).*

The crossing and transepts. – The open space beneath the dome is emphasised by the giant piers which surround it and mark the openings to the shallow transepts. That to the north serves as a baptistry and contains the dish shaped font carved in 1727 by Francis Bird, that to the south includes the exceptional portrait statue of **Nelson** by Flaxman and at the end the beautiful wooden doorcase of fluted columns enriched by garlands made up in 19C from a wood screen designed by Wren and carved by Grinling Gibbons.

(By courtesy of Architectural Press)

St Paul's: dome cross section.

Choir. – The marble high altar, covered by a massive post-war pillared baldachino, carved and gilded after drawings by Wren, fills the east end. Above, the gilding is reflected in gold and glass mosaics of the turn of the century, which also face the vaulting above the aisle (note the Christ in Majesty in the apsidal dome). In the foreground, warm in the light of red shaded candle lights, are the dark oak **choir stalls,** carved as only **Grinling Gibbons** and his craftsmen could carve – a long pillared range on either side beneath a crested canopy. Each stall differs in detail, in the flowers, leaves and fruits that make up wreaths and garlands, in the cherubs' expressions. Note that the stall backs, which form a screen on the chancel aisles, are also beautiful and can be seen from close to. The organ, originally a late 17C Smith instrument, and the case, again by Gibbons, have been divided and now tower on either side of the choir opening.

The wrought iron **railing,** originally the altar rail, the **gates** to the choir aisles, and the great gilded **screens** enclosing the sanctuary, are the work of **Jean Tijou,** wrought iron smith extraordinary. In the south choir aisle, against the first outer west pillar, is the statue of **John Donne,** Dean of St Paul's 1621-31 and metaphysical poet. As painted and as here subsequently carved by Nicholas Stone, he stands on an urn in the up-ended coffin (which he bought in his lifetime and kept in his house), wrapped in his shroud, crowned, but from his expression, much alive!

Crypt. – *Times of opening: p 49; 30p. Entrance off south transept.*

Between the OBE Chapel, simply decorated with royal banners, at the east end and the Wellington funeral gun carriage (1852) far away at the west, grouped in bays formed by the massive piers which support the low groined and tunnel vaulting, are the tombs, memorials and busts of men of all the talents of the 18, 19 and 20C, British, Commonwealth or who came from abroad and contributed to the national life – not all those commemorated are buried in the crypt:

– In the south aisle at the foot of the staircase are John Rennie (2nd recess), Walter de la Mare and Sir Max Beerbohm (north and west faces of pillar) and Christopher Wren, beneath a plain black marble stone with above him the inscription: *Si monumentum requiris circumspice.* Others commemorated in this aisle, known as Artists' Corner, include George Dance the Younger, Steer, Blake, Munnings, Landseer, Lawrence, Benjamin West, Frederick Leighton, Millais, Turner, Reynolds and Holman Hunt.

– In the north aisle are Sir Arthur Sullivan, Parry, William Boyce (on the floor), John Singer Sargent, beneath a relief by himself (choir face of dividing wall), Constable and Sir Alexander Fleming. In this chamber are a bronze bust of Stafford Cripps by Epstein (1953) and on the wall a plaque to Ivor Novello (south side).

– Down the steps in the Cornish porphyry sarcophagus is **Wellington.** Further on a plaque to the south commemorates Florence Nightingale.

Below the dome, at the centre of a circle of Tuscan columns lies **Nelson** beneath a curving black marble sarcophagus (originally intended for Cardinal Wolsey and subsequently proposed but rejected for Henry VIII). In the recesses to the south are the admirals Beatty, Jellico and Collingwood, and a bronze bust of W E Henley by Rodin (1903). Opposite on the north side are military figures, also T E Lawrence by Epstein. Only a handful of effigies were rescued from Old St Paul's in which were buried John of Gaunt, Thomas Linacre (*c* 1460-1524; founder of the Royal College of Physicians, teacher of Greek to Thomas More and Erasmus), Sir Philip Sidney, Sir Anthony van Dyck (modern plaque).

When visiting St Paul's take time also to explore the precinct, to spot the steeples of the nearby City Churches. Return to visit the churches, organising yourself to be present at midday for a service, concert, debate... (programme from the City Information Centre, St Paul's Churchyard, EC4; Tel. 01-606 3030; extensions 236, 237).

The CITY CHURCHES★★★

Rare men have designed cathedrals, as did Wren; none, at any time except Wren after the Great Fire, has been called on in a matter of years to draw plans for 51 parish churches and, as congregations collected additional sums, crown the west end of nearly every one with a tower or spire. Each church is different; every tower and steeple unique among its peers.

Before the Fire there had been 87 churches within the walls. Eleven were unharmed and it was decided after uniting some of the parishes to rebuild only 51 on former sites. By 1939, the construction of new roads in 19 and 20C, had reduced the total to 43 churches of which 32 were by Wren; nearly all were damaged, several totally destroyed during the war but the plans, although by their very nature not as elaborate or famous as those for the Cathedral, all existed and the churches were able to be reconstructed. There are now 39 City Churches in all of which 11 are pre-Fire, and 23 by Wren and, in addition, the towers of 9 former churches, 6 by Wren.

(National Portrait Gallery)

Christopher Wren.

Details of activities. – Twenty-four are still parish churches and 15 have become guild churches – some are both. *Most open throughout the week from 10am, some earlier, to about 3pm and conduct midday services, recitals, debates and counselling. For detailed information apply at the City Information Centre or at the churches themselves.*

Money for rebuilding the churches in 17C was granted under acts of parliament which increased the dues on coal entering the Port of London. By the time Wren was called upon to design the churches, and each parish made a separate request, houses were once more abutting all sides of the traditional site and the architect, therefore, ignored almost entirely all exterior walls and windows except those overlooking the street – the interest, therefore, lies in the spire, the entrance and the often irregular shape of the site and how the building fits into it. Inside note how the single side aisle (where there was no space for two) is turned to advantage, the unequal corners made to appear right angled, the interior is converted into a lozenge shape, a clerestory or lunettes light a barrel roof, how pillars present a cross, a circle, within a square, how the domes at St Stephen Walbrook and St Mary Abchurch are an essay before St Paul's. From a regard of the interplay of columns and complementing pilasters – fluted, circular, square, Corinthian or Ionic capitalled, look at the complementary cornice and decorated plaster vaulting. Examine in detail the superb 17C woodwork, much of it from Grinling Gibbons, workshop: the reredoses with gilded pelicans, the pulpits and sounding boards, often hilarious with garlanded cherubs. The churches, so individual and personal would seem to epitomise the phrase "small is beautiful".

All Hallows-by-the-Tower (RZ)   7/8C, 17 and 20C

Tower and Spire: 17C square brick tower. The lantern, encircled by a balustrade and supporting a tapering green copper spire, was added after the war making it the only shaped spire to be added to a City Church since Wren. The tower is the one climbed by Pepys on 5 September 1666 when he "saw the saddest sight of desolation that I ever saw".

The church, that time, was saved by Sir William Penn, whose son William, founder of Pennsylvania, had been baptised there on 23 October 1644. Four churches have stood on the site: in late 7C, a chapel erected soon after its parent house, Barking Abbey; 12 and 14C churches and finally 20C rebuilding. Inside modern sculpture has been grouped at the southeast corner before the baptistry where there is an exquisite **font cover★★** carved in 1681 by Grinling Gibbons for who, obviously, no cherub was anonymous. Ten exceptional **brasses★** dating from 1389-1591 (of which 9 may be rubbed – *by appointment only*) wall tablets, model ships in the Mariners' Chapel, the **Toc H** association chapel and lamp, give the church a distinctive atmosphere despite its inevitable "newness". In the crypt are tessellated Roman pavement fragments, 11C Saxon stone crosses.

All Hallows London Wall (PX)   G. Dance jr: 1765-1767

Open Wednesday midday – services.

Tower: Portland stone rising by stages from a pedimented doorway to an urn quartered cornice, pilastered lantern cupola and final cross.

The interior, lit by semicircular clerestory windows, has a particularly splendid gold "snowflake" patterned barrel vault.

St Andrew Holborn, Holborn Circus (KX)   Wren: 1686-1687, 1704

Tower: stout and square with angle buttresses; at the summit are an overhanging cornice and balustrade decorated at each angle with a great vase.

The City church escaped the Fire but was rebuilt nevertheless. Saxon, Norman and 15C churches all stood on the site; by 17C, however, the mediaeval church in which Henry Wriothesley, future Earl of Southampton and Shakespeare's patron, had been baptised with Henry VIII as godfather in 1545, had fallen into decay. Wren profited from the openness of the site to design a long basilical building of stone with windows in two tiers and a crowning balustrade. (Note the stone of the Resurrection – outside, north wall.)

The church was gutted by fire in 1941, but has been restored so that inside once more there is a panelled surround and square encasement of the pillars which support the gallery and continue as Corinthian columns. At the west end, in a recess, is the tomb, delightful with its shy child, of **Thomas Coram** (d 1751), sea captain and parishioner, transferred to St Andrew's from the Foundling Hospital in 1961, together with the font (1804), the pulpit (1752) and the case and organ, presented to Coram by Handel.

St Andrew-by-the-Wardrobe, Queen Victoria St (LY)   Wren: 1685-1695

Tower: square red brick with irregular stone quoins and a crowning balustrade.

The church was known as St Andrew juxta Baynard Castle until the Great Wardrobe or royal storehouse, previously in the Tower, was erected on a site closeby in 1361 (plaque in Wardrobe Place). Church, Wardrobe, Castle and St Ann Blackfriars, were all destroyed in the Fire; only St Andrew was rebuilt. On 29/30 December 1940, fire again gutted the church leaving just the tower and outer walls.

St Andrew Undershaft, Leadenhall St (RY)   c 1520

Tower: small and ancient, its square blackened stone outline misshapen by a staircase turret; the top is 19C and crenellated, the base probably early 14C.

The present 16C church, the third on the site, is named after the maypole shaft which stood before it until 1517 and, after being laid up, was finally burnt in 1549.

The nave, now bare of pews, is divided from the aisles by 5 slender shaft and hollow columns which support a plain glass clerestory. Flat wooden roofs cover the aisles and nave, the latter punctuated by 130 carved and gilded 16C oak bosses. The west window (originally at the east end) of Tudor and Stuart sovereigns, the Renatus Harris organ, the font, are late 16 and 17C; the altar rails of 1704 are by Tijou.

Most famous of St Andrew's **monuments★** (north side, east end) is the half-length ruffed figure in a decorated alcove of **John Stow**, 1525-1605, antiquarian whose *Survey of London and Westminster*, published in 1598 makes fascinating reading and remains a major source of every guide to London. The quill pen poised to "write something worth reading about" is renewed annually by the Lord Mayor.

St Anne and St Agnes, Gresham St (MX)   Wren: 1676-1687

Open only for Lutheran Services: English, Estonian, Latvian.

Tower: small square stuccoed stone with, above, an even smaller square domed turret, flaunting a vane in the shape of the letter A.

Mentioned c 1200 and rebuilt to the ancient domed cross plan within a square by Wren after the Fire, St Anne's had to be rebuilt again after the war. As in Wren's day the exterior is of rose-red brick.

St Bartholomew the Great★★, West Smithfield (LV)   1123, 19C

Tower: brick, square, castellated with a small vaned turret.

St Bartholomew was once a great, spacious church of which the present vessel was only the chancel. It was founded in 1123 by a onetime courtier, Rahere, following a pilgrimage to Rome: on land granted by Henry I he established both the hospital and an Augustinian priory of which he became the first prior. By 1143, when he died, the Norman chancel had been completed; by 1539 when Henry VIII dissolved the priory, the church was 280ft long with the west door where the gateway is now on Little Britain. Henry left the hospital untouched: the priory, valued at £693 9s 10½d four years earlier, he sold, after first demolishing the church nave and ordaining that the truncated building be used only as a parish church. The monarch's attorney-general, Sir Richard Rich, nevertheless paid him £1 064 11s 3d for the property which the family retained for 300 years. In that time the church fell into appalling disrepair: the Lady Chapel was

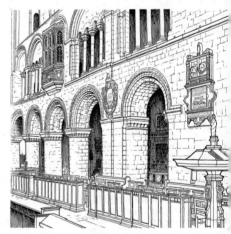

St Bartholomew the Great: the nave.

"squatted in", became a printers' workshop (where in 1724 Benjamin Franklin was employed) and later a fringe factory; the remains of the cloister became a stable, a thick layer of earth covered the church floor, limewash obscured the walls and murals, a brick receptacle, Purgatory, behind the altar, was filled with human bones...

Restoration, including the buying out of extraneous occupants, took from 1863-1896.

The building. — The gateway, a 13C arch, the original entrance to the nave, has above, a late 16C half-timbered gatehouse (restored 1932). The path through the churchyard is at the level of the mediaeval church. The porch, west front and other exterior flint and stone refacing dates from 1839 restoration by Sir Aston Webb, the **tower** erected, but not in the axis, at the west end of the curtailed church from 1628. The **vessel★** (west end obscured by the organ) is Norman with circular arches on massive round piers and plainly scalloped capitals and above, a gallery of small, rounded arches in groups of 4 slender columns within a relieving arch affording everywhere for so small a setting spacious perspectives of arch within arch. The clerestory, which was rebuilt in late Perpendicular style in 1405, reveals no later added carving except an **oriel** filling one south gallery arch inserted by Prior Bolton in 1520, stamped with his rebus — a bolt or arrow transfixing a tun or cask — and from which, behind the leaded lights, he could follow the service. The Lady Chapel completed in 1336 was rebuilt in 1897, except for the end north and south windows.

The **monuments: Rahere,** the founder, lies on a 16C decorated tomb chest beneath a crested canopy, all fashioned some 350 years after his death. The **font,** used at Hogarth's baptism in 1697, dates from early 15C and as such is one of the oldest in the City.

St Bartholomew the Less (LX)　　　　　Pre fire: George Dance, 1789, 19C

Tower : 15C square with a domed corner turret (within the hospital walls but just visible from the market).

St Bartholomew's Hospital, on the same site since its foundation by Rahere in 1123 and caring, nowadays, for some 500 000 in and out patients a year in massive new blocks, has retained buildings from the collegiate style reconstruction by James Gibbs of 1730-66. The north wing includes the great staircase with the vast murals by **Hogarth** (1734) which leads to the Great Hall hung with portraits by Kneller, Lawrence, Reynolds... The gatehouse from West Smithfield erected in 1702, contains an 18C statue of Henry VIII who gave the hospital to the City of London in 1546 — having sequestered the monastery of which it had previously been a part!

The 12C hospital church by the Great Fire period, appears on contemporary maps as a substantial building with a stalwart tower; by 18C, however, it was in decay so that it was renewed first by George Dance the Younger, in 1789 and again, in 1823, by Thomas Hardwick. Monuments, chiefly to hospital personnel, date from 20C back to 14C (vestry pavements).

St Benet's Welsh Church, (St Benet, Paul's Wharf) (LY)　　　　Wren: 1677-1685
Open only for Sunday services.

Tower: of dark red brick, defined squarely with white stone quoins, rises only two stages before being crowned by a small lead cupola, lantern and spire.

The church, at the time of the Great Fire, when it was already some 6 centuries old, stood directly behind Baynard Castle which fronted the river and which, like the church, was totally destroyed. The castle was not rebuilt and Wren designed for the now more open site, a small brick church with a hipped roof, rounded windows with carved stone festoons and a general country, Dutch, air. The tower is at the northwest corner so that inside it divides the north and west galleries supported on panelled Corinthian columns which rise, clearcut, above the base of the galleries. Below all is of wood — note the west doorcase decked with cherubs and crowning royal arms, a balustered communion rail, ornate table and behind, a high pedimented reredos with surmounting urns.

St Botolph Aldersgate (MX)　　　　　Nathaniel Wright: 1788-1791

Tower: small square and built of brick, topped by a cupola on which is perched a painted wooden turret flying a gilded vane.

The tower and oblong vessel with conventional rounded windows and clerestory are of dark red brown brick; this building was "improved" in 1829 by the addition of a pediment-ed east end in stucco. The interior is Victorian in atmosphere with 19C glass, red and yellow floor tiles, low slung tribunes, ceiling plasterwork of white roses in high relief and an east "window" transparency, a painting on glass by James Pierson (1788) of the *Agony in the Garden.* Wall monuments are a reminder that the present church is a 3rd rebuilding on the site by the gate in the City Wall; the position provides the natural dedica-tion to the 7C Saxon saint, patron of travellers.

St Botolph Aldgate (SXY)　　　　　George Dance the Elder: 1741-1744

Tower and Steeple: a white stone obelisk steeple stands on a four tier brick tower trimmed with stone quoins.

The site on the outer side of the gate through the City Wall and beside a bridge span-ning the moat (Houndsditch), had been occupied by a church for 1 000 years or more when George Dance came to rebuild it in 18C. Dance's interior was transfigured in 1889 by J F Bentley when he redecorated the church, fronting the galleries with balusters, geome-trically re-leading all but the east window, decorating the coved ceiling with a plasterwork design of shields and standing angels, leaves, garlands...

St Botolph without Bishopsgate (RX)　　　　　George Dance: 1725-1729

Tower and Steeple: a square brick tower rises directly from the Bishopsgate pavement to support a stone balustrade, clock tower, turret, cupola and crowning urn.

The church was rebuilt in 1725-9 on a 13C site. The south front, overlooking the former burial ground, is of brick trimmed with stone. Inside giant Corinthian columns support the galleries and wide coved ceiling, the east window is Victorian and there are 19C box pews.

The church hall at the west end was built to harmonise with the church in 1861 and restored after the war by the Worshipful Company of Fanmakers. 19C charity school children in Coade stone stand on either side of the doorway.

The CITY★★★

St Bride★, Fleet St (KY)

Wren: 1670-1684, 1701-1703

Steeple★★: the white, wedding cake spire rises by 4 open octagonal stages to a final open pedestal and tapering obelisk which terminates in a vane 226ft above the ground — Wren's tallest and most floating steeple. A baker made a fortune modelling wedding cakes after the spire when it was newly erected and inaugurated a lasting tradition. The baker's wife's silk dress is in the museum.

In 1940 Wren's church was gutted by fire leaving only the steeple and calcined outer walls standing. Before all was rebuilt the crypt was opened which had been closed since its use for burials from c 1720 until after the cholera plague of 1853, which killed 10 000 Londoners. Subsequent excavations have revealed a Roman ditch, walls, a pavement and the outlines of church buildings on the site dating back to Saxon times at least. *(Museum in the crypt.)*

The exterior was restored by Godfrey Allen to Wren's design with tall rounded windows between pedimented doors surmounted by circular windows; above a line of oval clerestory windows; at the east end a tripartite window beneath a pediment.

(After photo Pitkin Pictorials)

St Bride's steeple

The interior has been re-arranged to enclose the nave, now set with collegiate-style pews and fill the east end with a massive 17C style reredos. The decoration is 17C.

Associations. — St Bride's associations, more than its architecture, are what make it unique to many, however. Becket was born close by; King John held a parliament in the church in 1210; Henry VIII lodged in Bridewell Palace which lay between the church and the river, when he received Charles V in 1522; high ranking churchmen preferring, perhaps to live outside the City Wall, built town houses in the neighbourhood (Salisbury Sq) and since the clergy were the largest literate group in the land it was only natural that when **Wyken de Worde** acquired his master's, Caxton's, press on the latter's death in 1491, he should remove it from Westminster to St Bride's and Fleet St. By Wyken's death in 1535 (he was buried in St Bride's), the parish boasted several printers. Chaucer, Shakespeare, Milton, Lovelace, Evelyn, Pepys (born nearby and like all his family christened in the church), Dryden, Izaac Walton, Edmund Waller (poet), Aubrey, Ashmole, John Ogilby (mapmaker), Thomas Tompion, father of English clock and watchmaking, Addison; in 18C, Johnson and Boswell, Joshua Reynolds, Goldsmith, Garrick, Burke, Pope, Richardson (coffin in the crypt) and Hogarth; in 19C Charles Lamb, Hazlitt, Wordsworth, Keats, Hood, Leigh Hunt, Dickens, frequented the Street, local coffeehouses and taverns and the church. Today new pew backs are labelled with the names of contemporaries for St Bride's remains the printers' church, the Cathedral of Fleet St.

St Clement Eastcheap (PY)

Wren: 1683-1687

Tower: unassuming brick with stone quoins and balustrade.

The mediaeval St Clement's was the first City church to burn in the Great Fire; it cost £4 362 3s 4½ d to rebuild to Wren's design (in which there is no right angled wall!) and the architect was presented on its completion by the satisfied parishioners with "one third of a hogshead of wine" costing £4 2s 0d. The **panelled interior★★** has finely carved 17C door and organ cases (Purcell played on the organ), above the pulpit a massive sounding board, garlanded, swagged and gay with dancing cherubs. The marble font and cover, carved bread shelves, Stuart arms, sword rest, are all contemporary.

St Clement claims to be the church of the old *Oranges and Lemons* rhyme: its parish East Cheap, dates from the time of the Saxon market on the City's eastern hill; its association with oranges from when, in the Middle Ages, Spanish barges tied up at London Bridge to sell their oranges on the stone steps — all within cry of the church.

St Dunstan-in-the-West, Fleet St (JY)

Shaw: 1831-1833

Tower: neo-Gothic, rising from an arched porch to an octagon of slender open bays, superimposed by a crown of tapering finials and crocketed pinnacles.

The 19C church was a rebuilding, slightly to the north, on a site on which churches had stood since 1237; the 17C building narrowly escaped the Fire; the 19C was badly bombed in 1944. The exterior, apart from the tower, is chiefly remarkable for the additions which associate the church with Fleet St: the bust of **Lord Northcliffe** (1930), the public **clock**, made by Thomas Harrys in 1671 and for which he was paid £35, and its giant oak jacks; the **statues** from the 1586 Lud Gate: Queen Elizabeth, modelled during her lifetime (modern inscription) and originally on the gate's west face — purchased in 1786 for £15 10s and now in a pedimented niche over a doorway (to the right) in which stand statues of the mythical King Lud and his two sons (again of 1586 manufacture). Corbels at the main door show the visages of Tyndale (west) and John Donne (east), associated with St Dunstan's as were Izaac Walton (the *Compleat Angler* was printed in the churchyard), and the Hoares. John Shaw's church is octagonal with a high, star, vault; the altar, oriented to the north, is set in "choice panelling" — Flamboyant Flemish in style.

Since 1960s, one bay has been closed by an ornate 17C Romanian screen from the Antim Monastery, Bucharest. *(The community hold weekly services.)*

St Edmund the King and Martyr, Lombard St (PY)

Wren: 1670-1679, 1706-1707

Tower and Spire★: a distinctive black (lead covered) octagonal lantern and stout spire ending in a bulb and vane, rise from a square stone belfry. The corbelled parapet and inverted brackets at the tower base are decorated with flaming urns.

The façade, opposite Clement's Lane, is outlined by quoins and a central pediment; a round clock, decorated with a crown, overtops the other signs in the street.

The small oblong interior with squared apse and coved skylit ceiling, is chiefly remarkable for its woodwork: panelling and pierced galleries, finely carved pulpit with drops and swags, communion table with stalwart legs, font cover with 4 gilded apostles and semicircular rail, the urns on reredos and doorcases...

St Ethelburga Bishopsgate (RX)   15C and later

Turret: a square belfry and vaned turret stand slightly back from the mediaeval ragstone and brick repaired west wall on Bishopsgate's east pavement.

The early 15C church (two cinquefoil piscinas in the south wall), escaped the Fire but not 1939-45 bombings. It has a nave, 4 bay arcade and south aisle, besides an organ loft and gallery (1629; rebuilt1912), all within an overall dimension of 57ft. The furnishings date from mediaeval to modern, the accounts back to 1569.

St Giles Cripplegate★, the Barbican (MV)   14, 16, 19 and 20C

Tower: dwarfed, but in no way overpowered by the Barbican, St Giles' tower is built of stone below and brick above; corner pinnacles guard an open cupola merry-go-round shaped turret which sports a weathervane. (Peal of 12 bells; chiming clock.)

The latest rebuilding in St Giles' 900 year history came after high explosive and incendiary bombs had destroyed the interior in 1940. Almost every century previously had seen similar if not cómparable disasters, or enlargement, back to 1090 when a Norman church was first erected on the site outside the City Wall beside the postern gate on to the moor. Memorials, after so many vicissitudes, are few, although associations recorded by signature in the registers are many: **John Milton** (buried in the chancel, 1674; bust by John Bacon, 1793 – south wall), **Martin Frobisher**, navigator (buried in south aisle 1594), **John Foxe**, author of the *Book of Martyrs* (buried 1587), **John Speed**, mapmaker (buried 1629 below his monument on the south wall), **Oliver Cromwell** (married 22 August 1620), **Sir Thomas More, Ben Jonson, Shakespeare** (at the baptism of his nephew), Edward Alleyn, Prince Rupert, Holman Hunt, Sir Ebenezer Howard (pioneer of garden cities).

St Helen Bishopsgate★, Gt St Helen's (RX)   12-17C

Tower: a small square 17C white belfry turret, lantern, ball and vane, rise sturdily from the double fronted stone church; outside are a patch of grass and plane trees.

The two low west doors, side by side, beneath embattled gables typify St Helen's architecture and history. It began as a small parish church which by 1150 extended in two consecutive vessels from the present east wall to the south entrance (originally Norman arched). In early 13C a Benedictine nunnery was established in the church grounds and a conventual church built abutting St Helen's to the north; the nun's chapel was slightly wider and considerably longer than the existing parish church which was then extended to give the double front. The division between the churches was replaced in the late 15C by the present arcade of pillars and the last remaining screens were removed in 1538 when the nunnery was dissolved. In 1874 when Martin Outwich was demolished, 18 major monuments and brasses were transferred.

Furnishings. – In the north wall is one of several 13C windows (NW), the **Night Staircase** of c 1500, built from the dormitory to the church for nuns attending night services, the **Processional Entrance,** originally 13C, and, at the east end, the **Nuns' Squint** (since 1525 arranged as a memorial). Note the carved pulpit, the grotesque choirstall armrests from 15C Nuns' Choir and the two sword rests, one very rare being made of wood (1665).

Monuments★★: by the Nuns' Choir is the black marble slabbed tomb chest of Sir Thomas Gresham (d 1579); adjoining that of Sir Julius Caesar Aldemere (d 1636) with no effigy but a parchment and seal; within the railing, beneath the canopy is the marble effigy of Sir William Pickering, Elizabeth's Ambassador to Spain (d 1574) and opposite, Sir John Crosby (d 1475) and his first wife (d 1460), owner of the great City mansion, Crosby Hall. The **brasses,** 15-17C and rich in expression and costume detail, are in the transept and north aisle *(covered with carpets).*

Windows: there is 17C glass in the 3rd and 5th north windows and in the Holy Ghost Chapel. Shakespeare (north wall) was assessed for local rates at £5 6s 8d in 1597 but left the parish, according to the record, having paid off only the s and d!

St James Garlickhythe, Garlick Hill, Upper Thames St (MY)   Wren 1676-1683, 1713

Tower and Spire★: the tower, square, of stone ending in a balustrade, is quartered by pointed urns and crowned by the spire, added in 1713. This rises in a square 3 tier lantern, quartered by paired, advanced, columns, crowned on high by a vaned spirelet (*cf* St Michael Paternoster Royal).

Inside the tower, through the door decorated with a scallop shell, the emblem of St James of Compostella to who the church is dedicated, two tablets summarise the later history of the church which dates back to 10/11C. "This church", the upper plaque states, "was consumed by the late dreadful conflagration AD 1666; the foundation thereof was laid AD 1676; it was rebuilt and opened AD 1682 and completely finished AD 1683"; the inscription below continues, "The church was damaged by enemy action in 1940 and 1941; the work of restoration was completed in 1963".

It is an oblong church; it is also an equation: the slightly raised chancel occupies ⅓ of the total length; the aisles are each ⅙ of the width of the nave; 4 Ionic columns on either side divide the vessel into 5 bays, the two at either end being equal pairs, the centre ones slightly wider indicate transepts which are further underlined by the return on either side of the entablature.

The woodwork is principally 17C: note the dowel peg for the preacher's wig. Hatchments and **sword rests★**, complete with lion and unicorn supporters, recall six mediaeval lord mayors and others.

St Katharine Cree, Leadenhall St (RY)   1628-1631

Tower: the ragstone corner tower, late 15C below 16C above, rises to a parapet and small white pillared turret.

The present church is thought to be the third on the site which marked the corner boundary of the precincts of the Augustinian Priory of Holy Trinity, Christchurch, founded by Matilda, Queen of Henry I, in 1108 and dissolved in 1539. Note the two tiers of windows in the stone wall on Leadenhall St, straight headed with centres raised to include 3 lights each. Inside the nave remains with giant Corinthian columns supporting decorated round arches beneath the clerestory. High up, above the plain reredos, a rose said to resemble in its tracery that in Old St Paul's and glazed with 18C glass, leads one's eye back along the ceiling where the ribs, meet in central brightly coloured bosses, the badges of 17 City Companies. Note the wooden **sword rest★**.

St Lawrence Jewry, Gresham St (NX)   Wren: 1670-1687

Tower and Spire: stone, rising to a balustrade with corner obelisks which encloses a pedimented lantern set out of alignment with the base (which parallels the west wall) but in line with Gresham St. Above is a lead obelisk spire from which flies the original gridiron weathervane now also incorporating a replica of the incendiary bomb which caused the church's almost total destruction in 1940.

"St Lawrence, called in the Jury because of old time many Jews inhabited thereabout" was, according to Stow, a "fair and large" parish church. Built in 1196 and closely surrounded by houses, it perished completely in the Fire. Wren designed a building of modest outward appearance squaring up the interior by varying the thickness of the walls and decorating it with all the elegance behoving the City Corporation.

Today, where once were some of Grinling Gibbons' richest carvings, the dark, modern woodwork is plain and unassuming except for the organ case at the west end, which is after the 17C original and the screen dividing the north aisle, now the Commonwealth Chapel. The ceiling, coffered and decorated to Wren's original design with gilded plasterwork, emphasises the rectangular plan. Note at the southeast end, the pews for the Lord Mayor (sword rest), sheriffs, aldermen, sword and mace bearers... Sir Thomas Beecham's piano is now in the church, *(Piano recitals, Mondays, 1 to 1.45pm; organ: Wednesdays)*.

St Magnus the Martyr, Lower Thames St (PZ)
                                           Wren: 1671-1687, 1706

Tower★: the massive balustraded and urn decorated square block of stone supports an octagonal belfry, lead cupola, lantern and obelisk spire and, still higher, at 180ft, a golden vane. A 1709 clock projects over the churchyard.

St Magnus stood a stone sentinel from 1176 on an ancient Roman wharf at the foot of London Bridge. Wren rebuilt it on the same site. When, in c 1760, the houses and shops which lined the bridge were removed, Wren's building was curtailed to leave the tower as a church porch bestriding the bridge's east footpath. Its postern situation continued until 1831 when Rennie's bridge was constructed 100ft upstream.

The church today is hemmed in and overtopped by offices so that only the tower and north side lie open to the street. The interior, remodelled in late 18C, has a high barrel vaulted nave, punctuated by the deep recesses of the oval clerestory windows. Although much remains from 17C, inscriptions on the west gallery explain the decoration: the church was "repaired and beautified" in 1886 and 1924. Note the iron **sword rest★** dated 1708, and a small carved, shrine (right of the altar) of 16/17C.

St Margaret Lothbury★ (NX) Wren: 1686-1690, 1701

Tower and Spire★: from the square stone base (clock projecting over the street) topped by an iron railing, rise a lead covered cupola and slender obelisk spire balancing a gilded ball and vane.

St Magnus: sword rest.

While the derivations of Lothbury are speculative and various, the church's certain foundation dates back to the 12C. There were repeated rebuildings culminating in that by Wren in 1686-90. The unequal parallelogram inside is divided by Corinthian columns into a nave and chancel and shorter south aisle. The **woodwork★** especially attracts the eye: from a dark base of wall and column panelling and cut down box pews, rise in clear silhouette, a wonderful oak screen, exquisitely carved pulpit, massive sounding board, gay with dancing cherubs and a reredos with balustered rails.

The **screen★**, made c 1689 for All Hallows, Upper Thames St, and one of only two *(p 59)* to Wren's design, is divided into 4 paired arcs by two strand balusters; at the centre are pierced pilasters and above three broken pediments, the central one supported by a great carved eagle and filled above with a royal coat of arms.

The chapel with a dividing screen made from the altar rails of St Olave Jewry, has a reredos also from St Olave. The **font★** is attributed to Grinling Gibbons.

St Margaret Pattens, Eastcheap (PY)   Wren: 1684-1689 and 1698-1702

Spire★: the lead covered, and therefore, black spire, a polygon which sharpens to a needle point at 199ft where a gilded vane balances, rises from a square stone tower: the only ornament is the pinnacled balustrade at the tower summit.

The site at the corner of Rood Lane was possibly already occupied by a wooden church in 1067. The church as redesigned by Wren, is a plain oblong with a flat ceiling and round clerestory windows. The **woodwork★** is outstanding: to the east, the reredos, 17C, gold lettered and framing a contemporary Italian painting, is carved with fruit, a peapod, flowers; in front, turned balusters support the communion rail; a high boxed beadle's pew and below, a low "punishment bench" with ferocious devil's head, choir stalls, a finely carved eagle lectern, pulpit with hour glass aloft for all to see the sermon's duration. On the north side, the Lady Chapel has a former doorcase as reredos and dowel pegs on which to hang wigs on hot days; also in the church are the only two canopied pews in London (the ceiling of the south pew monogrammed CW 1686, is by tradition the one occupied by Christopher Wren).

"Pattens" was added for distinction to the dedication and according to Stow was after the pattens or iron shod overshoes sold in the abutting lane.

St Martin Ludgate, Ludgate Hill (LY)   Wren: 1677-1687

Tower and Spire★: from a lead covered cupola and lantern, ringed by a balcony, there rises a black needle spire, the perfect foil to the green cathedral dome.

The church by the mediaeval Lud Gate and with a west wall just inside the Roman perimeter, is said to have been built first by King Cadwalla in 7C; it was certainly rebuilt in 1439 and burnt down in the Fire. Wren cut off the hill frontage inside by means of stout pillars on which he rested a gallery and thick coffered arches. At ground floor level beneath the gallery the bays were filled with three doors with **cases★** richly carved by **Grinling Gibbons.** The remaining area is laid out as a square within a square by means of 4 inner columns on which rest the groined vault formed by the intersection of barrel vaulting above the nave, chancel and transepts.

St Mary Abchurch★, Cannon St (NY)   Wren: 1681-1686

Tower and Spire★: red brick with stone quoins, surmounted by a cupola, lantern and slender spire of lead, all to the miniature scale of the church.

The Fire consumed "a fair church", last of a line dating back to 12C. The site was minute, some 80ft square, and Wren, fascinated by the problem, decided to cover the new church with a **dome★**. This one, approximately 40ft in diameter, is different however: it cannot be seen from outside and inside it rises from arches springing directly from the outer walls. There are no buttresses and only one interior column.

Tall carved pews line the north, south and west walls as originally. Receipts in the parish records show that many of the greatest craftsmen of the day worked on the furnishings: the font and stonework, the gilded copper pelican weathervane (removed as unsafe 1764), the pulpit with garlands and cherubs' heads, doorcases, font rails and cover, the lion and unicorn and royal arms. Authenticated as is no other work in a City church, apart from St Paul's, by bills and a personal letter from **Grinling Gibbons** himself, is the **reredos★★**, massive in size, magnificent in detail and delicacy.

St Mary Aldermary, Queen Victoria St (NY)   Wren: 1681-1682, 1701-1711

Tower: Gothic with corner buttresses, robust pinnacles and gilded finials.

St Mary is "the older Mary Church" — older that is than the Norman St Mary-le-Bow. After the Great Fire, a benefactor appeared offering £5 000 to rebuild the church as it had been; Wren, therefore, built a Gothic church — for £3 457!

Despite successive remodellings of the interior there remain a Grinling Gibbons pulpit and rich west doorcase (with a peapod; from St Antholin qv) a 1682 font and, against the 3rd south pillar, an oak **sword rest** also of 1682, one only of 4 in wood to survive and uniquely carved with fruit and flowers by Grinling Gibbons.

St Mary-at-Hill★★, Eastcheap (PZ)   Wren: 1670-1676; John Savage: 1849

Tower: stock brick of 1780, overlooking Lovat Lane; stucco east end with great Venetian window by Wren, and projecting clock on St Mary at Hill.

A church is first mentioned on the site in 1177. The Wren **plan★**, almost square, is divided into 3 × 3 bays beneath a shallow central dome, supported on free standing Corinthian columns; at each corner are plain square ceilings at cornice height.

St Mary's is known for its **woodwork★★** which dates from late 17C (font cover), early 18C (great oak reredos, communion table, altar rails) and 19C work by **William Gibbs Rogers** (organ gallery — musical trophies — pulpit, garlanded with fruit and flowers, massive sounding board, beautiful curved staircase, lectern and turned balustrade). Box pews add a Dickensian atmosphere, 6 gilded and enamelled wrought iron sword rests a touch of pageantry.

St Mary-le-Bow, Cheapside (MY)   Wren: 1670-1683

Tower and Steeple★★: the massive square Portland stone base, advanced on the street, rises to the belfry, from which **Bow Bells** ring out, and which is surmounted by one of the steeple's two open balustrades. At each corner is an ornament which opens the theme, a play upon the word "bow" — a stone arch to a mason — evolved by Wren for this, his most famous steeple which culminates in a soaring obelisk spire. Ultimate fantasy: the **vane** is a great 8ft 10in winged copper dragon said, when Wren hoisted it into place in 1679, to have been bestridden by a rope-dancer!

Of the 17C building, the most costly of Wren's churches (the vessel completed in 1673 cost over £8 000, the steeple, 1671-80, nearly as much), the tower and steeple and outer walls only remained after the great fire of May 1941. Laurence King rebuilt it: the exterior after Wren, the interior to a more open plan. The twin pulpits are a reminder that it is in Bow Church that the now famous **lunch-hour dialogues** are held *(Tuesdays 1.05pm)*. The west end is filled at the centre by a majestic organ above an ornate doorway surmounted by the royal arms in full colour.

The **crypt** of rough hewn, Saxon type walls and round Norman arches and columns with cushion capitals, supplemented by new piles, supports extensive groined vaulting (restored). The church was presented in 1100 to the province of Canterbury and the crypt served, on occasion, as the seat of the supreme court which became known as the Court of Arches; subsequently arches or bow became incorporated in the church's name.

By 16C a Perpendicular style church had been built with a tower crowned by corner lanterns and supported by flying buttresses — the first allusion to the bow theme.

Bow Bell was originally a curfew bell, hence the sense of definition for those born within its sound (from 1472 it not only tolled at 9pm but also at 5.45am to wake local cockneys; it ceased only in 1874). Wren left space for a peal of 12 bells, though at first only 8 were hung — the first being the Great Bell of Bow (of nursery rhyme fame). In 20C the bells, shattered in fragments, were recast and the peal sounded again for the first time in 1961. Whether there was a peal at the time legend has it that Whittington was called by them to return to London town is unknown: if there were and the wind was right he would have heard them clearly.

St Mary Woolnoth, Lombard St (NY)   Hawksmoor: 1716-1727

Tower: rusticated stone below, Corinthian columned above, rising to twin turrets, linked and crowned by open balustrades.

The church, built in Saxon times possibly by someone called Wulfnoth, hence the name, was rebuilt in stone by William the Conqueror. A mediaeval parishioner was Sir Martin Bowes, Lord Mayor in 1545, who left his gilded helmet, gauntlets, sword, spurs and banner and who, with his three wives, is buried beneath the altar. The site was always hemmed in; Hawksmoor, however, made his building arresting by the use of heavily rusticated stone and idiosyncratic by his flat tower. The small area inside he planned beneath a shallow dome as a square within a square with clusters of 3 fluted Corinthian columns marking each corner and supporting a heavily ornamented cornice and beam.

St Michael, Cornhill (PY)   Wren 1670-7; Hawksmoor 1718-1724; G G Scott 1857-1860

Tower: of stone rising by 4 stages to strongly stemmed, ornamented corner pinnacles between which stand slim miniature pinnacles, braceleted by a balustrade.

The Gothic style tower was designed at the end of Wren's life by Hawksmoor, when the old tower which had survived the Fire had become unsafe; the neo-Gothic doorway, framed by small marble columns, carved stone covings and tympanum, by Giles Gilbert Scott, as part of an 1857-60 remodelling. Inside, the vaulting on tall Tuscan columns is by Wren; the Venetian windows by Scott; the carved bench ends in the Wren tradition by W Gibbs Rogers (19C); the font and large wooden pelican are late 17C...

St Michael Paternoster Royal, Upper Thames St (NY)   Wren: 1686-1694, 1715-1717

Tower and Spire★: square of stone rising to a balustrade quartered by urns. The spire, added in 1715, takes the form of a three tier octagonal lantern, marked at each angle by an Ionic column and urn; on high is a vaned spirelet (*cf* St James Garlickhythe).

The "fair parish church", as Stow described it, "new built by Richard Whittington", in place of the earliest known building of the mid 13C, was destroyed in the Fire; in July 1944 history was repeated. The south wall with 6 rounded lights and a balustraded parapet is of stone, the east end of brick, stone trimmed. Above the door is a cherub's head keystone. The rich red, gold, green windows include at the west end, young Whittington in a cap with his cat at his feet. **Whittington,** who lived in an adjoining house, founded an almshouse, also adjoining, and on his death in 1423, was buried in the church. The last part of the name Paternoster Royal is from La Riole, a town near Bordeaux from which the wine long imported by local vintners came.

St Nicholas Cole Abbey, Queen Victoria St (MY)   Wren: 1671-1681

Tower and Spire★: from a small square stone base marked by corner urns, rises an octagonal lead spire, lifting finally to a **gilded three master.**

St Nicholas' recorded history goes back to 1144 but even Stow "could never learn the cause of the name and therefore let it passe". The church was burned out in 1666 and again in 1941 so that it has had to be totally rebuilt. The stone exterior is pierced by tall rounded windows beneath corbelled, hoods and circled by an open balustrade.

St Olave★, Hart St (RY)   15C

Tower: the square mediaeval ragstone lower stage with 18C brick repairs above, is crowned with a lantern. A round faced clock projects back over the nave.

Wood (*c* 1050) and later stone (*c* 1200) parish churches have been piled on the site, the most recent rebuilding being after incendiaries had gutted the vessel in 1941. Throughout associations have been kept alive: the dedication to St Olaf, who in 1013 helped Ethelred against the Danes remains vivid in the new Norwegian flag; a bust (19C) of Samuel Pepys appropriately blocks the former south doorway (inscription outside) to what is still the Navy pew (small anchor on the bench end).

The churchyard gateway on Seething Lane, decorated exclusively with skulls is dated 1658 — opposite is the site, now a garden, of the Navy office of Pepys' day (burned 1673).

The church porch, into which one descends, like the major part of the church, is 15C. The interior is divided into a nave and aisle of three bays by quatrefoil marble pillars, probably from a former, 13C, church; the clerestory and roof are post war, as is the glass, except for the late 19C heraldic panels which had been removed for cleaning in 1939. Furnishings have been presented: the **pulpit,** made reputedly in Grinling Gibbons' workshop for St Benet Gracechurch (Wren; demolished 1867); Jacobean altar rails; four 18C sword rests. The monuments which, incredibly, withstood the fire, include tablets, brasses, effigies large and small of highly coloured or natural stone: **Elisabeth Pepys** (17C bust in an oval niche — high on the sanctuary north wall), the 17C kneeling and brightly coloured Bayninge brothers (below); Sir James Deane (17C kneeling figure with 3 wives and children — all in colour; north wall over 15C vestry door); Sir Andrew Riccard, Chairman of East India and Turkey Companies (17C standing figure — north aisle).

The **crypt** *(steps at west end)* of two chambers with ribbed vaulting, is a survival of the early 13C church.

St Peter upon Cornhill (PY)   Wren: 1677-1687

Spire: visible only from the churchyard at the rear and Gracechurch St: square brick tower crowned by small green copper dome and obelisk spire from which flies a vane in the form of a key (which measures 9ft and weighs 2 cwts).

The vessel exterior, again only visible from the churchyard, is stuccoed with rounded and circular east windows surmounted by a pediment. Inside there is a geometrical inter-play between the basilical ground plan divided by square pillars and the arcs of windows, tunnel vaulting, arches, underlined by a double plaster fillet, between nave and aisles and the outlines of the rood screen. The upper area is light and minimally decorated; the lower, to sill level, darkly panelled. The pews were cut down in 19C apart from two retained at full height for the church wardens (at the back). The oak **screen★**, one of two only in Wren's churches *(p 56)* and said to have been designed by the architect and his young daughter, has strong central pillars rising high to support a lion and unicorn; on the central arch are the arms of Charles II. Organ gallery, doorcases at the west end, sounding board with cherubs' heads, pulpit with domed panels and carved drops of fruit and leaves, add richness everywhere.

St Peter's upon Cornhill, one of the two hills upon which London was first built, claims to stand on the highest ground in the City.

Church of the Holy Sepulchre (St Sepulchre), Holborn Viaduct (LX)
15C; Wren 1670-1677, 19C

Tower: 15C square stone surmounted by 4 top-heavy crocketed pinnacles.

An early foundation, the church which stands "Without Newgate" was renamed at the time of the Crusades after the Jerusalem church "without the city wall". The porch, with fan vaulting, and the tower, though restored externally, date from 1450. The interior is furnished with a contemporary font and octagonal cover gay with cherubs' heads and at the entrance, the beautiful font cover rescued from Christchurch *(qv)* in 1940. The organ, built in 1670, reputed to have been played by Handel and Mendelssohn, and where Henry Wood at 14 officiated as assistant organist, has a superb case, including the royal mono-gram of Charles II. In addition there are mementoes: sword rests; the hand bell rung outside condemned men's cells at midnight in the old Newgate Prison; a brass plate to Captain John Smith, sometime Governor of Virginia who died in 1631 and is buried in the church; colours of the Royal Fusiliers, City of London Regiment; in the north, Musicians' Chapel, the ashes of Sir Henry Wood (1869-1944), windows, chairs, kneelers to British musicians of every period.

St Stephen Walbrook★ (NY)   Wren: 1672-1677, 1717

Tower and Steeple★: both are square throughout — the tower of ragstone rising to a trim balustrade; the later steeple of Portland stone through 8 stages all with the same outline, to two balls and a vane. The characteristic dome, green, turreted and also vaned can be seen at the rear.

St Stephens' is the birthplace of the Samaritans, founded in 1953 to befriend the suicidal and despairing; by 1976 there were 160 branches in the UK, 40 overseas.

In the 17C the church was seen by Wren as an experiment in the construction of a **dome★** in preparation for St Paul's. As in the cathedral it is the feature which impinges immediately. One other obvious resemblance is the ring of circular arches on which the cupola rests. St Stephen's ground plan is just oblong, the dome off centre, the bays delin-eated by free standing Corinthian columns, grouped to produce unexpected perspectives within the typically enclosing panelling and massively carved furnishings.

St Vedast, Foster Lane (MX)   Wren: 1670-1673, 1697

Tower and Spire★: a square stone tower, then an overhanging entablature which is the dividing line between the earlier construction and later fantasy, when Wren set a lantern on it with advanced triple pilasters at the corners through 3 stages, below the ribbed stone spire surmounted by a ball and vane.

The exterior with a pre-Fire curving southwest wall, retained by Wren when he accom-plished the church's rebuilding for the total sum of £1 853 15s 6d (the cheapest of all the City churches), is almost unnoticeable from Foster Lane. (The street's name is a corruption of Vedast, 6C Bishop of Arras to who the church was dedicated in 13C.)

The interior is entirely new. The floor has been marbled in black and white; pews aligned collegiate style beneath the **ceiling★**, reinstalled to Wren's design with a central wreath, cornice and end panels in moulded plasterwork, highlighted in gold and silver against a white ground — St Vedast's is the Goldsmiths' Church.

Towers and other places of Worship

St Alban, Wood Street (M X)   Wren: 1697-1698

Tower: Wren's pure Gothic tower with slim corner buttresses crowned by a balustrade and crocketed pinnacles, rises like a white stone needle out of the sea of traffic.

All Hallows Staining (R Y)

Tower: the 15C ragstone tower, battlemented but solitary since 1870 when its church of 1671 was demolished, is now dwarfed by overshadowing office blocks.

St Alphage, London Wall (opposite the rear of the City Business Library) (N X)

Tower Base: 14C pointed stone arches in black flint walls, mark the west tower of the chapel of Elsing Spital Priory dissolved by Henry VIII. (Revealed by 1940 bombs.)

St Augustine and St Faith, Watling St (M Y)   Wren: 1680-1687

Tower and Spire: the square tower of newly hewn stone ends in a pierced parapet quartered by obelisk pinnacles; above rise an almost black, tulip shaped, dome and lead spire — all rebuilt, since the war, to Wren's original design.

   The church was not reconstructed; instead new buildings were erected abutting the tower to provide premises for the Cathedral Choir School.

Christ Church★, Newgate St (L X)   Wren: 1704

Tower: slender, square and of stone, the tower rises by stages marked by urns and alternately solid and colonnaded, to a slim, decorated turret and vane.

   Christ Church was founded by Henry VIII on the site occupied from 1225-1538 by the Greyfriars monastery; close by was a second royal foundation, Christ's Hospital, the Bluecoat School (1552-1902). The church, destroyed in the Fire, rebuilt by Wren in 1667-91 on sufficient scale to accommodate the boys, is now a garden. The font cover, rescued by a postman in 1940 is in St Sepulchre's.

St Dunstan-in-the-East★★, St Dunstan's Hill, Lower Thames St (R Z)   Wren : 1697

Steeple: of Portland stone entirely. The spire is poised on flying buttresses with pinnacles canting the 4 tier tower.

St Martin Ongar, Martin Lane (P Y)

Tower: 19C solitary square brick and stucco tower marks the site of a mediaeval church.

St Mary Aldermanbury, Aldermanbury/Love Lane corner (N X)   Wren: 1670

Site: the 12C site, is now a garden, with only bases of the perimeter walls and pillars outlining the bombed Wren church. The stones were numbered and sent to Fulton, USA where the church has been rebuilt to the 17C plan.

St Mary Somerset, Upper Thames St (M Y)   Wren: 1695

Tower: slim, square and white, the tower rises from its garden setting to a parapet, quartered with square finials and obelisk pinnacles. Note the masks.

St Olave Jewry (N X)   Wren: 1670-1676

Tower: a two stage stone tower is topped by a beautiful **weathervane,** the three master fully rigged from St Mildred Bread St (Wren: destroyed 1940).

City Temple, Holborn Viaduct (K X)

Tower: high, square and pillared, surmounted by a square lantern, lead dome and cross.

   The history of the City Temple, the only English Free Church in the City, goes back to 1640 although occupation of the site on the viaduct dates only from 1874. The church is famous for its preachers, among who this century have been Dr Maude Royden, in 1917 the first woman to step into a pulpit, and Dr Leslie Weatherhead. Wartime bombing gutted the sanctuary so that the building now presents the contrast of a Victorian/Palladian exterior and modern interior.

Dutch Church, Austin Friars (P X)   Ansell and Bailey: 1955
   Ring for admission: Monday to Thursday, 11am to 3pm

Spire: slender lantern crowned by a spirelet and weathervane by John Skeeping.

   The church received a direct hit in 1940 and has been entirely rebuilt to a modern design with a hall interior and brilliant windows beneath a shallow curved roof.

   The foundation dates back to 1253, a rebuilding in 14C and an Augustinian monastery dissolved by Henry VIII; all that remained when in 1550 Edward VI granted the refugees of the Low Countries Austin Friars as a place of worship was the nave.

Spanish and Portuguese Synagogue, Bevis Marks (R X). — *Open for services.*

   The synagogue of 1701, successor to the one in Creechurch Lane (plaque) which was the first to be opened after the Jews had been invited to return by Cromwell in 1657, is known particularly for its rich appointments: the Ark, containing the hand-written Scrolls from which the Pentateuch is read, the raised Tebah, surrounded by twisted balusters, the 7 brass chandeliers from Holland.

   Bevis Marks is a corruption of Buries Marks, an abbreviation for the mark or site of the 12C mansion of the abbots of Bury St Edmunds. In 16C the mansion was acquired by Thomas Heneage whose name is perpetuated in the nearby lane.

   The City's only other synagogue, the Great Synagogue, Duke's Place, Aldgate, opened in 1722, rebuilt in 1790, was totally destroyed in an air raid.

■ The CORPORATION OF LONDON

The **City** is governed by the Corporation of London, which acts through the Court of Common Council. The latter, numbering 25 Aldermen and 159 Councilmen, is presided over by the Lord Mayor and meets in Guildhall.

Guildhall★ (NX). – *Open 10am to 5pm; Sundays May to September, Easter Monday, spring and autumn holidays, 2 to 5pm; closed 25, 26 December, 1 January, Good Friday.*

History. – "This Guildhall", Stow quoted in 1598 "was begun to be built new in the year 1411; ... the same was made of a little cottage, a large and great house... towards the charges whereof the (livery) companies gave large benevolences; also offences of men were pardoned for sums of money, extraordinary fees were raised, fines... during 7 years, with a continuation of 3 years more... Executors to Richard Whittington gave towards the paving of this great hall... with hard stone of Purbeck". All was complete by *c* 1440. The Great Fire left the outer walls and crypt standing. Rebuilding began immediately and in 1669 Pepys noted "I passed by Guildhall, which is almost finished".

In 1940 after 18 and 19C restorations and remodellings, history repeated itself. Reconstruction was once more completed in 1954 (west crypt: 1972; construction of a new west wing: 1974).

The City was granted its first charter by William the Conqueror in 1067; the first **Mayor** was installed in a building, of which no trace remains, probably on the present site in 1193; for at least 850 years, therefore Guildhall has been the seat of civic government.

Richard Whittington. – Whittington was four times Lord Mayor; in 1397, 1397-8, 1406-7 and 1419-20; he died in 1423, a man in his early sixties. He had come to London from Gloucestershire, where he was born the 3rd son of a local squire, entered the mercers' trade, married well and rose rapidly both in trade, from which he amassed a fortune and in the Corporation where he progressed from ward member to Lord Mayor. He was not knighted though an important part of his contact with the monarchy appears to have been as provider of considerable loans – legend has it that he concluded a banquet to Henry V by burning bonds discharged for the king for £60 000.

(National Portrait Gallery)

Richard Whittington.

Whittington's great wealth continued after his death as it had been in his lifetime, to be devoted to the public cause: the permanent establishment of Leadenhall Market, the construction of Greyfriars Library, half the cost of founding the Guildhall Library, repairs at Bart's, the foundation of a college (dissolved at the Reformation) and almshouses at St Michael Paternoster Royal, the rebuilding of Newgate Prison...

Such great personality, wealth, benefactions, were embroidered into legend until in 1605 license was granted for performances of a play (now lost), *The History of Richard Whittington, of his lowe byrth, his great fortune;* when an engraver, Renold Elstrack, about the same time portrayed him in classic pose with his hand upon a skull, popular protest was so loud that the engraver altered the plate to substitute in place of the skull a more endearing cat from which possibly a new legend developed.

Exterior. – Guildhall's front, a mixture of Classical and Gothic motifs, extends across 9 bays, rises to 4 storeys and culminates, on the four buttresses which divide the face into equal parts, in large and peculiar pinnacles. Crowning the central area are the City arms with griffin supporters *(1)*. All this dates from the restoration of 1788-9 by **George Dance the Younger** (which virtually obliterated Wren's and others' previous restorations). The **porch**, at the centre, however, is still covered by two bays of tierceron vaulting which is mediaeval.

Inside the **hall** also is in part mediaeval: the walls date back to the 15C and the chamber in which today's banquets are held is the same in dimension (152 × 49½ ft) as that in which Lady Jane Grey and others were tried.

A cornice at clerestory level bears the arms of England, the City and the 12 Great Livery Companies whose banners hang in front *(p 63);* below, the bays between the piers contain memorial statues, notably (north wall) a seated bronze of **Churchill** by Oscar Nemon; Nelson; Wellington; the Elder Pitt. Against the south, porch entrance, wall (far left) are the Standards of Length with above, the only remaining 15C window (right) and behind where the lord mayor sits at banquets, a canopied oak buffet on which are displayed the City sword and mace and plate.

---

(1) The City arms are composed of the Cross of St George, the sword of the patron saint, St Paul, on a shield supported by winged griffins, probably incorporated in 16C.

The CITY ★★★

Guarding the Musicians' Gallery are **Gog and Magog** — post-war replica giants, each 9ft 3ins tall, carved in limewood by David Evans after the figures set up in Guildhall in 1708, themselves descendants of 15 and 16C midsummer pageant figures who were said to have originated in a legendary conflict between ancient Britons and Trojans in 1 000 BC.

(After photograph, Pitkin Pictorials)

Gog and Magog.

Crypt. — *Open only on application to the beadle on duty.*

The crypt is divided into two: the western, pre-15C, part lies under the earlier hall which collapsed in the Fire, was repaired with a barrel roof by Wren and has recently been restored so that it now has a vaulted ceiling once more resting on four pairs of stone columns. The eastern 15C area below the hall, survived both 17 and 20C fires and is particularly notable for its size — it is the largest mediaeval crypt in London — and the 6 blue Purbeck marble clustered pillars which support the vaulting.

Clock Museum★. — *Open Monday to Friday 9.30am to 5pm.*

The 700 timepieces which make up the Museum of the Worshipful Company of Clockmakers range in size from long case (grandfather) clocks to minute watches, in date from 15 to 20C, in manufacture from all wood composition, in movement from perpetual motion (the ball rolls 2 522 miles a year) and in aesthetic appeal from a silver skull watch, said to have belonged to Mary Queen of Scots, to jewelled confections, enamelled, decorated, engraved, chased...

Library. — *Open Monday to Saturday 9.30am to 5pm. Newspaper and Exhibition Rooms closed on Saturdays, closed all public holidays. No ticket required (reference only).*

The library, founded *c* 1423, despoiled in 16C, refounded in 1824, possesses an unrivalled collection on the history and development of the City and, by extension, of London, including maps, prints, mss.

Two other nationally famous libraries with seemingly limitless resources and information on their special subjects *(both open Mondays to Fridays 9.30am to 5.30pm)* are: **City Business Library** (NX — Gillett House, 55 Basinghall St) and **St Bride Printing Library** (KY — Bride Lane, Fleet St).

Mansion House★ (NY). — *Admission only by prior written authority.*

The house dates only from 1739-52 — previously lord mayors remained in their own residences during the years of their mayoralty.

George Dance the Elder, the architect selected by the Corporation, designed a Palladian style mansion in Portland stone, before which modest staircases on either side at the front lead to a raised portico of six giant Corinthian columns, surmounted by an ornamented, triangular, pediment.

The interior, designed as a suite from the portico, leads to the dining or Egyptian Hall (named after an interior Vitruvius described as an Egyptian Hall and favoured by 18C Palladians but having nothing to do with Egypt). In the hall, giant Corinthian columns support the cornice on which the coved ceiling rests and the walled niches are filled with Victorian statuary on subjects taken from English literature from Chaucer to Byron. The Ball Room is on the second floor. The Lord Mayor is Chief Magistrate of the City and on the ground floor on the east side is a Court of Justice, with cells below, the only such appointments in a private residence in the kingdom.

Plate and insignia★★. — The Corporation plate, rich and varied, dates from 17C. The insignia includes much older pieces: the Lord Mayor's **chain of office,** *c* 1535 with later additions, suspends from a collar of SS gold links, knots and enamelled Tudor roses, a pendant known as the Diamond Jewel, an onyx, carved in 1802 with the City arms, set in diamonds; the **Pearl Sword,** 16C and according to tradition presented by Queen Elizabeth at the opening of the Royal Exchange in 1571; the 17C **Sword of State** and the 18C **Great Mace,** silver gilt and 5ft 3ins long.

Lord Mayor's Show★★. — The show is the lord mayor's progress to his swearing in before the Lord Chief Justice, an observance which dates back to the charter of 1215 which required that the mayor be presented to the monarch or his justices at the Palace of Westminster. The procession was, for centuries, partly by water — the mayor owned a civic barge in the 15C. In 1553 full pageantry became the order of the day with men parading their best liveries, trumpets sounding, masques and poems recited along the route. Today with the judges removed from Westminster, the oath is taken at the Royal Courts of Justice; the pageantry, after a decline in the 19C, has returned with floats and the new and old mayors progressing in the golden state and other horsedrawn coaches accompanied by outriders.

The Show on the second Saturday in November is followed on the Monday evening by the Lord Mayor's Banquet in Guildhall which by tradition (although not invariably) begins with turtle soup. The principal speakers are by invariable tradition the new Lord Mayor and the Prime Minister.

City Livery Company Halls

There are 84 companies of which 12 make up the so-called Greater Companies. Most are successors of mediaeval religious fraternities, craft or social guilds. The Great Fire, local fires, changes of fortune, incendiary bombs, have reduced the number of halls to 36 including the Master Mariners, transferred to the frigate HMS *Wellington* (moored in the Thames off the Victoria Embankment) and the Salters' to W1.

The halls are not generally open to outsiders. Special visits are arranged in summer by the City Information Centre – prior application essential.

Although in 1523 Henry VIII "commanded to have all money and plate belonging to any Hall or Crypt", many halls have collections or pieces dating back to 15C which they either managed to hide from the king or re-purchased.

MERCERS

GROCERS

DRAPERS

FISHMONGERS

GOLDSMITHS

SKINNERS

Mercers (NY). – *Ironmonger Lane.* 1958 rebuilding of earlier halls (1540, 1672-82) on the site of St Thomas of Acon Hospital. Major collection of plate dating from 15C.

Grocers (NY). – *Prince's St.* 1889-93. Elizabethan hall with 17C iron screen; courtroom with overmantel from late 17C hall; 16-20C plate; John Piper tapestries.

Drapers (PX). – *Throgmorton St.* 1868. Pillared and mirrored hall with full length portraits; silver from Elizabeth I to II.

Fishmongers (NPZ). – *London Bridge.* 1831-4. Neo-Greek building in a unique position with windows overlooking the river which enhances the rich interior gold leaf decoration (restored post war). Late 17/18C and 20C plate; the **Annigoni** portrait of the **Queen** hangs in the drawing room. On 20 June each year the company pays a "fine" of one red rose to the Lord Mayor imposed on Lady Knollys in 1381 for building a bridge across Seething Lane without permission.

Goldsmiths (MX). – *Foster Lane.* 1835. Exceptional plate in a lavish, baroque setting. The hall is also notable for its jewellery exhibitions.

Skinners (NY). – *Dowgate Hill.* Late 18C building, staircase and still aromatic sandalwood panelling of 1670; 18C plasterwork; hall 1850 with Frank Brangwyn decorations (1904-10); plate. Courtyard.

Merchant Taylors (PY). – *Threadneedle St.* Plate including a cloth yard with Henry VIII cypher.

Haberdashers (MX). – *Staining Lane.* Rebuilt 1956. Outstanding Elizabethan and 17C plate.

Salters. – *36a Portland Place.* The company owned a City hall from 1454-1941.

Ironmongers (MX). – *Aldersgate St.* 1924 Gothic stone porch; the small building is now surrounded by the Museum of London. Early 16C funeral pall. Late 15/18 and 20C plate.

Vintners (MY). – *Upper Thames St.* 1671, restored 1948; very fine late 17C panelling in majestic hall; staircase with outstanding balusters; 15C tapestry, 16C funeral pall; plate includes a double "milkmaid" cup, the Glass Tun etc. The monarch, the Vintners, and the Dyers own the swans upon the Thames, the company swans being marked on the bill as cygnets at the annual swan upping.

Clothworkers (RY). – *Mincing Lane.* 1955-8. 17/18C plate.

MERCHANT TAILORS

HABERDASHERS

SALTERS

IRONMONGERS

VINTNERS

CLOTH WORKERS

Apothecaries (LY). – *Blackfriars Lane.* 1632, rebuilt *c* 1670; pillared lamp over the old monastic well in the courtyard; interior remarkable for 1671 oak panelling, stone jars (one of 1566), apothecary vessels; chandeliers; banners from former state barge.

Armourers and Brasiers (NX). – *Coleman St.* 1840; large collection of 17/18C plate.

Barber-Surgeons (MX). – *Monkwell Sq.* Inigo Jones hall destroyed in the war; rebuilt on adjoining site (bombing exposed Roman fort and bastion). Superb 16/17C plate.

Cutlers (LX). – *Warwick Lane.* 1886-7. Elephant shaped poor box; sets of 17/18C spoons.

Founders (NY). – *St Swithin's Lane.* 1877-8. 16/18C plate.

Innholders (NYZ). – *College St.* 1886. Plate includes remarkable salts and spoons.

Stationers (LY). – *Stationers' Hall Court, Ludgate Hill.* 1800, 1887; splendid carved screen and panelling of 1670; 1800 ceiling (re-erected).

Tallow Chandlers (NY). – *Dowgate Hill.* Rebuilt 1670-2; Italianised 1880. Courtyard; 17C seating in courtroom; 16/20C plate.

Watermen and Lightermen (PZ). – *St Mary at Hill. (Not strictly a Livery company though dating back to Tudor times).* 1780; small hall in a pilastered building.

■ FINANCE

Wealth, resources, once visible in gold coin and bullion, now in the form of computer impulses on tape, quoted always it seems, in millions, existing as transactions, "futures", indexes... personal fortunes made or unmade as "confidence" rises or falls – though outside the common experience, the mystery – magic associated with the name of the City remains. The pervasive atmosphere of wealth is immediately recognisable in what has been for hundreds of years and remains a world centre of finance.

Bank of England (NY). – *Not open.* The Bank, massive, blank and undistinguished was designed by Sir Herbert Baker and erected between 1924 and 1939. It is taller and larger than its immediate predecessor by Sir John Soane whose Bank building was his life's masterpiece. Of this only the outer walls remain. An annexe of the Bank, erected since the last war, with a concave façade on New Change at the east end of St Paul's, is notable only for its size.

Bank of England.

The Bank, the concept of a Scot, William Paterson, was incorporated under royal charter in 1694 with a capital of £1 200 000 to finance in the modern way by raising loans and not by royal extortion as heretofore, the continuation of the wars against Louis XIV. It acquired its nickname a century later during the Napoleonic wars: the crisis had forced the Bank to suspend cash payments – Sheridan referred in the House to the "elderly lady in the City of great credit and long standing", Gillray drew a caricature which he captioned "The Old Lady of Threadneedle St in Danger".

The Bank has since weathered other crises, become a bankers' bank and in 1946 was nationalised. It supervises the note issue, national debt, exchange control regulations and acts as the central reserve. The governor is appointed by the Crown.

Royal Exchange★ (PY). – *Cornhill and Threadneedle St. Open Monday to Friday 10am to 4pm: Saturday to noon. A carillon plays English, Scots, Welsh, Irish, Canadian and Australian melodies at 9am, noon, 3 and 6pm.*

The exchange, modelled on that of Antwerp, was "first built with brick at the sole charge of **Sir Thomas Gresham** who laid the foundation 7 June 1565... On 27 January (1568) Queen Elizabeth came to view it and caused it to be proclaimed the Royal Exchange. But being consumed by the dreadful Fire in 1666 was rebuilt with Portland Stone by the City and Mercers' Company... King Charles II laying the first stone". This building, "esteemed the most beautiful, strong and stately of its kind in Europe" was designed by Edward Jarman on the same courtyard plan but bigger; in 1838 it was again burned down and a third, larger, building constructed.

The wide steps, monumental Corinthian portico and pediment with 10ft tall allegorical figures, provide an impressive entrance to an edifice once the very hub of the City. Between the façade and the tower at the rear, lies a hollow square lined by an arcade at ground and first floor levels where merchant brokers congregated besides "walking the central square" (glassed over in 1883). Around and on the outside walls are 19C portrait statues: in front, an equestrian bronze (lacking stirrups!) of Wellington (Chantrey); against the north wall, Whittington and Myddelton; at the rear, Gresham and above, the merchant's personal emblem as weathervane, a gilded bronze grasshopper.

Stock Exchange★ (PX). – *8 Throgmorton St. Visitors' gallery and film theatre open Monday to Friday 10am to 3.15pm; closed public holidays and 24 December (parties should reserve cinema seats in advance). Public entrance Threadneedle St.*

Trading in stocks and shares originated in 17C in this country, at first in the Royal Exchange and local coffeehouses. The first stock exchange, as such, was inaugurated in 1773 in Threadneedle St: in 1801 and 1971 this was replaced by ever larger buildings on the present site.

From a gallery inside the sleekly functional stone and glass edifice surmounted by a 350ft tower, the visitor looks through plate glass onto the trading floor below. Transactions are recorded by electronic equipment but also still "on the nod".

Baltic Exchange (RX). – *14 St Mary Axe. Visits only on written application.*

The Victorian building houses the world's only shipping exchange covering international chartering of ships and aircraft, also worldwide grain, oil and oilseed markets.

London Commodity Exchange (RY). – *Plantation House, Mincing Lane. Visits only on written application.*

In 1954 the cocoa, coffee, copra, cotton, essential and vegetable oils, hemp, ivory, jute, pepper and spices, rubber, shellac and sugar exchanges were incorporated to form the London Commodity Exchange.

Lloyd's (RY). – *Leadenhall and Lime Sts. Only open to parties by prior appointment.*

Until this century the biggest insurance corporation in the world possessed no exclusive office premises: Lloyd's Shipping Register was opened in 1900 and the two massive insurance offices on either side of Lime St in 1928 and 1957.

History. – In 1691 **Edward Lloyd**, coffeehouse owner near the Tower, took over Pontaq's at 16 Lombard St (plaque on Coutts), a French owned eating house frequented with relish by Pepys, Evelyn, Wren, Dryden, Swift... Under Lloyd, the house, at the heart of the business world and surrounded by literally hundreds of competitors, became the meeting place of merchants, shippers, bankers, underwriters, agents and newsmen. He inaugurated the still current system of port agents to provide shipping intelligence. In 1734 began the publication of the daily, *Lloyd's List,* and in 1760 of the annual *Lloyd's Register.* Edward Lloyd had died in 1712 (plaque in St Mary Woolnoth) and in 1769 his successors split: New Lloyd's moved into 5 Pope's Head Alley (the Lombard St house closed in 1785).

Through the good offices of John Julius Angerstein and the Mercers' Co, in 1774 Lloyd's transferred to more spacious quarters "over the northwest corner of the Royal Exchange" where it remained until this century. In 1771 the association became formalised by the institution of a minute book; in 1871 it was incorporated by act of parliament. (Policies are subscribed by members or underwriters acting for a syndicate of which there are now nearly 300; the requirements for membership are minimum assets of £75 000 and to be able to lodge a deposit of at least £10 000. Some £750 million is placed annually in premiums.) The organisation, guarded by doormen, resplendent in red frock coats with black velvet collars and gilt buckled top hats, covers everything except "life" it is said.

Old building. – The offices, opened in 1928, stand on the site in Leadenhall St of the former East India House company, chartered by Queen Elizabeth in 1600.

New building. – These offices in the 50s neo-Classical style were opened in 1957. Among Lloyd's traditions are the Captains' Room, first so-called in the Exchange when Lloyd's took over the Refreshment Room and the catering, and still the name of the members' exclusive dining room; Nelson mementoes; policies including that of 1680 at 4 % on the *Golden Fleece* bound for Venice from Lisbon; the Underwriting Room (340ft long in the new building – the Room, the former hall, is in the old building) furnished with "boxes" in the style of an 18C coffeehouse; the daily publication, the *Shipping Index,* recording movements of some 20 000 vessels... and the striking of the **Lutine Bell** for an overdue vessel, once for a loss, twice for a safe arrival. The bell came from a French frigate captured in 1793, sunk off Holland in 1799 when loaded with gold and specie valued at nearly £1.5 million and insured by the house but partly salved in 1857-61.

(After photograph, Pitkin Pictorials)

The Lutine Bell.

Lloyd's Shipping Register (RY). – *71 Fenchurch St.* The building, columned and turreted, is decorated with *art nouveau* figures and friezes towards Lloyds Avenue. *Lloyd's Register,* gives details of ownership, tonnage etc (as opposed to movements).

The City Markets. – Three of the main wholesale markets are still to be found in the City. (The other principal markets are New Covent Garden, Borough and Spitalfields.)

Smithfield (LV). – *London Central Markets. Time to visit: early morning to 3pm.*

Smithfield was opened as a wholesale and retail dead meat, poultry and provision market only in 1868. Previously the stock had come in live, driven into the City through Islington: from 12C for the summer Fair of St Bartholomew, from 1614 all the year round. After centuries of overcrowding on the site and chaos and congestion in the narrow streets, the livestock market was transferred in 1855 to the Caledonian Market, Islington. The buildings, erected in 1868 and since enlarged, are of red brick and stone with domed towers at either end; they extend over 8 acres, contain a railway depot below, cold stores... and 15 miles of rails capable of hanging 60 000 sides of beef.

Billingsgate Market (PZ). – *Time to visit: before 7.30am.*

Early, Billingsgate is alive: the smell of fish is in the air, gulls wheel and screech, lorries rev up, porters push barrows over the cobbles, men in white overalls, apparently unhurriedly, sell the daily harvest of some 400 tons of fish. Later there is just the hosed down 1875 arcaded building of yellow stock brick, crowned by a seated Britannia supported by dolphins poised with tails in the air. Note the fish weathervanes.

Leadenhall Market (PY). – *Gracechurch St. Open all day.*

Leadenhall, a retail market selling poultry, meat, fish, fruit, cheese and specialising in game, is at its most spectacular at the start of the season when the shop fronts are hung with grouse, partridge, pheasant... and at Christmas. The area was a market in Roman times *(p 47)* and then a manor which Whittington purchased and converted, in part, once more into a market under the Corporation – hence Whittington Avenue and the market's name after the house's lead covered roof. It was burned down in the Fire; rebuilt and rebuilt again in 1881 in the present form.

■ ADDITIONAL SIGHTS ON THE MAIN THOROUGHFARES

The City's network of alleys, courts, yards and steps — everyone's personal short cut — often enlivened by an old tavern, newly planted with half a dozen trees, arranged with benches, a fountain, a statue, would take a volume to describe. Their history — and often the City's — is reflected in their names: Pope's Head Alley, Puddle Dock, Glasshouse Alley, Bate's Court, Panyer Alley, Wardrobe Terrace, Seacole Lane, French Ordinary, Ave Maria Lane, Paternoster Row, Amen Court, Turnagain Lane...

FLEET ST - ST PAUL'S (JKL/Y)

Fleet St, named after the River Fleet which ran south from Hampstead and drained into the river at Blackfriars, has always itself had an east-west course; Lud Gate, in the ancient City wall, west of St Martin's (plaque) was called after the legendary King Lud (66 BC), said to have built the first gate on the site (demolished: 1760).

Temple Bar. — The bar has been the City's western barrier since the Middle Ages and is still where the sovereign pauses to receive and return the Pearl Sword from the Lord Mayor on entering the City. The present memorial pillar with statues of Queen Victoria and the future Edward VII surmounted by the City griffin, dates from 1880. It replaced the "bars" which had developed from 13C posts and chains and at various times constituted a high, arched building, a prison (thrown down by Wat Tyler in 1381), and finally an arch designed by Wren in 1672 and used, in the days of public execution, as a spike for heads and quarters.

Child & Co. — *No 1.* One of the country's oldest banks (now Williams and Glyn's), originally "at the sign of the Marigold" also known as the Devil Tavern (plaque).

Prince Henry's Room. — *No 17. Open 1.45 to 5pm daily; Sundays to 4pm; 10p.*
The upstairs tavern room is Tudor panelled with an ornate strapwork, Jacobean ceiling with a centre decoration of Prince of Wales' feathers and the initials PH. It is now overfilled with Samuel Pepys mementoes.

Cock Tavern (Ye Olde Cocke Tavern). — 17C overmantel panelled long bar and upstairs restaurant rooms; Dickens and Thackeray associations.

Fetter Lane. — At the top end are the Printer's Devil (pub, printing decoration) and the Daily Mirror.

The courts. — To the north are a series of narrow alleys: Crane, Red Lion, Johnson's, St Dunstan's, Bolt, Three Kings, Hind, Wine Office, Cheshire and Peterborough.

Dr Johnson's House★ (KX). — *Gough Sq. Open daily May to September 11.00am to 5.30pm (October to April 5pm); closed Sundays and public holidays; 20p.*
The typical late 17C house, where he lived between 1749 and 1759, was chosen by Johnson almost certainly for its long, well lit, garret, where he worked with his secretaries to complete his *Dictionary* which was published in 1755. The small rooms on each floor contain 18C furniture, prints, mementoes and the first edition. The work completed, he moved to chambers in the Temple, in 1765 to no 7 Fleet St (known purely coincidentally as Johnson's Ct), and finally to Bolt Ct where he died in 1784.

Cheshire Cheese. — *Wine Office Court.* The pub in a house rebuilt in 1667, has Johnson associations. It includes a restaurant, small beamed rooms and coal fires on 3 floors.

No 143 is Gothic with a 19C full length statue of Mary Queen of Scots between the first floor windows.

Bouverie and Whitefriars Sts. — *News of the World, Daily Mail, Evening News* buildings.

Reuters and Press Association. — *No 85.* The large white stone building was designed by Lutyens in 1935.

Daily Telegraph. — *No 135.* 1928 building in a ponderous mixture of styles.

Shoe Lane. — Ancient and winding like a mediaeval track.

Daily Express. — *No 121-8.* As much a landmark as when first built in 1931: all black and clear glass panels set in chromium, with straight lines throughout except for the rounded corner on Shoe Lane. (*Evening Standard* at the top of Shoe Lane).

Ludgate Circus. — The circus which was built in 1875 on the site of the Fleet Bridge to Ludgate Hill, includes a plaque (northwest angle) to Edgar Wallace (1875-1932).

Ludgate Hill. — A plaque on the south abutment of the 19C railway bridge states "In a house near the site was published in 1702 the *Daily Courant* first London daily newspaper". On the left, above the bridge is St Martin's Ludgate *(qv)*.

St Paul's Church Yard. — The statue within the circular railing is of Queen Anne, in whose reign the cathedral was completed.

Between the 19C offices on the south side is a narrow lane in which stands the **Deanery** built by Wren in 1670. Further on is the single storey circular building of the **City Information Centre,** and a paved court (Old Change) and garden — setting for modern sculptures, *Icarus* by Michael Ayrton and *The Young Lovers* by George Ehrlich. The streets and squares around Guildhall, particularly, are now an open air museum of post-war sculpture.

The Chapter House. — This perfectly proportioned red brick building with a crowning parapet and stone quoins marking the angles and centre, was built by Wren in 1710-14. Note the iron hand pump to the west erected by St Faith parishioners, 1819.

St Paul's Cross. — Paul's Cross (site marked on the pavement, north of the apse) which is known to have been in existence as a preaching cross in 1256, became the centre and symbol of free speech and so was removed by the Long Parliament in 1643. The monument in the garden with St Paul at the summit dates from 1910.

■ The TEMPLE★★ (J Y)

The Temple church dates back to 1185, when the order acquired the spacious site on the river bank in place of their first plot at the north end of Chancery Lane. The Templars were suppressed and their property assigned to the Hospitallers who, in turn, were dispossessed by Henry VIII. The church reverted to the crown; the outlying property remained with the lawyers to who the Hospitallers had previously leased it and who had formed themselves into the Societies of the Inner and Middle Temple which in 1608, were granted the safekeeping of the church.

TOUR

Inner Temple. – The Tudor **Inner Temple Gateway** (between 16/17 Fleet St), gabled, half timbered, 3 storeys high, each advanced on the one below so that the tunnel arch and pilastered stone ground floor are in shadow, dates from 1610 (reconstructed 1906). It leads into the lane, past 19C buildings to the church.

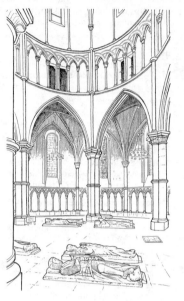

Temple Church.

The Temple Church★★. – *Open daily 10am to 4.30pm (4pm from 1 November to 31 March).*

The west doorway into the round church of 1160-85 is itself circular being Romanesque; the porch is rib vaulted and has a Perpendicular archway; the tower and clerestory are Romanesque – all dates from the period of transition. The exterior is of stone, the upper central tower is even crenellated; the later 13C hall plan chancel, also of stone, is alternately buttressed and pierced by tall pointed triple windows.

The round church is circled inside by an ambulatory, rib vaulted and walled by blind arcading with grotesque heads filling the spandrels between the pointed arcs. Six pillars of Purbeck marble, each of two stout, two slender, shafts heavily ringed midway, support curved Perpendicular arches; above is a Transitional triforium of rounded arcs bisected to form pointed arches which rest on slender, full capitalled columns; higher still are the round windowed clerestory and conical roof (dating from 1862 and restored to the same pattern after the war). On the stone floor are 10-13C effigies of knights – Templars and their illustrious supporters.

At the side is the door to the Penitential Cell of Templar times – a cubicle less than 5ft long. The chancel of 1220-40 is beautiful with slender shafted Purbeck columns dividing the nave and aisles and rising to form the ribs of the quadripartite vaulting. The dark oak reredos designed by Wren was carved by **William Emmett** in 1682 for £45. Note the heraldic floor brass with a Latin scroll winding between 29 shields, the 16 and 17C tombs at the west end.

The Inner Temple Hall, Treasury and Library were all rebuilt after the war.

King's Bench Walk. – The northern of the two ranges, in the largest Temple court, dates from 1678 and is by Wren (no 1 rebuilt). The mellow red brick fronts are marked by attractive doorways while beyond the east gate are two houses of especial note, no 7 of 1685 and no 8 of 1782.

Middle Temple. – In **Pump Court,** the cloisters (from Church Court) and the south side have been rebuilt (Edward Maufe), the north (except for 19C Farrar's Building) is late 17C.

Middle Temple Hall★. – *Open 10am to noon and 3 to 4.30pm (Saturdays 2 to 4pm); closed Sundays and holiday Mondays; enter through the 19C corner tower in Fountain Court.*

The great hall is Elizabethan and rich as only ancient oak timbers, panelling and fine carving can make an interior: the roof is a double hammerbeam, the finest of the period, 1574. The small panels in the high wainscot are bright with the arms of readers who instructed the mediaeval law students who not only ate but attended lectures and even slept in the 100 × 40ft hall. At the west end above the high table are royal portraits including Charles I (after van Dyck), Charles II (Kneller) and Queen Elizabeth, who by tradition, watched the first performance of *Twelfth Night* (1602) in the company of the benchers in the hall.

When the spectacular 16C carved screen at the hall's east end was shattered by a bomb the biggest jigsaw in the world was begun as splintered pieces were dug out of the rubble and fitted into place; it took years to complete but finally the screen was able to be reinstalled. The roof, incredibly, remained unharmed.

Up the steps from Fountain Court is **New Court** with its single building of 1676 by Wren.

Middle Temple Gateway and Lane. – The pedimented brick gateway with giant pilasters was erected only in 1684 although the lane is referred to as early as 1330 since it used to end in stairs on the river, affording a short cut by water to Westminster. Just inside the gate are two houses of 1693, their brick ground floors overshadowed by jutting timber faced upper storeys with 17C windows.

HOLBORN - NEWGATE ST (JKL/X)

Holborn *(See text and map pp 97 and 99).*

Staple Inn★. — Former Inn of Chancery *(p 98).*

Prudential Assurance Bdg. — The Pru, on the site of Furnival's Inn, is an all red building of the turn of the century. Many gabled, lancet windowed, it extends symmetrically on either side of a central tower, capped by a pyramid roof.

Daily Mirror Building. — A 170ft high curtain wall of stone on the street, is topped by yet taller buildings of glass extending down Fetter and New Fetter Lanes (1957-60).

Holborn Circus. — Prince Albert, mounted and with hat aloft, serves as a traffic island.

Holborn Viaduct. — The viaduct was built in 1863-9 to connect the City and West End — previously all traffic had to descend to the level of Farringdon St and climb up again. The bridge is an example of Victorian cast iron work: strongly, efficiently constructed and ornate with uplifting statues and lions.

Magpie and Stump. — *18 Old Bailey.* This pub grew to fame in the late 18C when public executions were transferred from Tyburn to Newgate.

Fleet Lane. — The lane, running east, recalls the existence of the notorious Fleet Prison which dated back to the 12C, was rebuilt after the Fire and only finally demolished in 1846 (Mr Pickwick made a brief but not painful stay).

Giltspur St (to Bart's). — At the junction with Cock Lane stands the **Fat Boy,** a gilded oak figure said to mark where the Fire stopped. The site, then known as Pie Corner, gave rise to the saying that the Fire began in Pudding Lane and ended at Pie Corner.

Central Criminal Court, the Old Bailey. — *The public are admitted when Courts are sitting, approximately 10am to 4.30pm with an adjournment for lunch.*

History. — This is the third Criminal Court on the site: the second was opened in 1774, the first in 1539. The 16C court was built because sickness and infestation, rife in the gaols brought "much peril and danger" to the judges — they still carry posies from May to September, traditionally to ward off gaol fever — and because no halls were available in which trials could be held; the Common Council, therefore, passed a resolution "that a convenient place be made... upon the common ground of this City in the old bailey of London". The site was hard by New Gate, the gate in the wall twice built by the Romans, on the main road west, enlarged in the early Middle Ages and by 1180 a City gaol, with Ludgate, taking in those who could not be crowded into the always overfull Fleet Prison.

Newgate became notorious for appalling conditions, for cruelty and barbarism. It was several times rebuilt; in 1423 with a bequest from Richard Whittington, in 1783 to designs by George Dance junior — it was broken open by Wat Tyler in 1381, fired by Gordon Rioters in 1780. Public executions, after these had ceased at Tyburn in 1783, were held outside (the Magpie and Stump did great business) until they were abolished in 1868. The gate was demolished in 1777; the prison, by then only used for prisoners on trial, in 1902. The bell once rung outside the condemned cell is in St Sepulchre's.

Among the most famous to have been tried were **William Penn** and another, in 1670 for preaching to an unlawful assembly in Gracechurch St; a tablet "commemorates the courage and endurance of the jury who refused to give a verdict against them though they were locked up without food for two nights and were fined for their verdict of "Not Guilty", from which developed the "Right of Juries to give their Verdict according to their convictions".

The building. — The Lady of Justice, a gold figure on a green copper dome, has been a dominant feature of the London skyline since she was placed on the then newly reconstructed Old Bailey in 1907. Cast in bronze, covered in gold leaf (regilded every 5 years and cleaned every August), holding scales and a 3ft 3in sword, she is 12ft tall and is neither blindfolded nor blind. The building is of Portland stone on a granite foundation, with a large entrance emphasised above the segmental pediment by figures of Truth, Justice and the Recording Angel. Inside all is marble — grand staircase, halls on two floors... and mural painting. The four original courts are large. After the war additional courts were required and an extension was added (1972).

Faced with Portland stone but otherwise bearing no relation whatsoever to Mountford's building, the annexe accommodates small, light panelled, modern, courts so that there are now 18 in all.

There are 60 cells; prisoners are brought daily from Brixton and Holloway — there is no gaol on the premises. No prisoner has escaped from an Old Bailey cell since 1907.

Post Office (HQ). — Plaques on the turn of the century building indicate the site of Greyfriars (f 1225) and Christ's Hospital which occupied the buildings from 1552-1902. Outside the main building stands the statue of Sir Rowland Hill, who in 1840, introduced the penny post — the uniform rate for a letter sent anywhere in the kingdom.

National Postal Museum. — *Open Mondays to Fridays 10am to 4.30pm; 7pm Thursdays; closed at weekends and all public holidays; special facilities on application for society and school visits, research, etc.*

The museum, established in 1965, claims to house what is probably the most important and extensive collection of postage stamps in the world. Of particular interest among the 250 000 stamps on display are the R M Philips **19C British Collection,** the Post Office collection of all stamps issued at home and overseas under British PO control since 1840 and stamp issues by members of the Universal Postal Union since 1878. A special feature is the story of the creation of the **penny black.**

Master Gunner. — Pub with Royal Artillery associations.

QUEEN VICTORIA ST - CANNON ST (LMN/Y)

Queen Victoria St is relatively modern having been cut through a maze of alleys and buildings only in 1867-71. It was the first City street to be lit by electricity.

Cannon St, in the Middle Ages Candelwriteystrete, the home of candle makers and wick chandlers, is now an area of vast offices at its west end where it was bombed, tailing off into late 19/early 20C constructions.

Printing House Sq. — Within ten years (1964-74) *The Times* constructed a new slate and glass building with the old square as forecourt and moved away to a still newer building in Gray's Inn Rd *(qv)*. *The Observer* remains in the east wing.

Printing House Sq got its name after the Fire, when, on the site of the Norman, Mount-fichet Castle and the later Blackfriars Playhouse, the King's Printer set up presses and began to publish acts, proclamations and the *London Gazette* (1666 — as *Oxford Gazette* 1665). The name remained after the printer had moved, in 1770, nearer to Fleet St. In 1784 John Walter purchased a house in the square and the following year began publication of the *Daily Universal Register,* altering its title on 1-1-88 to *The Times.*

No 146. — British and Foreign Bible Society.

Faraday Building. — 1932. Post Office international telephone headquarters.

College of Arms. — *Open only for heraldic or genealogical enquiries.*

The college, overlooking a forecourt behind splendid wrought iron gates, dates from 1671-88 when it was rebuilt after the Fire. Unlike, the churches with which it stands beautifully in perspective from the far side of the river, St Benet's and St Paul's, it was not designed by Wren, but by Francis Sandford, Lancaster Herald of the time and Morris Emmett, master bricklayer to the Office of Works. The mellow red brick building, formerly pedimented, now parapeted, has shallow return wings on either side of a full length terrace approached up shallow flights of steps at either end. The interior woodwork — staircases, panelling, pilastered and garlanded screen — is by William Emmett, contemporary of Grinling Gibbons.

Salvation Army HQ. — An imposing stone building, well back from the south side of the road, the rear dropping down to the level of Upper Thames St.

Financial Times (Bracken House). — A large post-war building by Sir Albert Richardson, employing small red bricks and red sandstone in no marked architectural style.

Temple of Mithras. — The stone temple with a double course of red tiles, 60ft long, 20ft wide, was erected on the west bank of the Walbrook in 2C AD when Roman legions were stationed in the City. All traces had long since vanished and even the Walbrook had altered course and level by 1954 when excavations preceding the construction of Bucklersbury House revealed walls laid in the outline of a basilica divided into a narthex, nave and aisles separated by columns and a buttressed apse at the west end.

The head of the god Mithras in a Phrygian cap, those of Minerva and Serapis, Egyptian god of the Underworld with a corn measure on his head, and other statuary fragments are now in the Museum of London. The temple itself, transposed to enable the office block to rise as planned, was then reconstructed in the forecourt.

The temple stood near the centre of the Roman city; to the south, on the Thames foreshore stood the governor's palace, to the northwest the basilica and forum which together occupied some 60 acres fronting what are now Cornhill and Leadenhall St and backing on to Fenchurch St.

Cannon St Stn. — The mid-Victorian viaduct and the station with its monumental towers crowning the train sheds high above the riverbank, stand on the site of two churches and the important mediaeval steelyard of the Hanseatic merchants.

London Stone. — *(Behind a grill in the wall of no 111, the Bank of China).*

A limestone fragment, touchstone of the legend on the plaque which states "its origin and purpose are unknown".

Martin Lane. — South to St Martin Ongar Tower *(p 60)* and **Ye Olde Wine Shades** (1663). This double fronted pub with painted boards outside, has been left as much as possible like a 17C tavern with dark wooden booths inside. It claims to be the oldest wine house in London having been originally the bar attached to the Fishmongers' Hall. It took its name from its position within the shadow of the hall.

The City Pubs — ancient and modern

There are now as many pubs as there once were churches in the City — namely some 200! Ye Olde Watling (MY), like so many, dates from before the Fire, was rebuilt in 1668 and again after a second baptism of fire, in 1947; the Square Rigger (PYZ), with decks aslant as though sailing a slight swell, has only recently been fitted out. Between the ancient and the modern, usually in a court or at the bend in an alley between main thoroughfares, are such 17 and 18C houses as Williamson's (MY) on the site of Sir John Falstaff's house and Ye Olde Dr Butler's Head (NX, reconstructed), named after King James' physician who established a number of taverns where a medicated ale was sold which the doctor claimed rejuvenated the imbiber! Among 19C pubs, all mahogany and cut glass mirrors, is the White Swan (KY) and, worth visiting for its Spy cartoons alone, the Punch Tavern (KY)... and then there are wine bars: El Vino's (JY)...

NB: Many City pubs do not open at weekends.

UPPER AND LOWER THAMES STS (KLMNPR/YZ)

Thames St in possibly Roman times and certainly the early Middle Ages, ran along the line of the river wall; by the 17C it served as a through route from the Wardrobe to the Tower, crossing the furriers' and vintners' quarters, lined by 8 churches and providing rear access to castles and mansions, quays, warehouses and markets, whose main thoroughfare was the river. Earthworks, under and overpasses, warehouse clearance, widening, promise to transform it once more into a major road.

Unilever House. – 1931. The vast stone building a rusticated ground floor, pillars, large sculptures and miles of corridors inside, stands on part of the site of **Bridewell Palace**, built by Henry VIII in 1522 as his residence during the visit of Charles V who elected to stay in Blackfriars Monastery on what was then the far bank of the Fleet. Edward VI gave the Bridewell to the City which converted it into an orphange and after the Fire rebuilt it as a prison, soon notorious as one of London's most evil houses (demolished 1864). Blackfriars Monastery, dissolved in 1538, was abandoned until in 1576 a theatre was founded in the cloisters where a professional children's company would rehearse before performing at court. Twenty years later James Burbage converted another part of the monastery into the Blackfriars Theatre for the performance of Shakespeare's later stage plays and those of Beaumont and Fletcher. The theatre, demolished in 1655, is commemorated in Playhouse Yard.

Mermaid Theatre. – *Puddle Dock.* In 1959 the disused warehouse at Puddle Dock came to life under Bernard Miles when, after conversion, it opened as the Mermaid Theatre, the first theatre within the City for three centuries. An apron stage and raked auditorium seating 500 are covered by the original tunnel vault.

The Mermaid, in addition to an adult theatre, has always specialised in children's entertainment and through the Molecule Club (f 1967) has demonstrated that science can be fun (documentary plays to musical accompaniment for 7-11 year olds) – 1 000 000 children excitedly crowded morning and afternoon performances in the first 10 years.

The site itself is historic as that of **Baynard Castle**. In *c* 1100 a fort was built on the river bank, pendant to the Tower downstream by one "Baynard that came with the Conqueror" according to Stow. When it burnt down in 1428 it was rebuilt by Duke Humphrey of Gloucester and was the scene in 1460 of Richard of Gloucester hearing the news that his plans to seize the crown were progressing (Richard III, 3 vii). Henry VII reconstructed it as a spacious palace and Lady Jane Grey heard there in 1553 that she was to be queen, before it finally disappeared in the Fire of 1666.

Samuel Pepys. – Pub with Pepys mementoes in a former warehouse.

Queenhithe Dock. – An unremarkable inlet is all that remains of what was London's most important dock above London Bridge.

Custom House. – *Not open.* The present house of rusticated stone and yellow stock brick, nearly 500ft wide, dates from 1813-17 with a central riverfront bay by Robert Smirke of 1825. Three storeys high, with three lanterns as sole decoration, it is the fifth to stand on this reach of the Thames.

CHEAPSIDE - KING ST (MN/XY)

Cheapside, originally West Cheap, was from earliest times until the Fire a microcosm of life in the City. *Ceap* meant to barter in Anglo-Saxon and local street names indicate the commodities sold first on stalls, later in shops; in addition craft and tradesmen lived in the houses in tributary lanes and alleys – Stow tells how Bow Lane was previously Hosiers' Lane and before that occupied by shoemakers. In mediaeval Cheapside there were 3 churches of which only one was rebuilt, St Mary-le-Bow (parishes before the Fire extended, on average, 3½ acres); facing Wood St was one of the crosses erected by Edward I to mark a halt in Queen Eleanor's funeral journey to the Abbey (1290; demolished 1643); there were also three communal fountains, of which the middle one was a place of public execution (Lesser Conduit at the west end, The Standard before St Mary-le-Bow (plaque on no 113) and the Great Conduit, east of Ironmonger Lane). Mansion House stands on a site adjoining the Stocks Market (named after the nearby stocks), which sold meat and other provender but was especially famous for its herbs and fresh fruit. It flourished from 1282-1737, the stall rents being allocated to the maintenance of London Bridge.

Cheapside. – Wide and commercial as throughout its history, it opens out west of St Mary-le-Bow into a small garden at the centre of which stands a statue of Captain John Smith (1580-1631), a leading settler of Jamestown, Virginia. In the Middle Ages the street was the setting for many a tourney, the contests being watched from upper windows by householders and by royalty, the lord mayor and aldermen from a balcony in the tower of St Mary-le-Bow, and recalled by Wren at the time of the reconstruction after the Fire in a window. **Bow Lane** on the east side of the church, narrow, winding, is still marked by old houses – Williamson's Tavern is in a 17C house.

King St. – This leads north directly to Guildhall crossing Gresham St by St Lawrence Jewry. Further east along Gresham St is **Gresham College**, a 1912 building. The college, under the will of Sir Thomas Gresham, was founded as a kind of free university in his mansion in Bishopsgate, Gresham House, which fronted on Old Broad St. The house was demolished in 1768, and the institution re-established in 1843 in a building on the present site. The lectures for graduate students are now held under the auspices of the City University whose main building is in St John St.

Poultry. – **Midland Bank**, by Lutyens (1924-39) with, high on the Grocer's Hall Ct corner a fat boy driving a goose to the Stocks Market (sculptor: Reid Dick).

EAST OF THE BANK: CORNHILL - LOMBARD ST (P/YZ)

From Mansion House there radiate: Prince's St (bordered entirely along one side by the Bank), Threadneedle St, Cornhill (named after a mediaeval cornmarket) and its continuation Leadenhall St, Lombard St and its continuation Fenchurch St, and finally King William St, constructed in 1829-35 as a direct route to the new London Bridge.

Freeman's Place. — Behind the Exchange with fountains at either end (south: bronze maiden beneath a pillared red granite canopy; north: mother and child by Georges Dalou, 1879) may be seen the seated figure of George Peabody (1869), the American philanthropist, founder of the trust to provide housing for the poor.

Jamaica Wine House. — The pub dates from 1652 when as the Pasqua Rosee Wine House, it was the first establishment licensed to sell coffee in London. Note the early percolator.

George and Vulture. — This pub, now Dickensian *(Pickwick Papers)* has been twice destroyed by fire in its 600 year old history. On the introduction of coffee in 1652 part of the then tavern became a chocolate, tea and coffeehouse.

P & O Deck (RY). — Tall new buildings line an open court at the back of which stands St Helen Bishopsgate. The beaver weathervane in the background is on the former Hudson's Bay House *(no 52 Bishopsgate)*. To the west stands Crosby Sq, the original site of Crosby Hall.

Lombard St, its name derived from the Lombard merchants of the late 13C and now synonymous with City banking, is lined with 19 and 20C buildings; association dignifies it; the gilt, the brightly painted bank signs, overhanging the pavement, distinguish it. Beginning with Lloyd's horse of 1677 (left), it continues with the 3 crowns of Coutts (right, no 15) the grasshopper, 1563, formerly Martins, now Barclays, (note the small arms decoration on the wall inside), the crown and anchor of National Westminster (right), the anchor of Williams and Glyn's (left), Alexander's artichoke (right), a cat playing a fiddle and further on the head of Charles II, both of the Royal Bank of Scotland (left) and at the end, a massive Barclays eagle in stone.

The Banker's Clearing House. — *No 10 (not open).* This is an 18C institution which grew out of the daily meeting in the streets of bank clerks, known as "clearers", to settle interbank accounts. From a post and one another's backs which they used as desks, the clearers migrated to a bay window, a room and finally a house, always in the same street.

N M Rothschild and Sons Ltd (NY). — Rothschild's achieved its status in this country when in its first years, under its London branch founder, Nathan Mayer, it took over at low cost and renewed drafts issued by Wellington which the government was unable to meet; ultimately they were redeemed at par — NMR increased his fortune, the government appointed him chief negotiator of future Allied war loans! Confidence in victory and his own intelligence service again increased his wealth, it is said, on the occasion of Waterloo, fought throughout Sunday 18 June. On the Monday, when only rumour was circulating. Nathan bought — the market rose; he sold — it plunged; he bought again, making a fortune as his personal messenger arrived from the scene confirming victory — Wellington's despatches arrived by messenger on Wednesday, *The Times* report was published on Thursday (22nd).

The clean lined building is postwar; the lane remains old and narrow, and is often blocked from end to end with waiting Rolls, Bentleys, Jaguars...

Square Rigger. — This pub has square rigged ships of 17 and 18C as its house theme.

Monument★. — *Open April to September, 9am to 5.40pm, October to March to 3.40pm; Sundays, May to September only 2 to 5.40pm; closed 1 January, Good Friday, 25, 26 December; 311 steps; 15p.*

The fluted Doric column of Portland stone, surmounted by a square viewing platform and gilded, flaming urn, was erected in 1671-77 in commemoration of the the Great Fire. The hollow column stands 202ft tall and 202ft from the baker's in Pudding Lane where the Fire began. The relief on the pedestal of Charles II before the City under reconstruction is by Caius Cibber. A later inscription blaming the papists for the Fire was finally effaced in 1831.

The **view★** from the platform is now largely obscured by the tower office blocks which, equally, mask the column at ground level. The monument does, however, remain a distinctive landmark from the river downstream.

The Monument : engraving of 1680.

ALDERSGATE ST, MOORGATE, BISHOPSGATE, ALDGATE
(MNPRS/VXY)

Aldersgate St. – A Saxon named Aldred, is said to have built the gate... James I entered the capital through it and in celebration it was rebuilt in 1617 but demolished in 1761.

London Wall, more or less, follows the line of the Roman Wall east to Bishopsgate, Houndsditch the course of the old ditch outside the wall; inside it was paralleled by Camomile St, Bevis Marks and Duke's Place. All along London Wall are outcrops of excavated wall (Barbican, St Alphage, All Hallows, Sir John Cass College, the Tower), usually with a Roman base and upper area of mediaeval construction.

West Gate (M X). – *Open midday during the week.*

This, the west gate of the Romans' north fort, including the outline of the guard turret, lies in a chamber off the west end of the underground carpark.

Museum of London★★. – *Open daily 10am to 6pm, Sundays 2 to 6pm; restaurant – cafeteria; special facilities on written application for adult and school groups.*

The best of modern architectural style buildings has been designed by Powell and Moya for the new museum. Faced with white tiles below, linked by a bridge to a purple brick rotunda set like an advanced bastion in the sea of Aldersgate traffic, in traditional City fashion it takes advantage of the disadvantages of the site to be an interesting shape as it turns the corner and surrounds the Ironmongers' Hall. Simultaneously it forms a base for a crowning brown glass and steel office block.

Open galleries inside divide into bays according to time and theme as the story of London is traced from pre-history to the present by exhibits as various as the head of the god Mithras, the Lord Mayor's Coach, maps, seals and charters, an 18C prison cell, shop fronts, interior panelling, a diorama of the Great Fire, material from the theatre and music hall, industrial machines, livery company plate, souvenirs of the women's suffrage movement. The development of domestic life and public utility services – gas, drainage, the Underground – are illustrated as well as political and fashionable London.

Barbican★. – Barbican, a City Corporation project on the bomb devastated site of a mediaeval stronghold and later overcrowded housing sector, incorporates flats, offices, shops, a pub, the City of London Girl's School, an arts centre with a theatre (future London home of the Royal Shakespeare Company), concert hall (London Symphony Orchestra), the Guildhall School of Music, an art gallery and library.

The city within the City was begun in 1962 and has, so far, been 15 years abuilding. The profile and layout are modern with 18 storey tower and lesser blocks and walkways grouped around inner garden courts, a lake at the foot of a stretch of the City Wall and the equally stalwart St Giles Cripplegate *(qv)*. The materials are rough surfaced cement, blue-red lustre bricks, wooden window frames and glass.

The Barbican.

Moorgate. – The gate giving access to Moorfields, the open common on which people practised archery, dried clothes, flew kites, was cut in the City wall in 1415; two and a half centuries later it was one of the main exits for thousands fleeing the Great Plague. It was demolished in 1760. The street overlooked by the City of London College, dates from the time of the rebuilding of London Bridge in 1831.

Finsbury Circus. – Mid 19/20C buildings surround the only bowling green in the City.

Bishopsgate. – The street, one of the City's longest, was the principal road to East Anglia in Roman and mediaeval times. The gate, said to have been rebuilt slightly west of the Roman gate by Bishop Erkenwald in Saxon times, was renewed several times, once even by the Hanseatic merchants, before being demolished in 1760.

Nos 105 and 108 *(first floor, either side of the road, Wormwood and Camomile St corners – RX).* Note the gilded mitres from the old Bishop's Gate.

Liverpool St Stn. – The station, erected in 1875 on the first site of Bethlehem Hospital (removed 1676) is vast, an iron Gothic cathedral, romantic or filthy and impractical according to taste. Adjoining is the Great Eastern Hotel gabled, mullioned, dirty outside, comfortable within and like the station the subject of dispute as to its future redevelopment. Close by is the Railway Tavern with steam locomotives' as the decorative theme.

Aldgate. – The street, after the Anglo-Saxon – *aelgate,* meaning free or open to all, was before that a Roman gate to the road to Colchester (Whitechapel Rd). In 14C Chaucer leased the dwelling over the gate and in 16C Mary Tudor rode through it after being proclaimed queen. It was demolished in 1761.

Aldgate Pump. – The proverbial pump is still extant.

Hoop and Grapes. – This pub is in a late 17C brick house with a wooden bay window.

Clapham village expanded into a fashionable residential area in the 17 and 18C as citizens moved out of London to avoid the plagues and the frequent City fires, notably the Great Fire which destroyed so many City merchants' houses. Residences were built around the common: mansions and terraces for the prosperous, houses in dependent streets for the more modest and, finally in the 19C, terrace houses and shops along the High St. The original inhabitants, others of low income and the very poor congregated round the railway, particularly Clapham Junction (known first as Battersea), built in 1845 and by the late 19C and still, Britain's busiest junction handling some 2 000 trains daily. The district remains densely populated, new housing estates replacing the old, the modern shopping areas and street markets as crowded raucous and vigorous as ever.

Public transport began modestly enough in the early 18C with a single stage coach making the journey daily from Clapham village to Gracechurch St. A century later (1827) the service had expanded into "short stage" coaches travelling several times a day to the City, Westminster, Piccadilly Circus and Holborn. By 1839 there were horse drawn omnibuses operated by twelve rival companies. 1870 saw the tube (Clapham Common station), 1903 the first electric tram and 1912 the first motor omnibus. Gone were the days of highwaymen on the common (the last hold-up was in 1801), of roads being so poor that it took several hours to reach the capital: Clapham, the site of a Roman battle, a mediaeval village, "pretty suburb" in the words of William Thackeray, had become a part of the great metropolis.

Among Clapham's famous men are William Wilberforce (1759-1833); Lord Macaulay (1800-59) who grew up in a house on the Pavement; Thomas Hood (1799-1845) who went to school on North Side; Lytton Strachey (1880-1932) who was born at Stower House; Henry Cavendish (1731-1810), who retired to a house in the road now named after him; Cardinal Bourne (1861-1935), Archbishop of Westminster, who was born at Larkhall Rise and ordained at St Mary's, Clapham. (The railway transport museum long in Clapham Junction has moved to York.)

Northeast of Clapham Common

Holy Trinity. – The church at the corner of the common was erected in 1776 to replace the parish church which had fallen into ruin. The rectangular stone quoined building with two tiers of plain, round headed windows, was increased, in keeping with growing local prosperity in 1872 by the addition of the giant columned portico and clock tower turret.

North Side. – The long mellow brick terrace with an archway in the end house dates from 1720. Many of the doorways, windows, iron gates and arches are original (nos 14, 17, 21). Clarence House is credited with being the home of Captain Cook (1728-79), Chase Lodge on the corner of The Chase, as the oldest house in Clapham.

Opposite no 28 is a grand Georgian Mansion which was for years the home of Sir Charles Barry, architect of the Houses of Parliament. (The house, with those adjoining, is now The Hostel of God.)

Cedar and Thornton Terraces (flanking Cedars Rd) epitomise hybrid Victorian – French Renaissance revivalism: round and flat topped windows with coarse iron infillings, cornices, balconies, are crowned by high pavilion slate roofs coronetted with ironwork.

Old Town (northeast end of North Side), and its continuation, Rectory Grove which leads to St Paul's Church, include a few modest Georgian houses and short terraces: nos 39-43 is a group of mellow red brick with uniform windows and dormers but a separate segmented pediment over no 39 and a wider arc over the adjoining doors of nos 41 and 43; no 16 has an attractive doorway; no 4, proudly sporting two royal warrants, an unusual façade with a projecting upraised and pillared porch and two half moon windows. No 23, St Peter's Vicarage, has round headed ground floor windows and an early iron gateway with an overhead arch. No 52 Rectory Grove is unique in its Coade stone decoration including a false arch on the side wall.

St Paul's Church. – By 1232, and probably long before, there was a parish church by the name of Holy Trinity in Clapham; by 1774-6 it had fallen into ruin and had been superseded by the new Holy Trinity; in 1814 a plain Georgian brick building was erected in which there are an interesting group of monuments (southeast end):

1401: a brass plate records the death of an unknown man William Tableer.

1589: Francis Clarke, a small ruffed figure at prayer remains from a larger monument to his father, Bartholomew, who rebuilt the manorhouse (now vanished).

1647: a bronze plaque to William Glanville, Merchant of Exeter, describes how he "never got to London as he died of fever in Clapham", a graphic reminder that in those days the capital was still a day's journey away.

1689: Sir Richard Atkins in full armour, his wife and three children. Only the almost lifesize figures remain from the great tomb and even these were "lost" in an underground vault for nearly two centuries. The Atkins were lords of the manor from 1590.

1715: Richard Hewer, naval administrator and friend of Samuel Pepys who retired to Hewer's house in the Chase where he died in 1703.

1849: a tablet records the death of John Hatchard, who with a capital of £5 in his pocket founded the bookshop in Piccadilly in 1797.

The Polygon, Pavement and High St have been almost entirely rebuilt.

Crescent Grove. – *Off Clapham Common South Side.* Only the grove, a wide arc and terrace of identical tall stucco houses, remains entire of the extensive Clapham Park Estate laid out by **Thomas Cubitt** as a series of squares and crescents in the 1870 s.

Map pp 5-8 (FG/V).

Clerkenwell recalls in name the mediaeval parish clerks who each year performed a cycle of plays outside the City at a local wellhead; Finsbury is named after the Fiennes family, the owners of the local manor (OE bury/burh/burg) who in 14C gave **Moorfields,** an unprofitable marsh, to the people of London as an open space – the first so designated. The outflow of artisans and cottage industry workers from the City, particularly after the Plague and Fire of 1665/66 caused poor quality housing and tenements to be erected up to the very walls of the Charterhouse, St John's Priory, Bethlem (on what is now City Rd) and other hospitals of which only one continues the tradition, Moorfields Eye Hospital, founded in 1805. Of the manor, open marsh, burial grounds, there remain Finsbury Sq, Finsbury Circus, Bunhill and the HAC Fields; of the crowded days of home industry and the tailors of the early 19C, the old rhyme and the Eagle Pub (Shepherdess Walk, City Rd): Half a pound of two penny rice, Half a pound of Treacle... Up and down the City Rd, In and out the Eagle, That's the way the money goes, Pop goes the Weasel.

■ THE PRIORIES

Charterhouse★. – History, ground plan, building styles and material have been superimposed and inextricably involved in Charterhouse's progress from small 14C priory to Tudor mansion, 17C hospital and boys' school to 20C residence for aged Brothers.

In 1535 the prior and brothers at the 150 year old Charterhouse refused to recognise Henry as head of the church and he dissolved the community, had the religious executed and removed treasure, timber, stone and glass for his own use. Within ten years, the house began a new life as a Tudor mansion under the Norths and Norfolks who Elizabeth visited several times – which did not prevent her having her host, the 4th Duke of Norfolk, executed in 1572 for intriguing with Mary Queen of Scots. In 1611 the house was sold to **Thomas Sutton** for £13 000 and letters patent were issued for the founding of a hospital for 80 old men and 40 boys under the name of the Hospital of King James in Charterhouse. Sutton (d 1612) lies in the chapel behind contemporary railings in an elaborate tomb by Nicholas Stone, including a vivid relief of a preacher failing to interest sleeping, yawning, talking, brethren. In 1872, the school moved to Surrey.

The Building. – *Open May to July, Wednesdays only (not after holiday Mondays) at 2.45pm. Rest of the year: special parties by application to The Master.*

The gatehouse, abutting a chequered 15C wall of flint and stone and with a contemporary wooden door, opens onto a second arch in a long, gabled range and the Master's Court around which the building now mainly depends. At one corner is the **Chapel.**

The **Great Hall,** with hammerbeams intact, is Tudor panelled with a 16C wooden screen and gallery and a carved stone fireplace of equally magnificent scale. Above, the **Great Chamber** or Tapestry Room, after the Flemish hangings along one wall, has a painted and gilded late 16C plaster ceiling, a painted fireplace and many old leaded light windows. In the tower is the vaulted, monks' treasure chamber with a squint upon the chapel altar.

Charterhouse : Great Chamber.

St John's Gate. – *Clerkenwell Rd. Open: museum 10am to 6pm. Tuesdays, Fridays and Saturdays; tours of the church and gatehouse, 2.30pm on the above days.*

The Grand Priory in the British Realm. – The Order, which developed from the First Crusade, as a religious order to look after pilgrims visiting the Holy Land, became a military order during the 12C. It left the Holy Land on the fall of Acre in 1291, establishing itself first in Cyprus, then Rhodes (1310), and finally Malta (1530) where it became a sovereign power. Priories and commanderies were instituted in many lands, the **Grand Priory of England** in Clerkenwell in 1144 to which were added the Templars' properties on their suppression in 1312. In 1540 Henry dissolved the Hospitallers and in 1546 issued a warrant *(in the library)* for the buildings to be dismantled (Protector Somerset later took the stone for his house in the Strand). St John's was re-established as an independent Protestant Order by Royal Charter in 1888.

The first aid and other work of the Ambulance Brigade is displayed in the museum.

The Gatehouse and Museum. – The 16C gatehouse, flanked by four storey towers, was the Priory's south entrance. Wide, vaulted, with the lamb of God and the arms of the order on the bosses, it contains the rooms which in the reigns of Elizabeth and James I were occupied by the Master of Revels, licenser of the plays of Shakespeare and Ben Jonson, and in the 18C by Edward Cave, publisher and printer of England's first literary periodical, *The Gentleman's Magazine* (1733-81), to which Dr. Johnson was a regular contributor. These rooms and the 20C Tudor style, Chapter Hall where the Maltese banners hang, contain pharmacy jars from the hospitals in Rhodes and Malta, silver-gilt filigree vessels, jewellery, enamelwork and a rare collection of beaten silver Maltese glove trays. In the library and museum are the illuminated Rhodes missal on which the knights took their vows, armour, portrait medals, the order's own coinage issued in Rhodes and Malta.

St John's Church and Crypt. — The Grand Priory Church of St John, once round and extending far into the square (note the brickwork in the tarmac), is now square with the 16 and 18C whitewashed brick walls hung with the mediaevally chivalric banners of Commonwealth Priories. The crypt is 12C, the only original Priory building to survive. Beneath the low quadripartite ribbed vaulting, it contains the recumbent 16C figures of the last Prior before the Dissolution, a worn cadaverous effigy, and the rich alabaster form of a Spanish grandee.

■ ADDITIONAL SIGHTS

Clerkenwell Green. — The nominal reminder of the Tudor village rallying point and open air, free speech centre in 18 and 19C of work people against the social and industrial injustices of the period, is now the site, in an 18C house, of the **Karl Marx Memorial Library** *(open for research by appt).*

Mount Pleasant. — The early 18C landmark, which is believed to have been ironically named as it was the local rubbish dump, in the 20C is one of the principal Post Office inland mail sorting offices and centre stage of the Post Office railway. The line, which is 50 years old, runs 70ft below ground from Paddington to Liverpool Street and Whitechapel, carrying the mail in automatically controlled trucks along 2ft gauge tracks. The "turnover" is nearly 2 million letters and 80 000 parcels a day.

New River Head. — *Thames Water Authority, Rosebery Av.* The neo-Georgian building contains a fireplace attributed to Grinling Gibbons and plaster ceilings c 1693 from the former water house on the site.

History. — The New River undertaking originated in 1609 when **Sir Hugh Myddelton** (statue on Islington Green), a City goldsmith and jeweller, put up the capital to construct a canal from springs in Hertfordshire to the City. The winding channel some 40 miles long (now 24) took 4½ years to dig and might well have ruined Myddelton but for the personal financial support of James I. Water for the capital at that time came from the Thames, from shallow wells and conduits deriving their supply from tributary streams, notably the Westbourne and the Tyburn. The New River Head was inaugurated in 1613 when water was carried down through wooden pipes to the City. Combined resources (Walthamstow, Chingford, Staines and Datchet) now supply London with 450 million gallons of water a day and double if necessary in summer — roughly each day the volume of the Serpentine.

Sadler's Wells Theatre. — *Rosebery Av.* Music house at the centre of late 17C fashionable pleasure gardens and medicinal wells, mid 18C theatre, Shakespearean and classical drama centre under **Samuel Phelp** in the 1840s, music hall, derelict ruin: such was the site's history when **Lilian Baylis** took it over and had a completely new brick theatre erected in 1931 as a north London complement to the Old Vic.

From 1934 the Wells specialised in opera and ballet to become the cradle of the future Royal Ballet and English National Opera, which in 1956 and 1968 respectively transferred to Covent Garden and the London Coliseum. The Well's itself now presents visiting opera and ballet companies.

The theatre is named after a builder, Mr Sadler, whose workmen in 1683 rediscovered the ancient medicinal wells.

Companies House. — *55-71 City Rd. Open Monday to Friday 9.45am to 4pm; closed on public holidays.*

The Register of Companies, dating back 130 years was transferred to Cardiff in 1976. Annual returns and accounts for the last 3 years of 650 000 companies, changes of directors and registered office addresses dating back 7 years are available on microfilm for immediate consultation *(Search fee: 5p).*

Wesley's Chapel and House. — *47 City Road. Chapel closed for repair until c 1978; house open daily 10am to 1pm, 2 to 4pm; closed 1 January, Good Friday, holiday Mondays, 25, 26 December; 10p.*

John Wesley, who is buried in the churchyard, laid the foundation stone of the chapel in 1777. The small house built for him next door is rich in mementoes: his desk, study and conference chairs, clock, clothes, part of his library, furniture and, in the minute prayer room, a small table desk and kneeler.

Bunhill Fields — *City Road. Open 7.30am to 7.30pm (October to March 4pm); weekends 9.30am to quarter of an hour after sunset, latest opening 9.30pm.*

Long before 1549 when the first wagon load of bones was delivered for burial from the overflowing charnel house in St Paul's Churchyard, the field had been given the name Bone Hill. Between 1665, when the City Corporation acquired it, to its closure in 1852, 120 000 were buried there including many non-conformists since the ground was never consecrated. Among the tombs are those of: William Blake (1757-1827), John Bunyan (1628-88), Susanna Wesley, mother of John and Charles (1669-1742)... In the adjoining Quaker yard is the grave of the founder of the Society of Friends, George Fox (1624-91).

HQ, HAC (Finsbury Barracks). — The buildings on the historic Artillery Fields, designated for archery practice in Tudor times, date from 1735 and 1857.

Covent Garden in ancient times. – Soho was a chase, named after the cry of the mediaeval hunt which often found in St Giles' Field; St Giles was a leper colony, established outside the town limits by Queen Matilda in 1117 (dissolved 16C); St Martin's was a church erected in the fields between Westminster and the City in early 13C and Covent Garden a 40 acre walled property belonging to the Benedictines of Westminster.

Henry's dissolution of the monastery at Westminster and confiscation of the garden was followed in 1552 by the first of the royal warrants which were to shape the area to its present form, give it its traditions and much of its character: Edward VI granted the land to the long serving Tudor diplomat and soldier, John Russell, later 1st Earl of Bedford. The 4th Earl, on payment of £2 000 – Charles I was ever impecunious – obtained a licence in 1631 to erect buildings "fitt for the habitacions of Gentlemen and men of ability" subject only to the approval of the King's Surveyor, Inigo Jones. Charles II, a lover of the theatre (and also of actresses) granted two royal warrants in 1660 which resulted in the building of two Theatres Royal, Covent Garden and Drury Lane.

■ COVENT GARDEN TODAY

The Piazza and St Paul's★. – The 1631 licence gave Inigo Jones the opportunity to design London's first square; he modelled it after those he had seen in Italy, with approach roads at the centre of two sides and the same two sides, to the north and east, lined by three storey, terrace houses of brick, above a pavement colonnade of stone which provided a covered way to shops and coffeehouses. Only those to the west of Russell St remain (rebuilt). The south side was filled by the garden wall of the earl's new town house which fronted on the more fashionable Strand. (In 1700, when fashion departed, Bedford House was demolished and the area developed.) The piazza's west end, although the earl declared that he could scarely afford the price of a barn, was designated as the site for a church, **St Paul's**, which Jones, declaring that it should be "the handsomest barn in England", designed with classical simplicity. It is of red brick (the easterly stone facing was a later addition) beneath a pitched roof which affords wide eaves; overlooking the square is the famous Tuscan portico in which on 9 May 1662 Pepys saw the first ever *Punch and Judy* show in England and in 20C Shaw set the opening scene of *Pygmalion*. The church, completed in 1633, has always been closely associated with actors, artists, musicians and craftsmen – a wreath of limewood, carved by Grinling Gibbons for St Paul's Cathedral, now decorates the west screen (beside the door).

Grinling Gibbons: limewood wreath.

The Market. – The market, begun by the monks, was regularised by letters patent in 1670 as it sprawled across the originally neatly gravelled piazza and onetime resort of gallants. In 1830 it was reconstituted when, with renewed royal permission, special market buildings were erected: Charles Fowler designed three parallel, west-east ranges running off a colonnade; in 1872 glass roofs were added and a separate, conservatory style, Flower Market built. By 20C when wholesalers had spread to all the neighbouring streets the whole quarter appeared to become the market from midnight to noon: it was brilliant with fruit and flowers, filled with vendors, buyers, porters, warm with open pubs and cafés – and blocked solid with lorries. In November 1974 the market emigrated to Nine Elms.

Present and future. – The Flower Market is to become two diverse museums: London Transport and the Theatre *(no scheduled date);* the 1830 market buildings, refurbished, are to be let as individual shops to craft workers, artists, architects, designers, photographers, film makers and small concerns, augmenting those established a century or more ago in the shadow of **Thomas Chippendale's** (d 1779) workshops. There are now armourers (Neal's Yd), barrow makers, bookbinders (Nottingham Ct, Neal St), chocolate makers (Neal's Yd), canvas cover makers, frame makers, jewellery makers (Dryden St), silversmiths, glass blowers and decorators (Neal St), potters, leatherworkers, theatrical costumiers... and at 43 Earlham St the **British Crafts Centre** with items for sale as various as jewelled rings, opalescent glass, big turned wood bowls...

Theatre Royal, Drury Lane. – The present Georgian theatre is the fourth on the site, one of London's largest (2 283 seats) and beautiful inside with symmetrical staircases, rising beneath the domed entrance to a circular balcony.

Killigrew's company, known as the King's Servants, opened in 1663 in the first theatre which was frequently patronised by the monarch who met "pretty witty Nell" there in 1665. After being burnt down the theatre was replaced in 1674 by one designed by **Wren** which knew a golden age under **Garrick**, the Kembles and Sarah Siddons and was replaced in 1794 by a third building which opened under **Sheridan's** management with his new play *The School for Scandal.* Fire again destroyed the theatre and the present house, to designs by **Wyatt**, was erected in 1812. Kean, Macready, Phelps, Irving, Ellen Terry, Forbes Robertson played there; Ivor Novello's dancing operettas have filled the stage, *My Fair Lady...*

The **Baddeley Cake** is a Lane tradition even older than the ghost; it is provided from money left by an 18C actor, Robert Baddeley, and is cut on stage after the performance on Twelfth Night. The ghost emerges from the left circle wall (where a corpse and dagger were found bricked up in 19C) to cross the auditorium and disappear.

Royal Opera House★. – Charles II's patent was eventually secured by John Rich whose earlier presentation in 1728 of *The Beggar's Opera* was said to have "made Rich gay, and Gay rich". He leased a site, erected a playhouse and in December 1732 opened his Theatre Royal, Covent Garden, with Congreve's *Way of the World* which he followed with a revival of *The Beggar's Opera*. A second theatre, designed by Robert Smirke, after the first had burned down, opened in 1809 with a double bill lasting nearly 4 hours, presenting Kemble and Mrs Siddons in *Macbeth* plus a musical entertainment. But the public not caring that rebuilding had cost £300 000 and convinced that seat increases were due to exorbitant fees paid to foreign artists, drowned the stage in what came to be known as the OP or **Old Price Riots.** After two months prices were reduced (pit: 3s 6d). A second fire in 1856 caused the present house to be built. The Classically pedimented theatre with a first floor portico was reorientated and made to front on Bow St, which afforded a site to the south on which a conservatory style arcade after the Crystal Palace and known as the **Floral Hall** was erected to serve as a promenade concert area and saloon. When the theatre fell into financial straits the hall was leased to the market and for 100 years served as an annexe to the fruit and vegetable, not the flower, market. Inside the theatre, decoration has always been white and gold with deep crimson and rose hangings. From the first there was a Crush Room.

Future plans and the model show the house's expansion to the west and upwards (in the 1858 style) for new dressingrooms, and facilities and south to include again the refurbished Floral Hall as a foyer and bar. The Sadler's Wells Ballet transferred to the house in 1956 when it was granted a charter by the Queen to become **The Royal Ballet.** The newly formed opera company received a royal charter in 1968.

Around performers (and characters) such as Patti, Melba, Caruso, Thomas Beecham, Lotte Lehmann, Elisabeth Schumann, Gigli, Conchita Supervia, Tauber, Flagstad... golden memories abound, legends grow – Patti in 1895 as Violetta wore a white dress studded with 3 700 diamonds – and two Bow St detectives joined the guests in Act 3 of *La Traviata* (Flora's party); Queen Victoria decided that the bearing of Italian choristers appearing in *Fidelio* was unmilitary and that as "Our soldiers can do better than that" extras to swell processions should be provided from the Brigade of Guards – and they still are!

The area's long standing theatrical association attracted builders of new theatres when the passage of the Theatre Regulation Act in 1843 broke the Covent Garden and Lane monopoly and some 40 new playhouses were licensed and erected in as many years.

■ ADDITIONAL SIGHTS

St Giles-in-the-Fields. – *(Map p 121).* The church was rebuilt in 1734 by Flitcroft after the styles of Wren and James Gibbs; the steeple rising directly from the façade, is reminiscent of St Martin-in-the-Fields.

Bow St. – "So called as running in the shape of Bent Bow" according to John Strype, the early 18C mapmaker. By the mid 18C when **Henry Fielding,** novelist, dramatist and magistrate and his half brother, John, the **Blind Beak,** moved into a house on the site of the present police station, the street had become the haunt of robbers and footpads. At once the Fieldings began their crusade for penal and police reform which included the organisation in 1753 of the **Bow Street Runners.** The white lights outside the present station (1881), the only such in the country, were suggested by Queen Victoria who, visiting the opera, considered the customary blue lights very dreary.

Samuel French. – *26-27 Southampton St.* The theatrical publishers and booksellers occupy the only two houses to survive of those built on the Bedford House garden when it was developed in early 18C. **Garrick** lived at no 27 while manager of Drury Lane (1747-76). The panelled shop walls are decorated with historic prints and play bills.

Moss Bross. – *Bedford St.* In 1881 Moses Moses with two sons as assistants, opened a second-hand clothes shop in King St, hanging a rail of coats outside when the weather was fine. A story is told of a customer, seen to be wearing his braces over his underclothes when returning topper and morning coat, being reproved with the words "Sir, we admit it sounded like a dead cert, but you really shouldn't have put our shirt on it".

Rule's. – *34-5 Maiden Lane.* Caricatures and prints recall the law, theatre and artists, in London's oldest restaurant and oyster bar, established in 1798 by Benjamin Rule and his sons, "who rush wildly about with dozens of oysters and pewters of stout".

Lamb and Flag. – *Rose St.* The tavern, the quarter's oldest, was known when it was built in 1623 as the Cooper's Arms and unofficially after 1679, when John Dryden on his way home to Long Acre was attacked outside, as the Bucket of Blood.

Clubs and Coffeehouses. – Two of the traditional clubs still flourish: the **Garrick** (1831) since 1864 in the house built for it in the new street which the club requested should be named after the actor (no 15). On the walls hang an unrivalled collection of theatrical portraits; the **Beefsteak** (9 Irving St *p 121),* dating from 1876, and always a dining club drawn from the worlds of politics, the theatre and literature.

Of the 17 and 18C coffeehouses for which Covent Garden was as famous as the City, none remain: **Will's** at no 1 Bow St, frequented by "all the wits in town" according to Pepys, **Button's** in Russell St, the **Bedford,** the **Piazza...**

Royal Masonic Institution. – *Great Queen St.* The Masons occupy the greater part of the street which includes 18C houses (nos 27-29) and the **Freemasons Hall** (1927-33).

■ SOHO *Map p 121*

Early maps and documents show a windmill where Gt Windmill St is now, two breweries on Brewer St, a bottle glass factory beside the cart track now Glasshouse St and big houses which now remain only as street names: Newport House (built *c* 1634, demolished 1682), Monmouth House, the residence from 1682 until his execution on Tower Hill in 1685 of the Duke of Monmouth, Karnaby House transformed in 60s into a brightly paved pedestrian precinct where shop after shop sold "gear". Leicester Fields was common ground, so that when the 2nd earl, nephew of Sir Philip Sidney, built a family mansion along the north side in 1631, an open space was left where local inhabitants could dry their washing and tree lined walks were planted for their pleasure. In 19C with the building of the **Alhambra** (1854), Daly's Theatre and the **Empire**, the square, which had been relaid in 1874, became famous as the dazzling centre of light entertainment, ballet, spectaculars and music hall. (**Leicester Sq** is now lined almost entirely by cinemas and eating houses.)

By mid 19C, through piecemeal development, Soho included the worst slums in the capital with 300 people to each acre or 30 000 in all — today there is a residential population of 3 000, and a working population of 10 000. To penetrate this foetid tangle three wide swathes were eventually cut: **Charing Cross Rd** in 1880, the upper part taking over the northern end of St Martin's Lane, a track dating back to the Middle Ages; **Shaftesbury Avenue** in 1886, named after the 7th earl, a great philanthropist and ardent believer in the necessity for slum clearance; finally, Kingsway in 1905.

Today Charing Cross Rd is known for its bookshops: Foyle's (no 119), Collet's (nos 52 and 66), Zwemmer's (no 78) and smaller shops stacked with long out of print editions; Cecil Ct dates back to 1670 and is becoming again as in the 18/19C a bookseller's close; Goodwins Ct is a narrow alley entirely lined by 18C bow windows of former shops.

People of all nations. – The indigenous Londoners of Soho have always been artisans, cottage industry workers, and, until planning regulations eliminated local factories, craftsmen in labour intensive factories. Refugees began to arrive in 17C, settling where their skills and labour would find a market: Greeks, fleeing the Ottoman Turks, Huguenots after the Revocation of the Edict of Nantes in 1685, refugees from the Revolution and 19C political changes, who established French restaurants and cafés — Wheeler's (19 Old Compton St) was founded by Napoleon III's chef — Swiss, Italians, Spaniards, and, most recently, Chinese from Hong Kong, Singapore and the docks who have transformed Gerrard St into a Chinatown and who at the Chinese New Year (a moveable feast in January or February) celebrate in traditional fashion with noisy processions led by lion dancers.

William Blake was born in Soho (1757), Hazlitt died there (1830); Edmund Burke, Sarah Siddons, Dryden, Sheraton lived there; Marx, Engels, Canaletto, Haydn lodged there; Mendelssohn and Chopin gave recitals at the 18C house in Meard St of Vincent Novello, father of Ivor and founder of the music publishers. John Logie Baird first demonstrated television in Frith St in 1926...

Churches and charities

St Anne's. – *Wardour St.* Since the war only the tower remains overlooking the churchyard in which are buried Hazlitt and the legendary 18C Theodore, King of Corsica.

Notre Dame de France. – *Leicester Place.* The church (RC), erected on the ashes of its mid 19C predecessor, is circular. Inside an Aubusson tapestry hangs above the altar, mosaics decorate the side altar, and outline paintings (1960) by **Jean Cocteau** the walls, notably the *Crucifixion* with the Virgin and only Christ's legs visible.

Our Lady of the Assumption. – *Warwick St.* The church, originally the chapel of the Portuguese, was rebuilt in 1788 after the Gordon Riots with an intentionally domestic appearance and only a pediment as decoration.

House of St Barnabas. – *Greek St. Open Wednesdays 2.30 to 4.15pm. Thursdays 11am to 12.30pm.*

The House of Charity, a temporary home for women in need, was built *c* 1750. The exterior is plain except for two obelisks at the entrance; the interior is one of the finest in Soho with a staircase with a wrought iron handrail, stucco walls and ceiling and first floor rooms with decorated Rococo ceilings.

Trades, streets, buildings today

Market: Berwick St market in all its colour and variety dates back to 1778, possibly 100 years earlier when the street began.

Media: Films from first features to commercial flashes are dreamt up, made, cut, etc. in Wardour St (once a furniture area), Soho Sq, Beak and Dean Sts.

Food shops, restaurants: the shops align Old Compton St, the restaurants — French, Italian and Greek — Romilly St and the three parallel streets running north; Chinese, Wardour St, Shaftesbury Av and Gerrard St.

Discos, drinking clubs, casinos, sex cinemas, strip clubs: proliferate.

Shops and workshops: there are timber merchants and silversmiths, tailors (tailoring remains the largest local cottage industry with pieceworkers supplying many of the famous houses in Savile Row), violin makers (3 where there were once 40) and jazz and pop instrument shops, the last in Shaftesbury Avenue, Charing Cross Rd and Denmark St — **Tin Pan Alley.** The jazz club, **Ronnie Scott's**, is at 47 Frith St *(open 8.30pm to 3am).*

Pubs: of the 60-70 in Soho, most date back to early 18C although, owing to industrious Victorian and mid 20C renovation, few look old. One is unique, the York Minster (49 Dean St) which for two generations has had a French host, father and son, and in consequence is known as the **French Pub.**

Dulwich's glory lies in its trees. The houses reflect the transition from 17C manorial village to small country town where 18/19C city merchants and gentlemen chose to reside (a triangular milestone on Red Post Hill indicates that it is 4½ miles equally to the Standard in Cornhill and the Treasury in Whitehall). Commuter trains and the car transformed it this century into a south London suburb; nevertheless, it remains rural in character with a main street, known as Dulwich Village, which divides at the green where Alleyn built his school.

■ DULWICH COLLEGE

Edward Alleyn: man of the theatre, founder of God's Gift. – Alleyn, born in 1566 the son of a City innkeeper, was by common consent one of the greatest actors of his day although Shakespeare disagreed and voiced his dislike in Hamlet's counsel to the Player King. His marriage in 1592 to the step-daughter of Philip Henslowe, theatrical business-man, leaser of plays, costumes, theatres, builder of the Rose Playhouse (1587), extended Alleyn's interests so that by 1605 he had virtually retired from the theatre and for £5 000, bought Dulwich manor. Having no heir, he established in 1613 a charity for "six poor men and six poor women and the education of twelfe poor children", which he named the Chapel and College of God's Gift (1616)

Old College and Chapel. – The buildings on the triangular site are entered through 18C iron gates surmounted by the Alleyn crest. Between the much altered two storeyed white building which still serves as almshouses, stands the central wing including the clock tower and door to the chapel where Alleyn is buried. The black marble stone dates from 1816, the original, very worn, is in the cloister. Note beside the reredos the two "poor Scholars" in 17C costume.

Dulwich College Picture Gallery★. – *Open Tuesdays to Saturdays: May to August, 10am to 6pm; September to 15 October, 16 March to 30 April to 5pm; 16 October to 15 March to 4pm; closed Sunday mornings (all day in winter), Mondays, Christmas Day, Good Friday and holiday Mondays.*

History. – Dulwich College Gallery, which was opened in 1814, is the oldest public picture gallery in the country. Edward Alleyn, as a man of substance, bought pictures, though not as a connoisseur one suspects – in 1618 he paid £2 for six royal portraits and later £2 13s 4d for a further eight crowned heads! His final collection of 39 pictures, including his own full length portrait, probably painted from a death mask, was later increased by 80 likenesses of contemporary authors and players: Michael Drayton, Richard Lovelace, Burbage, Nat Field (now principally in gallery III).

In 1811, virtually a double legacy of 400 pictures necessitated the construction of a special gallery. This gift originated with a Frenchman, **Noel Joseph Desenfans,** unsuccessful language teacher, who changed his profession to become the richest picture dealer of his day. Among his patrons was King Stanislaus of Poland who commissioned a gallery but abdicated in 1795 before paying for the paintings which Desenfans incorporated in his own collection and left to his widow and his friend, **Sir Francis Bourgeois,** a Londoner of Swiss origin, Royal Academician, landscape painter and inspired collector. He chose Dulwich as the gallery site; Mrs. Desenfans contributed £6 000, suggested Soane as architect and presented the furniture still on display.

The building. – Sir John Soane had a completely free hand in 1811 and three years later the gallery, much as it is today, was opened. The inconspicuous stock brick exterior belies the skilful inside plan: facing the central entrance, on the far side of two adjoining square galleries is the small domed mausoleum of the founders, Edward Alleyn, Noel Desenfans and his wife: symmetrically dependent on this central suite are oblong and final square, galleries of subtly varied dimensions.

The pictures. – **Aelbert Cuyp's** landscapes (gallery II), three superb **Rembrandt's** including *The Girl at a Window* and *Titus* (XI), 17 and 18C landscapes and pastorals by **Poussin,** Claude, Watteau and Lancret (XII); **Gainsborough** portraits of the Linley family (V), a **Reynolds** self portrait and portrait of *Mrs. Siddons* (VI) are among the most memorable pictures in the collection. There are also paintings by van Dyck (IV); Piero di Cosimo, Raphaël (VIII), Tiepolo, Canaletto, *The Doge's Palace,* Rubens (IX) and an urchin and *Flower Girl* by Murillo (X).

South via Dulwich Village and College Rd

Dulwich Village. – Pond House, Village Way, at the opening of Dulwich Village, is a three storey brick house with spanking white trims, an iron balustrade as delicate as lace edging the roof at the rear and a beautiful interplay of circular lines in steps, balustrades and porch before the round headed door.

Nos 60, 62 – **The Laurels, The Hollies** – date from 1767. The decorated ironwork canopy supported on iron pillars and extending across the pavement shaded the fare of the village butcher in the 18C.

Nos 92 and 95 – North and South Houses – not as old as the Cedar of Lebanon before them! Nos 97-105 is an 18C terrace, the last two houses very early 1700s.

College Rd. – On the pair, nos 13 and 15, note the early Sun Insurance fireplate. The small house at no 31, Pickwick Cottage, is said to be where Dickens envisaged Mr. Pickwick's retiring. Bell Cottage is a rare example of the once common small white weather-boarded local cottages; Bell House, of brick by contrast, dates from 1767.

Dulwich College, now nearly 1 400 strong, is housed in buildings of 1866-70 designed in Italian Renaissance style, complete with a stout campanile. Great crested iron gates mark the entrance on College Rd.

Pond Cottages (beyond the main road, Dulwich Common) is an 18C group overlooking the Mill Pond, several wholly or part weatherboarded. The **Toll Gate** is the last in use in the London area: charges are 2½ p for a car, 10p for "a score of beasts"...

Kingswood House. – *Accessible from beyond the Toll Gate or Alleyn Park.*

The castellated house built of ragstone in 19C baronial style, was known, when the owner was the founder of the meat extract firm, as Bovril Castle! The Jacobean style interior now serves as a library and community centre.

The brilliant green copper, needle spire, visible for miles, belongs to the neo-Gothic Church of All Saints in Rosendale Road.

EALING (Ealing)

Ealing Abbey, St Benedict's RC Church. – *Charlbury Grove.* The powerful mediaeval foundation which grew from the small number of Benedictines sent by Pope Gregory to England in the 6C, was dissolved in the 16C by Henry VIII. The re-established community has erected a new abbey, neo-Gothic in style and golden in colour (1897-1935).

Pitshanger Manor. – *Walpole Park, Ealing Central Library.* The south wing and central range only remain of the house built by **George Dance junior** in 1770, and bought by **John Soane,** as a country villa in 1800. Soane retained the south wing containing an upper and a lower room, both of modest proportions with finely moulded plaster decorations and added besides other rooms, an entrance of four colossal columns surmounted by standing figures before a high, ornamental screen. The hall, inside, lit by a raised lantern between tunnel vaults, is minute. Many features reappear in the house in Lincoln's Inn Fields.

St Mary's Parish Church. – The present heavy, dark brick construction of 1866 contains the tomb of John Maynard, successful lawyer to Stuart Kings, the Commonwealth, William and Mary, builder of Gunnersbury House and an expressive, late 15C brass to "Richard A'wnsh'm some tyme Mercer and Marchaunt of the stapyll (wool) of Calys and Kateryn his wyf" and their 3 sons and 6 daughters.

Gunnersbury Park. – In the park are two early 19C mansions acquired by the Rothschilds in 1835 and 1889 and now, in part, converted into a local history and 19C transport museum *(open April to September, Mondays to Fridays 2 to 5pm, October to March 2 to 4pm; closed Good Friday, 24, 25, 26 December).*

The Katyn Memorial to massacred Polish officers, a polished black granite obelisk crowned with a gold eagle, was erected in Kensington cemetery, an area in the park, in 1976.

FULHAM (Hammersmith)

Fulham, Parsons Green, Walham Green, all within a wide loop of the river were once separate riparian villages with the odd large mansion in its own grounds which ran down to the water's edge. Market gardens covered the fertile marshlands. The Bishop of London was the lord of the manor, a property of vast extent. Urbanisation came within a period of 50 years: in 1851 the population numbered 12 000; in 1901, 137 000.

The new **Charing Cross Hospital** *(Fulham Palace Road)* is the most outstanding modern building. Tall, capacious and clean lined, it dates from 1973 when it replaced the original Decimus Burton buildings of 1831 at Charing Cross.

Downstream from the bridgehead, **Hurlingham House,** an 18C mansion in its own wooded grounds is the last of the big houses which once lined the river bank. It is now a private club.

Fulham Pottery. – *210 New King's Road.* One bottle kiln *(not in use)* still stands tall on the site of a 7-9 kiln pottery established by John Dwight in 1671 and soon known for its stoneware and busts and statuettes in salt glazed earthenware. (The pottery is now supplier of materials and equipment to schools and craftsmen potters.)

All Saints Church. – Fulham Parish church has been a landmark at this bridging point of the river since the 14C, its square Kentish stone tower a twin to Putney church on the far bank, although the vessel was rebuilt in Perpendicular style in 19C.

Inside there is a rich collection of monuments and brasses: note the tombstones in the chancel floor, to William Rumbold standard bearer to Charles I in the Civil War and Thomas Carlos, whose coat of arms, an oak tree and three crowns, was granted to his father after he had hidden in the oak tree at Boxobel with Charles II after the Battle of Worcester, 1651. Fourteen Bishops of London are buried in the yew shaded churchyard.

Close to the church note the 19C Powell Almshouses with steep pitched roofs over a single storey, forming an L shaped building around a quiet garden.

Fulham Palace. – *Bishop's Avenue. Grounds only open.*

The palace, which was from the 7C to 1973 the official residence of the Bishops of London, retains the appearance of a modest Tudor manor. The gateway, a low 16C arch with massive beamed doors, leads through to the courtyard where the two storey red brick walls, except in the restored range to the right, are strongly patterned with a black diaper design. *(It is hoped at a future date to open the house as a local museum.)*

Bishop's Park, beside the river, was originally part of the palace grounds.

Greenwich is a place to visit selectively; besides the meridian, which one can bestride with a foot in each hemisphere, there are the wooded park rising from the river to the Old Royal Observatory, the delightful Queen's House, the Painted Hall and chapel of the Royal College, and the National Maritime Museum with some 1½ miles of galleries. These are arranged to appeal to anyone drawn by the British maritime tradition whether as sailor, historian or schoolboy, to those interested in painting, in astronomical and navigational instruments, charts, ships' models...

Access. – *In summer go or return by river bus from Westminster (allow 1 hour) or the Tower to Greenwich Pier. Trains (20 minutes) run from Charing Cross, Waterloo, Cannon St to Maze Hill (5 minutes' walk). There are local buses but no underground.*

Bella Court. – Greenwich had been in the royal domain since King Alfred's time and the site of a royal palace for 200 years when, in 1665, Charles II instructed John Webb to build him a new King's House on the site beside the river.

It was Humphrey, Duke of Gloucester, brother of Henry V, who first enclosed the park and transformed the manor into a castle, which he named Bella Court; it was he also who built a fortified tower upon the hill from which to spy invaders approaching London up the Thames, or along the Roman road from Dover. On Duke Humphrey's death in 1447, Henry VI's queen, Margaret of Anjou, annexed the castle, embellished it and renamed it **Placentia** or Pleasaunce.

Tudor Palace. – The Tudors preferred Greenwich to their other residences and Henry VIII, who was born there, magnified the castle into a vast palace adding towers and halls, a tiltyard and a royal armoury where craftsmen beat out and chased armour rivalling the suits from Italy and Germany and like them dramatically displayed at the Tower.

Henry also founded naval dockyards up and downstream at Deptford and Woolwich which he would visit by sumptuous royal barge and where he would inspect his growing fleet among which, from 1512 was the *Great Harry*, the first four-master to be launched in England. It set square sails on the fore and mainmasts, it had topsails on all four masts and top gallants on the first three. The docks were also accessible by a road skirting the wall which divided the extensive and quite magnificent royal gardens from the park. Overlooking the thoroughfare was a two storey gatehouse which, legend has it, Queen Elizabeth was approaching one day in 1581 when Walter Raleigh, seeing her about to step into the mire, threw down his cloak so that she might cross dryshod.

Palladian House and Pretty Palace. – Rich as the Tudor palace was, in 1615 James I commissioned **Inigo Jones** to build a house for his queen, Anne of Denmark, on the exact site of the gatehouse even to its straddling the Woolwich-Deptford road. Jones, at forty (b 1573) was known for his revolutionary stage settings; he proved equally inventive in his design for the Queen's House in which he favoured a plan based on the principles of the Italian architect, Palladio (1508-80). The road was crossed by means of a "bridge room". Work stopped on the death of Anne and was only resumed when Charles I offered the house to his queen, Henrietta Maria, whose name and the date, 1635, appear on the north front, and whose initials can be seen over the fireplace in the queen's bedroom "so finished and furnished, that it far surpassed all other of that kind in England".

English Mechanical Equinoxtial Dial *c* 1690.

The Tudor palace was despoiled during the Commonwealth, its collections sold and interior used as a barracks and prison; the Queen's House alone emerged relatively unscathed so that at the Restoration, Henrietta Maria could return to live there intermittently until her death in 1669 (in France). Charles II disliked the derelict palace, found the Queen's House too small for his court and in 1665 commissioned instead a King's House from John Webb, a student of Inigo Jones. The result was what is now known as the King Charles Block with its giant pilasters in groups of four at either end and at the centre where they are crowned by a pediment. With the exception of the Observatory, however, all construction had to cease for lack of funds long before Charles' "pretty palace" was complete.

Royal Hospital to Royal Naval College. – Work at Greenwich was resumed in 1694 when William and Mary, who preferred Hampton Court as a royal residence, granted a charter for the foundation of a Royal Hospital for Seamen at Greenwich on the lines of the Royal Military Hospital in Chelsea, and appointed Christopher Wren as Surveyor. Wren, as usual, submitted numerous plans, before proposing the one we know today which, at Queen Mary's insistence, retained the Queen's House and its 150ft wide river vista (only acquired at the demolition of the Tudor palace), incorporated the King Charles block and involved the construction of three additional symmetrical blocks, the King William (SW), Queen Mary (SE) and Queen Anne (NE, below which exists a crypt, sole remainder of the Tudor palace; *not open*). To complete the scheme the vista was focused by twin advanced cupolas before the refectory and chapel and the course of the Thames modified and embanked –

this was Wren's only major vista design to be realised. The project took more than half a century to complete and involved Vanbrugh, Hawksmoor, Colen Campbell, Ripley, "Athenian" Stuart... John Evelyn, who as he recorded in his diary, on 30 June 1696 "laid the first stone of the intended foundation at five o'clock in the evening... Mr. Flamsteed, the King's Astronomer Professor observing the punctual time by instruments", by June 1704 observed that the hospital had begun "to take in wounded and worn out seamen... the buildings now going on are very magnificent", but as treasurer he also noted that by 1703 the cost already amounted to £89 364 14s 8d (a list of donors in the entrance to the Painted Hall shows that the King gave £6 000, the Queen £1 000, Evelyn £2 000).

In 1873 the former hospital buildings were transformed into the Royal Naval College. The Queen's House, meanwhile, extended by colonnades and two wings in 1807 became first the Royal Hospital School and in 1937, the National Maritime Museum.

Royal yachts still moor at Greenwich.

■ MAIN SIGHTS

The Park. – Greenwich Park, palisaded in 1433, and surrounded by a wall in Stuart times, is the oldest enclosed royal domain. It extends for 180 acres in a great sweep of chestnut avenues and grass, to a point 155ft above the river crowned by the Old Royal Observatory and the General Wolfe monument. Beyond the Roman Villa and Great Cross Avenue are gardens with massed flowers before ancient cedars of Lebanon, a pond with wild fowl and a Wilderness with a small herd of fallow deer.

Royal Naval College★★. – *Open daily except Thursdays 2.30 to 5pm; closed Good Friday, 22 to 28 December.*

In 1873, when the Admiralty took over the Greenwich Hospital buildings as a centre of scientific instruction, steam and steel had just replaced wood and sail. Today, as a naval university open to both sexes and members of the NATO alliance, the courses include defence and nuclear science.

Court. – Walk to the embankment, past the white marble statue of George II, to see the classic view of the Queen's House framed by the advanced domes and the Observatory.

Painted Hall★. – Wren's domed building, designed as a refectory and forming a pair with the chapel was completed in 1703. In 1805 it was the setting for Nelson's lying in state before his burial in St Paul's. The hall and upper hall were painted in exuberant Baroque on the ceilings and upper hall walls by Sir James Thornhill: William and Mary, Anne, George I and his descendants, celebrate Britain's maritime power in a wealth of involved allegory. The artist portrayed the current monarch as he worked through each new reign (1708-27) and was paid £3 a sq yd for the ceilings, £1 for the walls.

The Chapel★. – The chapel by Wren was redecorated after a fire in 1779 by "Athenian" Stuart and William Newton as a Rococo interior in Wedgwood pastels. A delicate pattern of formal swags and panelled rosettes covers the upper walls and ceiling; corbels and beams are masked by a lacework of stucco. In contrast, blocking the apse, is *St Paul after the Shipwreck at Malta* by Benjamin West (1738-1820), who also designed the Coade stone medallions for the pulpit made from the top deck of a 3 decker.

National Maritime Museum★★. – *Open Easter to October 10am to 6pm (5pm in winter except Saturdays 6pm). Closed 1 January, Good Friday, 24, 25, 26 December. Restaurant; bookshop. Library, Print Room, navigational maps and charts accessible for research by appointment only; the Planetarium (in the late Victorian, South Building in the park, originally known as the New Physical Laboratory), is open only during performances, principally in school holidays; Half-Deck Club (in the East Wing), a centre for creative activities (7-15 years); apply for individual membership or school group.*

To follow the pageant of British naval history chronologically, begin in the Queen's House, continue in the West Wing and finish in the East Wing.

Queen's House★★. – This elegant white house was the first Palladian villa to be built in England; such style, proportion, sophistication, were hitherto unknown. Inigo Jones matched the beauty of a horse-shoe shaped staircase leading to the terrace (which formerly included the main entrance overlooking the Tudor palace), a first floor loggia on the park and crowning stone balustrade, with an equally attractive interior, which gradual restoration (effected, in places, by the removal of as many as 24 layers of paint) and refurnishing in 17C style, has recreated.

The house is particularly notable for the **Entrance Hall,** a perfect 40ft cube, encircled by a gallery and covered by a ceiling compartmented by richly carved beams in a pattern repeated in the black and white marble pavement – the original paintings were given to the duchess for Marlborough House *(qv)*. The other feature is the stairway, known as the **Tulip Staircase** after the graceful handwrought iron banisters which decorate the spiral. The flowers are not, in fact, tulips but French *fleur-de-lys*. On the first floor is the **Queen's Bedroom,** with a view of the river and a decor designed by Inigo Jones, apart from the ceiling which is by Thornhill. The East and West Bridge rooms with enriched plaster ceilings were added by John Webb in 1662.

Many of the museum's finest pictures are in the Queen's House, including the *Battles of Lepanto* (1571) and *Texel* (1673) and the greatest sea pieces by the Van de Veldes, father and son, who had a studio there in the 1670s. In addition there are pictures of Old Greenwich, 17C wall maps of the world, portraits of Drake and Hawkins, of Charles I by Mytens, Henrietta Maria by van Dyck and Inigo Jones by Dobson, 17C navigational instruments made of ivory, contemporary surveying and astronomical instruments (Barberini Collection), and more than a dozen accurate contemporary scale models of ships.

West and East Wings. – Nelson and Cook galleries *(opening 1977-8)* are major features in the west wing; elsewhere are the Barge House and New Neptune Hall – 17, 18C Royal and Admiralty barges, the development from early wooden boats to 19/20C steamships with replicas and vessels including 1907 paddle tug, *Reliant,* ships' figureheads and working models. Other galleries include Fishing and Whaling; the Royal Navy in the two World Wars and before and since; Arctic exploration... The pictures number some of the finest seascapes ever painted as well as pictorial records of historic naval battles, portraits of officers and heroic naval figures from Nelson to the present, momentous occasions. Artists are as diverse as Canaletto and Turner, Hogarth, Kneller, Lely, Reynolds, Gainsborough, Romney... (The collection is shown by rotation, except for certain pictures, always on view: the Canaletto, Turner's *The Battle of Trafalgar,* portraits).

The Old Royal Observatory★. – *Open same times as the museum.*

In 1675 Charles II directed Sir Christopher Wren to "build a small observatory within our park at Greenwich, upon the highest ground, at or near the place where the castle stood" for "the finding out of the longitude of places for perfecting navigation and astronomy". Originally map and chart makers fixed the zero meridian where they chose: Greenwich, Paris, the Fortunate Islands... The British reading began to be generally adopted with the inauguration in 1767 of the annual publication, the *Nautical Almanack,* which in combination with the marine chronometer and sextant, enabled navigators to find their longitude in relation to the Greenwich meridian. Map and chart makers soon also began to base their calculations on Greenwich. The standardisation of the meridian came finally when the speeding up of communications (railways and the telegraph) produced anomalies and even legal disputes – the time lag between London and Plymouth was 16 minutes. By 1884, when the Meridian Conference was called in Washington, 75 % of the world's charts were based on the Greenwich meridian and it and GMT were agreed as the standard which was ultimately adopted universally.

Flamsteed House. – As architect and a former astronomer, Wren designed in his own words, for John Flamsteed, first Astronomer Royal, a house of red brick with stone dressings, an upper balustrade and miniature canted cupolas "for the Observator's habitation and a little for pompe". Inside, beside the usual small 17C rooms, is the lofty **Octagon Room** beautifully proportioned, and according to John Evelyn, equipped already in the 17C, as now, "with the choicest instrument". Note the displays on the "history of the measurement of time" and the domestic quarters.

The Meridian Building. – This mid-18C addition of the same brick as Flamsteed House, was built to house the observatory's growing **collection★★** of telescopes of all sizes, and other instruments, many of which are still in their original positions. Note the 24 hours clock, Airy's Transit Circle through which the meridian passes and outside, the brass meridian of zero longitude, the clocks showing world time, the sundials (at the back), British Standard Measures and the red time ball. This was erected in 1833 on Flamsteed House to serve as a time check for navigation on the Thames: the ball rises to the top of the mast and drops at exactly 13 00 hours GMT. It was superseded in 1924 when the BBC began transmitting time signals, but is kept in operation.

Cutty Sark★★. – *Open 11 am to 6pm (5pm in winter); Sundays and Good Friday 2.30 to 6pm; 26 December 2.30 to 5pm; closed 1 January, 24, 25 December: 30p.*

Launched at Dumbarton in 1869 for the China tea trade, the *Cutty Sark* became famous as the fastest clipper afloat – her best day's run with all 32 000 sq ft or ¾ acre of canvas fully spread was 363 miles. In her heyday she brought tea from China and later wool from Australia, chasing before the wind like the cutty sark or chemise of the witch, Nannie, in Robert Burns' poem, *Tam O'Shanter,* from which she took her name and witch figurehead. She was converted into a nautical training school in 1922 and transferred to dry dock at Greenwich in 1955. In her hold are papers, charts, mementoes and models, illustrating the history of the clipper trade and her own story in particular. In the lower hold is a lively collection of boldly coloured figureheads.

(After photograph, Pitkin Pictorials)

The Cutty Sark.

Gipsy Moth IV. – The 11 ton, 53ft, ketch in which the late Sir Francis Chichester, circumnavigated the world alone in 1966-67, stands nearby looking incredibly small.

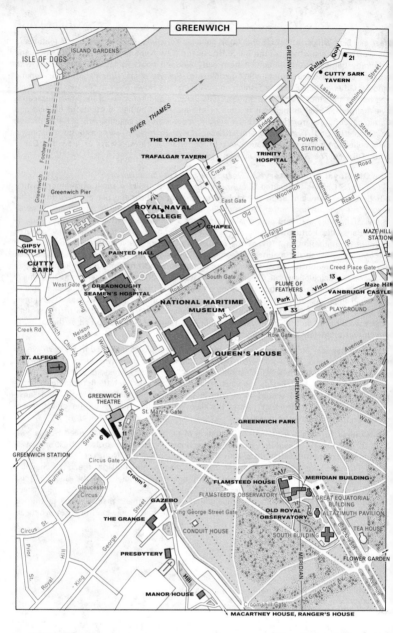

■ THE TOWN

The tall parish church of St Alfege stands at the central crossroads while shops selling antiques and maritime mementoes, books and bric-a-brac, restaurants, pubs and private houses, line the main streets and alleys. Façades and even a few complete buildings date back to the late 17C, 18 and early 19C. The **Dreadnought Seamen's Hospital,** on the corner of King William Walk, was designed in 1764 by James "Athenian" Stuart.

St Alfege's. – The somewhat gaunt, early 18C church with an elegant Doric portico, is by **Hawksmoor,** the superimposed tower by John James. Inside there are no pillars, although the span measures 65 by 90ft. On the site where Alfege, Archbishop of Canterbury, suffered martyrdom at the hands of Danish invaders in 1012, churches were erected which witnessed Henry VII and his queen at worship, the baptism of Henry VIII, heard Thomas Tallis, the father of English church music, playing the organ for 40 years (console in SW corner) and saw his burial also that of General Wolfe, parishioner and Commander of the British Army at the capture of Quebec (d 1759). Two other parishioners were Lavinia Fenton, the original Polly Peachum in *The Beggar's Opera* and John Julius Angerstein. The registers *(visible on request)* which, date back to 1615, vividly portray the large families, child mortality, the decimation of plague years and contrasting, usual, longevity.

Croom's Hill. – Croom's Hill, already an established local thoroughfare in 15C, was taken as a natural western boundary, when the park was enclosed. The west, or right side of Croom's Hill, is lined all the way up by 17, 18, early 19C houses. The east side includes, at the bottom, the Greenwich Theatre, built in 1968 in the shell of a Victorian music hall and a terrace of five humble 17C tenements (nos 3-11) with weatherboard backs. Opposite are **Georgian terraces** – the first the oldest, the second marked with a central bow and main doorway (C Day Lewis, Poet Laureate, lived in No 6 from 1968-72). Further up,

The Grange, an early 17C building with 18C additions, stands on a site recorded as having been given in 818 by a daughter of Alfred the Great to Ghent Abbey. The small square gazebo with a pyramid roof and carved plaster ceiling, beside the road, was built in 1672.

The **Presbytery** is a relatively low brick mansion with large gabled dormers and pilasters on brackets supporting the upper floor. Built in the 1630s the house is a rare example of so early a domestic building to remain exteriorly so unaltered.

The **Manor House** of red brick, two storeys high, overlooking the heath, is typical of 1697, even to the hooded porch with a finely carved shell motif.

At the hilltop are houses built in 1674 on land filched from the royal domain by Andrew Snape, Serjeant Farrier to Charles II and, according to Evelyn, "a man full of projects". Snape's speculative building can be seen in the large, rambling **Macartney House** (now private flats) built of mellow brick and stone with a roof balustrade and tall rounded windows overlooking the garden, and the Ranger's House.

Ranger's House★. – *Open daily including Sundays 10am to 5pm (4pm November to January); closed Good Friday, 24, 25 December.*

The mansion was originally a small brick villa with a stone balustrade lining the roof and steps leading up to an elegant stone frontispiece decorated with a mask. Rounded wings in pale yellow brick were added during the house's ownership by Philip, 4th Earl of Chesterfield (1694-1733), politician, diplomat and wit. The resultant south gallery, 75ft in length with a compartmented ceiling and three fine bow windows commands, its satisfied owner declared, "three different, and the finest prospects in the world" – the gardens are still as beautiful.

The **Suffolk Collection** of 53 paintings inside, includes an outstanding series of full length family portraits by William Larkin (*fl* 1610-20) all in the finest clothes of the period, embroidered, slashed, jewelled, lace collared and ruffed and complete with pompom shoes. Daniel Mytens (1590-1647), Cornelius Johnson (1593-1661), and other fashionable painters were also patronised to record family traits.

East of the College

East of the College lie Park Row and the **Trafalgar Tavern** of 1837 where bars and dining rooms, named after the personalities and events of Nelson's time, overlook the river from cast iron balconies resembling the galleries of a man o'war. In the early 19C the tavern was the setting for the Liberal ministers' "whitebait dinners" and later was described in *Our Mutual Friend* by Dickens who used to meet there with Thackeray and Cruikshank.

In the old and narrow Crane Street, is **The Yacht Tavern,** at least a century older and also overlooking the Thames. High Bridge, beyond, is fronted by a small white, importantly gabled and crenellated charity building, the **Trinity Hospital** with the date 1616 on the gateway tower.

Ballast Quay. – The terrace of neat 17C, early Georgian houses (note the 1695 Morden *(qv)* estate marks), and **Cutty Sark Tavern,** rebuilt with a great bow window in 1804 on the site of earlier inns, ends in the four square Harbourmaster's Office (no 21) which for 50 years, until the 1890s, controlled colliers entering the Pool of London.

Park Row, Park Vista and Maze Hill lead up to Blackheath along the east side of the park. In Park Vista are the early 18C plain two storey, brown brick, **Manor House** (no 13), the **Vicarage** (no 33) a rambling 18C house incorporating Tudor fragments, and the small white 18C public house, the Plume of Feathers.

Vanbrugh Castle. – The caricature of a mediaeval fortress, stands at the top of the hill, built and lived in by the architect and playwright himself, Sir John Vanbrugh, from 1717-26 while Surveyor to Greenwich Hospital. Gothick towers; turrets, high walls, crenellations and all – it preceded Strawberry Hill *(qv)* by some 30 years.

HAM HOUSE ★★

Open Tuesdays to Sundays, holiday Mondays 2 to 6pm (October to March, noon to 4pm); closed Mondays (except holidays), 1 January, Good Friday, 24, 25, 26 December: 20p. NT.

Ham House was at its prime under **Elizabeth Dysart, Duchess of Lauderdale,** "a woman of great beauty but greater parts... a wonderful quickness of apprehension and an amazing vivacity in conversation... (who) had studied... mathematics and philosophy; but... was restless in her ambition, profuse in her expense and of a most ravenous covetousness; she was a violent friend, and a much more violent enemy". She lived in dangerous times – her father, William Murray first Earl of Dysart, had literally been youthful "whipping boy" for Prince Charles, future Charles I; Elizabeth, it was said, became for a time the Protector's mistress. Her first husband, Sir Lyonel Tollemache, founded the line who, as Earls of Dysart, remained owners of Ham House until modern times when it was presented to the National Trust; her second, the Earl, later Duke of Lauderdale, favourite of the Stuart restoration, was a learned, ambitious, vicious character. A double portrait, *Both ye Graces in one picture,* by Sir Peter Lely in the Round Gallery presents them graphically – the toll of years is clearly evident in the duchess of whom there is an earlier portrait on the same wall.

The Lauderdales, according to their contemporaries, "lived at a vast rate". They enlarged the house, which had been built to the conventional Jacobean plan in 1610, and modified the front to give a continuous roof line with a horizontal emphasis. A family idiosyncracy for inventories and hoarding furniture, paintings, hangings, and bills for structural and decorative alterations, has enabled the house to be returned to its 1678 appearance

HAM HOUSE★★

when it was described by John Evelyn as "furnished like a great prince's". The gardens have been relaid to the 17C plan.

Exterior. – The fabric is brick with stone dressings; the building, three storeys beneath a hipped roof with a five bay centre recessed between square bays and typical, canted Jacobean outer bays. The fine iron gates and piers date from 1671 although for another century the house's most usual approach was by water; the present forecourt with the Coade stone figure of **Father Thames** by John Bacon, was laid out in 1800.

(By courtesy of the V & A)

Ham House from an engraving c 1730.

Interior. – Paintings, in this house, bring to life the period of Charles II, the Cavalier generals, the women at court – young, fair, delicately complexioned and far from innocent. Furniture, doors, doorcases, fireplaces and ceilings display the craftsmanship of the period – frequently Dutch for Dutch craftsmen were well established long before the accession of William III. The remarkable ceilings show the progress from geometrical type plasterwork bands to garlands and spandrels (compare the original, north and later, south rooms).

Ground Floor. – The house has an impressive entrance in the Great Hall, increased above by the Round Gallery with a decorated plaster ceiling by Kinsman (1637). Lely portraits adorn the gallery while below are Hoppner, Kneller, Reynolds paintings of Dysarts of 17, 18C.

The most notable features of other rooms on the ground floor are the gilt leather wall hangings and 1679 cedar side tables in the Marble Dining Room (parquetry replaced the marble paving in 18C), the artificially grained and gilded panelling, fashionable in 1670s, the chimney furniture of silver, considered very ostentatious by contemporaries. In the Duchess's Bedchamber are damask hangings and a plum and yellow bed (note the carved cherub feet), in the Yellow Bedroom or Volury Room, an oyster work veneered writing desk, and picture of the south front of the house in 1683 in the White Closet. The altar cloth of "crimson velvet & gould & silver stuff" in the chapel is original.

Upper Floor. – Lady Maynard's suite contains 17C Flemish tapestries after Poussin and miniatures by Hilliard, Oliver and Cooper, the Museum Room, examples of the original vivid upholstery, a prayer book of 1625 and ledgers and bills of the alterations to the house and the 1679 inventory which has enabled the rooms to be arranged as in Elizabeth Dysart's day. The North Drawing Room is sumptuous, epitomising the Lauderdale passion for luxury and display in a plaster frieze and rich ceiling (1637) above walls hung with English silk tapestries (woven by ex-Mortlake workers in Soho), carved and gilded wainscoting, doorcases and doors; furniture, carved gilded and richly upholstered surrounds a 17C Persian carpet; the fireplace is exuberantly Baroque... Equally opulent is the Queen's Suite, rich with late 17C garlanded plaster ceilings, grained wainscoting and carved wood swags above the fireplaces; the furniture includes then fashionable Oriental screens, English japanned chairs, a small Chinese cabinet on a gilded stand and 18C tapestries. In the heavily ornate closet with painted ceiling and the original satin brocade hangings, note the carved "sleeping chayre".

HAMMERSHITH (Hammersmith)

The buildings of North Hammersmith are known not for architectural merit but for their function: **Wormwood Scrubs** *(Du Cane Rd)*, stock brick and white stone buildings, profusely chimneyed, turreted and betowered, was constructed behind high walls by convicts from 1874-90 as the last prison to be built in London; **Hammersmith Hospital,** in close proximity, was built in 1904, the original buildings being in red brick and stone, and now stands enlarged by utilitarian annexes built for the expansion of specialised services and the Royal Postgraduate Medical School and Wolfson Institute. (Two other famous hospitals in the borough are Queen Charlotte's, Goldhawk Rd and the Royal Masonic, Ravenscourt Park.)

In Wood Lane, juste south of the Western Avenue/Westway flyover, on the site on which it was first built for the 1908 Olympics, is the **White City Stadium.** Within sight is the **BBC Television Centre** *(Wood Lane),* the only building with any style in the area. The original block, which dates from the early 1960s, is in yellow-brown brick and glass in the form of an open horseshoe with sides of unequal length and affords an interplay of curve and straight wall, of mounting heights and varied texture.

Shepherd's Bush Common, overlooked by the old Shepherd's Bush Empire, now a BBC TV Theatre, tree fringed and an incredible 4 acres in extent, serves only as a traffic island at the juncture of Wood Lane, the Uxbridge Rd, the M41, Goldhawk Rd, Holland Pk Av.

St Paul's Girls' School, Brook Green (south side), of red brick and stone with a formal entrance, carvings and segmental pediments, dates from 1903-4 when the school was founded. The music wing of 1913 is named after the composer and onetime music master **Gustav Holst** *(St Paul's Suite for Strings).* Further towards Hammersmith Rd but still within the calm of the green, are terraces of modest late 18/19C houses. At the end of Shepherd's Bush Rd by the fire station is the **Hammersmith Palais,** opened in 1919 and still vibrating as London's favourite dance hall.

Hammersmith Broadway is pounded by traffic going west to get onto the M 4 and the Great West Rd, south to Putney Bridge and east to Hyde Park Corner along Cromwell or Hammersmith Rds. This last is marked on its south side by the red brick, turreted and narrow windowed buildings in 1881 Early Gothic style, of the old St Paul's School, (now LEA Welfare Service) and on its north side by the West London Hospital, the extensive offices of J Lyons and, at the road's union with Kensington High St, by **Olympia.** The hall's front was refaced in 1930 but the actual building dates from 1884 (which explains the staircases); the rear extension was added in 1936.

St Paul's, Hammersmith. – *Open Sundays 8.30, 11am and 6.30pm; 1pm Thursdays.*
The parish church stands halfway between the broadway and the bridge, grand in size, pink stone in fabric, neo-Early English in style with a tall tower surmounted by high pinnacles. It dates from 1882 when it replaced a 17C chapel of ease which, although restored and enlarged in 1864 proved too small to accommodate the teeming population: 1801, 5 000; 1861, 25 000; 1881, 72 000; 1901, 112 000.

The furnishings include 17C octagonal pulpit, carved with cherubs' heads and garlands, from the Wren church of All Hallows, Thames St, late 17C chairs (in the chancel), 17 and 18C monuments. Note the one erected by the church benefactor, Sir Nicolas Crispe before his death in 1665, to "that Glorious Martyr King Charles I of blessed Memory" in the form of a bronze bust (Le Sueur).

Two big houses once bordered the Hammersmith riverside, both downstream from the bridge: **Craven Cottage,** an 18C cottage *orné* with Egyptian style interiors, burnt down in 1888 and now perpetuated as the name of Fulham football ground (Stevenage Rd) and 17C **Brandenburgh House,** the residence of Queen Caroline of Brunswick when she attempted to claim the rights of consort on the accession of her husband as George IV (the house was demolished after her death in 1821).

Hammersmith Bridge to Chiswick Mall

Upstream the embankment has developed gradually since the early 18C, modest houses being built singly or in terrace groups, the characteristic feature, besides the clouds of sometimes centuries' old wisteria, a balcony from which to watch, in olden days, sailing barges making for the harbour and now, yachts racing, oarsmen at practice.

Lower Mall. – Pleasingly notable in Lower Mall are, among the 18/19C group, no 6 (Amateur Rowing Association) with a balcony and bow window supported on slender, blue painted irons above the entrance to the boathouse; no 10, Kent House, with symmetrical bay windows, medallion decorations after Adam on the yellow brickwork and contemporary, late 18C, ironwork; the Blue Anchor, the later, Victorian, Rutland, then, marking the lower end of Furnival Gardens, Westcott Lodge, two storeys beneath a plain brick coping, the front door the last of the six bays, with an Ionic pillared porch which forms a canopied balcony above. At the garden's upstream end are the pier and a plaque which indicates the site of the creek and "harbour where the village began".

Upper Mall. – The Upper Mall opens with the 1726 Sussex House, stone urns at the corners of the brick coping and segmentally pedimented doorway flanked by Doric pilasters. The **Dove** which has had a licence for 400 years, although the present building only goes back a couple of centuries, was a coffeehouse in 18C – James Thomson is said to have written the words of *Rule Britannia* in the upstairs room.

In the next group, **Kelmscott House,** 3 storeys high, 5 bays wide, plain, with dormers behind the brick coping, dates from the 1780s. In the 19C it was lived in consecutively by George Macdonald poet and novelist (1867-77) and **William Morris** (until his death in 1896). Morris put a loom in his bedroom, held meetings in the stables, and in the studio drew the illustrations and designed the founts for the fine books he printed in the nearby no 14 and published under the imprint of the Kelmscott Press.

Frank Brangwyn, Morris' apprentice from 1882-4, moved to no 51 Temple Lodge, Queen Caroline St, nearby in 1899. Adjoining the house he built a lofty studio *(temporary exhibitions and recitals)* to accommodate the large canvases which brought him fame.

One of the largest on the Mall is early 19C **Rivercourt House;** the former Linden House, now the London Corinthian Sailing Club is a century earlier (much refurbished) – note the Ionic pillared but otherwise very different doorways. (Before the clubhouse looking like a glassed-in crow's nest above the riverside wall, is the race officer's box). Two pubs, the Old Ship Inn and the Black Lion, mark the end of the Mall, the latter set back from the river behind a garden with a brick arcade from an old riverside factory.

Hammersmith Terrace. – Nothing could be more urban than Hammersmith Terrace: 16 identical brick houses of 3 and 4 storeys built as a single block – yet it dates from the mid 18C when all around were fields, market gardens, vineyards and famous strawberry fields. Householders have included Philippe de Loutherbourg (artist and scenic designer at Drury Lane in 18C, no 13), Sir Emery Walker (antiquary and typographer, collaborator with Morris at the Kelmscott Press, no 7), and for more than 50 years, Sir Alan Herbert – APH – writer, lover and ardent protagonist of the Thames (1890-1971, nos 12-13).

Upstream is Chiswick Mall *(p 46)*; inland are St Peter's Sq with substantial 1830s houses of three storeys, bay windows and Ionic pillared porches, simultaneously planned dependent streets with smaller houses and cottages and St Peter's Church, a yellow stock brick landmark with pedimented portico and square clock tower on the Gt West Rd. It dates from 1829, the sculpture before it of a reclining woman by Karel Vogel, from 1959.

Hampstead Heath was the common of Hampstead Manor in Charles II's reign, an area where laundresses laid out washing to bleach in 18C and since earliest times, a popular place of recreation (vast one day fairs; *Easter, Spring and Autumn holiday Mondays*) Hampstead Village developed from a rural area of a few substantial houses (Fenton) manors and farms and later into a fashionable 18C spa when the chalybeate springs were discovered in what has been ever since, Well Walk. It was 4 miles only from the centre of London and by the time enthusiasm for taking the waters had subsided, builders had begun the erection of houses and terraces, the development which continues to this day. Finally, in 1907 came the tube. Throughout its history it has attracted writers, artists, architects, musicians, scientists.

The village, irregularly built on the side of a hill, has kept its original street pattern, main roads from the south and southeast meet and continue north; between is a network of small roads, groves, alleys, steps, courts, rises, places...

Swiss Cottage. – The chalet was built as the latest style in tavern design in 1840 and was so novel that it gave its name to the small locality beginning to develop between Hampstead and St John's Wood. Buses – it became a terminal in 1856 – then the tube (1868) brought transformation to a Victorian suburb now replaced by modern apartment blocks.

The chalet, more brightly painted than a stage set, still exists (café) at the centre of an island site.

The attractive, irregular buildings of **Swiss Cottage Civic Centre** (Avenue Rd, by Swiss Cottage Stn) by **Sir Basil Spence** include a library and swimming pool, opened in 1964. A temporary building houses the Hampstead Theatre Club.

East of Heath Street and Hampstead High Street

Downshire Hill going east from the foot of Hampstead High Street has some good Regency houses. **St John's Church** marks the Keats Grove fork, white and upright with a small domed bell turret, Classical pediment, large name plaque and square portico, a chapel of ease dating from 1818. **Keats Grove** is lined by early 19C houses and cottages irregular in height, detached and terraced, bay windowed, balconied with canopies, many with flowered front gardens.

Keats House. – *Keats Grove. Open daily 10am to 6pm; Sundays 2 to 5pm; closed New Year's Day, Good Friday, Easter Saturday, 25, 26 December.*

The small Regency house, known as Wentworth Place, was erected in 1815-16 as a semi-detached pair with a common garden, by two friends with who Keats and his brothers, in lodgings in Well Walk, soon became acquainted. In 1818, Keats came to live with his friend Brown in the left hand house; shortly afterwards Mrs. Brawne and her daughters became tenants of the right hand house. He wrote poems, the *Ode to a Nightingale,* in the garden; he journeyed; he became engaged to Fanny; he became ill; in September 1820 he left to winter in Italy and in February 1821 he died.

"His short life" in Edmund Blunden's words "was of unusual intensity; it insisted on being recorded in many ways". These records are now assembled, chiefly in the Chester Room added in 1838-9 when the two houses were united. The original rooms are furnished much as Keats and Fanny Brawne must have known them.

The **Keats Memorial Library** *(available to students by appointment only)* is in the local library next door.

Off Hampstead High Street in the **Old Brewery Mews** is a conversion to offices of the third building on the site – the first, of timber, dated from the 17C; modern houses have been erected round the former yard. Further north off Heath Street, **Flask Walk,** starting as a pedestrian precinct, includes a Victorian pub and tea merchant and continues, to pass on the right, Gardnor House built in 1736 with a full height and rounded bow window at the back. The 18C Burgh House standing high on the left in New End Square is known locally for its panelled music room *(open only for functions).* It was at no 40 Well Walk that **John Constable** lived from 1826 to his death. Christchurch Hill with its Georgian cottages leads to the mid 19C Church with a soaring spire visible for miles.

West of Heath Street and Hampstead High Street

Church Row. – The fine 1720 terrace of brown brick houses with red dressings, tall windows, straight hoods on carved brackets shading the Georgian doors, is separated from the uneven line on the north side, by a line of tall trees planted down the centre of the wide road. The range along the north pavement, older, younger and more varied, includes cottages, a weatherboarded house with oversailing bay, full style town houses of 3 storeys with good ironwork... **St John's,** the parish church at the row's end, obscured in summer by the trees, was built boldly on an ancient site in 1744-7 with a spire rising from a battlemented brick tower, banded in stone. The interior, with giant pillars supporting arches in the tunnel roof, galleries on three sides and box pews, was twice enlarged in 19C to accommodate Hampstead's rapidly growing population: 4 300 in 1801, 47 000 in 1881.

Frognal, to the west, once a manor, hence all the roads of the same name, includes buildings as typical and various as University College School, large and neo-Georgian with Edward VII in full regalia standing above the entrance door; Kate Greenaway's house (no 39) designed in 1885 by Norman Shaw in true children's story book appearance with rambling gables and balconies; and the Sun House (no 9 Frognal Way) by Maxwell Fry at his 1935 best, in stepped horizontals in glass and gleaming white.

Holly Walk. – The path north from the church, bordered by the 1810 cemetery extension crowded with funeral monuments, rises to the yellow and pink washed, three story houses of Prospect Place (1814) and delightful cottages of Benham's Place (1813). Holly Place,

816, is another small enclave with, at the terrace centre, St Mary's, one of the earliest RC churches to be built in London, founded by the Abbé Morel, refugee from the Revolution who came to Hampstead in 1796. At the summit begins one of the village's mazes, as steps and alleys every few yards lead down to Heath St.

Mount Vernon junction. — The triangular junction of Windmill Hill, Hampstead Grove and Holly Bush Hill, weighed down by the institutional late 19C National Institute for Medical Research, is redeemed by **Romney's House** (plaque), picturesquely built of brick and weatherboarding in 1797, and the tall 18C group: Volta, Bolton and Windmill Hill, all of brown brick. The iron gateway of 1707 by Tijou at the end belongs to Fenton House.

Fenton House★★. — *Open Wednesdays to Saturdays 11am to 5pm or dusk if earlier, Sundays 2 to 5pm or dusk; closed 1 January, Good Friday, all December; 50p. N.T.*

Exterior. — The red brick house built in 1693, is Hampstead's finest besides being one of its earliest and largest. The front, with a recessed door is less attractive than the back of seven bays beneath a hipped roof with a central pediment repeated in miniature over the pilaster-ed garden door. In 1793 the house was bought by a Riga merchant, Philip Fenton, after who it is still named; in 1952 it was bequeathed, with furniture, pictures and porcelain to the National Trust.

Interior. — The house is a treasure trove: furniture and pictures form a background to 18C porcelain — English, German and French, and the Benton-Fletcher collection of early **keyboard instruments** — some 18 in number plus an early 17C Flemish harpsichord lent by HM The Queen Mother. The instruments range in date from a five sided Italian spinet, encased in cypress wood, with a keyboard of boxwood, with ebony accidentals, signed Marcus Siculus faciebat 1540, to an Arnold Dolmetsch clavichord of 1925. (The instruments are for the most part kept in good playing order and are accessible to students. There are frequent concerts). On the ground floor are harpsichords (1770 English, 1612 Flemish), the most important part of the English porcelain collection (Bristol, Plymouth, Chelsea Bow, Worcester), some of the German figures, and an Oriental room; on the landing Staffordshire figures and a Trubshaw grandmother clock. On the first floor are German figurines, teapots; Worcester apple green porcelain in satinwood cabinets, the most important piece of English porcelain in the collection, a Worcester pink-scale vase and cover probably decorated in London (Drawing Room), 17/18C Chinese blue and white porcelain, 18C English harpsichords, an early 17C Italian and mid 18C English spinet, and on the top floor 18C square pianos, 17 and 18C harpsichords, 17 and 20C clavichords, and a 17C spinet and virginal.

Admiral's Walk, on the left, leads to Admiral's House, built in the first half of 18C and given its nautical superstructure including, in his time, a couple of cannon with which to fire victory salutes, by the colourful Admiral Matthew Burton (1715-95) after who the house, now resplendent in "tropical whites", remains named. It was the home of Sir George Gilbert Scott from 1854-64 — he made no alteration. The adjoining Grove Lodge also white, probably older, was Galsworthy's home from 1918 until his death in 1933 and where he wrote all but the first part of the *Forsyte Saga*. Lower Terrace, at the end of Admiral's Walk, is where Constable lived from 1821-5 before moving to Well Walk.

North of Hampstead village (Hampstead Heath)

Whitestone Pond. — The pond and the milestone (Holborn Bars 4½ — in the bushes at the base of the aerial) from which it takes its name, are, at 437ft, on London's highest ground. The flagstaff is thought to stand on the site of an Armada beacon, the link with the signal south of the river on Shooter's Hill, Blackheath, visible on a clear day, and even more distinctly at night. (In 18/19C military and admiralty telegraphs stood on Telegraph Hill — west.)

Jack Straw's Castle. — The white weatherboarded inn, rebuilt in 1962-4, was first mentioned in local records in 1713. The name is thought to be derived from the possibility that supporters rallied on the spot before going to join Straw in Highbury and Wat Tyler in central London in the Peasants' Revolt of 1381.

Standing on its own at the junction of the two roads, Heath House, a plain early 18C mansion of brown brick is chiefly remarkable for its commanding position and the visitors received by its 18/19C owner, the Quaker abolitionist, Samuel Hoare: William Wilberforce, Elizabeth Fry and the leading politicians of the day.

Vale of Health. — The Vale, a cluster of late 18, early 19C cottages, mid-Victorian and now a few modern houses and blocks, built in a dip in the heath and connected by a maze of narrow roads and paths, all unnamed, has at various times been the home of Leigh Hunt, the Harmsworth brothers, Rabindranath Tagore, D H Lawrence, Edgar Wallace, Compton Mackenzie. The origin of the Vale's name is unknown — until 1677 it was a marsh; the houses only began to be named from 1841.

To the west of North End Way are **Golders Hill Park,** a landscaped park with tall trees, lawns, shrubs and serpentine paths providing a perfect intermediary between the West Heath to its southeast and the formal **Hill Public Garden** with its never ending rectilinear pergola, sweet with wisteria, roses and trailing plants. (Inverforth House, rebuilt in 1914 is now a wing of Manor House Hospital.)

Bull and Bush. — The 1920s building with a modern inn sign, turn of the century paintings of Florrie Forde and a verse of the music hall song outside, reputedly stands on the site of a 17C farmhouse. In 18C it became for a brief time Hogarth's country retreat, then a tavern, patronised by Joshua Reynolds, Gainsborough, Constable, Romney...

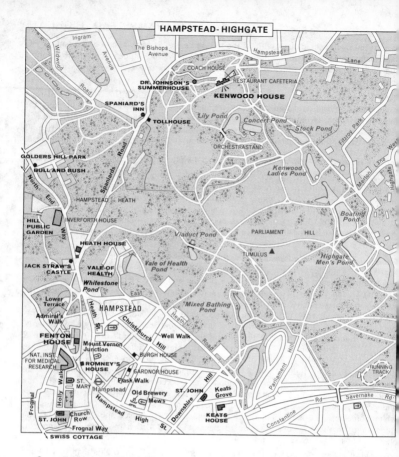

Opposite is the gabled brick house (now a speech and drama college) where Anna Pavlova lived from 1921-1931. The Elder Pitt, Earl of Chatham, retired to a house, since demolished, at North End in 1767 (d 1788); Dame Henrietta Barnett, living in what is now Heath End House, devised her campaign for what was to become, with the aid of the architect, Sir Raymond Unwin, Hampstead Garden Suburb.

Spaniards Inn and Tollhouse. — The inn and tollhouse have slowed traffic on Spaniards Road into single file since they were built in the early 18C. The small brick tollhouse stands on the site of an entrance to the Bishop of London's Park, the white painted brick and weatherboard pub on that of a house said to have been that of a 17C Spanish Ambassador. In 1780, the Gordon Rioters, having sacked Lord Mansfield's Bloomsbury town house, stopped to ask the way to Kenwood but were so plied with drink by the publican that they had not moved by the time the military arrived.

■ KENWOOD HOUSE★★ (Iveagh Bequest)

Open daily 10am to 7pm — 5pm October, February, March; 4pm November to January; closed Good Friday, 24, 25 December; cafeteria.

"A great 18C gentleman's country house with pictures such as an 18C collector might have assembled". — William Murray, younger son of a Scottish peer, acquired Kenwood, then a 50 year old brick house, in 1754, two years before he was appointed Lord Chief Justice and created **Earl of Mansfield.** He intended Kenwood as his country place where he could holiday and entertain, and in 1764 invited his fellow Scot, **Robert Adam,** to enlarge and embellish the retreat. The architect transformed it both outside and in and left so strong an imprint that all subsequent additions were in his style.

Kenwood was purchased by Lord Iveagh in 1925 and bequeathed to the nation in 1928. The house's contents, including much Adam furniture, had previously been sold and he filled it instead with the remarkable collection of pictures he had formed at the end of the 19C. Contemporary furniture is gradually being acquired.

Exterior. — The pedimented portico with giant fluted columns, frieze and medallion was, typically, Adam's contribution to the north front; the south front, from which there is a splendid view down to the lake *(concerts in summer),* Adam raised to three floors at the centre (decorating the upper floors in his own style) and prolonged on either side by, respectively, the Orangery and Library.

Dr Johnson's Summerhouse (west of the flower garden). — The summerhouse was provided by Henry and Hester Thrale for their guest at Streatham Place where he was a constant visitor from 1766-1782. It was rescued and re-erected on the present site in 1962.

Interior. — Of the rooms on either side of the hall, the most remarkable are the Music and Ante-Rooms (cornice and doorcase related in motif to the preceding enriched columns and entablatures), the Adam Library and Orangery.

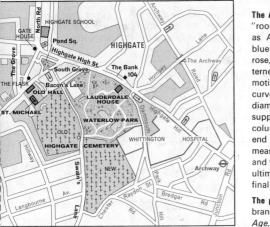

The Adam Library★★. — The "room for receiving company" as Adam described it, is in blue and white, gold and old rose, everywhere richly patterned with Adam designed motifs. At either end of the curved ceiling is an apse, its diameter marked by a beam supported on fluted Corinthian columns. From the door at one end the length of the room is measured in mirrored niches and tall, draped windows and, ultimately, columns before final curved bookcases.

The paintings★★. — A Rembrandt, *Self-portrait in Old Age,* the lusty *Man with a Cane* by Frans Hals, the ringletted young girl *Guitar Player* by Vermeer, Cuyp and van de Velde seascapes and a Turner, *Fisherman upon a Lee Shore,* occupy just the Dining Room. Portraits by the English school people other rooms: beautiful Gainsborough women, including *Mary, Lady Howe* in pink silk with that special flat hat, *Lady Hamilton* by Romney and children, sentimental, patient, delighted, by Raeburn *(Sir George Sinclair),* Reynolds *(The Brummell Children)* and Lawrence *(Miss Murray).* A portrait of different interest is that by John Jackson, after Reynolds, of the Lord Chief Justice, the Earl of Mansfield, creator of Kenwood.

■ HIGHGATE

Highgate Village developed from 16/17C when one or two decided it was the place to build their country seats; in 17C came rich merchants with their mansions; in 18C the prosperous... The mid and later 20C has continued the tradition. Nevertheless Highgate remains a village in character, centring on Pond Square and the High Street.

Small houses and cottages line three sides of the irregularly shaped Pond Square, from which the ponds disappeared in the 1860 s.

South Grove. — Along the south side of **Pond Sq** are the early 18C Church House (no 10), the Highgate Literary and Scientific Society at no 11 and Moreton House (no 14) a brick mansion of 1715. **Rock House** (no 6) opposite, with overhanging wooden bay windows is 18C and, on the far side of Bacon's Lane, **Old Hall,** late 17C, plain brick with a parapet and at the back a great bow window, topped by a pierced white balustrade. Bacon's Lane recalls that the philosopher was a frequent guest and died at Arundel House, which stood nearby.

St Michael's. — The church of 1830 with a tapering octagonal spire stands before **Highgate Cemetery.** This is in two parts: the New (south of Waterlow Park) in which are interred **Karl Marx** (d 1883; bust by Laurence Bradshaw 1956), George Eliot (1819-80), William Foyle (1885-1963), William Friese-Greene (1855-1921); and the Old, opened in 1838 and in which lie buried Michael Faraday (1791-1867), the Rossettis, Charles Cruft (first dog show 1886). The latter is also remarkable for its 19C monumental masonry. *(The New cemetery is open on application at the gate in Swain's Lane.)*

The Flask on Highgate West Hill corner is a period country pub.

The Grove. — This wide, tree planted, road branching off to the right, presents, behind open railings, late 17/early 18C terrace housing at its satisfying best; rose brick in colour, of dignified height, with segment headed windows and individual variations.

Highgate High Street. — The street is lined by small, local shops and pubs with houses above: the **Gate House Tavern,** stands on the site of a 1386 gate house to the Bishop of London's park (18C house at the rear); no 46, Fisher and Sperr, antiquarian bookseller, with a small paned bay window, dates from 1729; no 23 opposite, Englefield House with straight-headed windows and modillion frieze is early 18C; nos 21 and 27 next door are slightly later.

Just inside **Waterlow Park** stands **Lauderdale House,** in origin 16C but remodelled in the 18C in small country house style. This is the house about which the tale is told that in 1676, Nell Gwynn not yet successful in obtaining titled recognition for her princely 6 year old son, dangled him out of a window before his father threatening to drop him, whereupon Charles called out "Save the Earl of Burford" (the future Duke of St Albans).

Opposite, fronting the upraised road, is The Bank, a row of brick houses: nos 110, 108 and 106, Ireton and Lyndale Houses are early 18C, no 104 Cromwell House (so called for uncertain reasons since 1833) of now mellow red brick with a solid parapet and an octagonal, cupolaed, turret of 1638.

The tree lined **North Road,** begins with the 19C red brick buildings of Highgate School (f 1565; now 700 strong) on the right and opposite a late Georgian terrace, nos 1-11, followed by individual houses of the same period (nos 15, 17 — plaque to A E Housman — 19) and at 47, 49 another early Georgian group. Beyond stand the clean lined Highpoint One and Two designed by Lubetkin and Tecton in 1936 and 1938; the first with two Erechtheum caryatids supporting the porch; one facing front, but the other — fed up perhaps? — at the half turn!

HAMPTON COURT ★★★ (Richmond on Thames)

Open May to September, weekdays 9.30am (Sundays 11am) to 6pm; March, April, October 9.30am (Sundays 2pm) to 5pm; November to February to 4pm; Palace and park closed 1 January, Good Friday, 24, 25, 26 December; State Apartments 50p (20p October to March); Mantegna cartoons (Lower Orangery) 15p.

The three builder patrons. – **Wolsey** purchased the manor site at Hampton from the Knights of St John of Jerusalem in 1514: Henry VIII purloined it in 1530.

It was the age of the *Field of the Cloth of Gold* (1520 – painting in the Cartoon Gallery), of splendour and display, of unbridled ambition and meteoric careers. Thomas Wolsey, the son of an Ipswich butcher, appointed to a chaplaincy in the household of Henry Tudor while still in his early thirties, rose, under Henry VIII, to be Archbishop of York (1514), Lord Chancellor (1515), Cardinal (1515), Papal Legate (1518). Celebrating his position and wealth were his houses in and around London: Whitehall, Hampton Court and Moor Park (Herts).

Construction of Hampton Court in 1515 proceeded apace. The plan was the accustomed Tudor one of consecutive courts with surrounding buildings: Base Court, Clock Court, Carpenter's Court, hall chapel. It measured 300 × 550ft overall and contained some 500 rooms of which 280 were kept prepared for guests. The residence was richly furnished throughout with panelled and tapestry hung walls painted and gilded ceilings and was peopled by

Hampton Court: east front.

the cardinal's personal household of 500. Wolsey's wealth, it was said, exceeded the king's, his mansion outshone the royal palaces. His power in the kingdom approached the absolute until after 15 years, he fell, disgraced, and within months had died (1530).

Sumptuous as Hampton Court was, **Henry VIII** enlarged and rebuilt much of it. He added wings on either side of the central gateway, a moat and drawbridge; he constructed the Great Hall, the Great Watching Chamber, the annexes around the Kitchen Court including the Haunted Gallery, the Fountain Court, the tennis court wing, the south front overlooking the Pond Garden. He built a tiltyard (where the restaurant and walled gardens are now) and planted a flower garden, kitchen garden and two orchards.

Edward VI, who had been born at Hampton Court, his two sisters and the early Stuarts resided at the palace when the season was fine or the plague rife in London.

Unlike other royal residences it was reserved for Cromwell and so preserved with its contents – notably the wood carvings and paintings. Charles II returned to initiate the modern garden layout but the palace, through the next 140 years, remained virtually unaltered and uncared for.

To **William** and **Mary,** the third and last of the palace's true builder patrons, Hampton Court offered delight and a splendid potential which they immediately began to realise through Wren and Talman and an unrivalled team of artist-master-craftsmen – Grinling Gibbons, Jean Tijou, Antonio Verrio, Morris Emmett, C G Cibber, the king's Dutch architect, Daniel Marot, and the great gardeners, George London and Henry Wise.

Wren began work in 1689 and, after schemes to demolish the 200 year old Tudor palace had been discarded, designed and rebuilt the east front entirely, and the south front to enclose between the façades, the State Apartments – two suites each including a guardroom, presence and audience chambers, drawing room, state bedroom and closet or dressing room and known respectively as the King's Side (overlooking the Privy Garden to the south) and the Queens' Side (overlooking the Fountain Garden to the east). The smaller informal royal apartments on the Fountain Court he also rebuilt anew but left the Base Court much as it was only adding the colonnade and a new south range to the Clock Court. To achieve such massive works, the crenellations, irregularities and forest of turrets of Henry's castle palace (still to be seen in an anonymous painter's view of *Hampton Court from the Thames),* were swept away and replaced by the classic Renaissance style of the 17C, executed in brick with stone centrepieces, enrichments and surrounds to the long ranges of tall, circular, square windows which emphasise the horizontal lines of the building, crowned by a seemingly infinite balustrade.

Queen Anne's contribution was to have Wren design and Grinling Gibbons decorate a small Banqueting House overlooking the river and start the decoration and furnishing of the State Apartments, only finally completed under George II, the last monarch to reside at the palace. It was in his reign that William Kent decorated the Cumberland Suite, with typical 18C plasterwork. In 1771-3 the Great Gatehouse was rebuilt; two storeys being lopped off in the process. In 1839 Queen Victoria opened the State Apartments, gardens and Bushy Park to the public.

NB: *the map and key on page 94 are numbered in the sequence in which the apartments are visited – as courtiers would have approached the monarch in the king's rooms, in the reverse order in the queen's. The official (HMSO) guide provides details of each gallery and room throughout; to avoid repetition subjects are grouped below under points of particular interest with their situation.*

THE PALACE★★★

Tudor timberwork, panelling, carving

Wolsey's Closet (30): the cardinal's original furnishings: linenfold panelling (restored); frieze with Tudor badges, mermaids and Wolsey's motto as running motif; ceiling of timber with plaster and lead mouldings, a chequerwork of Tudor Roses, Prince of Wales' feathers, Renaissance ornament — all coloured and gilded.

Wolsey's Rooms (4): (misnamed as used by guests, not the cardinal); 16C linenfold and later, plain panelling and an elaborate ceiling decorated with Wolsey's badges.

Great Hall (36): (106 × 40 × 60ft high); built in 5 years (1531-36) with Henry VIII so impatient to see it finished that men even worked by candlelight. The magnificent hammer-beam roof is enriched with mouldings, tracery, carving and elaborate pendants relieved with gilding and colours.

Great Watching Chamber (35): built in 1535-36 at the entrance to the Tudor State Rooms (destroyed), with an elaborately panelled ceiling set with coloured bosses displaying Tudor and (Jane) Seymour devices between ribs which curve down to form pendants.

Chapel Royal (33): built by Wolsey but lavishly transformed by Henry VIII when the fan vaulted wooden ceiling was erected and gilded pendants added *(see also below)*.

Grinling Gibbons: "Master Carver to our Workes in the room". Gibbons' work and that of his assistants in cornices, friezes, doorcases, provides a superb finish to the king's staterooms especially. Overmantels, picture frames, swags and drops are each different and minutely executed: petalled and stamened flowers in garlands, lush, ripe fruit, gay billing doves and spying cherubim. Whether highlighted with gold leaf as in the chapel, the carvings are rich as only wood is rich, be it yellow-green limewood, pear or ancient oak. The principal Gibbons' carvings are to be seen in:

- **First and Second Presence and Audience Chambers** (5, 6, 7): overmantels and door friezes of ribbons, roses, tulips, crossed sheaves, ropes of primroses and oak leaves, trumpets and cornucopia, drops of leaves, flowers, fruit, peapods and acorns.
- **Drawing Room** (8): elaborate frame to Isabella of Austria, headed by a crown of fruit and flowers and descending in drops including garlands, putti, birds, flower chains.
- **King's Bedroom and Dressing Room** (9, 10): limewood frieze of birds, leaves, wheat, overmantel of ribbons passing through wreaths and frieze including pot plants!
- **Queen's Gallery** (13): doorcases (*Triumph of Venus* in marble by John Nost).
- **Cartoon Gallery** (27): four doorcases; the very long drops framing the tapestry over the fireplace cost £25 the pair.
- **Banqueting House** *(not usually open):* very fine door, mirror and window cases.
- **Chapel Royal** (33): reredos between Wren's Corinthian pillars and segmental pediment; a wreath of cherubim above drops on either side of a framed oval.

Tapestries

Great Watching Chamber (35): 16C Flemish — *the Vices and Virtues* — possibly purchased by Wolsey in 1522; three others of scenes from Petrarch.

Haunted Gallery (32): hangings probably from Queen Elizabeth's collection; (ghostly screams heard in the gallery are said to be those of Catherine Howard begging Henry to save her from the scaffold).

Great Hall (36): mid 16C Flemish — *History of Abraham* (also Queen's Audience Chamber).

Queen's Gallery (13): Brussels tapestries woven to Gobelin designs in 1662.

Cartoon Gallery (27): the gallery was especially designed by Wren (1699) to display seven of the ten tapestry cartoons designed by Raphaël (1515), purchased by Charles I in 1623. The cartoons on the lives of St Peter and St Paul are now in the V & A, their place being taken by tapestries woven later after the cartoons.

Prince of Wales Staircase: the illustrations of the battle between the English and Dutch fleets at Solebay in 1672 are attributed to William van de Velde; they were woven by Francis Poyntz at the factory built by James I at Mortlake.

Wolsey's Rooms (4): the scriptural hangings are 17C north Italian needlework.

Chairs of State and royal beds

First Presence and Audience Chambers (5, 7), King William's and Queen Anne's Bedrooms (9, 14), Queen's Drawing Room (15, Queen Charlotte's bed designed by Robert Adam with a painted dome and delicate embroidery), Prince of Wales Bedroom (20) and King's Private Dressing Room (25).

Paintings

The royal collection at Hampton Court dates back to Tudor and Stuart times with Henry VIII and Charles I as the major patrons.

The pictures are not grouped by school or subject as in a museum, but hang, in some cases, still in the position for which they were painted (Kneller's *King William III on horseback*), in others where they can be seen as a panorama (the two series of *Court Beauties*) or the juxtaposition is of especial interest (*Henry VIII* and his friend the savant, *Erasmus*). The description below is intended only to indicate the scope of the collection and a few highlights. *Exact locations, since the pictures may be moved and are frequently sent out on loan, should be sought from the keepers.*

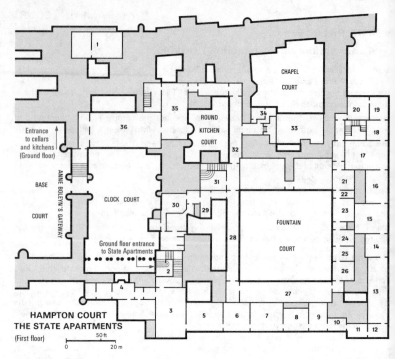

Entrance to cellars and kitchens (Ground floor)

BASE COURT

ANNE BOLEYN'S GATEWAY

CLOCK COURT

Ground floor entrance to State Apartments

CHAPEL COURT

ROUND KITCHEN COURT

FOUNTAIN COURT

HAMPTON COURT THE STATE APARTMENTS
(First floor)

50 ft
0   20 m

Pictures of particular historical interest. — Henry VII and VIII and their wives, Margaret of York and Jane Seymour (after Holbein); Henry VIII (after Holbein); Edward VI (born and christened in the palace); Queen Elizabeth; Tudor portraits including the poet, Henry Surrey; an anti-papal allegory by Girolamo Treviso (only survivor of Henry's extensive collection); Hampton Court, showing the Long Water reaching the east front and a view from the south before Wren's alterations and in the time of George I (details of the gardens) — **Wolsey's Rooms** (4).

Henry VIII (contemporary portrait) and Erasmus — **King William's Dressing Room** (10).

Historical paintings of Henry VIII's reign; *Field of the Cloth of Gold*, the *Journey to France* (1520); *Family Group* of Henry VIII, his children and including a posthumous portrait of Jane Seymour, *The Windsor Beauties* (Charles II's Court) by Lely — **Communication Gallery** (28).

William III on horseback (1701) by Kneller; *The Hampton Court Beauties* (Queen Mary's Court) by Kneller — **1st Presence Chamber** (5).

Mantegna (c 1431-1506): *Cartoons of the Triumph of Caesar.* 9 giant paintings of a triumphal procession, ending with the portrait of an ashen, withered, Caesar, high on his chariot. The Cartoons, possibly the earliest pictures on canvas to survive, were bought by Charles I in early 17C — **Lower Orangery** *(15p).*

Early Italian paintings (13-15C): *Madonna and Child* by Gentile da Fabriano; altarpiece by Duccio — **Prince of Wales Presence Chamber** (18).

16 and 17C Italian paintings including Titian *(The Lovers),* Giorgione *(Shepherd with a pipe),* Tintoretto, Veronese *(Marriage of St Catherine),* Correggio, Andrea del Sarto — **King's Side and Private Dining Room** (23).

18C Venetian artists including Sebastiano and Marco Ricci — **Public Dining Room** (17).

Early 16C German, and Dutch: *Christ at the Tomb* by Holbein, *Adam and Eve, Children of Christian II of Denmark* by Mabuse — **King William's Dressing Room** (10).

16C German and Flemish paintings: the *Massacre of the Innocents* by Pieter Brueghel the Elder (the picture originally included many murdered children; for political reasons the painter had later to disguise the bodies as parcels etc) — **Queen Mary's Closet** (12).

16 and early 17C portraits of ladies of the court including Margaret Lemon, the artist's mistress by van Dyck — **Queen's Private Chapel** (21).

17C portraits including Jeffrey Hudson, the dwarf attendant of Queen Henrietta Maria, by Mytens — **Queen's Audience Chamber** (16).

Frescoes and ceiling paintings by Antonio Verrio (17C) on the **King's Staircase** (2) in the **King's Bedroom** (9), **Dressing Room** (10, very light-hearted), **Queen's Drawing Room** (15); by James Thornhill in the **Queen's Bedroom** (14, portrait medallions of George I and II, Queen Caroline, Prince Frederick) and **Holy Day Closet**; by William Kent on the **Queen's Staircase** (31).

Ironwork and arms

King's Staircase, Queen's Staircase (2, 31): the stylised wrought iron balustrades, which line three sides of the open stairwells, were made to designs by **Jean Tijou,** a French Protestant who came to England by way of the Netherlands, and often worked with Wren.

Prince of Wales Staircase: Tijou festoon (below landing) also gate in the East Front.

King's Guard Room (3): the display of more than 3 000 arms were arranged by William III's gunsmith.

Features of the exterior and auxiliary buildings

Trophy gates: built as the main gates in George II's reign with lion and unicorn supporters on the inner piers.

Moat and Bridge: constructed by Henry VIII; the moat was filled in, the bridge buried by Charles II; in 1910 the work was excavated and the bridge found to be complete apart from the parapet which was renewed and fronted by the King's Beasts.

Stone animals on the battlements: the weasels date from the construction by Henry VIII of wings with characteristic 16C diapered brickwork, flanking Wolsey's gatehouse.

Henry VIII's arms: the royal arms appear in a (renewed) panel beneath the central oriel in the Great Gatehouse; also on Anne Boleyn's Gateway (Base Court side).

Terracotta roundels: the medallions of Roman emperors on the turrets and three other pairs inside were bought by Wolsey for Hampton Court in 1521. They were originally painted and gilded and cost £2 6s each.

Anne Boleyn's Gateway: so-called because the king embellished it during the queen's brief reign; bell turret, 18C; Base Court side, Elizabeth's badges, initials, date 1566; Clock Court side, Wolsey's arms in terracotta (restored) and cardinal's hat.

The Astronomical Clock: the clock in what was the main Court of Wolsey's house, was only brought to the palace (from St James's) in the 19C. It was made for Henry VIII in 1540 by Nicholas Oursian and on the 8ft dial are indicated the hour, month, date, signs of the zodiac, year and phase of the moon. It ante-dates the publication of the theories of Copernicus and Galileo and the sun, therefore, revolves round the earth.

Chimney Stacks: the brick stacks are a delightful example of Tudor fantasy.

Kitchens and Cellars *(access-Base Court; open April to September):* The King's Beer Cellar beneath the Great Hall (note the wooden piers supporting the floor above, the stone pier beneath the hearth) and the New Wine Cellar, beneath the Great Watching Chamber, stored the home brewed ale and imported wine for the royal household of 500.

Tudor Tennis Court *(access: the Broad Walk, open April to September):* built by Henry VIII and still played on regularly. The windows are 18C.

East Front entablature: Caius Cibber carved the entablature (1694-6) combining the William and Mary cipher with crown, sceptres, trumpets... He also carved many of the palace's finest window and arcade ornaments (Fountain Court round window surrounds).

Royal Mews Museum *(access: south front; 5p)* royal carriages, harness and miniature cars given to the Queen, Prince Charles and younger members of the family are displayed in the Upper Orangery where William III's orange trees used to overwinter in tubs.

ER 1568: on the bay window stonework overlooking the Knot Garden (south front); the lead cupola and octagonal turret date back to the 16C.

Lower Orangery: the plain building by Wren now houses the Mantegna Cartoons *(15p).*

■ THE GARDENS★★★
Open 9.30am (2pm on Sundays) until dusk.

The gardens bear the imprint, now faint now clear, of the men who created them; the Tudor, Stuart, Orange monarchs, the designers and the great gardeners. In the 50 acres surrounding the palace, features have been levelled, schemes abandoned; fashion has translated 17 and 18C box edged *parterres* into lawns or woodland, growth transformed man size yew obelisks into 30ft green-black cones; new species, have been introduced; the half mile long herbaceous border along the Broad Walk laid...

Wolsey planted a walled flower garden in the confined area between the river and the forward south front. Under Henry VIII and the Tudors, this became the brightly coloured formal **Pond Garden** and **Knot Garden,** the last a velvety conceit of interlaced ribands of dwarf box or thyme with infillings of flowers, replanted this century within its walled Elizabethan site. A gazebo crowned mound erected by Henry VIII by the river with a spiral approach, flanked by gaudily painted King's Beasts, was levelled in 1700, the beasts being preserved to stand in the court before the main entrance, the soil used to construct the raised Queen Mary's Bower and Queen's Terrace on either side of the Privy Garden. Henry's tiltyards and five observation towers, covering 7 acres to the north, have also vanished, transformed into a series of walled, old fashioned rose gardens, overlooked by one remaining tower (adjoining the restaurant) — roses cost 4 pence for 100 bushes in Tudor times.

Charles I had a tributary of the Colne River diverted to Bushy Park to form the 9 mile Longford River; enclosed 10 miles as a deer park and commissioned Francisco Fenelli to sculpt the Diana Fountain, originally for the Privy Garden.

Charles II, who discovered the royal parks to be in a sad state of neglect, had the Long Water canal excavated and lime trees from Holland planted in the vast semicircle and three radiating avenues which still provide a "set piece" from the palace. (The giant goosefoot or *patte d'oie,* with the canal as the central claw extending from the palace front to the horizon was very much in the architectural style of current garden design in France under Le Nôtre.)

William III was a "Delighter" in gardening; Mary "particularly skill'd in Exoticks", for which she sent botanists to Virginia and the Canary Islands. Garden designers included Wren, Talman, Marot, gardeners George London and Henry Wise.

William determined to have a fountain garden. The Long Water was curtailed to its present ¾ mile and **Great Fountain Garden** laid out in the 10 acres between the semicircle of limes and the palace east front. 13 fountains played in a formal scrollwork setting of

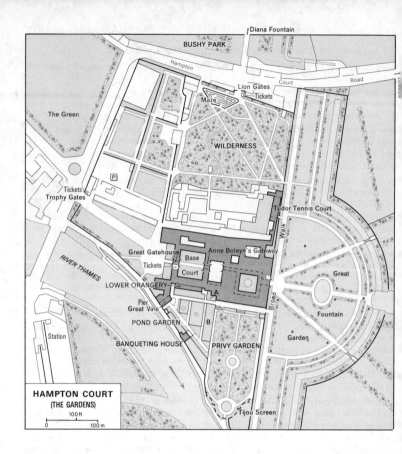

HAMPTON COURT
(THE GARDENS)

100 ft
0 ———— 100 m

dwarf box hedges (a Dutch fashion), obelisk shaped yews and globes of white holly. Under Queen Anne, eight fountains at the circumference were removed, the box hedge arabesques replaced by grass and gravel; in Queen Caroline's time the fountains were reduced to the present singleton. The yews in the 19C grew as they willed and only in the 20C have they been gradually trimmed to allow, between, beds glorious with tulips and bright bedding plants, spectacular vistas from the palace front.

Tijou designed the ironwork gates to the NE and SE lime avenues across the side arms of the Long Water, the Lion Gates and the unique 12 panel **screen,** a climax at the river end of the Privy Gardens – allusive with Scottish, English, Irish and Welsh emblems, and delicate as black lace. His bill for the work came to £2 160 2s ¼d.

The **Broad Walk,** nearly half a mile long was planned by Wren and Queen Caroline to separate the Privy and Fountain Gardens. The border is now 12ft wide and an almost permanent ribbon of colour throughout the seasons.

To the north of the palace, where Henry VIII had his orchard, William laid out a Wilderness – the name for a geometrical garden of espaliers, clipped yews, hollies and box hedges and including within its 9 acres a circular **maze,** replaced in 1714 by the present triangular version *(2p).* In its turn the formal Wilderness has been replaced, though not in name, by natural woodland, golden in early spring with a million daffodils.

From the same period, the turn of the 17/18C, and the only memorial to Wren's grand design for a new north front, is the **Chestnut Avenue** in Bushy Park. To view the chestnuts in flower – 274 of them planted 42ft apart, extending over a mile and bordered on either side by 4 files of limes – remains a mid-May event to this day. Beyond the fountain, west of the avenue is a "new" – 20 year old! – 100 acre **Woodland Garden** *(open from 8.30am)* where, on either side of the stream, patrolled by waterfowl and a black swan, beneath the trees, are rhododendrons and azaleas and azaleas and rhododendrons – white and purple, sugar pink and gold, tawny orange, shocking pink, red...

Under George III, Capability Brown planted in 1768 the **Great Vine,** an incredible plant with a girth of 78 inches and an annual crop of 500-600 bunches of grapes *(on sale late August/early September).* The massive wistaria, near the Vine House, dates from 1840.

HAMPTON COURT GREEN

At the palace entrance, around the green and extending towards the bridge are houses built for and lived in then and later by those associated with the court, particularly in the late 17 and 18C. Of most interest are those extending back from the early 19C hotel on the bridge road, which recede also in date: Palace Gate House, The Green, **Old Court House,** the home of Sir Christopher Wren from 1706-23, Court Cottage, the 18C bow windowed **Faraday House** where Michael Faraday lived in retirement from 1858-67, and Cardinal House. Back from the road are the Old Office House with a hipped roof and the small square, white weatherboarded, **King's Store Cottage** (George III plaque).

Beyond is the long brick range of the Tudor **Royal Mews,** built round a courtyard and now converted into flats.

Holborn, meeting place in the Middle Ages of roads from the north to the City, to Oxford and the west; site of the Bishop of Ely's palace – in Richard, Duke of Gloster's mind when he requested: "My lord of Ely, when I was last in Holborn, I saw good straw-berries in your garden there, I do beseech you send for some of them" (R III; 3 iv). There were also manors and a market at the crossroads, open fields on which beasts grazed, archery was practised, duels were fought and washing laid out to dry. Today the manors are transformed into Lincoln's Inn and Gray's Inn – two of the four Inns of Court – the chapel and place of the episcopal precinct remain in name, the fields are less in extent but still open, the produce market is a world diamond centre...

Lincoln's Inn Fields. – By 1650 a developer, who had purchased the common fields to the west of Lincoln's Inn twenty years before, had surrounded them on three sides with houses. Of that period, one, **Lindsey House** remains, probably designed by Inigo Jones (Since divided, nos 59-60, west side). The brickwork was originally all exposed, giving greater emphasis to the segmental pediment, the accented window and giant, wreathed, pilasters. 18C houses in the square, include, the Palladian style nos 57-8 dating from 1730, no 66, Powis House of 1777 with a pediment marking the centre window. On the north side nos 1-2 are early 18C, 5-9 Georgian, and no 15 with an Ionic columned doorway, frieze and pediment, mid-century.

The square's south side is almost entirely occupied by official buildings: the neo-Jacobean Land Registry, neo-Georgian Nuffield College of Surgical Sciences (1956-8) and 19-20C Royal College of Surgeons and the six storey, 1960s, Imperial Cancer Research Fund.

The Old Curiosity Shop. – *Portsmouth St, corner of Lincoln's Inn Fields.*

The half timbered, little house on the corner is said to date back to the late 1500s and so be one of the oldest in London.

Sir John Soane's Museum★. – *13 Lincoln's Inn Fields. Open Tuesdays to Saturdays 10am to 5pm; closed 1 January, Good Friday, 25, 26 December.*

In 1833 Soane obtained a private Act of Parliament to ensure the perpetuation of the Museum after his death. A stipulation was that nothing should be altered in any way, hence, house and collections are of interest not only in their own right but as an insight into his mind and those of other collectors of the period.

Born in 1753 (d 1837), the son of a country builder, Soane made his way through his talent: he worked under George Dance Junior and Henry Holland; he won prizes and a travelling scholarship to Italy (1777-80) while at the Royal Academy where, in later years, he was Professor of Architecture. He held the important office of Surveyor to the Bank of England (1788-1833) for which he successfully executed the most original designs ever made for a bank. He acquired as his town house, no 12 Lincoln's Inn Fields in 1792, no 13 in 1805 as his museum and in 1824, built no 14 as a further annexe.

Interior. – The rooms are small, passages narrow, the stairs not "grand" (note the wedge shape of the stairs in no 13 following the line of the house site), but mirrors behind flying arches (library), windows on inner courts, ceilings slightly arched and decorated only with a narrow border, or, as in the breakfast room of no 12, painted to resemble an arbour, give an illusion of space and perspective. Fragments, casts and models are distributed through-out the galleries and along balustrades at ground level, while below ground, in the Crypt, are the Gothic Monk's Parlour and the Sepulchral Chamber containing the sarcophagus of Seti I (c 1392 BC), celebrated on its acquisition in 1824 by Soane with a three day recep-tion. On the first floor, past the Shakespeare recess on the stairs, in the drawing rooms and former offices are models, prints and architectural drawings (8 000 by Robert and James Adam, 12 000 by Soane), rare books and a glorious 16C illuminated ms by the Italian, Giulio Clovio.

The ground floor with dining table and chairs, desk, leather chairs, the domed breakfast room, the portrait of Soane at 75 by Lawrence, is highly evocative. His collection of pic-tures, mostly assembled on folding planes in the picture room, includes original drawings by Piranesi and 12 of Hogarth's minutely observed paintings (from which the engravings were made) of the *Election* and the *Rake's Progress*. Elsewhere are paintings by Canaletto, Reynolds and Turner.

Lincoln's Inn★★. – *Open at restricted periods, apply at the porter's lodge.*

The site belonged to the Dominicans until 1276 when they went to Blackfriars, and then to the Earl of Lincoln who built himself a large, walled mansion which he bequeathed as a residential college, or inn, for young lawyers.

The buildings. – The buildings, principally of brick with some stone decoration, date from the late 15C. The self-contained collegiate plan of intercommunicating courts is entered through a main gateway and the surroundings enhanced by beautiful and extensive gar-dens *(open noon to 2.30pm).*

The **gatehouse** on Chancery Lane, built of brick with square corner towers and a four centred arch filled with the original massive oak doors, dates from 1518. Above the arch are the arms of Henry VIII, the Earl of Lincoln and Sir Thomas Lovell.

Once through the arch, the gabled buildings immediately south of the court, known as the **Old Buildings,** are all Tudor redone in 1609 and all of brick. The **Chapel** *(open 12.30 to 2.30pm)* on an open undercroft, was rebuilt in 1620-23 and is stone faced with later 19C pinnacles and additions to the west end. The windows illustrate with arms and names men who have been benchers and treasurers since the Middle Ages: Thomas More, Thomas Cromwell, Pitt, Walpole, Newman, Canning, Disraeli, Gladstone, Asquith...

The **Old Hall,** with paired bay windows at either end, dates from 1490. Inside linenfold panelling adorns an early 17C oak screen which is notable especially for the busts carved on the end pilasters and Hogarth's painting of 1748, *St Paul before Felix.*

Towards Lincoln's Inn Fields is **New Square,** built with identical four storey ranges with broken pediments above the doors in the late 17C and incorporating in the south range an archway to Carey St, wide and ornate with differing pediments on either side.

The **New Hall** and **Library** are mid 19C of red brick, diapered in the Tudor manner.

Gray's Inn★. – *Open to the public at all times.*

The most northerly of the four Inns of Justice dates from the 14C in its foundation from the 16C in its buildings, many of which, however, have had to be renewed since the war. The main entrance is from High Holborn through the **Gatehouse** of 1688, distinguished, above the wide arch, by a bay window flanked by niches; Dryden's publisher kept a bookshop in the house for many years in the late 17C.

South Square, just inside, which, except for no 1 of 1685, has been entirely rebuilt, has at its centre an elegant bronze statue of **Francis Bacon** *(p 28),* the inn's most illustrious member, designer of the gardens *(not open to the public)* delighted in by Pepys and Joseph Addison and which many, besides Charles Lamb, consider "the best gardens of the Inns Court". The very fine wrought iron garden gateway is early 18C. The hall, which was burnt out, has been rebuilt to its 16C style with stepped gables at either end and late Perpendicular tracery and inside, Elizabethan panelling to set off the late 16C screen which was saved from the fire.

Staple Inn★. – *Holborn.* Lying just inside the limits of the City, Staple Inn was one of the Inns of Chancery, where law students passed their first year of studies. Originally the home of wool merchants, Staple Inn became a dependant of Gray's Inn and is now occupied by the Institute of Actuaries.

For the row of half timbered houses to have survived on such a site since 1586-96, when they were built, seems incredible – true they have been restored (19C) and the backs rebuilt (1937) but the character remains and gives an idea of the pre-Fire City. The west house of 2 gables, is the taller with two floors overhanging; the east range has 5 gables each marked by an oriel and again two floors overhanging. An arched entrance at the centre leads to the Inn surrounding a central courtyard at the rear. The east and west red brick ranges were erected in 1731-4 and 1757-9. Much of the rest has had to be rebuilt, including parts of the hall which dates from 1581 and possesses an original hammerbeam roof. (The nearby **Barnard's Inn,** also an Inn of Chancery, was rebuilt in the 19C and is now entirely commercial.)

St Etheldreda's (RC), Ely Place and Hatton Garden. – The church has had a chequered history. It was erected in 1291 as a chapel to the Bishop of Ely's town house (St Etheldreda was the founder of Ely Cathedral). In the 14C John of Gaunt resided in the mansion from the time the Savoy Palace was burnt down in 1381 until his death in 1399, converting it the while into a minor palace, visited by monarchs in his and later owners' lifetimes.

At the Reformation, the property passed to Protestants and in 1576, when it extended over an area bounded today by Holborn, Leather Lane, Hatton Wall and Saffron Hill, at Queen Elizabeth's command, to **Sir Christopher Hatton,** her "dancing chancellor".

Hatton, whose portion included the famous garden, built a fine house and made such improvements that when he died in 1591 he was in debt to the crown for £40 000. The third Christopher Hatton followed Charles II into exile, selling the property to builders who retained only the name as they erected slum tenements.

Ely House and St Etheldreda's, under Protestant jurisdiction since the Reformation, deteriorated, except from 1620-24 when leased by the Spanish Ambassador as his residence. By early 17C the crypt had become "a public cellar to sell drink in"; the Commonwealth made Ely Place a prison, the 75ft hall, all that remained of the house, and the church, a military hospital (1643). The precinct escaped the Fire but a century later was purchased, through the crown, by a Mr Cole who demolished the hall, built the pleasant four storey brick terrace with pilastered straight hooded doorways, which still lines the east side of Ely Place and, while retaining the church for his tenants, stripped it of such mediaeval furnishings as remained. The church's vicissitudes continued until finally, in 1873 Ely Place again came up for auction and the church was repurchased to become the first pre-Reformation shrine to be restored to the Catholics in the country.

St Etheldreda's. – Such age, so eventful a history and finally repeated bombing, have left little but the outer walls and undercroft of the 13C building. New stained glass windows depict the five English martyrs beneath Tyburn gallows and on the aisles the arms of the pre-Reformation bishops of Ely – note the 4 cardinals' hats. Against the east wall is a carved mediaeval wood reliquary.

The crypt. – The chamber has 8ft thick bare masonry walls, modern abstract single colour windows, blackened mediaeval roof timbers, a floor of London paving stones. The six supporting roof columns were placed down the chamber's centre in 19C.

Hatton Garden. – The Garden, built up in the 1680s and today the centre of diamond merchants and jewellery craftsmen, is less a place to window shop than to let the imagination play. Halfway down are the London Diamond Club (no 87, west side), a white stucco house 6 bays wide with a triangular, pedimented door and, on the opposite side, the former Charity School (no 45) dating from 1696 with an important pedimented doorway, flanked on either side by the painted figures of 17C charity schoolchildren.

Gray's Inn Rd. – The commercial road north to King's Cross is marked at its top end by three hospitals – the Eastman Dental (no 256), the Royal National Throat, Nose and Ear and the Royal Free. The last, is in a Classical style building of 1842 with additional wings on either side of 1855 and 1876, built originally as the Light Horse Volunteer Barracks.

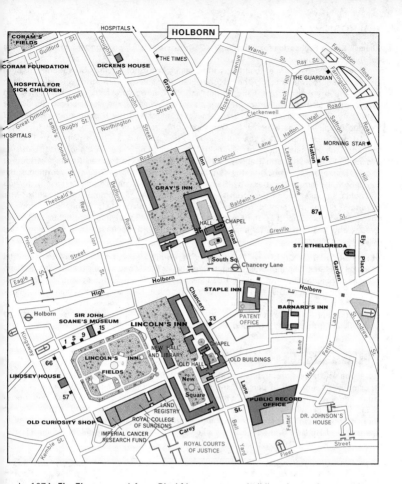

In 1974, **The Times** moved from Blackfriars to a new building, brown in appearance, strongly horizontal in line from the ribbon windows which bound it. Round brown piers which at the north end support the building, at the south advance and increase in height to form a colonnade before the plate glass curtain of the entrance hall. Inside can be seen an old press, the headstone which decorated the building in Printing House Sq and which, modified and with hands on the clock, appears on the editorial page. (There is also a maquette of the Henry Moore sundial, formerly at Blackfriars and now in Brussels.)

The other national newspapers outside the City are the *Morning Star* at 75 Farringdon Rd in a plain building of concrete and brick by E. Goldfinger erected in 1949 and *The Guardian* at 119 Farringdon Rd. .

Dickens House. – *48 Doughty St. Open Mondays to Saturdays 10am to 5pm; closed Sundays, holiday Mondays, Easter Saturday and one week at Christmas; 40p.*

Charles Dickens and his family lived in the late 18C house in Doughty St for nearly three years, from April 1837 – December 1839. During this stay, he completed *Pickwick Papers,* wrote *Oliver Twist* and *Nicholas Nickleby* besides articles, essays, sketches and letters. The house which contains portraits and mementoes, is particularly interesting for the letters and manuscripts – he had a terrible hand! – the early small paperback parts in which the novels were first issued, the prompt copies he used for his public readings and the original illustrations to his works.

Coram's Fields. – A children's park *(adults admitted only if accompanied by a child)* extends over part of the area once occupied by the hospital buildings of which a cloister remains.

In his sixties, **Thomas Coram,** a successful sea captain, trader and founder-trustee of the Colony of Georgia, was so distressed on his visits to London by the hopeless plight of infants and small children, abandoned in the streets to die, that he determined to better their lot. Campaigns, petitions to George II, determination, won a charter of incorporation in 1739 and wide support from the rich, the noble and the prominent, money to purchase 56 acres of Lambs Conduit Fields – 20 for buildings and playing fields, the remainder to provide revenue for the hospital by development.

By Coram's death at the age of 83 in 1751, the hospital was soundly established; hundreds of children had been saved. The patronage of artists, begun by Hogarth at the foundation, had already provided outstanding paintings and would continue with gifts and donations by the least and the greatest such as Handel.

In 1926 the hospital was sold and subsequently demolished. The children were moved to new buildings in Berkhampsted; in 1954 these in turn were sold and a policy of fostering inaugurated for the 2-300 children in the foundation's care. Meanwhile the Governors had bought back the site of the present museum building and adjoining Coram Children's Centre. (Coram's tomb is in St Andrew's, Holborn.)

Thomas Coram Foundation for Children. – *40 Brunswick Sq. Open Mondays to Fridays 10am to 4pm, closed public holidays; 20p.*

The 1937 neo-Georgian building with a seated bronze of Thomas Coram after Hogarth before it, incorporates notably the 18C hospital oak staircase with an open well, in which stands a jaunty peasant boy, hand on hip, and the Courtroom exactly rebuilt with dark red walls setting off the moulded ceiling and plaster enrichments, the mantelpiece with a relief of Charity Children given by Rysbrack, the oval mirror and the 8 contemporary views of London hospitals (Charterhouse by Gainsborough), framed in gilded roundels.

Of particular interest are the full length portrait of *Thomas Coram* painted in 1740 by Hogarth, the Roubiliac bust of *Handel* (both on landing), the *March of the Guards to Finchley,* 1746 by Hogarth (lobby), the portrait of *Weber,* part of the Raphaël cartoon of the *Massacre of the Innocents,* the surprising *Worthies of Great Britain* by Northcote, the full length governors' portraits by Ramsay, Benjamin Wilson, Thomas Hudson, Joshua Reynolds. In cases round the room are a Georgian silver gilt communion service, pewter porringers, Hogarth's punchbowl of blue and white Lambeth-delft, Handel's fair copy of the *Messiah* and other mss, the keyboard of the organ he presented, rare letters and autographs, the 1739 royal charter and hundreds of coins and tokens left by destitute mothers with their children.

Hospital for Sick Children. – *Gt Ormond St.* Within 20 years of Coram's foundation the Hospital for Sick Children was being erected close by. Today within a small radius there are the Homeopathic and Italian Hospitals (both 19C foundations) and the National Hospital for Nervous Diseases on the site of another 19C children's hospital. Ancilliary research institutes, clinics, departments of London University, nurses' homes, now line the streets but the primary association with children remains through the work of the almost entirely rebuilt and vastly extended Gt Ormond St.

HYDE PARK ★★ (Westminster)

Place of relaxation, free speech, fashion: since 16C, of military manœuvres and encampments, and still of parades and royal salutes; a place, since 1800, for burying pet dogs; more recently for boating, swimming and cracking the ice on Christmas morning for a dip in the **Serpentine** (Lido, 1930). A place for listening to the band, sitting out the interval in a "prom" concert, for watching birds – over 90 species have been recorded in the park and Hudson Bird Sanctuary, marked by the Jacob Epstein sculpture **Rima** (1925).

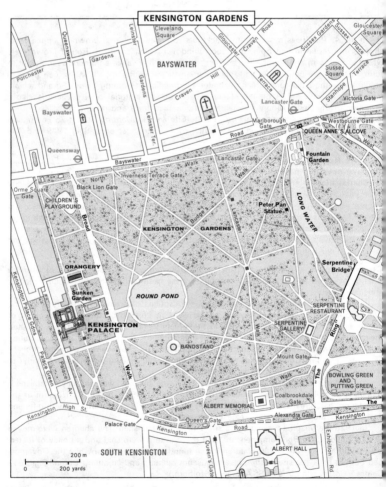

The acres were once, in Saxon times, part of the Manor of Eia which until "resumed by the King" in 1536, belonged to Westminster Abbey. Henry VIII enclosed the area and having stocked it with deer, kept it as a royal chase. In 1637 it was opened as a public park and the crowds came to watch horse-racing and other sports only to be debarred when it was sold by the Commonwealth to a private buyer who, to Pepys' indignation, charged for admission. At the Restoration the contract of sale was cancelled and the park again became public although access was restricted, since it was surrounded by a high wall which was only replaced by railings in 1825.

The activities of those who frequented and made use of the park were even more diverse in 18 and 19C than now: the last formal royal hunt was held in 1768; pits were dug along the east and north boundaries to supply clay for bricks to build the new houses of St Marylebone and Mayfair; gunpowder magazines and arms depots were sited in isolated parts; there was a large reservoir on the eastern boundary; soldiers were executed against the wall in the northeast corner — at the same time it was a fashionable carriage and riding promenade — first round the road known as the Tour, then the Ring (a small inner circle) and ultimately along the Ring Rd or along the Row **(Rotten Row)**. It was a convenient place for duels and a common spot for footpads (Horace Walpole wrote to all his friends about being robbed in the park in 1749).

Speakers' Corner is a relatively modern feature of the park, the government only having recognised the need for a place of public assembly and unfettered discussion in 1872.

The south end of the park was transformed in 1825-8 by the erection of a triple arched **screen,** crowned by a sculptured frieze, and a **triumphal arch** surmounted by a colossal equestrian statue of Wellington (Turner painting in Apsley House). Arch and screen, both designed by Decimus Burton, were intended as a royal progress from the palace to the park. In 1883 the arch, however, was moved to its present position, the statue transferred to Aldershot and replaced by a quadriga (1912). A new statue of the duke mounted on Copenhagen, guarded by a Grenadier, a Royal Highlander, a Welch Fusilier and an Inniskilling Dragoon, cast from captured guns, was placed before the entrance to Apsley House. Other monuments at Hyde Park Corner are *David leaning on Goliath's sword* (1925; Derwent Wood), the memorial of the Machine Gun Corps and the Royal Artillery War Memorial in front of St George's Hospital.

Inside the park is the 18ft, so-called, Achilles statue by Richard Westmacott cast from captured cannon and incidentally after an antique horse tamer on the Quirinal Hill, Rome and no god and said to have embarrassed the women who presented it to Wellington by its nakedness. Opposite is Byron meditating on a rock, in his own words "a worst bust".

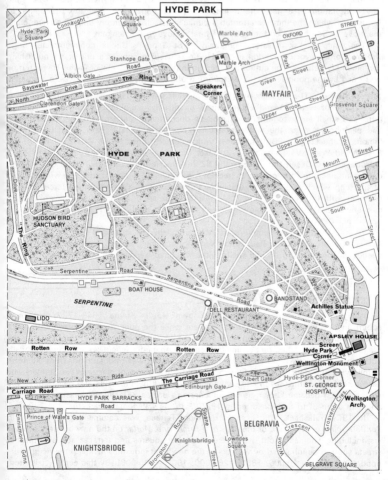

Kensington Gardens★. – The gardens, originally 20 acres and extended finally to 275, were at their prime under Queen Mary, Queen Anne and Queen Caroline, consort of George II and the Royal Gardeners, Henry Wise (portrait in the palace) and his successor in 1728, Charles Bridgman. The original style of geometric and formal wildernesses was transformed in 18C when the octagonal basin, or **Round Pond** was constructed in line east of the State Apartments. With the pond as focal point, borders were planted around it with flowers and small trees and avenues radiating north and southeast and due east to the New River, now the Serpentine and the Long Water, its northern continuation terminating in the Fountain Garden and Queen Anne's Alcove. Other features of the period which persist are the Broad Walk recently re-planted and the **Orangery★** with a massive stone centrepiece by Hawksmoor (1704). Later additions are the Edwardian sunken garden in which pleached limes surround brilliant flower beds and a long canal and, in 1912, the statue of **Peter Pan** by the Long Water.

The two parks meet where the Long Water and Serpentine are spanned by the **bridge** designed by John Rennie in 1826-8.

The most wondrous single event to have taken place in the park was, of course, the Great Exhibition of 1851 after which it resumed its role defined a century before by the Elder Pitt as one of "the lungs of London".

IMPERIAL WAR MUSEUM ★ (Lambeth Rd, Southwark)

Open daily 10am to 5.50pm; Sundays 2 to 5.50pm; closed 24, 25, 26 December, 1 January, Good Friday; Reference departments, Art, Documents, Printed Books, Film, Firearms, Photographs, Information Retrieval, Sound Records, open by appointment Monday to Friday 10am to 5pm; film shows Saturday and Sunday, weekdays (except Mondays) during holidays.

The museum covers all aspects of warfare, military and civil, allied and enemy, involving Britain and the Commonwealth since 1914 *(see also pp 43, 82 and 133)*.

History. – The museum of what Churchill termed the Age of Violence, stands on the site of a 19C madhouse. It was founded in 1917, opened in 1920 at the Crystal Palace, transferred in 1924 to South Kensington and in 1936 to the present building. This, to which the dome and giant columned portico were added by Sydney Smirke in 1846, originally comprised the present 900ft wide central area and extensive patients' wings since it was designed in 1812-15 to serve as the new Bethlem Royal Hospital or Bedlam, as it was known, which dated back to the founding of the Priory of St Mary of Bethlehem in Bishopsgate in 1247. In 1547 this had been seized by Henry VIII but then handed over to the City Corporation as a hospital for lunatics. It was transferred, after the Great Fire, to Moorfields where the inmates afforded a public spectacle. A century and a half later came the move to Southwark and in 1930 the final remove to Beckenham.

The white obelisk milestone, originally at St George's Circus, commemorates Brass Crosby, Lord Mayor of London in 1771 who refused to convict a printer for publishing parliamentary debates. The authorities thereupon imprisoned the mayor in the Tower but he was freed by the populace and press reporting of Commons' proceedings was inaugurated.

The exhibits. – The museum in no sense glorifies war but honours those who served. A wide range of weapons and equipment is on display: armoured fighting vehicles, field guns and small arms, together with models, decorations, uniforms, posters, photographs and paintings. Among the more notable exhibits are a Mark V Tank, "Ole Bill" (most famous of the London "B" type buses which carried troops to the Western Front in the First World War); V1 flying and V2 rocket bombs, a magnetic mine; the Eighth Army crusader's cross, Desert Rats' jerboa, the NZ 2nd Division fernleaf; the VC and GC. Historic documents include Montgomery's "receipt", as Churchill termed it, the typewritten sheet of foolscap which was the Instrument of Surrender of all German armed forces signed, complete with the corrected date, 4 May 1945. There are numerous mementoes of famous men and women – many unknown until all too often a final act of bravery or skill brought posthumous award.

10 000 paintings and sculptures reflect particularly the individual's lot in war: Orpen, Augustus John, Nevinson, Paul Nash, Kennington, Piper, Moore, Topolski, painted food queues, people sleeping in tube shelters, the wounded, service life, boredom...

ISLINGTON (Islington)

For south of the Angel see Clerkenwell.

Islington, "a pleasantly seeted country town" (John Strype, 1643-1737) became a suburb in 17C when the better off came there while the poor, numbering some 300 000, erected shacks and tenements on Finsbury and Moorfields when all fled the City after the Plague and the Fire. Islington became fashionable: tea gardens were set up around the wells (Clerkenwell, Sadler's Wells etc); taverns flagged the old well trodden roads from the north – following the course for centuries and until the coming of the railways, farmers and herdsmen drove cattle, sheep and swine south, resting them in fields and pens around the village, which became known as one of London's dairies. (Finally the beasts were driven down St John St to Smithfield, or, in 19/20C, to the Caledonian Market.)

In 19C, **Cruikshank,** who lived in Highbury Terrace, was commenting graphically in *London going out of Town* or the *March of Bricks and Mortar* on the new builder developers, including Thomas Cubitt, who were laying out squares and terraces and ever meaner streets soon to be inhabited by workers in the new light industries invading the neighbourhood (pop. 1801 – 10 000; 1881 – 283 000; 1901 – 335 000). By this century Islington, and the Angel in particular, had become a synonym for slums, grime and grinding poverty, hilarious, raucous cockney kids, rough pubs, the Cally Market, the gas-lit glories of Collins Music Hall.

Since the war restoration and repainting have returned terraces and squares to their precise, well groomed lines; slums have been largely replaced by 4 to 8 storey blocks of brick, reminder of the locality's past as a major London brickfield.

Islington and Highbury

The Angel. – Five main thoroughfares converge on the ancient crossroads; now awaiting building redevelopment.

Ducan Terrace, Colebrooke Row. – The brick, or brick and stucco three floor houses with shallow first floor iron balconies, built in long uninterrupted terraces (apart from postwar rebuilding in Colebrooke Row) date from 1761.

Charlton Place, a crescent and diameter complete, of 3 storey houses with rounded doorways and ground floor windows, leads off, left, to Camden Passage.

Camden Passage. – *Upper Street. (Tuesdays to Saturdays).* The quaint old alley, lined with small shops, arcades, two restaurants, a refreshing Victorian pub, and the newly built " Georgian Village ", becomes a flea market on Saturdays. On weekdays precinctual quiet returns and the small specialist shops can be searched for antique furniture, *art nouveau* ornaments in china and opalescent glass, Sèvres porcelain, heavy plate cameras, silverware, military mementoes, almost inaudible clocks.

Agricultural Hall. – *Between Upper St and Liverpool Rd.* The interest of the hall, built in 1861-2 for the annual Smithfield Show, lies not in its exterior (domed with a giant entrance arch flanked by towers with pavilion roofs) but in its interior which measures 384 × 271ft, with a 150ft span iron and glass roof. From cattle show, military tournament and revivalist meeting hall, setting in 1888 for a bullfight and from 1891-1939 of Cruft's Dog Show, it is to become a leisure centre.

Islington Green. – The shaded triangular green is pinpointed at its centre by a statue of Sir Hugh Myddelton. A plaque marks the site (north side) were from 1862 until the middle of this century, Collins Music Hall was boisterous with song.

Canonbury. – Canonbury is crossed by a network of streets and squares lined by early 19C terraced houses of which **Canonbury Square***, since it is complete and beautifully proportioned, is the prime example. Minor connecting roads such as Canonbury Grove with small country cottages overlooking a New River backwater and others, like Alwynne Rd in which later 19C villas and semi-detached houses stand in the shade of tall plane trees, add to the atmosphere. Also in Canonbury is that north London landmark the Tower.

Canonbury Tower. – *(Now leased by a repertory drama company).* A square dark red brick tower 60ft high is all that remains of the manor rebuilt in 1509 on land owned in 13C by St John's priory. In 1570 Canonbury was acquired for £2 000 as his country residence by Sir John Spencer, Lord Mayor and owner of Crosby House in Bishopsgate who largely rebuilt his out-of-town house. Buildings which now abut the tower date from the 18/19C. Of the five late 18C houses overlooking Canonbury Place, the most imposing is the pedimented two storey **Canonbury House,** with a central door framed by slender Ionic Pillars.

Highbury Place. – By 19C Highbury had fallen into the hands of undistinguished developers except for Highbury Place, 1774-9, Highbury Terrace, 1789, Highbury Crescent, 1830s, where detached and semi-detached villas had been erected for the more opulent.

Holloway

The villages of Lower and Upper Holloway merged in 19C. The high street, Holloway Rd, continued north to what, since 1813, has been known as the **Archway** after the viaduct designed by John Nash to span the road (A1) cut 80ft below through the hill. Nash's bridge endured until 1897 when it was replaced by Alexander Binnie's metal construction.

Highgate Hill is the site as it has been seen since 1473 of a hospital, the Whittington, originally a "leper spytell". On the hill is the Whittington Stone, traditionally where, in 1370 Whittington heard Bow Bells telling him to turn again for London town *(p 61)*. Sitting on a stone *(left pavement)* is a marble cat.

Pentonville Prison. – *(East side).* The prison (1840), hemmed in by neighbouring flats, fronts the main thoroughfare, the portcullis inside the arched door when it opens one of the few signs of its purpose. Most famous of those executed in Pentonville are Dr Crippen (1910) and Roger Casement (1916).

Caledonian Market Tower. – The tower, on the site of the 18C Copenhagen Tea Garden and Tavern, remains, a landmark although the general meat market closed down in 1939 and the wholesale in 1963. White, Italianate, it rises to a square loggia with a pointed roof. The farmers, drovers, butchers who thronged the market, the banks, post office, shops and offices, the vast sheds, the 10 000 head of cattle and 8-10 000 sheep and pigs that weekly from 1876-1939 arrived, driven along the two main roads or transported by rail, have all vanished to be replaced by a still life of undulating lawns, overlooked by the low red brick ranges of borough apartment blocks and the new hall of residence of the N London Polytechnic. The only other reminder of the "Cally" are the distinctive 18/19C square brick Lamb, Lion and White Horse pubs, which marked 3 of the 4 corners of the 70 acre site.

Holloway Prison. – *Parkhurst Rd (west of Caledonian Rd, north end).* Holloway, erected in 1849, a women's prison since 1903, has a mediaeval appearance complete with turreted and castellated entrance. It is scheduled for rebuilding as a hospital prison.

Michael Sobell Sports Centre. – *Hornsey Rd (junction with Tollington/Isledon Rd) open daily 9am to 11pm; Sundays 10am to 10pm; admission 10p or by membership.*

Circular, massively built of ribbed rough cast and brown tinted glass, the centre which opened in November 1973, is used weekly by 6 000 schoolchildren, 9 000 adults to practise golf, archery, cricket, fencing, boxing, judo, badminton, weight-lifting, play squash, snooker... to skate – the glass and lighting transforming the figures on the ice into a silent, Lowry-like scene. It was launched with £1 100 000 from Sir Michael Sobell for the building, equipped from a further £1 000 000 from the Variety Club of Great Britain and designed free by Richard Seifert.

KENNINGTON (Lambeth)

Map pp 5-8 (F/YZ).

Kennington and Vauxhall were transformed from a rural hinterland of marshes, manorial estates, market gardens and even vineyards, into a prosperous and, finally, densely populated inner London area by the construction of Westminster Bridge in 1750. Until that time communication with the capital had remained by cross-river wherry as it had been in 1339 in the days of the Black Prince when he was granted the manor of Kennington and Vauxhall by his father Edward III. The Prince, whose way to the river is still marked by Black Prince Rd, built a splendid palace, it is said, although nothing remains, Henry VIII having pulled it down in 1531 (plaque on NAAFI, 160 Kennington Lane). James I vested the manor in the royal heir as Duke of Cornwall which it remains to this day. By the time Prinny was traversing the manor on visits to his new Pavilion in Brighton (1815), the paved Kennington Rd provided easy access to the capital for those who preferred to live outside and, coinciding with the increased commercialisation of the riverside, tempted others to move inland. Kennington Rd, Kennington Park Rd, Kennington Lane and a network of streets which gradually grew up between them, were bordered first by Georgian houses and terraces (Kennington Rd: nos 104, 121 (1770), 150, Kennington Park Rd: nos 80 and 180), later by Victorian houses and bay windowed cottages.

Vauxhall Gardens. – The gardens, on a site north of Harleyford Rd, were greatly favoured by Evelyn and Pepys who frequently "took water to Fox-hall, to the **Spring Garden** and there walked an hour with great pleasure". In the 18C the garden of flowers, arbours, shaded walks, light refreshments and simple pleasures was modernised and provided music, sophisticated meals and pastimes, including nightly firework displays. But as the crowds thickened, knavery increased; the gardens became notorious and in the 19C they closed. **Cuper's Gardens**, where the South Bank is now, equally famous, were shorter lived.

Lambeth Palace. – *Open only occasionally for charity and groups by appointment.*

The primate, requiring a seat close, but not too close, to the crown, in 12C obtained a parcel of land on the far side of the river from Westminster, then accessible by wherry and public horseferry. Lambeth House, as it was first called, was commenced in 1262. Despite 19C additions and alterations, the mellow red brick palace, with its high, crenellated wall, 1499 gateway, 1450 Lollards' Tower, remains mediaeval in appearance. Especially notable inside are the hammerbeam roofed Great Hall, Library and Guard Room.

Greater London Fire Brigade headquarters and pier. – *Albert Embankment.* The service of 6 460 with 114 land stations, 578 fire fighting appliance vehicles, 2 fireboats, answers some 93 500 fire calls each year. *(See also p 22.)*

The Oval. – The ground was a market garden when acquired in 1845 as a cricket ground by the newly formed Surrey County Cricket Club. At the east end are iron gates erected in memory of Sir Jack Hobbs (d 1963); to the north the gasometers. Arriving by air from Europe, the ground stands out as the unequivocable landmark of south London.

Kennington Park. – Halfway along the road frontage, as the inscription in gold letters announces, is a "Model house for families erected by HRH Prince Albert". This is, in fact, a re-erection of the prototype workman's cottage commissioned by the Prince for the 1851 Exhibition. The park was enclosed in 1852 when, after centuries as common grazing and popular meeting ground, it had served as the gathering point of some 200 000 Chartists determined to march on Westminster, although in the event they didn't.

Streets and squares. – Vauxhall Bridge traffic flows into Bridgefoot, once known as Vauxhall Cross, but now increased to six main roads, one, Nine Elms Lane leading to the New Covent Garden Market (transferred from central London in 1974). Off the Albert Embankment (1866-9), Black Prince Rd includes Woodstock Court a model, two storey, precinct constructed around a fountained court (1930) and **Lambeth Walk,** grass verged and overlooked by new flats, far removed from the aged housing and cockney gusto of the war time song. Kennington Park Rd has a very long, late 18C, terrace down its east side (91-165), appealing as a unit and for its entrances (no 125); on its west side Cleaver St (beside the City and Guilds of London Art School) leads to the large, late Georgian, **Cleaver Sq.** Off Kennington Lane is **Courtenay Sq,** in which around spring flowering trees, two storey 1837-9 brick houses are delightfully transformed by white painted, summerhouse shaped, canopies supported on ironwork trellis pillars before each modest front door. Kennington Rd is notable for two long terraces, the first early 19C, centrally pedimented with sash windows and door frames painted white, doors apple green, the other (nos 121-143), with more individuality, dating from 1770s (LMH settlement: no 131).

The village of Kensington was for centuries manorial, with a few large houses at the centre of fields growing root vegetables for London. It increased slowly from small houses lining the main road to squares and tributary streets as estates and separate parcels of land were sold. Among the famous mansions were Nottingham House later Kensington Palace, Camden House, Notting Hill House later Aubrey House, Holland Park House and, on the site of the Albert Hall, Gore House, until 1823 the home of William Wilberforce and for 12 years from 1836, the residence of "the gorgeous" Lady Blessington whose circle included poets, novelists, artists, journalists, French exiles: Wellington, Brougham, Landseer, Tom Moore, Bulwer Lytton, Thackeray, Dickens, Louis Napoleon...

■ KENSINGTON PALACE★★ *(Map p 100)*

Entrance: NE corner. Open 10am (2pm Sundays) to 6pm (5pm February and October, 4pm November to January); closed 1 January, Good Friday, 24, 25, 26 December; 15p.

"The house is very noble, tho not greate, the Gardens about it very delicious". — Since its purchase in 1689 by William III, Kensington Palace has passed through three phases: under the House of Orange it was the monarch's private residence with **Wren** as principal architect; under the early Hanoverians it was designated as a royal palace with **William Kent** in charge of alterations, particularly painted redecoration; since 1760 it has been a residence for members of the royal family other than the sovereign.

"Kensington is ready" wrote Queen Mary to her husband, William, in July 1690 and, disliking Whitehall, she moved in. The house was not ready, nor would it be free of builders and carpenters until 1702 when it had grown from an early 17C Jacobean house, rebuilt in 1661, to the rambling mansion around three courts which it is today. Throughout Wren kept to a style befitting a house — it was known as Kensington House in 17 and 18C — a modest two, two and a half storeys in red brick beneath slate roofs.

Decoration was limited to the finely carved William and Mary monogram in the hood above the entrance to the Queen's Staircase and the royal arms on the pediment of the turreted clock tower. When Hawksmoor, working for Wren in 1695-6, designed the south front, the style was embellished only by the addition of a central attic screen topped by Portland stone vases. Subsequent external modifications were of a minor character: a Georgian doorway acceding to the Queen's Staircase, a portico on the west front.

The **State Apartments** are approached up the Queen's Staircase designed by Wren.

The Queen's Apartments: Gallery, Closet, Dining and Drawing Rooms, Bedroom. — The 84ft gallery is rich in carving, with cornice and doorheads by **William Emmett** and sumptuous surrounds to the gilt Vauxhall mirrors above the fireplace in the gallery by Grinling Gibbons in 1691. Portraits in the rooms are personal: *Peter the Great* in armour by Kneller in commemoration of his visit in 1698, *William III* as king and Prince of Orange, *Queen Mary, Anne Hyde* by Lely and in the adjoining closet where the final quarrel (1710) took place between "Mrs Freeman" and "Mrs Morley", *Sarah Duchess of Marlborough* by Kneller. In the Dining Room there is a painting of the ten year old Princess Mary as *Diana* by Lely, in the Drawing Room of *Queen Anne* in profile by Kneller, as she appears on coins and medals. Kneller also painted the first Royal Gardener, *Henry Wise.* The furniture includes an 18C mahogany cabinet (gallery), a late 17C inlaid cabinet, 17-18C Oriental porcelain and a fine Thomas Tompion barometer of *c* 1695, one of many possessed by William III who was a chronic asthmatic (drawing room). In the bedroom are a state bed of James II and an ornate, mid 17C, cabinet with Boulle mounts, marquetry and semiprecious stone inlays.

Privy and Presence Chambers, King's Staircase and Gallery. — The lofty rooms designed by Colen Campbell in 1718-20 for George I, bear William Kent's strong decorative imprint. The **Privy Chamber,** above busts of distinguished 17-18C scientists and David Garrick, blue and white Oriental porcelain and Mortlake tapestries of the months, has an allegorical ceiling of George I as Mars; the **Presence Chamber,** a red and blue on white ceiling in the Pompeian manner (the earliest in England and later popularised by Adam). Remaining from 17C are the cornice and the Grinling Gibbons pearwood overmantel.

The **King's Grand Staircase,** built by Wren in 1689, was first altered in 1692-3 when the Tijou iron balustrade was incorporated and for George I by Kent who covered walls and ceiling with illusionist paintings including a dome and gallery of contemporary courtiers.

The King's Gallery. — The gallery which extends almost the length of the south front was intended as the setting for the greatest pictures in the royal collection and decoration was, therefore, limited to an elaborately carved cornice, enriched window surrounds and the practical and ornamental wind-dial connected from its position over the fireplace to a vane on the roof. The most notable pictures now are the large *Jupiter and Antiope* by Rubens, van Dyck's *Cupid and Psyche* and Allori's *Judith with the Head of Holofernes.*

Although the 19C **Victorian Rooms** were redecorated by Queen Mary, who was herself born in the bedroom, all else was personally possessed and epitomises Queen Victoria and her family — furniture, inlaid pieces, ornaments, portraits, photographs, busts, dried flowers under glass domes, beading, tasselling, commemorative china... The **Council Chamber** at the far end of the east front, contains mementoes notably of the 1851 Exhibition including the famous picture of the opening, crowds in the Crystal Palace and exhibits — a garish jewel casket with inlaid portraits of the royal family, a massive carved Indian ivory throne and footstool. Only the ceiling of arabesques, figures and medallions remains of Kent's Baroque decoration in the **King's Drawing Room** but in the **Cupola Room,** high and square with a vault patterned in blue and gold, are trophies and gilded Classical statues and busts divided by fluted pilasters and a colossal marble chimneypiece.

■ KENSINGTON VILLAGE *(Map pp 5-8)*

In 1846 when Thackeray and his daughters moved into a house in Young St, the eldest described the High St as "a noble highway, skirted by beautiful old houses with scrolled iron gates", while Thackeray himself noted that there were "omnibuses every two minutes". Within a few years the population was to multiply from 70 to 120 000 and shops extend the full length of the High St. Today the same street, second only to Oxford St among the country's prime retailing locations, is bright with chain stores and run of the mill small shops. On the north side of the road (nos 26-40) is the Antique Hypermarket, a rich store-house of polished Victorian jewellery, 18 and 19C silver, china, porcelain. Below are larger pieces, particularly furniture, and a pullman car at the back where one can get "a refreshing cup of tea".

Kensington Palace Gardens and Green. — The private avenue, guarded at either end, is now the preserve almost exclusively of ambassadorial residences and embassies of which the most remarkable is the modern Czechoslovakian complex at the top, Notting Hill end. The old houses, dating back to mid 19C when the palace kitchen gardens were sold and the site developed are, to varying degrees, Italianate in style but all sufficiently opulent for the avenue to have been given the sobriquet, Millionaire's Row.

Kensington Church St. — The street of clothes and ornament, oriental prints and better antique shops, is joined, from the west at its lower end by a winding country style lane bordered by trees and bookshops and small houses; higher up are modern blocks and the individual houses large and small, erected on the former Camden House estate. At the street's southwest corner on the High St, approached through an unusual vaulted cloister is the parish church of **St Mary Abbots**. The dedication dates back to 11/12C but the present church with a towering 278ft high spire, is 19C Early English style rebuilding.

Kensington Sq. — The square, one of the oldest in London with houses dating from 17-19C is as varied in design as the people who have lived in it. The two oldest houses are nos 11 and 12 in the southeast corner where a cartouche over the door announces the owners as Archbishop Herring 1737, Talleyrand 1792-4 and previously the Duchess Mazarin 1692-8, Henrietta Mancini, niece of the cardinal. Other residents have been Sir Hubert Parry (no 17), John Stuart Mill (no 18), Mrs Patrick Campbell (no 33).

Holland House and Park. — *Open dawn to dusk.* The east wing and George VI Hostel by Sir Hugh Casson serve as a youth hostel, the courtyard before the restored central range as a stage for a summer theatre *(June to August)*. The 18C garden ballroom is now a restaurant. The woodland has been re-established and the gardens replanted after long neglect.

It is 100-200 since the house was in its heyday and approaching 400 since Sir Walter Cope, City merchant and courtier built the first large house in the scattered village of Kensington. The mansion, characterised by Dutch gables, and known as Cope's Castle, was lavishly furnished, equipped with a library and soon became a place of entertainment for king and court. Advanced wings on either side of the central range, were added by Cope's daughter whose husband, in 1624, for soldierly and other services was created Earl Holland. The tradition of hospitality was maintained in the 2nd earl's time and extended when his widow married **Joseph Addison**. In mid 18C the politician, Henry Fox, bought Holland House and was himself created Baron Holland. He was rich, a spendthrift and corrupt; he knew everyone, entertained lavishly and fathered, as his second son, **Charles James Fox**, who continued to frequent the house when it passed to his nephew, 3rd Baron Holland, politician, writer, literary patron and with his wife, the last great host of Holland House. Among those who dined and visited frequently were the Prince Regent, Sheridan, Wilberforce, Canning, William Lamb the future Lord Melbourne, Byron, Thomas Moore, Talleyrand, Louis Napoleon, Macaulay (whose own house, Holly Lodge, stood on the site now occupied by Queen Elizabeth College), William IV, and almost the last visitor, Prince Albert — little wonder that Sydney Smith in a bread and butter letter to his hostess had once written "I do not believe all Europe can produce as much knowledge wit and worth as passes in and out of your door".

Commonwealth Institute★. — *Kensington High St. Open daily 10am to 5.30pm. Sundays 2.30 to 6pm; closed 1 January, Good Friday, 24, 25, 26 December. Restaurant, library and resource centre (appt desirable); school's service (by prior booking — dining hall, activities room, etc.); shop.*

The striking building lying back from the main road, with its 5 peaked, green copper roof, on glass curtain walls, was opened by the Queen in 1962. Sixty-nine years before her great, great, grand-mother, Queen Victoria, had performed a similar ceremony in a Renais-

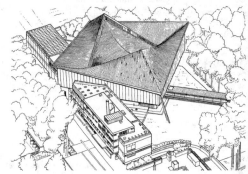

(After photograph by Aerofilms)

Commonwealth Institute.

sance style building equally outstanding in its time, the Imperial Institute of which only the Queen's Tower remains *(p 109)*. Inside wide circular galleries on three levels present an uncomplicated and colourful view of the Commonwealth with the aid of backdrops such as the Snowy Mountains and artefacts from Nigerian house posts to a Manx cross, a model of the Brunei Saifuddin Mosque in its water village, a festival dragon from Hong Kong...

Leighton House★. – *12 Holland Park Rd. Open weekdays 11am to 5pm; closed Sundays, Good Friday, Easter Saturday, holiday Mondays, 25, 26 December.*

Lord Leighton (1830-96) Victorian painter supreme, "high priest of the cult of eclectic beauty" as he has been described, remains most originally reflected in the house which he built for himself in 1866. In it the High Victorian art of the domestic rooms contrasts with ceramic tiles from the Middle East and others in brilliant blues by **William de Morgan** on the hall and stairs and even more exotically in his creation of an **Arab Hall.** This has a mosaic floor around a cool fountain and, on the walls, sets of 13, 16 and 17C tiles from Rhodes, Damascus and Cairo, tiles bearing inscriptions from the Koran, flowers and birds, brought back from their travels by Leighton himself and his friends, including Sir Richard Burton.

At the west end of Kensington is Earl's Terrace, a uniform brick range of large houses of 1800-10 overlooking a slip road parallel to the High St and, just behind, **Edwardes Sq** with west and east ranges of more modest 3 storey houses built between 1811-20 as a single undertaking – even to the balcony, garden and square ironwork. In contrast, in the square's southeast corner stands a robust Victorian pub, the Scarsdale, "established in 1837". Just south again is Pembroke Sq with Georgian ranges on three sides, matching iron balconies and, again, a pub in the southeast corner.

■ ADDITIONAL SIGHTS *(Map pp 5-8)*

Brompton Oratory. – *Open daily 6.30am to 9pm, Sundays 6am to 8.30pm.*

With a Renaissance style exterior, a ribbed and lanterned dome, and an interior lofty with marble pillars, a cupola and saucer domes, a nave so wide as to be a hall in itself, dependant chapels and Classical statues of the saints, the church appears crystalised much in the aspect it must have had when Cardinal Manning preached at the official opening in April 1884.

In front of the building is a characteristic monument to Cardinal Newman (d 1890).

Institut Français. – The institute buildings although in *art nouveau* style, date only from 1939; the number of students enrolled in the Institut and Lycée respectively is 1 250 and 2 250 of who many are English. The French community in London now numbers 20 000.

Baden-Powell House. – The house built in 1961, signalled outside by a bareheaded statue of B-P, is primarily a hostel for visiting scouts. There is a memorial exhibition to the founder inside which can be viewed by appointment.

Michelin House. – The 1910 building is a genuine example of the *art nouveau* style. The decoration is grandiose, the theme on the tiled front being the initial M and tyres which appear in the patterning and, three dimensionally, as supports to the gable containing the upper area of the colossal central window. On the sides and at the rear, is a **frieze** in which each panel illustrates a turn of the century motor car rally – note the strokes to indicate speed!

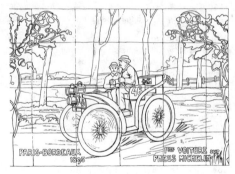

Michelin House: ceramic panel, Sloane Ave.

Royal Marsden and Brompton Chest Hospitals. – The Royal Marsden Hospital was built in 1859, the Brompton in 1844-54. Attached to the first is the Cardiothoracic Institute and to the second the Institute of Cancer Research (including the Chester Beatty Research Institute), both part of London University.

South of the Old Brompton Rd there are 19C artisan cottages in Elm Row and its immediate vicinity, still surrounded by small gardens brilliant with flowers throughout the summer, and a typical mid 19C development of tall houses, cream stuccoed with advanced pillared porches in Onslow Gardens and the local maze of intersecting roads. Of greater well-being are the fine Cubitt built houses in **The Boltons,** white stuccoed in a mandorla crescent layout.

Brompton Cemetery. – The vast necropolis, founded in the mid 19C, contains hundreds of neo-Gothic, Egyptian, Baroque style, tombs.

Portobello Rd. – *Notting Hill Gate. Market: all day Saturdays.*

The winding road, once a cart-track through the fields from the Notting Hill turnpike, comes unhurriedly to life on Saturdays as people arrive to search the shop tables and stalls between the Chepstow Villas crossroads and Elgin Crescent. Victoriana and later silver and chinaware, a stamp stall, small items, provide the interest; the approach past 19C houses with colourful front gardens, the lack of traffic, Wally, softly grinding a peg-leg organ as his brilliantly coloured macaw perches on his arm, the milling pubs at every corner, create the atmosphere.

■ MUSEUMS and COLLEGES (Kensington)

The Great Exhibition Inheritance. — The exhibition of 1851, the first in the international field and initially bitterly and often spitefully opposed in parliament, was conceived, planned and opened in less than two years so steadfast was Prince Albert. Joseph Paxton's glasshouse or **Crystal Palace,** covered 19 acres in Hyde Park. It was tall enough to enclose the giant elms on the site, capable of rapid erection through the use of prefabricated unit parts and was beautiful to boot! Inside were the products of 13 937 exhibitors demonstrating man's inventiveness and 19C British achievement in particular. It was an exhibition which excited everyone: Queen Victoria, Wellington and some 6 039 195 others and it made a net profit of just under £200 000.

The Crystal Palace was dismantled and re-erected at Sydenham (burnt down 1936); the financial profit Prince Albert proposed should be spent in establishing a great educational centre in south Kensington by buying land on which have become established the world famous museums and colleges to be found there today. In the event 86 acres were bought and there began a sequence of construction still in progress.

1856:	William Cubitt erects a utilitarian glass and iron building known as the "Brompton Boilers" along the Cromwell Rd to house former 1851 exhibits and various art collections.
1861-1863:	Commemorative Exhibition statue erected (now sited behind Albert Hall).
1861:	Prince Albert dies; the Albert Memorial (1864-72) erected through national appeal. 1876 unveiled.
1862:	International Exhibition held on site now occupied by Natural History Museum.
1867-1871:	Albert Hall built on site of Lady Blessington's Gore House as national memorial to Prince Consort, following a further public appeal.
1867-1871:	Huxley Building erected, Exhibition Road (originally as the Science Schools).
1873-1880:	Natural History Museum.
1875:	National School of Music later (1883) Royal College of Music founded in building, since 1903 the Royal College of Organists.
1881-1884:	City and Guilds College; rebuilt 1962 as Imperial College extensions.
1883:	Royal College of Music (transferred from previous building).
1887-1893:	Imperial Institute. Buildings demolished 1957-65, save for existing central tower, to assist expansion of Imperial College.
1899-1909:	Victoria and Albert Museum.
1909-1913:	Royal School of Mines (now part of Imperial College).
1914:	Science Museum.
1933-1935:	Geological Museum.
1960-1964:	Royal College of Art beside Albert Hall, first stage of a development to centralise College buildings scattered in south Kensington.

Albert Memorial★. — Proverbial as the epitome of mid-Victorian taste and sentiment, the memorial which stands at the summit of 4 wide flights of granite steps, was designed by Sir George Gilbert Scott as a neo-Gothic spire of 175ft and, as such, ornamented with mosaics, pinnacles and a cross. A 14ft bronze figure of the Prince Consort sits at the centre surrounded by allegorical statues and a frieze of 169 named portrait figures of architects, artists, composers, poets.

Royal Geographical Society (f 1830). — Against the outer wall are statues of Scott and Livingstone. The many gabled brick house was designed in 1874 by Norman Shaw. The map room *(open Monday to Friday 9.30am to 5.30pm)* contains 30 000 old and historic maps besides the largest modern private collection in Europe.

Down Exhibition Rd on the east side is the Mormons' Hyde Park Chapel (1960) with a needle spire of gilded bricks.

Albert Hall. — The round hall was designed by Capt Fowke, a Royal Engineer. Nearly ¼ mile in circumference, built of red brick with a shallow glass and iron dome, it is the foil in shape and ornament to the memorial since its only decoration is an upper frieze of figures illustrating the Arts and Sciences. Reunions, pop and jazz sessions, exhibitions, boxing, political meetings, conferences and concerts, particularly the eight week series of **Promenade Concerts,** fill the hall with up to 7 000 people at a time.

The Albert Memorial.

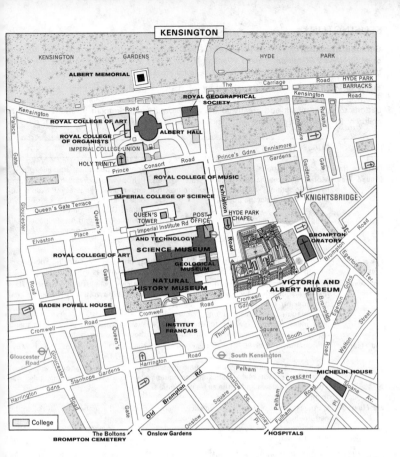

Royal College of Art. — The Darwin Building, designed by Cadbury-Brown with eight floors of studios and workshops is built of purple brown brick, dark concrete and glass. It dates from 1961 and, uniquely in such a district, is without applied adornment.

Royal College of Organists. — The small building, 4 floors tall, 3 bays wide, designed by another RE, Lt H H Cole, in 1875 almost disappears beneath an ornate decoration (F W Moody) of chocolate brown panels patterned in cream, a frieze of putti carrying musical instruments, garlands incorporating the VR monogram around the door.

Royal College of Music. — The college is an architect's building of 1883, as opposed to an RE's; Sir Arthur Blumfield, designed in dark red brick and grey slate, stepped and decorated gables between pavilion roofed towers and finally quartered his construction with pepper pot turrets after the French style. Inside is the highly prized **Museum of Instruments,** including the Donaldson Collection of 300 instruments, Handel spinet and Haydn clavichord. *Museum open by appt only: Mondays, Wednesdays in term: 10p.*

Imperial College of Science and Technology★. — The schools which go to make up Imperial College, extend from either side of the Royal College of Music in Prince Consort Rd south to the Science Museum, apart from the small enclaves occupied by Holy Trinity Church (1909 replacement of a chapel of 1609 itself a rebuilding of the chapel of a former leper hospital), the Edwardian, Post Office Building and the Underground exit. With the exception of the neo-Georgian 1909-13 Royal School of Mines of stone with an apsed entrance flanked by giant sculptures, the buildings date from the mid'50s. They are vast but homogeneous in proportion and human in scale, cleaned lined, in single, right-angled and hollow square ranges, surrounding interconnected quadrangles; the fabric, in general, is glass supported on steel or concrete. From one of the quadrangles, guarded at its foot by a pair of lions, rises the old Queen's Tower, 280ft high, brick and stone below, green copper and gold turreted at the summit, last relic of Colcutt's Imperial Institute (1887-93), erected following the Colonial Exhibition of 1886; history has been neatly and imaginatively preserved in the midst of the present.

Geological Museum★. — *Exhibition Rd. Open daily 10am to 6pm, Sundays 2.30pm; closed 1 January, Good Friday, 24, 25, 26 December. Library daily 10am to 4.30pm; closed 1 to 2pm Saturdays.*

The museum developed as a result of the Geological Survey of Great Britain of 1835 when specimens were accumulated which in 1935, the centenary of the Survey (now the Institute of Geological Studies, Princes' Gate), were established in the present building. There are four displays on the ground floor: The Story of the Earth, Treasures of the Earth and Britain before Man, complete in themselves and also appetizers, respectively for the top and first floors, where economic geology is demonstrated as fuel, building and fission material and Britain is presented systematically in 18 areas by maps, specimens, relief models, which show everything from the soil in your garden to the layers beneath it. The most concentrated ground floor display is of gemstones — diamonds, rubies, sapphires, garnets, emeralds in their original form and after cutting.

KENSINGTON★★

Science Museum★★★. – *Exhibition Rd. Open daily including holiday Mondays 10am to 6pm, Sundays 2.30 to 6pm; closed 1 January, Good Friday, 24, 25, 26 December. Library open daily (except holiday weekends) 10am to 5.30pm. Passage to the Natural History Museum.*

Where to begin? – This factory-laboratory of man's continuing invention extends over 7 acres; there are innumerable working models, handles to pull, telephones to listen to, buttons to push, which add greatly to the interest and enlightenment of adults as well as children. Broadly from the main entrance each of the 5 floors exhibits:

FLOOR	SUBJECTS	NAMED OBJECTS
Entrance Hall	Special exhibitions; publications	Foucault pendulum (model).
Ground Floor	Motive and mechanical power (water wheels, hydraulic turbines); steam boilers, turbines; hot air, gas, oil and electric power	Pelton wheel; Watt beam pumping and rotative engines; Parson's turbine and dynamo; Lenoir, Akroyd, Stuart, Diesel engines.
	Weighing and measuring	Standards bearing royal ciphers; million volt impulse generator.
	Transport (road and rail): roads, bridges, tunnels; fire engines	1888 Benz, 1734 fire engine.
Lower Ground	Children's gallery; firemaking, locks, 19C domestic appliances	Byrant & May firemaking appliances, Temple of Vesta fire machine.
1st Floor	Hand and machine tools; iron and steel; glass; textile machinery; sewing machines; printing, papermaking, typewriting machines, agriculture; gas manufacture, distribution; meteorology	Bramah, Maudslay, Roberts, Nasmyth, Whitworth's, Arkwright's machines.
	time measurement – water to quartz, crystal clocks; map-making, surveying, astronomy	Wells Cathedral clock, Ramsden's theodolite, star dome.
2nd Floor	Photography (1835-1976), cinematography	Niepce, Daguerre, Fox Talbot, Muybridge, Marey, le Prince, Edison.
	Chemistry, structure of matter, atomic physics and nuclear power; mathematics and computers – navigation (at sea and in the air); ships, docks, diving	Cockroft and Walton's apparatus; cyclotron; Harwell atomic pile.
3rd Floor	Magnetism and electricity, acoustics, thermal instruments, optics; early physics; geophysics; telecommunications, space exploration, aeronautics, aero-engines	George II's collection of scientific instruments; Kater's pendulum; Baird's receiving set, Watson Watt's, radar apparatus.

If massive beams pumping up and down, pulses and radio waves, computer art, printing machinery, mean nothing, select a subject and look at it as you would in an encyclopaedia: time (1st floor), public transport (ground floor), musical boxes (3rd floor), shapes in the form of mathematical models, polyhydra (2nd floor) or, mesmerised by Foucault's pendulum (entrance) stand and stare, literally, at the earth's turning.

Natural History Museum★★. – *Cromwell Rd. Open daily 10am to 6pm, Sundays 2.30 to 6pm; closed 1 January, Good Friday, 24, 25, 26 December. Passage to Science Museum.*

History and the building. – The museum has accumulated about 40 million specimens; the collections continue to grow by some 350 000 specimens a year of which 250 000 are insects. Such increase would not have surprised **Hans Sloane** whose own collection, beginning with plant specimens from Jamaica soon outgrew his house, the house next door, the accommodation at Chelsea Manor. The BM, founded in 1753 as a result of his bequest, trebled in size almost immediately and continued to expand so that by 1860, despite new wings and annexes, the galleries were chaotic and quantities of objects were unable to be shown. It was decided to separate natural history, the nucleus of Sloane's original collection. Land was available in Kensington but it took 20 years before the new museum was ready to be opened to the public (1880). The building (apart from a recent departmental annexe) expresses the solemn reverence and sense of mission in public education of the 19C; Alfred Waterhouse, the architect, took as his model 11/12C Rhineland Romanesque cathedral architecture, producing a vast symmetrical building, 675ft from end pavilion to end pavilion with, at the centre, twin towers 190ft high above a rounded, recessed entrance, ornate with decorated covings and pillars. The fabric is washed out terracotta pink and pale slate-blue; everywhere are lifelike carvings of animals, birds, fishes.

The collections. – Elephants, rhinoceroses, hippopotami in the central hall announce immediately that despite the cathedral door, this is the Natural History Museum. The plan is simple: to the left are the species alive today, to the right the extinct – except at the top where the plant gallery is preceded by a cross section of a **Douglas Fir** which was 25 years old when Edward III died in 1377. On the *first floor,* up the grand staircase, there are mammals to the left and rocks, minerals, gemstones and meteorites to the right.

On the *ground floor* to the right, fossils range in size and complexity from bacteria to dinosaurs; to the left, by the entrance, birds are systematically displayed through their physiology and by classification so that one can see together a single group in all its amazing variety of size, adaptation and plumage. At the end is a room of British birds set in their habitat and just before, a brilliant gallery of insects (including butterflies). Far back on the left side is the **Whale Hall,** a place once seen always remembered with its colossal suspended skeletons and models and, nearer the entrance the new **Human Biology Hall** with modern displays skillfully dissembling the complexity of the subject.

In 1938, Baron Rothschild bequeathed the **Tring Zoological Museum** (Herts) to the nation, where mammals, and insects and the major bird collections are now housed.

Victoria and Albert Museum★★★. – *Page 162.*

■ THE ROYAL BOTANIC GARDENS★★★

Open daily from 10am (except Christmas and New Year's Days) to between 4pm in midwinter, 8pm in midsummer; museums open at 10am, houses at 11am, close at the latest at 4.50pm weekdays, 5.50pm Sundays. Photography and sketching in the houses restricted: apply to the director. Admission: 1p.

There are a refreshment pavilion (Pagoda area), tea bar (Orangery – river direction), drinking fountains, numerous toilets (see map). A limited number of invalid chairs are available for hire (5p for 3 hours); apply in advance to the director.

Kew Gardens are pure pleasure. Colour and the architecture of the trees, singly – the weeping willow, the stone pine – or in groups, delight at all seasons. The layman will spot common-place flowers and shrubs and gaze on delicate exotics, gardeners check their knowledge against the labels for this 300 acre garden is the superb offshoot of laboratories (under the Ministry of Agriculture) engaged in the identification of plants and plant material from all parts of the world, and in economic botany. The curatorship of the biggest herbarium in the world, a wood museum, a botanical library of more than 100 000 volumes and the training (3 year course) of student gardeners are also within the establishment's province.

The botanical theme of the gardens, as opposed to the purely visual, began under Princess Augusta who was personally responsible for the inauguration of a botanic garden south of the Orangery and the enlargement of the gardens from seven to more than 100 acres. On moving into the White House *(see below)*, Prince Frederick had employed William Kent not only to rebuild the house but to landscape the garden. On the prince's death in 1751, the Dowager Princess of Wales, guided by the Earl of Bute, a considerable botanist if no politician, appointed William Aiton as head gardener (1759-93) and William Chambers as architect (1760). Under Aiton, a Scot who had worked at the Chelsea Physic Garden, his son who succeeded him (1793-1841), and Sir Joseph Banks (d 1820), voyager, distinguished botanist, naturalist, biologist, and finally director, plants began to be especially collected from all parts of the world for research and cultivation. By 1789, 5 500 species were growing in the gardens.

In 1772 on the death of Princess Augusta, George III combined the Kew and Richmond Lodge gardens and had them landscaped by "Capability" Brown. The Palace, Orangery, Queen's Cottage, Pagoda remain as colophon to the royal epoch.

The Gardens. – Major plantings and flowering seasons are indicated on the map overleaf, colour keyed to draw your attention to flowers in areas possibly not previously explored.

Plant Houses. – *For opening times see above. The Alpine House opens seasonally 10am to noon and 1pm to closing time, the Tropical Waterlily House in summer only.*

The Palm House★★. – The house was designed by **Decimus Burton** and the engineer, Richard Turner, as a purely functional building – it measures 362ft in length, is 33ft high in the wings and 62ft at the centre. It is constructed entirely of iron and glass, has curved roofs throughout, took four years to erect (1844-1848) and "came off" in a way no similar building, including the 1851 Crystal Palace, has done before or since. Inside are palms and a variety of tropical trees and shrubs (coffee, cocoa, bananas); outside roses – mostly hybrid teas – in a formal garden watched over by the Queen's Beasts (stone replicas of those designed by James Woodward to stand outside Westminster Abbey at the coronation in 1953).

Temperate House★. – The house, again by Burton, but 20 years later and including crested ridges, octagons, wings, ornamentation, epitomises Victorian conservatory construction. Inside note the camellias, rain forest and dragon trees.

Aroid, Tropical Waterlily, Conservatory and T-Range houses present the exotic and beautiful, jungle, statue-like succulents and cacti by turn.

KEW: A ROYAL RESIDENCE

Early mansions. – Once upon a time there was a palace at Richmond which included in its domain the Old Deer Park, guarded by a keeper's lodge; this (on the site occupied since 1769 by Kew Observatory) was rebuilt and in 1721, sold to the future George II and his consort, Queen Caroline who laid out around the renamed **Richmond Lodge,** elaborate gardens in which she included typical 18C ornamental statues and follies.

In 1730, Frederick, Prince of Wales, although on unfriendly terms with George II leased a house only a mile away. The residence, the **White House,** "an old timber house" built in the late 17C, was redeemed in the diarist Evelyn's eyes only by the "garden (which) has the choicest fruit of any plantation in England". Frederick and Augusta rebuilt the house (known also as Kew House) on a site now marked by a sundial, in which the princess remained after Frederick's death in 1751, devoting herself particularly to the garden.

King George III (1760-1820) and Queen Charlotte found with an increasing family – they had 15 children – that Richmond Lodge was too small, and on Princess Augusta's death in 1772 moved into the White House. This also rapidly proved too small and, in 1773, the **Dutch House** was leased for the young Prince of Wales (the future George IV) and his brother as well as other houses on Kew Green.

Not satisfied, however, George III commissioned **James Wyatt** to design a new "Gothic" enterprise to be sited on the riverbank. The **Castellated Palace,** as it was known, was never completed, but like the White House was demolished, leaving alone of all the cousin-hood of royal residences, just the Dutch House or Kew Palace, which was occupied, until her death in 1818, by Queen Charlotte. In 1899 it was opened as a museum.

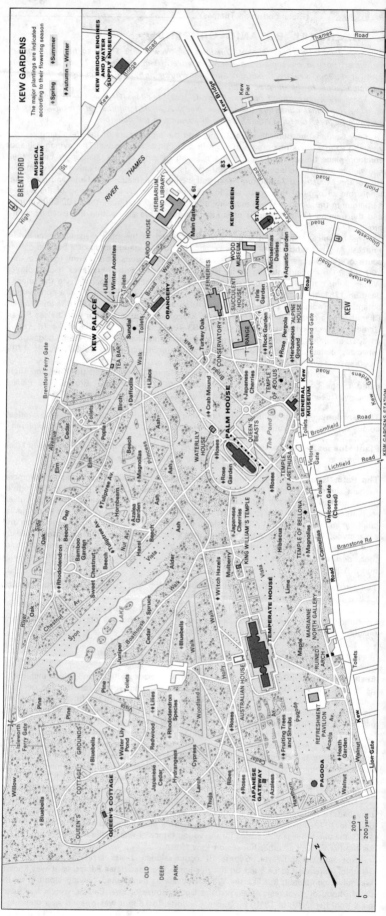

KEW GARDENS

The major plantings are indicated according to their flowering season

◆Spring ◆Summer
◆Autumn ◆Winter

Kew Palace★★ (or Dutch House). – *Open 11am (2pm on Sundays) to 6pm; closed from 29 September to Easter Sunday; 15p.*

The dark red brick building immediately recognisable by its Dutch attic gables and notable for the richness and variety of the brick laying, cutting and moulding, was built by Samuel Fortrey, a prosperous London Merchant of Dutch parentage, who commemorated his house's construction in a monogram and the date, 1631 over the front door.

At the rear is the **Queen's Garden,** a formal design of pleached alleys of laburnum and hornbeam, *parterres,* a gazebo and including only 17C plants.

Interior. – The interior is that of a small country house of George III's time. Downstairs the rooms are all panelled: the King's Dining Room in white 18C style, the Breakfast Room in early 17C style and the Library Ante-Room in re-set 16C linenfold. Upstairs, apart from the white and gold Queen's Drawing Room, formally set out with lyreback chairs for a musical evening, the rooms are wallpapered with new paper printed from the delightful original blocks and intimate with family portraits by Gainsborough and Zoffany. In the

king's rooms note the embossed terracotta paper in the wig closet and in the bedroom a russet red paper patterned in dark green with matching hangings. Downstairs in the Pages' Waiting Room, is an exhibition of minor royal possessions – silver filigree rattles, alphabet counters, snuff boxes, lists of Prince Frederick's gambling debts, the queen's code of bell pulls...

Other buildings and monuments. – Under Princess Augusta, William Chambers set about constructing typical 18C garden follies: temples, a ruined arch, an **Orangery★** (1761) and a **Pagoda★** (1761), a garden ornament *(not open)* 163ft and ten storeys high, still the climax to a long vista.

The Queen's Cottage. – *Open summer weekends and bank holidays only.*

Two storeyed beneath a thatched roof, typical of "rustic" buildings of the period (1770) but designed, in this case, purely as a picnic house by Queen Charlotte.

The **Main Gates** are by Decimus Burton (1848 – the lion and unicorn on the original gate are now above gates in Kew Rd). The **General Museum** by the pond, dates from 1857-8, when it replaced the original Museum of Economic Botany, the first in the world in 1847. The **Japanese Gateway★** was imported for the Anglo-Japanese Exhibition of 1912.

(After photograph, Pitkin Pictorials)

The Pagoda.

■ KEW VILLAGE

Kew Bridge. – Three span stone bridge *(p 152).*

St Anne's. – The nave and chancel were constructed of brick in 1710-14 on the site of a 16C chapel once frequented by Tudor and Stuart courtiers. In 1770 the church was lengthened, a north aisle built on and books and furnishings were presented by George III, who in 1805 added the royal gallery (note the fine Queen Anne arms and hatchments). In the churchyard lie Gainsborough (d 1788) and Zoffany (d 1810).

Kew Green. – The most attractive houses on the green are those on either side of the main gates to the gardens. Dominating the north, river, side are Kew Herbarium (collection of 7 million dried plants and library – *open only to specialists),* a three storey Georgian house and extensive annexe, followed by an irregular line of 18/19C houses of brick with canted bays, canopied balconies, rounded doors and windows in arched recesses... (nos 61-83). On the far side of the gates, backing onto the gardens, are a line of onetime royal "cottages", including, behind the coaching porch at no 37, Cambridge Cottage, now the Wood Museum *(enter from inside the gardens).*

Kew Bridge Engines and Water Supply Museum. – *Entrance off Green Dragon Rd. Open weekends 11am to 1pm and 2 to 6pm (5pm from 1 October to 31 March); closed Good Friday, 24, 25 December; 40p.*

One engine is in steam, others waiting to be fully restored in this museum which demonstrates the development of **James Watt's** basic idea through half a century of improved efficiency and increasing scale. The Boulton and Watt of 1820, brought up to Kew when the pumping station was built in 1837, has been put in steam first. Awaiting the voluntary engineers are a Maudslay, 90 and 100inch Cornish beams, installed in 1845 and 1869 which pumped 6½ and 10 million gallons daily, an 1856 Bull.

Buildings in 19C were, for the most part erected round the engines with no provision for bringing in replacement parts so confident were our forefathers that their engines would last indefinitely. Exteriors were functional, the interiors dominated by giant columns, slender pillars and staircases enabling one to climb to cylinder and beam levels. The standpipe tower outside is a local landmark nearly 200ft high.

Musical Museum. – *368 High St, Brentford (150 yds from Kew Bridge in a disused 19C church). Open April to October, Saturdays, Sundays 11am to 5pm; 50p.*

Inside an acoustically rewarding neo-Gothic church is a collection of some 200 mechanical reproducers of music – pianolas, organs, a wurlitzer...

KING'S CROSS (Camden)

King's Cross, St Pancras and Euston Stations are each as near the centre as was permitted when they were constructed respectively as the Gt Northern terminus (1852), the Midland (1864) and the London and North Western (1837). Today the front of Lewis Cubitt's **King's Cross**, apart from the clock tower (clock from 1851 Exhibition) is largely masked by an advanced single storey hall providing covered access to the platforms at the rear; **St Pancras** remains as Sir George Gilbert Scott designed it, a combination of mediaeval Gothic in brick with Italian terracotta. **Euston** is modern (1968), clean lined, with exposed plain black piers supporting glass panels with the interior recessed west of the centre to provide a colonnade. Two white courses, one clearly bearing the name, provide a strong horizontal line. A statue of Robert Stephenson, chief engineer of the London Birmingham line (1838) stands in the forecourt.

British Rail, Collectors' Corner. – *National Carrier's Ltd Garage, Cardington St. Open Tuesdays to Saturdays 9am to 5pm; closed Bank Holidays.*

Bits and pieces for sale to railway enthusiasts: signalling equipment, badges and buttons, lamps, enamel and cast iron signs...

KNIGHTSBRIDGE - BELGRAVIA ★★ (Westminster)

Knightsbridge. – This present synonym for elegant living with luxury stores and larger shops lining the main road, and antique and rare shops tucked away behind, was until *c* 1800 an unkempt village beside a stone bridge across the Westbourne River (where Albert Gate is now). It was outside London and, as such, a place for spitals, cattle markets and slaughterhouses, taverns, footpads and highway robbers, pleasure gardens frequented by Pepys and his friends; it was a highway crowded with travellers from the west and men and carts bringing in produce to the central markets. Only in later 18/early 19C, did houses and shops begin to line the road in solid terraces: in 1813 Benjamin Harvey opened a linen draper's and in 1849 **Harrod** took over a small grocer's which by 1901-5 had prospered and enabled him to rebuild, in terracotta brick crowned by towers and cupolas, to today's familiar outline. Inside, in addition to the general joy of the items for sale, the food halls remain a prime example of *art nouveau* wall tile decoration. The other major local building in brick is the Hyde Park barracks, dark red, angular, with a tower block, designed by Sir Basil Spence in 1970-1.

The triangle between the main highway and the track to Brompton village developed as a residential area around a series of squares in true Georgian fashion and, besides obviously being desirable places in which to live, present an interesting progression: **Trevor Sq** 1818, **Brompton** 1826, **Montpelier★** 1837. Slightly to the west and only slightly later, but quite different to the trim stucco ground floors and basements with brick above, neat windows and doors and slender balconies, are the seemingly disproportionate, all stucco ranges with pillared square porches of the mid-Victorian **Ennismore Gardens** (All Saints, 19C Early English in style, is the Russian Orthodox Church.) Interlacing the squares are small streets, mews, closes, alleys, lined by one-up one-down cottages, colour-washed and transformed, the handkerchief sized front gardens (Rutland St) ablaze with flowers.

Between Brompton Road and Sloane Street there grew up a fringe of small streets such as **Yeoman's Row** (1768) and Beauchamp Place, lined by modest brick terraces – the shops in the latter now as various as their appearance: reject china, oriental porcelain, handmade shoes, silver, antiques, restaurants, rare maps... Almost simultaneously, in 1773, Sloane St was developed, followed by the land to the rear which came to be known as Hans Town. In the late 19C the area, together with Cadogan Place and Sloane Gdns, to the south, was rebuilt to Victorian architectural taste in unfading red brick *(p 26)*. Sloane St equally has been rebuilt, but piecemeal.

The most distinguished buildings today in the area are the **Danish Embassy,** 1976-7 by Ove Arup in Sloane St and in Pont St, **St Columba's** of 1950-55 by Edward Maufe, perfectly sited with its green cupolaed, square stone tower in the street's axis.

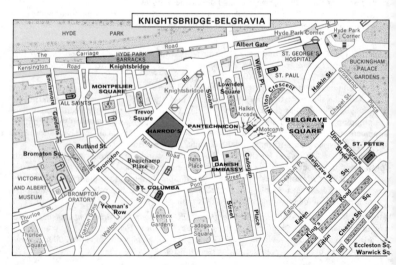

Belgravia. — Most remarkable of all was the development of the area east of Sloane St: within 6 years, 1821-27, maps show the land, which was part of the Grosvenor estate, developed from the Five Fields and market gardens, bordered along Upper Grosvenor Place by St George's Hospital (f 1733; rebuilt in Classical style in 1829), houses and stables, into the well defined plan of Wilton Crescent, Belgrave Sq, Eaton Sq and the roads parallel to the King's Road, after so many centuries a public thoroughfare. Impetus for such a development came from George IV's decision to transform the Queen's House into Buckingham Palace — only the king's and Nash's undertaking took longer, in fact was never completely accomplished. Belgravia, so rapidly built, on soil brought from the newly excavated St Katharine Dock, is **Cubitt** territory.

Belgrave Sq★★. — **George Basevi** was the architect. The square of 10 acres has twinned, but not identical, sides with Corinthian centres and ends, urns and balustrades, statue decorated attic screens, prominent pillared porches, all in gleaming white stucco; a uniform 3 storeys, cornice and floor above. The ironwork matches that enclosing the garden in which a bay has been cut at the southeast corner for a bronze statue of Simon Bolivar. The end of each range is carefully designed; three corners are canted allowing two roads to enter with a house between, facing onto the square.

Basevi also probably designed and Cubitt built the adjoining squares and streets extending far into Pimlico with New, now Eccleston, and Warwick Sqs. Upper Belgrave St, Belgrave Place, Eaton Sq, Chester Sq, echo the same theme for, incredibly, apart from a few streets of older houses, Belgravia, 150 acres in extent, is constructed to the basic terrace design of Basevi, varied by the addition of combinations of a restricted number of related forms of ornament to afford, overall, a strong family resemblance.

St Peter's. — The church was erected as part of the project but off-centre because of the King's Rd thoroughfare and therefore lost effect. The design is Classical.

Wilton Place, Wilton Crescent. — Wilton Place predates by a century the Perpendicular style St Paul's Church, erected in 1843 on the site of guards' barracks and still recalled in local street and pub names. The place's 17C brick terraces lead into the crescent, ringed on its inner perimeter and across the diameter by stucco terraces (*p 25* — outer side rebuilt). Between the crescent and Lowndes Sq (a different estate separately developed and largely rebuilt this century), are a maze of small streets, overlooked by colour washed cottages, new small houses, towering apartments and garden precincts. In Motcomb St stands the **Pantechnicon,** now Sotheby's, built in 1830 with an august Doric columned front and inside, on every floor, people's onetime treasures awaiting auction; on either side and in W Halkin St and Halkin Arcade are small shops where through the windows one sees prints, modern watches, pottery from Mexico, carpets, antiques and customers sitting in leisurely consideration.

LEWISHAM (Lewisham)

December 1836 saw the opening of the first railway, the Deptford-London Bridge line on which 20 000 people travelled in the first week. Already the villages of Lewisham, Lee, Lee Green, Catford and New Cross were being urbanised; in the next century the population was to multiply fifty fold to 250 000.

Parish Church of St Mary's. — *High St.* The sturdy building of Kentish ragstone with an imposing portico and a low square tower, ornamented at the crest, which dates from 1775, stands on an ancient site. A board inside lists early incumbents, Richard of 1267, or his undated predecessor, Yeonomy of Ghent. On the opposite corner, in Ladywell Rd is the late 17C vicarage, with a pedimented doorway and modillioned eaves.

Pentland House and Manor House. — *Old Road, Lee High Rd.* Next to 18C, white stucco, Pentland House stands the timelessly elegant Manor House, built in 1788 of brick and from 1797-1810, the residence of the banker, Sir Maurice Baring (now a public library).

Note further along the High Rd, on the opposite side, the mid 19C Merchant Taylor's Almshouses and Boone Chapel (Wren, 1683).

Church of the Resurrection (RC). — *Kirkdale, Upper Sydenham.* The low fortress building of yellow brick is lancet windowed and buttressed (DA Reid: 1973-4). Surmounting the plain wooden door is a bronze and lead relief of Our Lord showing his wounds as the shroud drops away (Stephen Sykes). The circular Church of the Annunciation (Beckenham Hill Rd) of 1964 by Roy Lancaster has an interesting thorn crowned roof.

St Antholin Spire, Roundhill. — *Dartmouth Rd, Dulwich.* The slender stone spire by Wren with dragon's head weathervane, purchased in 1874 on the church's demolition by a City master printer to adorn his estate, now stands beside a cedar, at the centre of a modern housing estate.

■ HORNIMAN MUSEUM★

London Rd, Lewisham. Open: 10.30am to 6pm; Sundays 2pm to 6pm; closed 24, 25 December; refreshment room. Education centre, library (anthropology and zoology); aquarium.

Tribal masks, Buddhas, lutes and bagpipes line your path, until suddenly there is the walrus... for this museum is one of great variety, re-arranged and displayed in modern manner but continuing the enquiring tradition of its founder, Frederick John Horniman (1835-1906), tea merchant and MP. Successful private views decided Horniman to construct a museum which he had designed by Harrison Townsend (1901) in *art nouveau* style and then presented "as a gift, to the people of London".

Map p 135.

The Mall's alignment was traced at the time of the Stuarts but its completion as a thoroughfare dates only from 1910 when **Sir Aston Webb** transformed it into a processional way from the palace to Whitehall with monuments to Queen Victoria at either end: the memorial before the palace, and, on the site of the former LCC office, the massive curved arch with a sovereign's gateway at the centre, known as **Admiralty Arch** after the adjoining Admiralty buildings. The Mall is now the traditional processional way – George V was the first to ride along it to his coronation.

The south side opens with the 19C Admiralty extension and the pebble and flint Citadel which served as the operational centre for Churchill, the cabinet and chiefs of staff from 1939 to 1945. Beyond is the greenery of the park. The north side is regal.

Carlton House Terrace★, Carlton Gardens. – Carlton House, built of brick in 1709, purchased by Frederick, Prince of Wales in 1732 and refaced in stone in 1772 taken over by the Prince Regent, who with Henry Holland and at a cost of £800 000 transformed it into what was briefly the country's most gorgeous mansion. The king, however, was by then tired of the house and it was demolished (1829) and the government commissioned **Nash,** who had just completed the Regent's Park scheme, to design a similar terrace surround for St James's Park. In the event only the two terraces on the north side were constructed.

Seen from the Mall, the white façades, each 31 bays wide with central pediments and angle pavilions, giant Corinthian columns and balconies, appear even more majestic as they stand upraised on squat, white painted, fluted, cast iron columns. The entrances are on the north side, porched, flanked by Tuscan or Ionic pillars, paired in some cases, beneath continuous balconies; the end houses are advanced to complete the composition. Among those now occupying the houses in the terrace are Crockford's at no 16, the National Portrait Gallery (annexe) at nos 14-15 *(details of exhibitions in the press)*, the Institute of Contemporary Arts at Nash House (no 12), the **Royal Society** at no 6, the Turf Club at no 5...

At the west end is **Carlton Gardens** where four grand houses surround a small grass plot shaded by plane trees: no 1 was once the residence of Curzon, no 2 of Kitchener and no 4 of Palmerston. This last house, demolished and rebuilt Classically in grey stone in 1933, was the headquarters from 1940-45 of the Free French Forces and is distinguished by a tablet inscribed with General de Gaulle's famous call to arms to the French people broadcast on 18 June 1940.

On the site of Carlton House between the two terraces at the top of the steps down to the Mall is the Grand Old Duke of York who, according to the nursery rhyme, marched 10 000 men to the top of the hill then marched them down again and whose 124ft pink granite column was just high enough, according to his contemporaries, to place him out of reach of his creditors!

At the west end of the terrace, a second stairway is marked by the slim bronze statue of George VI by William McMillan, before a circle of plane trees.

Marlborough House. – *Pall Mall. Tours by arrangement with the Administration Officer, weekdays only, when not in use for conferences; 5p.*

While John Churchill, **Duke of Marlborough,** was winning the final victories in the seemingly endless War of the Spanish Succession (Blenheim 1704, Ramillies 1706, Oudenaarde 1708) and the duchess was waiting on and quarrelling with the queen and supervising the construction by Vanbrugh of Blenheim Palace (1705-24), Wren, in two years (1709-1711), designed and completed Marlborough House. It was of red brick with straight headed windows and slightly advanced wings at either end on the garden front. The mansion was altered in 1771 by William Chambers and enlarged in the 19C to include additional storeys, a balustrade, the Prince of Wales' feathers and the deep front porch. The house eventually passed to the crown and is now the Commonwealth Information Centre.

The interior decorations include vast mural paintings celebrating Marlborough's victories. The ceiling paintings, created originally for the Queen's House, Greenwich, by Gentileschi and presented to the duchess are in the Blenheim Saloon.

Against the wall in Marlborough Road is a large *art nouveau* bronze fountain group in memory of Queen Alexandra (1926) and on the corner overlooking the Mall, a life-like relief by Reid-Dick of Queen Mary.

Queen's Chapel★. – *Marlborough Road. Open to those attending morning service or by arrangement with the Administration Officer.*

The chapel was intended for the Infanta Maria of Spain but was completed for Charles I's eventual queen, Henrietta Maria, in 1625 by **Inigo Jones.** It was the first church in England to be designed completely outside the Perpendicular Gothic tradition and stood originally within the palace walls.

The pedimented exterior of rendered cement with Portland stone dressings has three principal windows at the west end, of which the central one is arched above the unobtrusive, straight headed, door. Inside, at the east end, is a broad Venetian window and, framed by a richly detailed cornice, a splendid, curved white and gold coffered ceiling. The greyish-green walls are the original colour, the royal and other galleries, lower panelling, stalls and lectern are mid 17C. The beauty of the small edifice lies in the perfection of its proportions, the simplicity of interior adornment enriched at the east end by being highlighted in gold. The choirboys wear Tudor scarlet and gold.

St James's Palace★★. – *Pall Mall. The chapel is open to the public for Sunday Services.*

Henry VIII's "goodly manor" became in 1532 a crenellated, turreted palace entered through the **Gate House** at the bottom of St James's, even then a regular thoroughfare. The original and early palace buildings, considerably more extensive before the fire of

1809 which destroyed the east wing, are of the traditional 16C Tudor red brick with a diaper pattern and stone trim along the line of crenelations. With later additions they now surround only four courts, the Colour, Friary, Ambassadors' and Engine.

St James's was the last royal palace to be built as such in the capital and became the chief residence after Whitehall had been burned down in 1698. Although no longer the sovereign's residence it remains the statutory seat — proclamations are made from the balcony on Friary Court, ambassadors are accredited to the Court of St James.

Inside there remain the so-called Holbein ceiling in the **Chapel Royal,** of which the Tudor Gothic windows can be seen from outside (right of the gateway), and the imprint of successive architects and designers, Wren, Grinling Gibbons, Hawksmoor, Kent and William Morris. The splendid State Apartments *(open only for special functions),* are hung with full length portraits of Stuart and Hanoverian monarchs.

Many kings and queens have been born or died in the palace. Charles I spent his last night there, in the guardroom, before walking across the park to the Banqueting House and his execution on 30 January 1649.

It is a romantic building with gateway towers standing out against the sky and at dusk when the quiet courts are lit by crowned wall standards.

(After photograph, Parke and Roche, France)

St James's Palace.

Clarence House. — The distinctive white stucco home of Queen Elizabeth, the Queen Mother, was built in 1825 by John Nash for the Duke of Clarence, the future William IV.

Lancaster House★. – *Stable Yard. Open when not serving as government conference and hospitality centre.*

The mansion, designed by Benjamin Wyatt in 1825 for the Duke of York, who died in 1827, was for years in the 19C the town house of the Marquesses of Stafford and the Dukes of Sutherland when it became the setting for balls and soirees. Inside the Corinthian porticoed, square edifice of mellow Bath stone, is an opulent magnificence of mixed Baroque decoration — not for nothing did Queen Victoria on a visit declare to her hostess "I have come from my house to your palace". Beneath the coved and painted ceilings, the vast pictures, the gilding and chandeliers of the state apartments, a great marble staircase by Charles Barry divides and turns and turns again to enter the Grand Gallery, enriched with a painted ceiling by the Italian, Guercino, and most impressive when thronged by people at an evening reception.

Queen Victoria Memorial. — The memorial planned by Sir Aston Webb, with the seated figure of the queen appearing on the east side, is the climax of the processional way. The white marble statue, 82ft high with a gilded bronze victory at the summit, when completed in 1910, appeared overpowering and necessitated the heightening and refacing with Portland stone of Buckingham Palace's east front.

■ ST JAMES'S PARK★★

London's oldest royal park. — Henry VIII was the inaugurator of London's royal parks and this, the oldest, goes back to 1532 when Henry exchanged the building occupied by a community founded before the Conquest as a "spittle for mayden lepers" for land in Suffolk. After demolishing the hospital, according to Stow, the king "built there a goodly manor, annexing thereunto a park, closed about with a wall of brick now called St James's Park, serving indifferently to the said manor and, to the manor or palace of White Hall".

In Tudor times the park was stocked with deer. James I, a lover of wild life established a menagerie of animals and exotic birds. Charles II aligned aviaries along what came to be called Birdcage Walk, added the acres now known as **Green Park** (1667) and walked regularly, in the early morning, up a path which came to be known as Constitutional Hill. Strongly influenced by the formal gardens of Le Nôtre which he had seen during his exile in France, the king had the park laid out according to the standard goosefoot (or *patte d'oie*) design. The marshy ponds were systematised into a west-east canal from the west end of which extended two avenues — one along the line of the Mall, although blocked by the houses of Charing village and so leading nowhere!

In 19C when Nash was commissioned to design a project for the park's improvement, in addition to the terraces *(see opposite),* he landscaped the park itself after Repton, transforming the long water into a lake with islands (on which the duck and wildfowl originally on the "decoy" have flourished ever since), planting trees and shrubs. At the same time he replaced the high surrounding wall by iron railings.

The park today is known especially for the pelicans and wildfowl upon the lake and brilliant borders which surround it. There are views from the bridge of Buckingham Palace and Whitehall.

Mayfair is named after the annual cattle and general fair which was held in May but became so unruly and the neighbourhood so notorious that it was officially closed in 1706. In 1735 the architect, Edward Shepherd took a 999 year lease on the site and opened a food market for the sale of fish, fowl, herbs and vegetables. Around the square and dependant streets he erected small houses, a practice renewed by his heirs so creating Shepherd Market. Development elsewhere arose as a rich overspill from the City.

Piccadilly★★. – *(North side from Hyde Park Corner; for south side see St James's p 136.)*

The street is called after the house of a tailor from Somerset who made a fortune manufacturing the frilled lace borders, or pickadills, fashionable Elizabethans attached to their ruffs and cuffs. He bought a plot adjoining Great Windmill St and built upon it an imposing family mansion, Pickadill Hall.

The street's north side is still lined at the west end by late Georgian houses occupied by a diminishing number of clubs and notably at no 94 by the **Naval and Military** or In and Out Club, as it is known after the piers at the entrance (f 1862). The modest town house of 1756-60, two storeys high, with a Venetian window beneath a central pediment, was formerly the residence of George III's son, the Duke of Cambridge (1829-50) and from 1854-65 of Lord Palmerston.

Burlington House★. – In 1664 the 1st Earl of Burlington bought a plot on which to build a town house near the courtly St James's development; the 3rd earl, an architect in his own right, with **Colen Campbell** in 1715-6, remodelled and refaced the house in the Palladian style. In the 19C the house was twice remodelled, the second time in 1867-73 to its present neo-Italian Renaissance appearance.

Inside, the modifications were equally drastic as the house was converted to the use of the **Royal Academy** (f 1768) with a central grand staircase and exhibition galleries.

The academy's treasures *(on view in the Private Apartments from March to October)* include splendid pictures by members (Reynolds, Gainsborough, Turner...), 18C furniture, Queen Victoria's paintbox, **Michelangelo's** unfinished marble tondo, *Madonna and Child.*

At the centre of the courtyard is a bronze statue of Sir Joshua Reynolds (1723-92), first PRA; in the ranges on either side are the libraries and rooms of learned societies.

The back of the building was remodelled in 1869 in ornate Italian style with towers, an upper portico of giant columns and a colossal porch, and suitably decorated with more than 20 magisterial statues. On completion the building became for many years the headquarters of London University and is now the Museum of Mankind.

Museum of Mankind★. – *6 Burlington Gardens. Open daily 10am to 5pm, Sundays 2.30 to 6pm; closed 1 January, Good Friday, 24, 25, 26 December.*

The Ethnography Department of the BM is so extensive that it exhibits the principal objects from its collections from tribal societies in rotation, usually to a geographical or cultural theme. The greatest treasures are on permanent display: shadow puppets from Java, cult masks from Ceylon, an ivory mask from Benin, also a brass queen's head and bronzes, an Ashanti gold pectoral disc mounted in a silver-gilt dish, wooden spirit figures from the Solomon Islands, pre-Columbian gold, an Aztec crystal skull and coiled rattlesnake and, in a separate room, Mexican, turquoise mosaic, masks.

The **Burlington Arcade★★** along the west side of Burlington House, is delectable with embroidered waistcoats and jewellery, tobacco, pipes and cigars, cashmere scarves and camelhair pullovers, ivory and jade, behind bright shopfronts. It was built in 1819 and every night the beadle still closes the gates at either end.

(After photograph, Parke and Roche, France)

Burlington Arcade.

Albany is named after Frederick, Duke of York and Albany, he of the column, second son of George III.

The prince was compelled on account of his debts to sell the 18C house, designed by **Sir William Chambers,** to a builder who converted it into chambers or the bachelor apartments which remain, increased in number, to this day. The building, as altered by **Henry Holland** in 1804, is in the shape of an H, the rear a stuccoed court on Vigo St enclosed by two lodges between neighbouring 18C houses. The front, with a forecourt on Piccadilly, is of brick with a central pediment, and porch. Distinction has always come to Albany through its residents, today as in 19C when they included Gladstone, Macaulay, Byron...

Park Lane. – The Lane is now studded with hotels where it was previously graced by the town residences of local estate owners: Grosvenor House, in 1930, replaced the early 19C mansion of the Duke of Westminster; the Dorchester also in 1930, the mid 19C Dorchester

House; the London Hilton replaces a short terrace; the Londonderry stands on the site of Londonderry House of 1765 and the Inn on the Park and Intercontinental (Hamilton Place) on the site of the Earl of Northbrook's residence.

Oxford St. — The Road to Oxford, to Uxbridge, Tyburn Rd, are the names under which the street appears on old maps. By mid 18C it was built along almost entirely on the south side and the Harley estate had been laid out around Cavendish Sq. A turnpike just before the junction with Tyburn, now Park, Lane, marked the boundary and the capital's separation from the place of public execution at the crossroads formed by the meeting of the Roman Watling St now Edgware Rd, Bayswater Rd, Tyburn Lane and Tyburn Rd. The gallows, first a tree, then a gibbet and finally an iron triangle from which several could be hanged together, was the centrepiece of the gruesome area which was also a place of public punishment and torture. The crowds would mass to see the spectacle, often accompanied by side-shows, until 1783, when hangings were removed to Newgate. A stone in the park railing at the opening of Bayswater Rd marks the site.

Marble Arch. — The triumphal arch of Italian marble with three closely patterned iron gates but lacking a crowning quadriga or statue *(see p 176)* was designed by **John Nash** in 1828 as the royal entrance to Buckingham Palace. The construction of the east front made the arch superfluous and it was rebuilt on its present site in 1851 as the boundary of what was soon to become and has remained, London's prime shopping street.

Gordon Selfridge confirmed the street's status when he erected a vast and imposing shop in it in 1908: windows below displayed wares in a new way; colossal Ionic columns soared above through three floors to be crowned by an attic and balustrade; a canopy protected the entrance. No enterprise since, whether chain or department store, and all are represented along the street, has erected so distinctive a building.

Mayfair's three squares. — The squares were laid out in the first half of 18C: Hanover c 1715, Grosvenor in 1725, Berkeley from 1737. Little survives except the plane trees now overlooked from three sides of Berkeley and four sides of the others, by phalanxes of 20C office blocks with only the exceptional 18C or 19C house between.

Hanover Sq. — **St George's** was constructed in 1721-4 as part of the quarter's development. It remains in address, a feature of the square, the free standing portico projecting across the street pavement and west tower with a lantern after St James' Garlickhythe, producing a distinctive landmark to the south. Inside all is white with the detail picked out in gold... and on the pavement, waiting for who knows who (since no one seems sure where they came from) two cast iron game dogs.

Grosvenor Sq. — The 18C square comprising 6 acres and, therefore, one of London's largest, might be said to have been as effectively redesigned in the 20C as it was in the 18C — even the garden, originally circular with a central statue of George I, is now square with a memorial to Franklin Roosevelt on the north side. The first American resident (at no 9) was **John Adams,** the first Minister to Britain and later President. Today the neo-Georgian buildings to north, east and south are almost all US State Department offices while the entire west side, since 1961, has been filled with the embassy designed by **Eero Saarinen.**

Berkeley Sq. — The bottom west corner remains. The 1740s houses were built after Berkeley House, erected in 1664 overlooking Piccadilly, had given way in 1733 to Devonshire House which, in turn, was demolished this century (Berkeley St across the old site is dominated at no 45 by the headquarters offices of Thomas Cook). Nos 45-46 in the square, stone faced with balustraded balconies and pediments at the first floor windows are 18C (Clive of India lived at no 45) as are those on the far side of no 47 (rebuilt 1891). The brick and stucco house of 4 floors, at no 50, is occupied by Maggs, the antiquarians who display in beautifully proportioned rooms, equally attractive books, maps and autographs. Note the ironwork in first floor balconies and lamp holders at the steps to each house, complete with torch snuffers. No 52, on the corner, has a front also on **Charles St** where 18C houses continue, some less grand than in the square and some refaced or remodelled in the 19C as in the case of no 37 where three houses have been combined as premises for the English Speaking Union. The street ends in a confusion of backs and fronts and finally a small 19/20C pub in a cobbled yard.

Bourdon House, 2 Davies St at the square's northwest corner (now Mallett's antique dealers), was built in 1723-5 as a manorhouse amidst fields and orchards. It remains small square and of brick, two storeys with a third added above the cornice, pedimented to the south above a pedimented doorway, with a second door on the street. Fine 18C interior.

The streets of Mayfair. — Other than in the residential streets with their occasional Georgian houses, attention in Mayfair concentrates on the shop windows.

Bond Street★. — Old and New Bond Sts began as far back as Tudor times as a lane continuing northwards the line of St James's St. It is named after Sir Thomas Bond, treasurer to Henrietta Maria, who gave £20 000 to the impecunious Duke of Albemarle, demolished his mansion and began to build what are now Old Bond St, Dover, Stafford and Albemarle Sts completed by the construction in 1720 of New Bond St. As the streets developed there came to live in them Nelson and Emma Hamilton, Byron, Boswell, Beau Brummell... and to line the pavements, stores, tailors, haberdashers, chemists. Today's shops and even the Antique Bazaar (124 New Bond St), specialise in the unique, the perfect, the luxurious, whether in handmade chocolates, leatherwork, stationery, perfumery, cigars, porcelain, a jewel, optical instruments, watches, a piece of furniture, a picture... In the street are **Chapell's** (50 New Bond Street), **Sotheby's** (no 35) who began in 1744 as book auctioneers, produced a turnover of £826 in the first year and are now the biggest firm of art auctioneers in the world, their notable rivals, **Philipps'** (7 Blenheim St, New Bond St), whose first big sale was on 9 February 1798, when they auctioned Marie Antoinette's pictures.

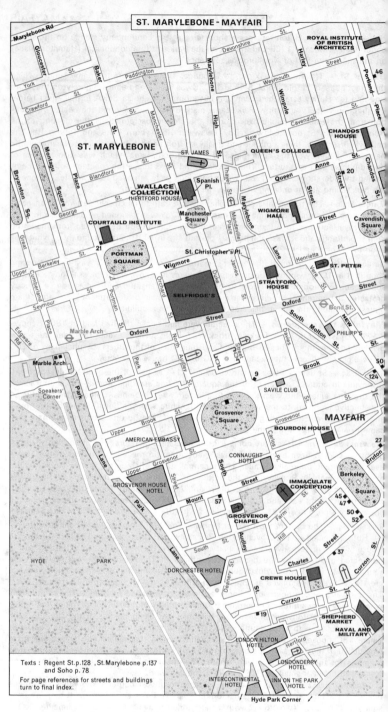

Texts : Regent St.p.128 , St.Marylebone p.137
and Soho p. 78
For page references for streets and buildings
turn to final index.

Savory and Moore, at 143 New Bond St, retains an early 19C shop front and interior. As famous are **Partridge** (no 144), **Asprey's** (27 Bruton St), **Marlborough Fine Art Galleries and Graphics** (39 and 17 Old Bond St), **Agnew's** (no 43) and **Sac Frères** (no 45) who deal only in amber. Antique dealers have overflowed into Brook St, site also of the Savile Club (69-71).

South Molton St has become a pedestrian precinct with pavement cafés, small restaurants, a shop smelling of and selling coffee, a clockmaker...

Albemarle St is lined by 18C houses occupied at no 7 by the National Book League and no 21 by the Royal Institution (f 1799; **Michael Faraday Laboratory** – *open: Tuesdays, Thursdays 1 to 4pm; 20p*).

Savile Row retains its tailors and a laboratory for the restoration of works of art.

Mount St is different again as it extends from the northwest corner of Berkeley Sq in a straight line, past the Connaught (that epitome of late 19C luxury hotel building and comfort) to the park, with one side and sections opposite, lined by tall, irregularly gabled terracotta brick houses of 1888, 1893... Below window after window displays choice objects: antique furniture, porcelain, pictures, Oriental screens... On one corner is a butcher, his shop faced inside with turn of the century tiles.

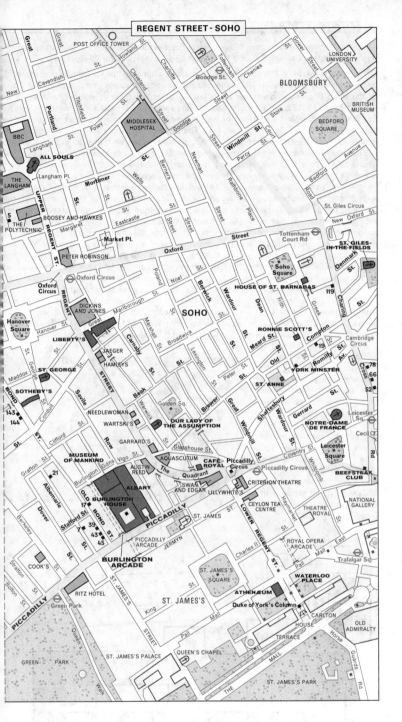

The Church of the Immaculate Conception. – *Farm St.* The church of the Jesuit community, built in 1844-9 has a notable high altar, meticulously designed by Pugin.

South Audley St. – Halfway along the street is the **Grosvenor Chapel** of 1739 with a distinctive, Tuscan portico, square quoined tower and octagonal turret.

Purdeys, gun and riflemakers, established in 1881 would hardly be noticeable at no 57, were it not for the richly coloured royal coat of arms above the door.

Curzon St. – This street is different again, being part residential and part commercial. There are 18C houses along the south side at the Park Lane end – Disraeli died in 1881 at no 19 – and behind it the maze of streets, archways and paved courts that is **Shepherd Market★,** a quarter of Victorian and Edwardian pubs and houses with small, inserted shop fronts which serve as pavement cafés, tourist antique (brass) shops...

Crewe House (no 15), standing back behind trees and lawns is the only surviving example of a type familiar in engravings, as an 18C gentleman's London mansion. Sometime residence of the Marquess of Crewe (d 1945), the house was built in 1730 by **Edward Shepherd** and subsequently enlarged and altered to its present seven bays with large bow fronted wings at either end. The entirely white stucco is relieved and ornamented by the curves of Venetian windows, a pillared, square porch and above, a triangular pediment.

Open Mondays to Saturdays 10am to 6pm (Tuesdays and Thursdays to 9pm, June to September), Sundays 2 to 6pm; closed 1 January, Good Friday, 24, 25, 26 December.

Origin and habitat. – The collection was founded, after more than a century of discussion, by parliamentary purchase in 1824; the nucleus was not the spoils of monarchy as so many of the older European collections were, but 38 superb pictures assembled by **John Julius Angerstein** (1735-1823), City merchant, banker, owner of a mansion in Greenwich, a town house at 100 Pall Mall and friend of Sir Thomas Lawrence whose portrait of him can be seen in the Historical Gallery (B on plan). The pictures, for which £57 000 was given and which included Titian's *Venus and Adonis*, Rubens' *Rape of the Sabines*, Rembrandt's *Woman taken in Adultery* and *Adoration of the Shepherds*, five paintings by Claude, Hogarth's *Marriage à la Mode* series and Reynolds' *Lord Heathfield*, remained in Pall Mall, where 24 000 people came to view them in the first seven months.

Only in 1838, fifteen years after Angerstein's death, was the new gallery completed in Trafalgar Sq. This building, on the site of the Royal Mews and at first shared with the Royal Academy (before the latter's removal to Burlington House), was intended to provide an architectural climax to the square; it succeeded better, however, in its internal arrangement than in its monumentality of which the most spectacular feature in the long, disproportionately low and subdivided front relieved by a small dome and turrets, is the great pedimented portico composed of Corinthian columns after those of the recently demolished Carlton House. (The Carlton House columns had been frugally preserved by the authorities who, however, had not noticed their friable condition so that no economy was effected since, the design having been approved, more solid ones had to be made!)

The 1973-5 extension is the fifth to William Wilkins' original building and affords additional space not only for the permanent collection but occasional special exhibitions based on the gallery's pictures supplemented by private and international loans complemented by furniture, sculpture and fine art from other museums *(see press for details)*.

There are now more than 2 000 paintings in the collection; they represent the jewels in the public domain from early to High Renaissance Italian paintings, early Netherlandish, German, Flemish, Dutch, French, Spanish pictures and the masterpieces of the English 18C. (The fuller representation of British painting, particularly the more modern, and of 20C work of all schools, including sculpture, is in the Tate Gallery.)

Gainsborough : Mr and Mrs Andrews.

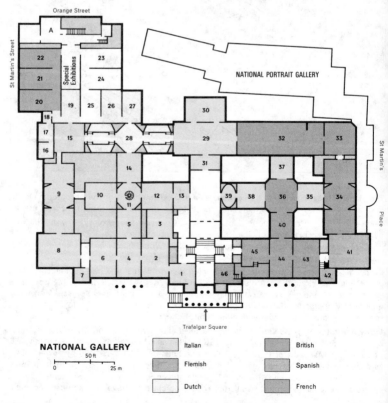

NATIONAL GALLERY

50 ft

0   25 m

Italian   British

Flemish   Spanish

Dutch   French

The arrangement. – Italian paintings occupy all the west galleries (beginning with 13 and 14C in 1 and 2) and continue broadly in chronological sequence round the vestibule and central, publication's room, to 18C in galleries 35, 38, 39 midway along the east side; the early German, early Netherlandish, Flemish and Dutch schools lie to the northwest, French from north to south of the east wing and British and Spanish in the farthest east galleries.

GALLERY	SCHOOL AND DATE		ARTISTS (and some famous titles, but not necessarily the only work on view)
1-2	Italian	13/14C	Wilton Diptych (? French); Duccio; Giotto (Pentecost); Masaccio.
3-5	Florentine	15C	Uccello (St George and the Dragon); Botticelli; Fra Angelico.
6	Central	15C	Piero della Francesca.
7		15C	Leonardo da Vinci, Cartoon (Madonna and Child).
10	Venetian	15C	Bellini (The Doge, St Dominic); Antonello da Messina; Giorgione
12-13	Northern	15C	Mantegna; Pisanello (Virgin and Child, Vision of St Eustace); Crivelli (Annunciation).
14	Milanese	15C	Leonardo (Madonna on the Rocks).
8, 9, 15	Central and Venetian	16C	Michelangelo (Entombment); Andrea del Sarto; Raphaël (Pope Julius II); Correggio (Madonna of the Basket); Titian (Noli me Tangere, Bacchus and Ariadne, Death of Actaeon, Vendramia Family, Portrait of a man, Self-portrait); Tintoretto; Veronese
30	Italian	16C	Moretto, Romanino, Savoldo.
29, 31		17C	Domenichino frescoes.
29, 37		17C	Caravaggio (Supper at Emmaus); Carracci; Guido Reni; Guercino.
35, 38, 39		18C	Canaletto (Venice); Tiepolo (Allegory with Venus and Time); Guardi; Longhi.
19, 26-28	Dutch	17C	Rembrandt (two Self-portraits, Saskia in Arcadian costume, Hendrickje Stoffels, A Woman Bathing, Jacob Trip, Old Man in an Armchair, Woman taken in Adultery, Belshazzar's Feast, A Man in a Room); Frans Hals (Family Group in a Landscape).
16-18, 28	Dutch	17C	Interiors and domestic scenes by van Hoogstraten, Jan Steen, Vermeer (Young Woman standing at a Virginal); Pieter de Hoogh; sea and landscapes by Cuyp, de Cappelle, van de Velde, van Ruisdael.
20-22	Flemish	17C	Van Dyck (Charles I on horseback and the beautiful courtly, double portrait, Lady Elizabeth Thimbleby and Dorothy, Viscountess Andover); Rubens (The Judgement of Paris, View of Het Steen, Le Chapeau de Paille).
23	Early German	15/16C	Dürer (The Painter's Father); Cranach (Cupid complaining to Venus).
24	Early Netherlandish	15/16C	Jan van Eyck (Marriage of Giovanni Arnolfini and Giovanna Cenami); Rogier van der Weyden (Portrait of a Lady, St Ivo); Mabuse (A Little Girl), Bosch, Brueghel the Elder.
25	Netherlandish	16C	Holbein (The Ambassadors, Christina of Denmark); Spranger.
34	British	17/18C	Hogarth (Marriage à la Mode series, Shrimp Girl); Reynolds (Anne, Countess of Albemarle, Lord Heathfield); Gainsborough (Mr and Mrs Andrews, The Morning Walk, The Painter's Daughters, The Watering Place); Constable (The Haywain, The Cornfield, Salisbury Cathedral, Weymouth Bay); Turner (The Fighting Temeraire, Calais Pier, Rain, Steam and Speed); Stubbs (The Melbourne and Milbanke families).
41-42	Spanish	18C	Velazquez (The Rokeby Venus, St John on Patmos); El Greco (Christ driving the Traders from the Temple); Murillo (Self-portrait, Boy leaning on a Sill); Zurbaran; Goya (Duke of Wellington).
32	French	17C	Poussin (Landscape, Bacchanalian Revel); Claude (A Seaport, Hagar and the Angel, Embarkation of the Queen of Sheba); Philippe de Champaigne (Cardinal Richelieu, full length and triple profile).
33		18C	Watteau, Chardin, Boucher, Lancret, Nattier.
36, 40		19C	Vernet, Delaroche.
43		19C	Ingres, Delacroix, Courbet, Corot.
44		19C	Manet (La Servante des Bocks); Monet (Beach at Trouville, Westminster); Renoir (Les Parapluies); Pissarro.
45		19C	Douanier Rousseau (Tropical Storm with a Tiger); Degas (Woman drying herself); Seurat (Une Baignade); Cézanne (Les Grandes Baigneuses, Old Woman with a Rosary); Van Gogh (Sunflowers).
46		19C	Monet (Water lily paintings).

The greatest private collection of paintings in the country is the Royal Collection which may be seen, in part, at Hampton Court and Windsor Castle and in temporary, wonderful, small exhibitions in the Queen's Gallery.

There are also considerable collections or one or two outstanding paintings in the great houses mentioned on pp 180-184.

Pictures from the Royal Collection are frequently out on loan and few have been mentioned by name as this guide is no catalogue. Always enquire, therefore, on the spot for works by any particular artist. The final index states, but not exhaustively, the names of many artists mentioned in the guide.

Open Mondays to Fridays 10am to 5pm, Saturdays to 6pm; closed 1 January, Good Friday, 24, 25, 26 December. Temporary exhibitions in Carlton Gardens (p 116).

Chronologically the arrangement begins at the top *(lift)* with pre-Tudor sovereigns and ends four floors down in the basement with 20C; on no account try to visit the gallery all at once.

The gallery is heaven on earth! Inside the Victorian-Italian-Renaissance building is everyone English one has read about or read: Tudor monarchs to 20C poets, men of science, politics, letters, music, the stage, diarists, architects, people in the social whirl... The act of foundation of 1856 states that paintings shall be collected for their subject, but portraiture having been a major *genre* since Holbein was court painter to Henry VIII there are works by (or copies after) the greatest British and visiting artists including van Dyck, Mytens, Honthorst, Lely, Kneller, Gainsborough, Reynolds, Romney, Zoffany, Lawrence, Sargent, Orpen, Rothenstein, John, Gunn, the miniaturists Samuel Cooper, Nicholas Hilliard and Isaac Oliver, sculptors Roubiliac and Epstein and caricaturists and etchers Landseer, Max Beerbohm, Phil May, Spy, Low...

Top Floor: The Tudors to the Regency. – Throughout there are the royal portraits from Henry VII, Henry VIII (Holbein) to Queen Elizabeth in youth and majestic old age, the Stuarts, George IV (Lawrence). Grouped by association on the walls are their contemporaries: Thomas More and his family, Wolsey; Mary Queen of Scots; court favourites: Essex, Leicester, Raleigh, Buckingham; Purcell; Shakespeare – the best authenticated portrait – Ben Jonson, Marvell, Donne, Milton, Dryden, Swift, Pope, Addison and Steele, Johnson and Boswell (both by Reynolds); Pepys, Evelyn; Wren, Vanbrugh, Hawksmoor, Caius Cibber; Oliver Cromwell and the generals of both sides; the Cabal, the Kit-Cat Club (self portrait by Kneller); there are Fanny Burney in her stylish hat, self-portraits by Reynolds and Gainsborough, Garrick superbly painted by Gainsborough, Sterne by Reynolds...

First Floor: The Victorians and Edwardians. – There is a statue of unabashed sentimentality of the young Victoria and Albert. There are politicians in abundance, Melbourne, Gladstone, Disraeli, many in caricature; there are the reformers, explorers and generals; Darwin and T H Huxley; Barry and Pugin, the Scotts; Gilbert and Sullivan; Tennyson, the Brownings, Dickens, George Eliot, the Brontë sisters (by Branwell); Ellen Terry; Ruskin; the Pre-Raphaelites; Oscar Wilde, Aubrey Beardsley, Whistler, Steer, Sickert, George Moore, Max Beerbohm...

Mezzanine floor: 1914-18 War.

Basement: 20C poets and writers including the Bloomsbury Group, Lady Ottoline Morrell, Edith Sitwell, the poets of the Thirties, Auden, MacNiece, Day Lewis; T E Lawrence; Bernard Shaw; politicians... and a thousand others.

OSTERLEY PARK ★★ (Hounslow)

Open Tuesday to Sundays and Bank Holidays, April to September 2 to 6pm; October to March 12am to 4pm; closed Mondays (except Bank Holidays), Good Friday, 24, 25, 26 December, 1 January; car park; restaurant; 20p NT.

Osterley is the place to see **Robert Adam** interior decoration at its most complete – room after room is as he designed it: ceilings, walls, doorcases, doors, handles, carpets, mirrors and furniture – especially chairs standing in the exact positions for which they were designed. Osterley is also the place to look at trees: in the avenue of mixed species, four files wide leading to the house, shading the lawns...

The country seat of two City gentlemen. – **Sir Thomas Gresham** bought Osterley Manor in 1562 and immediately began to build a country house adjoining the old manorhouse, a late 15C Tudor brick building surrounding three sides of a courtyard. When Gresham's mansion was complete, Queen Elizabeth honoured her financier and merchant adventurer by a visit to the "house beseeming a prince" (1576), which on his death in 1579, passed to his stepson Sir William Read, husband of Lady Mary of Boston Manor *(see opposite).* In 1711 the mansion was purchased by another City grandee **Francis Child,** clothier's son from Wiltshire, who came to seek his fortune in London in the 1650s, had found it, been knighted, elected Lord Mayor (1698) and become banker to Charles II, Nell Gwynn, Pepys, John Churchill, future Duke of Marlborough, King William and Queen Mary... He had started as a goldsmith's apprentice; moved to a second house where he married the owner's daughter, inherited the family fortune and business which he transformed to suit the times. Money – gold – was accumulating rapidly through increased trade in Tudor and Stuart times but was easily stolen; merchants, after finding that even deposits in the Tower were vulnerable – Charles I seized £130 000 from the vaults in 1640! – placed their bullion with goldsmiths usually for a fixed time; the smiths with Francis Child as a forerunner, began to lend the cash out at interest and became the City's first bankers. Child's Bank (now amalgamated with Williams & Glyn's) "at the sign of the Marigold" – the building had been a tavern and there were no street numbers – can still be seen at No 1 Fleet St.

The old banker, he was 69 when he bought Osterley, never lived there himself; it was his grandchild, namesake and heir who, in 1756, began the transformation which was to continue for more than twenty years by which time the house was owned by Francis Child's great niece, Sarah Sophia who in 1804 married the future 5th Earl of Jersey; the 9th Earl presented Osterley to the nation in 1949.

Exterior. – The square form with corner towers of Sir Thomas Gresham's house remains, though enlarged and encased by new bricks and stone quoins in 18C by the first of the two architects employed on the transformation. Sir William Chambers in addition reduced

he courtyard to provide a hall and contin-
ous passage round the house and comple-
ed the Gallery and Breakfast Room before
eing superseded in 1761 by the now more
ashionable, Robert Adam. The Scotsman
ade two contributions to the exterior, the
rand portico at the front and, at the rear, a
orseshoe staircase with delicate wrought
on and brasswork combined (1770).

Osterley Park : rear staircase.

nterior. — By 1773 Horace Walpole,
siting from nearby Strawberry Hill, wrote:
The old house is so improved and enriched
hat all the Percies and Seymours of Sion
ust die of envy... There is a hall, lib-
ary, breakfast room, eating room, all
hefs d'œuvre of Adam, a gallery 130ft
ong, a drawing room worthy of Eve before
he Fall''.

The **Hall** is wide with apses at either
nd, a ceiling compartmented and filled
vith floral scrolls and a black and white
marble pavement. Trophies on blue panels
ll the spaces between pilasters, Clas-
ical statues flank the curved fireplaces.
part from the statues, Adam personally designed every item, even to the door handles, such
vas his attention to detail.

The lobby (note the ceiling), the staircase, with Adam designed iron balustrade, decor-
tive panels and cornice and three beautiful lamps and the north passage, lined with
rchitectural drawings and armchairs of painted beech-wood with cane seats (c 1790),
ead to the **Library.** In this room it is the furniture which is outstanding: there are lyre back
rmchairs, a pedestal desk veneered with harewood (stained sycamore) and inlaid with
notifs matched in the side tables, all made in about 1775 by John Linnell, leading cabinet
naker of his day probably to his own designs under Adam's supervision.

The **Breakfast Room,** in an amazing lemon yellow with strong blue rococo type ceiling
rnament is by Chambers; tables and pier-glasses, however, were designed by Adam and the
yre back mahogany armchairs probably by Linnell.

The **Eating Room,** at the opposite end of the passage is again an all Adam room: motifs
rom the ceiling decoration of vines and ivy leaves reappear over the doors; wall panels,
edestalled urns, sideboard (for which the 1767 drawing is in the passage), side tables,
eautiful swagged, oval pier-glasses and again a set of superb lyre back chairs of carved
nahogany (18C custom required that the chairs be set formally, against the wall, and that
ate-leg tables be brought in for dining).

Chambers, it is believed, designed the **Gallery** which runs the length of the house.
Marble chimney pieces, Classical doorcases and the lighter Rococo style white frieze on
n ochre ground are set off by the original peagreen walls, as in the 18C hung with paint-
ngs. The portraits at either end are by Hoppner, the views of Osterley in the late 18C
fter the water colourist, Anthony Devis. The laquerwork is 18C Chinese, the furniture
hought to be by Adam and the gilded pier-glasses and intervening girandoles, heart shaped,
arlanded, supported by nonchalant mermaids, are the Scotsman in his lightest vein.

The **Drawing Room,** rich with gilding and ornament, has a ceiling studded with flower
illed patterae framing a gilded panache of ostrich feathers. Pale pinks and greens, gold,
ed reappear in cornice and carpet (made at Moorfields) and in the doorcases from which,
n turn, motifs are taken for the fireplace and as part of the inlaid design and ormolu decoration
of the two harewood veneered commodes. The serpentine sofas and chairs after the early
French neo-Classical style, are the combined design of Adam and Linnell; the Adam drawings
or the pier-glasses, dated 1773, are in the Study Room.

In the **Tapestry Room,** the Adam motifs for ceiling and fireplace fade into insigni-
icance beside the richness of the Gobelins' tapestries woven for the room, signed and
dated by (Jacques) Neilson, 1775, an artist of Scots origin in charge of the works in Paris
rom 1751-88. On a rich crimson ground, framed in gold, is the Boucher series, *The Loves
of the Gods,* and between are flower filled urns, garlands, cupids at play... Chairs and sofa
are upholstered in tapestry after the same style.

The adjoining **State Bedroom** is in cool greens. Note the Child crest of an eagle with
an adder in its beak on the four poster, and the gilded chairs, upholstered in green-gold
velvet, oval backs supported on reclining sphinxes — one of Adam's most graceful designs
(1777). The chimney glass, surmounted by the Child crest, is declared in the house inventory of 1782 to have been the "first plate made in England".

The interest of the **Dressing Room,** which forestalled a fashion for the Antique, lies
n Adam's application of what he took to be Etruscan decorative themes, in fact, Greek,
to an 18C interior: even the chairs are made to conform in colour and patterning, though not
in shape, to the theme. The study is hung with Adam architectural drawings.

Boston Manor. — *Brentford. Open May to September, Saturdays only 2.30 to 5pm; 5p.*
Cedars and house have grown old together: the house dates back to 1622 when Lady
Mary Read began construction of the property she had acquired from Sir Thomas Gresham by
settlement and marriage; the trees to 1670 when James Clitherow, whose portrait by Kneller
still hangs in the house (state bedroom), gave £5 136 17s 4d for the mansion and grounds
which he landscaped with cedars and a lake.

PADDINGTON (Westminster)

Map pp 5-8 (B/VX).

Paddington still numbered less than 2 000 souls in 1800; by 1900 it exceeded 125 000. Within the century it had become a canal junction and a railway terminal, bus services – horse drawn – had been inaugurated, also the metropolitan and district underground railway.

The Canal. – In 1795 Paddington was linked to the **Grand Union Canal,** completed two years earlier to unite the industrial Midlands to the capital; and in the same year work began under a Cornishman, William Praed, on the construction of a canal from Uxbridge to Paddington. This, by 1801, was in use transporting produce from the market town and passengers in vast numbers on outings (half-a-crown to Uxbridge); a further plan in 1874 resulted in the canal which skirts Regent's Park's northern boundary, continues through Camden Town to King's Cross and Mile End to come out on the river at Limehouse in the heart of dockland. Today, in summer, motorised barges run excursions from Camden Lock *(50p)* to Little Venice and British Waterways operate a Zoo Waterbus from **Little Venice,** the small backwater basin, near Paddington, overlooked by luxury apartments in modern rendered cement terraces.

Paddington Station. – The GWR and the station were the undertaking, in 1850, of **Isambard Kingdom Brunel.** The station radiated 19C confidence beneath an extensive wrought iron and glass roof mounted on cast iron pillars; there were four platforms approached by ten tracks. The accompanying hotel (1850-2), by Hardwick the Younger, was French Renaissance and Baroque inspired, decorated with allegorical sculpture.

The underground. – The railway, the Metropolitan, was the first section to be constructed of what is now the London Transport Underground. The line, which ran from Praed St to Farringdon by way of King's Cross was opened on 10 January 1863 and within five years had been extended to South Kensington and Westminster and, in the east, to Moorgate. The carriages were open trucks and although the smoke and dirt going through the tunnels was asphyxiating, 9½ million passengers travelled on the new line in the first year.

The bus service. – Omnibuses were introduced to London from Paris on 4 July 1829 by the coachbuilder, George Shillibeer. He brought over a "handsome machine", as the papers called it, drawn by 3 horses abreast and with a capacity of 16-18. Long and short stage coaches were not licensed to take up or set down passengers "on the stones", in other words the pavements of central London, so Shillibeer discreetly ran his first omnibuses outside the central limits, from Paddington Green to the Bank by way of the New, now Marylebone, Road.

The development. – In 1827, after the gallows had at last been removed, development of the area between the Bayswater and Edgware Rds was undertaken and 150 years later has been renewed, maintaining the original layout of squares, crescents and terraces.

PUTNEY (Wandsworth)

Putney's transformation was precipitated by the arrival of the railway in mid 19C. Evolution previously had been gradual, from settlement beside the ford to substantial village where Oliver Cromwell held a council of war round the communion table in St Mary's in 1647. Even the erection of a wooden toll bridge in 1729 – the first above London Bridge – had little effect. In the wake of the railway came builders... The early association with the river remains – rowing clubs still line the Surrey bank, oarsmen practise in midstream; the **Boat Race** over the 4½ mile course to Mortlake is rowed each spring as it has been ever since 1845.

St Mary's Parish Church. – The church at the approach to the bridge *(p 152)* was burnt out in 1973 so that all that remains are the 1836 outer walls and the 15C west tower.

Putney High St, Putney Hill. – The bustling High St with, halfway along a Tudor style, gargoyle decorated pub, the Old Spotted Horse, still includes tall 19C house-fronts.

At the start of Putney Hill, near the crossroads, are to left and right, no 11, The Pines, a monstrous tall grey attached Victorian House where **Swinburne** lived and no 28A, a pink washed Georgian villa with a firemark set like a beauty patch on its pale wall.

Lower Richmond Rd. – The road which makes its way upriver from the bridge, is marked at the start by the mid 18C, **Winchester House,** built low in now darkened brick, overlooking the river, and the White Lion, a flamboyant Victorian pub of 1887 with two caryatids standing out on the corner like a ship's figurehead.

Beyond, punctuating the straggling line of village and antique shops and small Victorian houses are three more pubs of different vintage: the late Georgian, Duke's Head on the river, the 19C, gabled Spencer Arms and, just before the common, the Georgian, French Revolution. On the Lower Common is All Saints Church (1874), notable for its Burne-Jones windows *(open only during services)*.

Five educational establishments in Putney are interesting as typical examples of their respective periods:

Putney High School for Girls. – *Lytton Grove, Putney Hill.* 1893 in tall Victorian houses.

Whitelands Training College. – *West Hill.* 1930 brick buildings with Tuscan style roofs set in extensive grounds, increased by modern, angular, but harmonising annexes.

Wandsworth School. – *Sutherland Grove.* A vast 1970s brick, rough cast and glass institution, redeemed by its proportions.

Putney College for Further Education. – *Putney Hill.* Late 1960s concrete and glass.

Mayfield Comprehensive School. – *92 West Hill.* A modern Powell and Moya building.

The proposal. – It was a superb plan: the government wanted something done with Marylebone Fields (enclosed by Henry VIII, divided under the Commonwealth into manor farms of which the leases reverted to the crown in 1811) and they required direct access from north central London to Westminster. **Nash** proposed a tree landscaped park with a serpentine lake bounded by a road along which, on all except the north side left open for the view of Primrose Hill and the heights of Hampstead and Highgate, there would be terrace palaces, divisible into three bay town houses for the noble and fashionable. Within the park would be a circus, ringed by houses facing both in and outwards and, surmounting the upraised centre, a valhalla; elsewhere would be a *guinguette* or summer pavilion for the Prince, approached along a wide avenue (the Broad Walk) in the axis of Portland Place, numerous villas half-hidden in the trees and, to mark the northern boundary, the Union Canal *(qv)*; in sum, the park would become the most exquisite garden suburb.

The approach was to be up Robert Adam's Portland Place, a most successful speculation begun by the brothers in 1774 as a private road lined by substantial mansions and closed at the bottom by Foley House, whose owner insisted on an uninterrupted view which dictated the 125ft width. To link the place and park and traverse the psychological barrier of the New Road (Marylebone Rd), would be a circus with, at the centre, St Marylebone Church (not then built). Nash hoped to extend Portland Place, which he greatly admired, due south across Oxford St and Piccadilly by means of circuses and so arrive in the axis of Carlton House. From Oxford Circus south the street was to be lined with shops and houses behind a continuous colonnade which would provide shelter below for shoppers and fashionable promenaders and balconies to the houses above; under the street was to be a much needed new sewer system for central London.

The realisation. – In essence the plan survived – considering that it was subject to government commissions and the hazards of land purchase; the *guinguette,* all but seven of the villas and the would-be double bath Crescent disappeared although an Inner Circle was laid out as a botanic garden, now transformed into **Queen Mary's Garden**; the approach from Portland Place was modified to the open armed Park Crescent and Park Sq; the extension of Portland Place being out of line, was given a pivoted turn by the construction of the circular All Souls, and the angle at the south beautifully swept round by means of the Quadrant. The plan took eight years to achieve, from 1817-25; New St, as it was called at first, was a fashionable and glittering success – it was the age of Beau Brummell; the houses along the park were taken; the Prince, by now George IV, had unfortunately tired of Carlton House but it remained the focal climax until 1829 when it was demolished and replaced by Waterloo Place *(see below)* and Carlton House Terrace *(qv)*. Nash personally probably only designed a few of the **terraces★★**, houses and shops, but he set the style and different architects, among them Decimus Burton, in accordance with the practice of the day, drew up plans which were formally submitted to Nash to ensure homogeneity before being executed. The common theme was the use of giant columns, generally Ionic or Corinthian to emphasise the centre and ends of the long façades which, in addition, were usually advanced and sometimes pedimented or given an attic screen decorated with statuary. Columns, of a different order, forming an arcade or framing doors or ground floor windows, balustrades and continuous first floor balconies of iron or stucco, united the long fronts into single compositions.

Round the park★★★

Starting at Park Crescent and bearing west, then crossing the open park (Zoo *qv*) and the Broad Walk, and returning to the crescent, the principal terraces (named after the styles of some of George III's 15 children) and other major buildings are:

Park Crescent (1821): paired Ionic columns in a continuous porch, and a balustrade and balcony emphasise the classical curve. The Doric lodges once adjoined iron gates closing the crescent, and those opposite, the square, from the main road.

Park Sq, East and West (1823-4): single Ionic columns.

Ulster Terrace (1824): the idiosyncracy appears in two closely positioned pairs of bay windows at either end.

York Terrace (1821; west end now named **Nottingham Terrace**): 360yds long or nearly half the width of the park, the terrace comprises two symmetrical blocks, York Gate in the axis of St Marylebone Church *(qv)* and some detached houses. The sequence of column orders is giant Corinthian in the mansions at either end, Ionic above Doric colonnades in the pedimented main blocks and Ionic in the houses at York Gate.

Cornwall Terrace (1822): the 187yd front, marked at either end and the centre by Corinthian columns, is divided into a number of receding planes. Note through the trees the modest 18C brick houses and old pub on the far side of Baker St/Park Rd, also the lodge with rounded windows and pitched slate roof.

Clarence Terrace (1823): heavily accented Corinthian centre and angles above an Ionic arcade.

Sussex Place (1822; **London Graduate School of Business Studies**): the most surprising, finialled, slim, óctagonal cupolas, in pairs, crown the ends and frame the pedimented centre of the curved terrace; below the domes are canted bays and, between, a continuous line of Corinthian columns (the far side from the park was rebuilt in a modern buttressed style in brick in 1972).

Royal College of Obstetricians and Gynaecologists (1960): the 4 storey brick building has a stone wing at right angles encompassing the low recessed entrance and over it, the hall.

Hanover Terrace (1822-3): pediments coloured bright blue as a background to plasterwork and serving as pedestals for statuary silhouetted against the sky, mark the terrace. Hanover Gate has a small, octagonal lodge with heavy inverted corbel decoration and niches with statues beneath a pitched slate roof and central octagonal chimney.

The Mosque (1977): the 140ft minaret, white with a small gold coloured dome and finial crescent, is a delicate addition to the skyline. The mosque itself has a pale grey façade, pierced by tall, four centred, arched windows of five lights each and blind arcades supporting a drum, crowned by a huge, gold coloured copper dome. To the rear are the extensive new buildings of the Islamic Cultural Centre. It stands on the site of one of Nash's villas (Albany Cottage) and was designed by Sir Frederick Gibberd.

Hanover Lodge, one of the 18C villas, with a large modern brick addition, and **The Holme,** another villa, are now both annexes of **Bedford College** (f 1849 in Bedford Sq and part of London University) which is itself on the site of South Villa and St John's Lodge, rebuilt and enlarged this century in red brick.

Winfield House: the neo-Georgian house of 1936, now the residence of the US ambassador, is on the site of St Dunstan's Lodge where the organisation for blinded exservicemen was founded in 1915. The lodge was designed by Decimus Burton in 1825 for the 3rd Marquess of Hertford *(qv)* who, it is said, used it as a harem.

Outside Gloucester Gate, on the east side of the park is **Cecil Sharp House** *(2 Regents Park Rd; open Mondays to Saturdays 9.30am to 5.30pm; closed 1 January, Good Friday Easter Saturday, all holiday Mondays, 25, 26 December),* headquarters of the English Folk Dance and Song Society and containing a huge and colourful mural by Ivon Hitchens. Down Albany St is **Park Village West,** the most attractive of the two dependent streets to the terraces. The small houses and modest terraces, although in his country cottage style, were not designed by Nash who was by then engaged on Buckingham Palace. Note particularly the charming Tower House.

Gloucester Gate (1827): angle pediments with plasterwork against red painted tympana and surmounting statues, mark the main terrace.

Danish Church. – The neo-Gothic church in stock brick dates from 1829 when it was built for the St Katharine Royal Hospital Community *(qv).* In 1950 the church was taken over by the Danish community whose own building in Limehouse had been bombed. Inside are a coffered ceiling, below the windows shields of English queens from Eleanor to Mary, and beside the modern fittings, John the Baptist and Moses, two of the four figures carved in wood by the 17C Danish sculptor **Caius Cibber** for Limehouse. Outside to the right, is a replica of the Jelling Stone.

Cumberland Terrace (1826): the three part, 267yd façade, is underlined by Ionic pillars which reappear in the triumphal arches between the blocks. Grouped above, on the pedimented centre, are Britannia accompanied by arts and science, and before the figures, squat vases.

Chester Terrace (1825): the longest unbroken façade (313 yds) has Corinthian columns rising from ground level to emphasise the ends, centre and mid points between; at either end triumphal, named, arches lead to the access road to the rear.

Cambridge Terrace (1825): small coupled, rusticated columns mark the ground level.

Cumberland Terrace.

Cambridge Gate (1875): the totally Victorian, stone faced block with pavilion roofs, stands on the site of the Coliseum, a large circular building with a portico and glazed roof used for exhibitions and panoramas (or dioramas).

Royal College of Physicians. – The three storey, tesserae faced, building, extending squarely forward to afford a recessed entrance encased in glass, contrasts with a long polygonal construction of black brick to one side covering a hall. It was designed with marked success by Denys Lasdun in 1964.

Down the street★ *(Map pp 120-121)*

Portland Place. – In 18C the street, closed by gates to the north, overlooked by Foley House at the south end and houses by James Adam along either side, was a fashionable promenade. Foley House was replaced in 1864 by the high Victorian, pavilion roofed, Langham Hotel. James Adam's houses, except no 46, have long since disappeared. In 1934 the **Royal Institute of British Architects** celebrated their centenary by erecting a tall stone corner building (no 66) adorned on the façade and on the pillars framing the entrance,

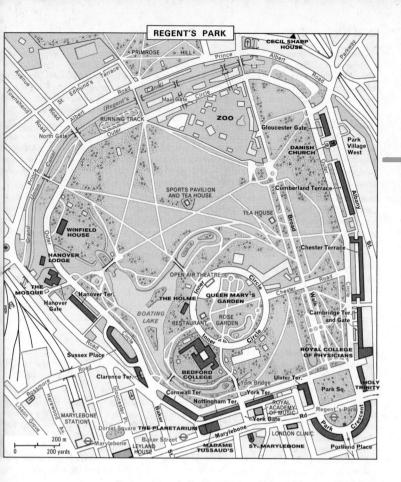

with reliefs. Statues of Lord Lister, who lived in Park Crescent and Quintin Hogg, founder of the Regent St Polytechnic in 1882, signal the ends, the BBC, designed by engineers in 1931, and since doubled in size, the turn. Above the main entrance to Broadcasting House, looking down Upper Regent St, is a statue by **Eric Gill**, of Prospero and Ariel.

All Souls. – *Langham Place*. The fluted, candle-snuffer, spire set on a ring of columns mounted at the centre of a circular portico of tall Ionic pillars, gives All Souls a unique silhouette. Nash constructed this, his only important church, in 1822-4 as the pivot around which his triumphal way was to proceed south and so designed it to be the same from whatever angle it was viewed. The fabric is Bath stone; inside is a traditional, galleried hall church which has been splendidly restored. The unusual undercroft is supported on inverted brick arches. The BBC morning service comes live from All Souls.

Regent St★. – The street, which in 18C included chapels, a theatre and large and small façades, was related by the colonnades designed by Nash, to run from Oxford Circus to Carlton House. Named the New Street, it was so successful that it brought about its own architectural downfall; the shops beneath the colonnades and round the sweep of the **Quadrant** had windows filled with fashionable wear, fripperies and delicacies but they had no room to expand beyond the small ground floor showrooms, so that from the turn of the century the Classical style fronts began to be demolished and replaced piecemeal by the large,

All Souls Church.

dignified buildings of today with plate glass windows, upper floors and "all mod con". The only colonnade section, and that rebuilt, is beneath the London County Fire Office at the south end.

Among the places and shops of note are the **Polytechnic** (west side, no 309), Boosey and Hawkes (295); at Oxford Circus, Peter Robinson; Dickins and Jones, Liberty's *(see below)*, **Jaeger, Wartski's** (specialists in Fabergé jewels), **Garrard's**, the Crown Jewellers responsible for the royal regalia, Aquascutum, **Hamleys**, the Needlewoman, the Café Royal *(see below)*, and opposite, Austin Reed and Swan and Edgar; in Lower Regent St are Lillywhite's and further down, the Ceylon Tea Centre (tea restaurant; small museum).

Liberty's. — The shop, founded by the son of a Buckinghamshire draper, Arthur Liberty, in 1875 on a borrowed £1 500, was soon dignified by the name of an emporium and associated with the Aesthetic Movement. From the first it was known for its silks and within three years was producing its own materials after old Indian prints; the riches are even more varied today: silks, lawns, wall papers, oriental carpets and bronzes, bamboo, china and glass, furniture, leather, jade and modern jewellery, scarves...

Café Royal. — The "café", now a multifloored restaurant with a hall where the National Sporting Club meets, a Masonic Temple and banqueting rooms, began as a tiny eating house opened in 1863 in Glasshouse St by a Burgundian and his wife. Daniel Nichols, as he anglicised his name, built up a reputation for good wine and good food, prospered and moved to the fashionable site in the Quadrant. In France the Second Empire was at its height; in Regent St the Café Royal adopted a new name and as house emblem a crowned N wreathed in laurel leaves! In 1890s the café became the meeting place of writers and artists — Oscar Wilde, Lord Alfred Douglas, Aubrey Beardsley, Whistler, George Moore, Max Beerbohm, Augustus John, Orpen...

Piccadilly Circus. — The circus, for which there have been innumerable plans since the war, was adorned with **Eros,** the memorial fountain to the philanthropist, Lord Shaftesbury, in 1892.

The south front is occupied by the Criterion, a Victorian building with pavilion roofs now divided but originally in 1870s a hotel and restaurant with a marble hall with a mosaic ceiling. Incorporated in the block and actually on the site of the 17C St James's market, is the Criterion Theatre (1874), largely underground and one of the first to be lit by electricity.

Waterloo Place★. — The wide street which swept straight up to Carlton House lost its climax when this was demolished in 1829 although it gained a vista across the park to Whitehall. With the years it acquired a focal point in the Duke of York's column *(qv)* and Classical façades of the Athenæum and the former United Service Club.

The **Athenæum** by Decimus Burton (1828-30), a square stucco block, in deference to the Club's foundation as a meeting place for artists, men of letters and connoisseurs, was given Classical touches in the torches, Roman Doric pillars supporting the porch, the gilded figure of Pallas Athene and the important Classical frieze.

Please write should you notice alterations in buildings mentioned.

RICHMOND ★★ (Richmond upon Thames)

Richmond, possessing what has been called the most beautiful urban green in England, grew to importance between 12 and 17C as a royal seat and, after the Restoration, as the residential area of members of the court — Windsor, Hampton Court and Kew are easily accessible. In the courtiers' wake followed diplomats, politicians, city financiers and merchants, professional men, dames and their schools, and finally, with the coming of the railway in 1840, prosperous Victorian commuters.

On the east side of the main road are reminders of the growing village in the parish Church of St Mary Magdalene with its 16C square flint and stone tower, early brasses and monuments (Edmund Kean), 18C houses (Ormond and Halford Rds), 19C cottages (Waterloo Place), the Vineyard dating back in name to 16/17C when local vines were famous, and the rebuilt almshouses of 17C foundation — Queen Elizabeth's, Bishop Duppa's and Michel's.

Around the Green

Richmond Green★★. — The Green, overlooked by the Old Palace, scene of Tudor jousting and since the mid 17C, of cricket, lies back from the bustle and traffic of the main road, George St.

Along the east, Greenside, are 17 and 18C houses and at the south end a series of narrow lanes, running into the high street, overlooked by the small front windows of jewellers, antique shops, pubs... At the corner there is a widening into a paved court, lined by the last of the enfilade of 18C houses and by two pubs, rebuilt on ancient sites, the Princes' Head and the Cricketers. Abutting is a group of six, two storey brick houses with straight hooded doorways, built between 1692-1700 by John Powell (who lived himself in no 32 which he also built) and known as **Old Palace Terrace.**

Continuing round are **Oak House, Old Palace Place** and **Old Friars.** The first two date back to 1700 and the third to 1687 (date on a rainwater head); Old Friars, so named as it stands on part of the site of a monastery founded by Henry VII in 1500, was extended to the right in the 18C to include a concert room for the holding of "music mornings and evenings".

Maids of Honour Row★★. — The famous row dates from 1724 when the future George II gave directions for "erecting a new building near his seat at Richmond to serve as lodgings for the Maids of Honour attending the Princess of Wales". There are four houses in all, each three storeys high with five bays apiece, pilastered, with friezed door cases, and small gardens behind 18C wrought iron gates and railings. The brick is mellow; the proportions are perfect.

Richmond Palace: royal residence through six reigns. – Henry VII, parsimonious where his son was prodigal, nevertheless, after a disastrous fire, "rebuilded (the palace) again sumptuously and costly and changed the name of Shene and called it Richmond because his father and he were Earls of Rychmonde" (in Yorkshire). This palace, the third on the site, was to be the last. The first residence, a manor house, erected in the 12C, was extended and embellished by Edward III, who died in it in 1377, was favoured by Richard II, his grandson while his queen, Anne of Bohemia, was alive, but demolished at her death in 1394; a new palace, the second, was begun by Henry V but completed only forty years after his death in the reign of Edward IV who gave it with the royal manor of Shene, to his queen, Elizabeth Woodville, from who it was confiscated by Henry VII. In 1499 it burned to the ground.

The new Tudor palace conformed to standard design: service buildings of red brick, preserved today in the gateway, enclosed an outer or Base Court, from which a second gateway led to an inner or Middle Court, lined along one side by a Great Hall of stone with a lead roof. The Privy Lodging, which included the state rooms, surrounded another court. Domed towers and turrets crowned the construction which covered ten acres, and was by far the most splendid in the Kingdom. Henry VII died in his palace; Henry VIII and Catherine of Aragon frequented it; Queen Elizabeth held court in it particularly in springtime, and died there; Prince Henry, James I's son, resided there and added an art gallery to house the extensive collection of royal paintings, increased after the prince's death (in the palace) by the future Charles I who also resided there notably during the plague of 1625. At the king's execution the palace was stripped and the contents, including the pictures, were sold. By the 18C little remained and private houses – the Old Palace, Gatehouse, Wardrobe, Trumpeters – were constructed out of the ruins on the site.

The Old Palace and the Gatehouse. – On the south side are two houses, the first castellated, bay windowed and with a central doorway, incorporating Tudor materials, notably brickwork, from Henry VII's palace, the second the original outer gateway of the palace (note the restored arms of Henry VII over the arch).

The Wardrobe (in Old Palace Yard *i.e.* the Base Court of the Tudor Palace). – Note the blue diapered Tudor walls incorporated in the early 18C building, now a terrace, also the 18C ironwork.

Trumpeters' House★. – *Old Palace Yard.* The main front of this house converted *c* 1701 from the Middle Gate of Richmond Palace, overlooks the garden and can be seen through the trees from the riverside path. The giant pedimented portico of paired columns was formerly guarded by stone statues, after which the house is still named. For a brief period in 1848-9 it was occupied by Metternich.

Richmond Riverside

Old Palace Lane, lined by modest, wistaria covered, 19C houses and cottages, leads from the southwest corner of the green to the river.

Asgill House★. – The house which stands at the end of the lane overlooking the river from a site once within the palace walls, was built *c* 1760 as a weekend and summer residence for the City banker and sometime Lord Mayor, Sir Charles Asgill. In pale golden stone with strong horizontal lines and a central bay advanced and canted for the full three storeys, it was one of the last of its type to be built overlooking the Thames.

The river path continues past the Trumpeters' House and beneath **Richmond Bridge★★** *(qv),* which in 1777 replaced the horse ferry (note the milestone-obelisk at the town end), to re-emerge as the riverside promenade below Terrace Gardens (between Petersham Rd and Richmond Hill).

Richmond Hill. – The view gets ever better as one climbs the steep road lined by balconied terraces.

At the top, overlooking the park stands Ancaster House, a brick mansion with big bow windows, built in 1722 to designs principally by Robert Adam. The house is now attached to the Star and Garter Home opposite, opened in 1924. (The British Legion poppy factory is at the Richmond end of Petersham Rd.)

The **Wick** and **Wick House,** both on the west side of the road and both enjoying the view across the bend in the river towards Marble Hill, were built in 1775 and 1772, the latter by Sir William Chambers for Sir Joshua Reynolds.

The park gates which mark the hilltop are dated 1700 and are attributed to Capability Brown.

Richmond Park★★. – The countryside had been a royal chase for centuries when Charles I enclosed 2 470 acres as a park in 1637. It is the largest of the royal parks and is known today for its **wildlife** which includes badgers and herds of red and fallow deer, its majestic **oak trees** and the **spring flowers** (rhododendrons) of the Isabella Plantation.

On a fine day there is a **panorama★★★** from the top of the Henry VIII mound (said to have been raised to allow the king to survey the field) which extends form Windsor Castle to the dome of St Paul's.

Among the houses in the park are Pembroke Lodge *(cafeteria),* a rambling late 17/18C house at the centre of colourful walled and woodland gardens, Thatched House Lodge, the home of Princess Alexandra and White Lodge, built by George II in 1727 as a hunting lodge and since 1955 the junior section of the Royal Ballet School.

The railway has never come to Roehampton and so its transformation to a residential suburb from a Surrey village, ringed by Georgian family mansions, came about only this century through the combustion engine — Roehampton Lane, so long a winding country road, is now a 4 lane highway. The different periods are marked by modern blocks of flats and houses grouped in long terraces following the contours of the slopes on the east side of Roehampton Lane and the Georgian mansions almost all shaded by magnificent cedars of Lebanon, and now occupied by educational establishments, which continue to give the town its special character.

High St. — Still with a few small 19C houses with shops on the ground floor (note the ironmonger, 1885, in a tall weatherboarded corner house) and containing within its ambit three pubs : the Angel, rebuilt this century on a traditional site, the 18C brick Montague Arms, and at the junction with Roehampton Lane, the rambling white weatherboarded 17-18C, King's Head.

The 200ft spire, to the south, is the dominant feature of **Holy Trinity Parish Church**, built of Corsham stone in 1898.

Manresa House. — *Battersea College of Education, opposite the High St.* This Classically plain 4 storey brick house with a slate roof was built in 1750 by Sir William Chambers for Lord Bessborough.

Downshire House. — *Garnett College, Roehampton Lane.* The two storey, square, parapeted house of red brick dates from 1770. Note the garden and contemporary Cedar Cottages.

Queen Mary's Hospital. — (1915) *Westminster Hospital Group.* The hospital, behind tall iron gates, occupies **Roehampton House,** a wide, parapeted brick mansion, four storeys high, built by Thomas Archer in 1712 and extended in 1910 by Lutyens with curving arcades on either side of the forecourt to new wings and pavilions. Adjoining is the Roehampton Artificial Limb Fitting Centre.

Mount Clare. — *Minstead Gdns.* The white, Palladian style, house of 1772 with twin curving staircases and a balustraded portico added in 1780, is superbly sited on the crest of a hill. It is now overtopped by two great cedars planted in 1773 by Capability Brown.

The Froebel Institute occupies **Grove House** (junction of Roehampton and Clarence Lanes), **Ibstok Place** and **Templeton,** respectively a low white stone and stucco mansion of nine bays built by James Wyatt in 1777 to which an Italian wing was added in 1850; a long low early 18C mellow brick house with dormers in the tiled roof and an attractively irregular front and a tall, late Georgian, plain brick house with, at the back, a terrace extending the width of the house overlooking a garden enclosed at one end by yew hedges and shaded by two massive cedars.

Two strange houses mark Roehampton's north end: a deeply thatched white cottage of irregular shape (by Rosslyn Park RFC, at the Roehampton — Rocks Lanes, Upper Richmond Rd junction) and the Coach House (no 1 Fitzgerald Av, Upper Richmond Rd West), a 19C Gothick folly with disordered gables, pepperpot roof turrets, phoney Latin plaque, wall sundial — an Arthur Rackham illustration in a suburban street!

■ MORTLAKE

Mortlake, now known for its brewery and as the finishing point of the Boat Race, by contrast with Roehampton was reputed as early as 16C for its salt glaze pottery and in 17C for its **tapestry works** (recalled in Tapestry Court, no 119, north side of the High St). Examples of the hangings, prized for the fineness of the weaving and elaborate borders may be seen in the V & A, at Hatfield House, Hampton Court, Kensington Palace and in the House of Lords (arms of Charles II).

St Mary the Virgin Church. — The church was largely rebuilt in 19/20C except for the brick vestry with its corner door shaded by a square hood on carved corbels which is 17C and west tower where a 17C superstructure stands on foundations laid by order of Henry VIII. (A collection of salt glaze pottery may be seen on application.)

Sir Richard Burton's tomb. — *St Mary Magdalen churchyard, North Worple Way.* Sir Richard's widow had a Bedouin tent in stone erected as his memorial on the explorer's grave in 1890.

The north, river, side of Mortlake High St is bordered by short ranges of old cottages and several 18C houses: nos 115 Acacia House, 117 Afon House with an off centre door and unusual, peaked, roof, the L-shaped, brick, 119 and, most notably, **no 123,** a splendid two storey house of dull red brick built *c* 1720 and subsequently extended. The pedimented porch on Tuscan columns is repeated at the top of a short flight of steps at the back where it overlooks the garden and river; chandeliers alight inside *(not open)* add a romantic note. The house, then known as The Limes, was where Turner stayed when painting his Mortlake Terrace pictures, *Early Morning* and *Summer Evening.*

Rotherhithe. — The village served as a mooring to Olaf in 1013 when he supported King Ethelred against the invading Danes, as a Tudor dockyard in the reign of Henry VIII and as a berth to which the *Mayflower* returned after her historic voyage in 1621.

The Angel Inn. — An 18C, partly weatherboarded, inn painted white, overlooking the river.

Mayflower Inn. — *117 Rotherhithe St.* The inn, which dates back in part to the 16C, contains *Mayflower* and later 17C mementoes. It claims an ancient licence to sell British postage stamps and has permission also to sell American stamps.

St Mary's Church. — The present St Mary's on a 1 000 year old site dates from 1715. The brick building with a stone trim, is crowned by an octagonal obelisk spire collared by thin columns (rebuilt 1861), which is visible from the river. Inside, a wooden framed barrel roof stands on four massive pillars which are, in fact, plaster encased tree trunks, carpentered as would be a mast. The communion table is of wood from the *Temeraire;* the altarpiece includes rich garlands by **Grinling Gibbons**, "signed" with open pea-pods. The church flies the White Ensign so numerous are its Royal Navy associations.

Behind the church is 17C Peter Hills School, 3 storeyed, 3 bayed, with coloured figures of a contemporary schoolboy and girl above the door.

Scandinavian seamen's mission churches. — St Olave Kirk (1926), the Norwegian mission, stands at the entrance to the Rotherhithe Tunnel, the hospital and the rebuilt, attractively spare Swedish Church (1966) in Lower Rd and in Albion Rd respectively. The 1957 Finnish Mission with a spectacular belfry, has an interior east wall of stone, dark and running as a sea swell.

Deptford. — The riverside village, became important under Henry VIII as a yard building ships later numbered among the fleet which defeated the Armada (1588). It was also at Deptford that Queen Elizabeth boarded the *Golden Hind* in 1581 to dub Francis Drake knight for his circumnavigation of the globe and where Christopher Marlowe was stabbed to death in a tavern brawl (1593). In 17C John Evelyn, who kept a journal as keenly observed if not as gay as Pepys', had a house there, Sayes Court where he cultivated a fine garden and which briefly, in 1698, and to his regret since he was a bad tenant, he leased to Peter the Great while the latter learnt the art of shipbuilding in the yards.

St Paul's. — The church of 1712-30 by Thomas Archer has a lofty semicircular stone portico supporting an impressive steeple and, inside, great Corinthian columns upholding a richly sculpted plaster ceiling.

St Nicholas'. — St Nicholas stands on a site occupied by Deptford parish churches since Saxon times. Of particular interest in the post-war reconstructed interior are the extended reredos by St Nicholas' 17C parishioner, **Grinling Gibbons**, with swags of leaves, flowers and fruit, a pea-pod, the ciphers and coat of arms of William and Mary. There is also a weird carved relief, an early work by Grinling Gibbons, known as the *Valley of Dry Bones.* The Jacobean pulpit is supported on a cherub believed to have been a ship's figurehead; the table and sanctuary chairs are contemporary.

The laurel wreathed skulls on the gate posts originally dominated crossed bones and since so many privateers sailed from Deptford, it is claimed that the carvings inspired the traditional skull and crossbones flag. More honourably, the church so steeped in naval history, has the privilege of flying the White Ensign.

Bermondsey. — *(Map pp 5-8,* **HY**). The square on the site of the ancient Bermondsey Abbey has been the setting since 1950 of the revived **Caledonian Market** *(Fridays 7am to 5pm).* The biggest flea market in London displays on open stalls, silverware, copper, Victorian jewellery, small furniture, telescopes and ships' compasses, china dolls' heads, books, bronzes, a fawn silk parasol with a deep fringe...

St Mary Magdalen. — Adjoining is the parish church founded in 1290, rebuilt in 1691 and twice restored in the 19C. It retains 12C carved capitals (from the Cluniac monastery, Bermondsey Abbey, once on the same site), 17C woodwork, boards inscribed with 18C charity donations, three hatchments vividly painted with armorial bearings (north gallery) and tombstones in the aisle pavements giving a sad insight into 18C infant mortality.

ROYAL AIR FORCE MUSEUM ★★ (Grahame Park Way, Hendon) _____

Open daily 10am to 6pm (Sundays from 2pm); closed 1 January, Good Friday, 25, 26 December Restaurant; car park (Colindale underground: ½ mile).

The RAF's Lightning Mach 2 aircraft concludes the history of aviation, the Service and its predecessors which the museum, uniquely, recounts in two aircraft hangars of 1915 (from the old Hendon airfield which once stood on the site) and a modern central building.

In the **Main Aircraft Hall** *(ground floor)* is a panorama of aircraft presented in chronological order from a Sopwith Camel to a Vickers Vimy. In the centre is the Camm Collection of 10 planes including the famous Hurricane.

The **historical galleries** *(first and ground floors, start on the top)* recount the story of early experiments as illustrated by components, mock-ups and trophies, including two British Empire Michelin Trophies awarded to the British pilot flying the greatest distance in a British plane: Moore-Brabazon won No 1 in 1910 for a distance of 19 miles.

British Empire Michelin Trophy no 1.

Other exhibits such as the signature board from the pub at Brasted near Biggin Hill, the portrait of Douglas Bader, evoke memories of the Battle of Britain. There is a gallery of winners of the VC and GC, and there are cases displaying escapers' equipment...

St James's was the gift of Charles II at the Restoration to his loyal courtier, Henry Jermyn, later Earl of St Albans, who speedily developed the empty fields into an elegant suburb for members of the re-established court.

The founder of the West End, as he has since been described, laid out his estate around a square from which roads led from the centre of each side (not, as became the custom from the corners): to the east was a large market, and beyond, the Haymarket, to the north, Jermyn St, the local shopping street, and, in the axis of Duke of York St, the church. The community was self-contained even to a railed enclosure in the square for the fashionable to promenade.

At the end of the Stuart monarchy, vacated private houses were taken over by the clubs which had originated in taverns, coffee and chocolate houses where men of similar calling, like interest, congenial company, made a practice of meeting regularly. The encounters developed into subscription groups with reserved quarters and finally took over the houses in which they met, employing the owner or publican as manager and enhancing the amenities, particularly the food for which many became famous. In the period of Beau Brummell (1778-1840), and the Prince Regent, the clubs were known as the resort of the wealthy and the fashionable and as infamous gambling centres. Numbers grew until by the turn of the 19/20C there were nearly 200 in the West End, now there are fewer than 30. Their character has also changed from 18C flamboyance, to 19C silence and reserve and now to a modified social function or gaming.

Berry Bros façade.

St James's was always and remains a masculine world of bespoke boot and shoemakers, skirtmakers and hatters, sword, gun and rod makers, antique and 18C picture dealers, wine merchants, cheese vendors, safe makers, jewellers traditional and modern, fine art auctioneers. Although banking and property companies have invaded St James's St it is still the address of eight of London's principal clubs, Pall Mall of five.

St James's Sq★. — The square, with a Classical equestrian statue of William III (1807) beneath very tall plane trees, is encircled by modern offices and 19C residences except on the north and west sides where there are still Georgian town houses. Of them the most notable are no 4 of 1676, remodelled in 1725 — Ionic porch, rich cornice and continuous iron balcony; no 5 of 1748-51 with 18, 19C additions; no 13 of 1740 with faked mortar uprights to give an all-header effect to the blackened brick wall; no 15, Lichfield House, of 1764-5 — a perfect Classical stone façade with fluted columns marking the doorway and embracing the upper floors beneath a pediment (note also the continuous iron balcony); and no 20 built by Adam in 1775 with no 21 its 20C mirror image. No 14 (of 1896) is the **London Library,** no 12 with a stucco front and Tuscan pillared porch is possibly by Cubitt (1836) and nos 9-10, Chatham House, the Royal Institute of International Affairs (f 1920). The houses date from 1736 and no 10, in its time, has been the residence of 3 PM's: William Pitt, Earl of Chatham, 1757-61, Edward Stanley, Earl of Derby, 1837-54 and William Gladstone, 1890.

St James's Church★. — Wren, the automatic choice of architect in 1676 for the new parish church, built a plain basilica of brick with Portland stone dressings and balustrade and a square tower. Plain glass windows, segmental below and tall and rounded above, line the north and south walls and a tripartite and superimposing Venetian window fill the east end. Consistent with the church's parochial origin, the entrance was placed in the south wall overlooking Jermyn St until 19C when the local emphasis had changed and a new entrance was made from Piccadilly.

The galleried interior is roofed with a barrel vault and entablature, richly decorated with plasterwork, fashioned from mouldings made from bomb damaged fragments. The organ case with figures on high, is original as is the altarpiece of gilded wood with garlands of flowers and fruit, framing a pelican with her young, also a marble font in the form of a tree of life with Adam and Eve on either side, all carved by **Grinling Gibbons.**

The London Brass Rubbing Centre. — *St James's Church Hall, access: Church Place. Open weekdays 10am to 6pm; Sundays noon to 6pm, exhibition free.*

The centre has replicas of brasses from churches in all parts of the country *(small fee).*

St James's St★. — The wide street, unnamed but clearly marked in early 17C maps as the approach from Piccadilly to the palace, developed as part of the quarter and by the end of the century was lined on either side by town houses including those of merchants who fled the City after the Great Plague and Fire of 1665 and 1666. It retains much of the atmosphere of the good life with individual shops, restaurants and clubs. Starting from Piccadilly, the most famous include:

White's Club (no 37): established in 1693 from a coffeehouse of the same name, this club, the oldest and Tory in character, occupies a house of 1788 to which the famous bow window was added in 1811. The façade was renewed in 1852;

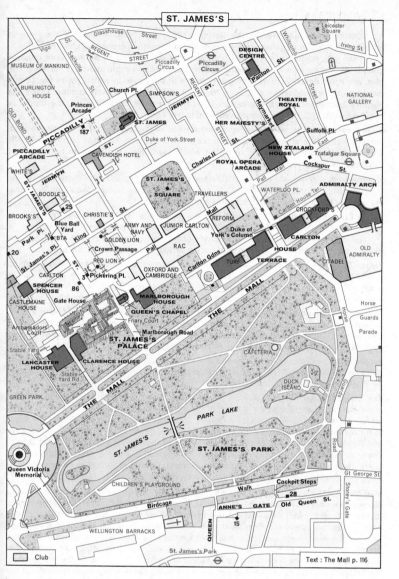

Boodle's Club (28): dating from 1762, the club is in a house of blackened brick and stucco of 1765. On either side are identical porches and at the centre a rounded Venetian style window with below a bay window added in 1821;

The Economist (25): the 1966-8 complex which houses a gallery, bank and offices, besides the journal, consists of three canted glass towers around a paved court;

Brooks's Club (61): founded as the rival Whig club to White's in 1764 by Charles James Fox and the Duke of Portland, the club is in a house built of yellow brick and stone designed by **Henry Holland** in 1778 in which year it took over the famous Almack's of Pall Mall;

Royal Overseas League (f 1910: 50 000 members): the brick buildings and annexes now almost fill the side street, Park Place. No 14 was formerly Pratt's.

Blue Ball Yard. — The far left end of the yard is lined by stables of 1742, now garages, but still with round niches in the walls where iron hay baskets once hung. Above are the old tiled cottage quarters and, in the corner, the pink Stafford Hotel.

British Tourist Authority. — *No 64, Queen's House. Open for personal inquiries, April to October, Mondays to Fridays 9am to 6pm (9.15am to 5.30pm in winter); Saturdays 9am to 2.30pm (9.15am to 12.30pm in winter). Tel 01-629 9191.*

St James's Place. — The L shaped street is lined by 18C houses which become more ample and include decorative fanlights and continuous iron balconies where the street widens at the turn. The corner is remarkable as siting, side by side, examples of a great Palladian style residence, **Spencer House** of 1756-66 and adjoining, Castlemaine House, of 1959-60, a block of flats, strongly horizontal in line, designed by **Denys Lasdun.** At the street end (no 20) is the Royal Ocean Racing Club, a neat Georgian town house. On St James's St corner are a gunsmith (67a) and, adjoining, a locksmith and safemaker (68).

Carlton Club (69): the club, which originated as "Arthur's", was formed in 1832 by the Duke of Wellington. It is now in an early 19C Palladian stone building which incorporates rooms once part of White's Chocolate and Gaming House.

No 74, formerly the Conservative Club, was designed by **George Basevi** and **Sydney Smirke** in mid 19C, in modified Palladian style including a canted bay window.

135

Constitutional Club (1883), the Savage (1857), the National, the Flyfishers are at no 86, a club house in golden ochre stone, a magnificently Victorian building of 1862.

At the end, relating to the corner opposite, are two buildings by **Norman Shaw** in terracotta brick and stone, with asymmetric gables, friezes and an angle tower. At the lower end also, are: **Byron House** (7, 8, 9): 1960s on the site of the house in which Byron awoke one morning on the publication of *Childe Harold* in 1811 to find himself famous; **Lobb's** the bespoke bootmaker; **Lock's** the hatters (6) (the firm dates back to 1700, the topper in the window to 19C, the bow windowed shop to late 18C);

Berry Bros & Rudd (3): wine merchants "established in the XVII century". A half timbered passage beside the shop (note the wall plaque: the Republic of Texas legation 1842-5) leads to **Pickering Place**, reputed, though it would seem to be too small, to be the site of the last duel in London.

Haymarket. – *(From the north end).* **Fribourg and Treyer** (no 34), the "purveyors of fine cigars, snuffs and tobaccos since 1720" occupy a small bow fronted shop, rich in aroma, old tobacco jars and boxes, meerschaums and Wedgwood.

Design Centre★. – *(no 28). Open daily 9.30am to 5.30pm. Wednesdays and Thursdays to 9pm; closed 25, 26 December. Design Index available for consultation.*

The ordinary building of 1954-5 houses changing exhibitions of well designed products from machines to toys, textiles to fishing tackle, manufactured in Britain.

Panton St. – The street recalls Col Panton, card player and gambler, who in an evening in 1664 won enough to purchase "a parcel of ground at Piccadilly". This he laid out as a narrow, shop lined, street one of which in 1770, was taken by William Stone, Wine and Brandy Merchant, eventually transformed into a coffeehouse and later a chophouse (extant).

Theatre Royal, Haymarket★. – When **John Nash** designed the theatre in 1821 with a great pedimented portico, he resited it to stand, unlike its predecessor of 1720, in the axis of Charles II St and so enjoy a double aspect. The interior, which has been remodelled, is most elegantly decorated in deep blue, gold and white.

Her Majesty's. – Opposite, on the corner of Charles II St, is the fourth theatre on the site, a Victorian, French pavilioned, building with an ornate but efficient interior plan, constructed by Beerbohm Tree as his own in 1895-7.

New Zealand House. – Since 1957-63, the 15 storey tower above a 4 storey podium, 225ft in all, has stood sentinel at the bottom of the street. It is glazed overall, banded in stone, recessed at ground level to provide a canopy. Incorporated in the ground floor is the **Royal Opera Arcade★,** a delightful row of bow fronted shops designed as a covered way by Nash and Repton in 1817 as part of their transformation of the exterior of the then Royal Operahouse to harmonise with other buildings in the Haymarket and the nearby Suffolk Place (note the big corner house, now American Express). George III in bronze on horseback in Cockspur St, completes the scene – the future king was born in St James's Sq.

Pall Mall. – The ancient way from the City to St James's Palace is named after an avenue planted to its north which served as an alley for the game brought over from France early in the 17C and much favoured by the Stuarts. When St James's was developed, the avenue was cut down, the road lined with houses, none of which remain, and renamed after the old alley. Since the 19C it has been famous for the clubs along its south side: the **Travellers** (no 106) founded in 1819 with a rule that members must have travelled a minimum of 500 miles (now 1000) in a straight line from London outside the British Isles; the **Reform** (nos 104-5) established, in opposition to the Carlton, by Whig supporters at the time of the Bill in 1832, the latter on the renumbered site of Julius Angerstein's house and both in 19C Italian palazzo buildings. The **RAC** is in a vast building of 1911 by the constructors of the Ritz; the **Oxford and Cambridge** (no 71), the last on the south side, was founded in 1830 by Lord Palmerston at the British Coffeehouse, in Cockspur St. The **Junior Carlton** (no 30), one of two clubs on the north side, is in another 19C palazzo and the **Army and Navy** (f 1839) in an ornate Sydney Smirke house of 1848-51.

Leading away from such spaciousness (beneath 59-60), **Crown Passage,** winds between an ironmonger, picture and bullion dealers, the 19C Red Lion, to King St where there is the Victorian, Golden Lion, all cut mirror glass and mahogany.

Piccadilly★★. – *(For the north side of Piccadilly see p 118).* The shops have restrained displays of merchandise of such variety that window shopping is diverting – silk, leather, cashmere, tweed; wines and spirits, fruit and preserves; books; china, glass and kitchenware; military memorabilia; umbrellas, sticks; hairbrushes, rifles and guns.

Jermyn St★ boasts shirtmakers, pipemakers, antique dealers, antiquarian booksellers, a chemist with real sponges, men's Turkish baths (no 92), a provision merchant (Paxton and Whitefield, 93) selling countless varieties of cheese over a wooden counter; modern jewels (Andrew Grima, 80), restaurants, bars, chambers and the Cavendish, a luxury hotel, on the site of the famous Edwardian rendez-vous. Between Piccadilly and Jermyn St are two parallel arcades, Princes', and the **Piccadilly★,** bright, with bow fronted shops.

King St includes two world famous shops: **Spinks** (no 5), specialists in coins, medals, and orders (besides antiques of all kinds) and **Christie's** (no 8), the fine art auctioneers, founded in 1766 at the time of the height of the grand tour.

Hatchard's, the bookshop in Piccadilly (no 187) which was established by John Hatchard in 1797 with a capital of £5, is still in the original 18C building with small paned bow windows on either side of the entrance.

Simpson's, beautiful in proportion, simplicity, sophistication, dates from 1935.

The **Ritz Hotel** *(map p 121)* marks the end of the south side of Piccadilly. It was built at the height of the Edwardian era, in 1906, to a French design. Inside all was gilded Louis XVI decoration and marble.

Map pp 120-121.

St Marylebone village had just begun to expand along its High St and the inconsequential winding of its Lane through the fields beside the Tyburn River, when, in the early 18C, Edward Harley, 2nd Earl of Oxford, began the development of Cavendish Sq. By the end of the century this had evolved into the most complete grid layout of streets of any area in London: although superimposed on the village as on the surrounding waste land, the two original streets survive, the **Lane** and the **High St** — the only two between Oxford St and the Park not to conform to the rectangular theme.

■ THE SQUARES

Cavendish Sq. — The square was designed in 1717 as a focal point north of Oxford St with a chapel of ease, St Peter's to the west, dependent residential and service streets and a local market (the street name Market Place remains on the far side of Oxford Circus). Development northwards proceeded only spasmodically, attendant on the closing in 1778 of the Gardens, after the style of Vauxhall, the demolition of the "palace" or hunting lodge, in 1791...

The square retains a pair of stone faced Palladian houses of the 1770s at the centre of the north side, which are now linked by a bridge against which stands a moving, dark bronze, *Virgin and Child* by **Jacob Epstein** (1950). There are late 18/19C houses, much altered, along the east side — Nelson lived in 1787 at no 5 and, 100 years later, Quintin Hogg (d 1903), founder of the London Polytechnic (Upper Regent St).

St Peter's Chapel. — *Vere St.* The attractive small dark brick church with quoins emphasising the angles and a square turret and open belfry, is unexpectedly spacious inside including galleries supported on giant Corinthian columns with massive entablatures. The architect was **James Gibbs**, the date 1721-4, making St Peter's, possibly the experimental model for St Martin-in-the-Fields.

Portman Sq★. — At the northwest corner there remain two of the finest houses that ever graced the square, nos 20 and 21, now respectively the **Courtauld Institute of Art** (London University) and the **Heinz Gallery of Drawings and Plans,** an annexe of the RIBA *(both only open for special exhibitions).* No 20 was built and furnished in 1744-6 for Elizabeth, Countess of Home by **Robert Adam.** The adjoining houses appear as a single unit, Adam's doorway only facing into the square and the pillared porch of the Heinz Gallery, standing on the approach street (Gloucester Place). Curving, shallow stepped, staircases are a feature of both houses, the Adam one being particularly remarkable.

Manchester Sq. — The last of the three principal squares dates from 1776 when the 4th Duke of Manchester built a town house, Manchester House on the Portman estate. The square which developed before it, in the next 12 years continued to be named after the house although this was bought as his residence by the Spanish ambassador who built a chapel, St James' in the adjoining street, henceforth known as Spanish Place. In 1872, the house was again sold, the new owner being Richard Wallace, Marquess of Hertford who renamed the property **Hertford House** and entirely remodelled it as the setting for his collection *(p 166).* The square itself is attractive with late Georgian houses.

■ THE STREETS

Marylebone High St and Marylebone Lane wind south towards Oxford St, coming out near Stratford Place, the approach to the Palladian **Stratford House** (Oriental Club).

Of the network of over 100 streets and mews which intersect, always at right angles, north of Oxford St, seven, at least, are known for some special reason:

Wigmore St. — The street is one in which to look in the varied small shop windows, to wander off up Marylebone Lane, to pass through on the way to a chamber music concert or recital at the **Wigmore Hall,** to decide what one would most prefer to collect from the shops in St Christopher's Place — military tradition, buttons, porcelain...

Gt Portland St. — The old street, rebuilt in 19/20C, was widely known in 1930s and again in 1950-60s as the Mecca of second-hand car dealers (no more). At the top end are the Royal National Institute for the Blind (no 224) and the Royal Orthopaedic Hospital (no 234), a turn of the century building with only the theatre rebuilt. At the east end of Mortimer St, stands the Middlesex Hospital, founded in Windmill St in 1745, since 1754 on the present site, entirely rebuilt in 1925-36 and extended in 1960s.

Portland Place. — *Page 128.*

Chandos St. — The street remains named after the palatial residence the Duke of Chandos failed to erect because of the bursting of the South Sea Bubble in 1720. At the end, in the solo position, resembling one of his own immaculate drawings, is Robert Adam's perfectly proportioned **Chandos House** (Royal Society of Medicine). Built of Portland stone in 1771, it is 4 bays wide, 3 floors high, and unadorned except for the off-centre square porch, and the 18C iron railings and lamp holders, complete with snuffers.

Harley St. — Seemingly every door, three steps up from the pavement, is emblazoned with consultants' brass plates. Architecturally the street is a mixture, dating back from the present, through the terracotta brick and stone of mid 19C to the original Georgian. Nos 43-9, with a Tuscan pillared, stucco portico, is **Queen's College,** the oldest English school for girls, founded 1848 and at no 47 occupying the home of Florence Nightingale. A recent addition is Harmont House (no 20), a block of flats in dark blue-black brick which turns the corner into Queen Anne St and, inside, overlooks a court with a water garden and flying bronze sculpture.

Wimpole St. – Elizabeth Barrett, before her marriage to Robert Browning in 1876, lived at no 50, demolished when the street was largely rebuilt at the turn of the century.

Baker St. – The wide thoroughfare was 100 years old when Sherlock Holmes in 1880s went to live at 221B – a number no longer fictitious since the street, originally in two sections and with 85 the top number, was united and renumbered in 1930! Hansom cabs, gas lamps, the fog, private houses with rooms to let, inevitably have vanished, romance remaining only in some of the small shops in the side streets, quiet in the twin early 19C squares to the west: **Montagu**, notable for the shallow ground floor bow windows which mark every house and **Bryanston**, for its long stucco terraces, ribbed by giant attached columns. The parallel Gloucester Place has attractive small doorways, ironwork balconies and railings towards the upper centre.

■ MARYLEBONE ROAD *(Map p 129)*

The line of Marylebone, Euston and Pentonville Rds was laid in 1756 as a by-pass from the City to Paddington and west London. It was known along its full length for its first 100 years as New Rd; the division into named sections came in mid 19C when it became absorbed into the surrounding areas. The principal landmarks today include: St Marylebone Station and Leyland House west of Baker St, the underground station, Mme Tussaud's and the Friends Meeting House (nos 173-7).

Madame Tussaud's★. – *Open daily 10am to 6.30pm (5.30pm October to March, weekends 6.30pm); closed 25 December only; £1, children under 16, 55p.*

History. – Mme Tussaud, born in 1761, perfected her modelling skill by "doing" the French royal family for the waxworks museum opened by her uncle in Paris in 1770. She lived through the Terror taking deathmasks of its victims – Marat, Robespierre... In 1802 she brought the waxworks, by then her's, and her children, to England and for 33 years travelled the country before settling in 1835 in Marylebone. She was 74. At 81 she made a self portrait: a stiff, small figure, mercilessly revealed; at 89, in 1850, she died.

(By courtesy of Mme Tussaud's)

Madame Tussaud.

The museum. – The exhibition is divided into a series of halls: the conservatory, where sports, film, TV personalities of the present stand; The Grand Hall which is peopled by historical, political, military, royal figures from Henry VIII and his wives to Chairman Mao, General Montgomery, prime ministers, the Royal Family, Mme Tussaud herself; the Chamber of Horrors, built like the inside of the Bastille with the murdered Marat at the centre, an actual guillotine, the death masks of Louis XVI, Marie-Antoinette... and in the cells, the most infamous 20C British murderers. Illusion is carried further as one walks below decks aboard HMS *Victory* at Trafalgar with Nelson dying amidst the smoke, sound and fury.

The Planetarium. – *Performances on the hour from 11am to 6pm (5pm October to March; 6pm weekends); closed 25 December only; 55p, children under 16, 30p.*

Moon, planets, stars are described in words and tracked in film projected to spangle the dome.

St Marylebone Church. – The church by Thomas Hardwick, was completed in 1817, a large balustraded building with a three stage tower ending in gilded caryatids upholding the cupola. Nash saw it as a potential focal point from the park in the axis of York Gate and ennobled Hardwick's edifice by the addition of a pedimented Corinthian portico.

The road continues with the London Clinic on the south side, and on the north, the Royal Academy of Music of red brick and stone, overlooked by reclining figures in the large segmental pediment (1911) and, beyond, the distinctive thin stone tower of **Holy Trinity** ascending from a pillared square base to a tall, egg-shaped cupola, by **Soane** (1878). Below are a Classical pedimented portico and an outside pulpit added in 1891. The church is now the office of the SPCK.

Behind the church is the **White House,** an early modern apartment-hotel block, erected in 1936 to a star shaped plan, 9 storeys tall and faced overall in white ceramic tiles.

■ ST JOHN'S WOOD *(Map pp 5-8, BC/V)*

St John's Wood developed rapidly in the first half of the 19C. The rural days, dating back to the Middle Ages when as the property of the Knights Hospitallers of St John, it got its name, were swept aside as Marylebone began to overflow and Nash's development of Regent's Park made it a potentially desirable residential area. It was, moreover, within three miles of the City and Westminster. Cleverly the developers departed from the current urban styles and erected Italian type villas, broad eaved, in pairs, surrounded by good sized gardens. By 1824 when Edwin Landseer (d 1873) moved into a house in St John's Wood Rd, a colony of artists had begun to gather which much later included Sir Lawrence Alma-Tadema (d 1912) and W R Frith (*Derby Day:* d 1909).

The villas have now largely disappeared, replaced everywhere by apartment blocks and neo-Georgian houses; the small High St has been modernised. Two long standing landmarks, however, do remain:

St John's Wood Church. – *Prince Albert Road*. The church is of the same date, 1813, and by the same architect, Thomas Hardwick, as St Marylebone Parish Church and like it has a distinctive, cupolaed turret.

Lord's Cricket Ground. – The first match to be played at Lord's was MCC (Marylebone Cricket Club) v Herts on 22 June 1814. The club, originally at the White Conduit in Islington moved to Marylebone and altered its name accordingly in 1788 when Thomas Lord, the grounds-man, discovered and leased a site in what is now Dorset Sq. In 1811 Lord lifted the, by now, sacred, turf first to a field which proved to be in the course of the Regent's Canal and then to what, by purchase, has become the permanent ground. The first Test Matches at Lord's were played in 1884.

The **Ashes** (of a bail), portraits and cartoons, memorabilia from batting lists to snuff boxes, can be seen in the **Memorial Gallery** *(open during the season on match days)*. The main gates were erected in memory of **Dr W G Grace** (d 1915) in 1923, Father Time (removing the bails) on the grandstand in 1926.

SOUTH BANK ★ (Lambeth)

The area on the south bank remained rural until the construction of Westminster and Blackfriars Bridges and their approach roads in the mid 18C. The evolution of public transport developed the area from village to town and spa, where the modestly wealthy such as Henry Thrale built out-of-town residences. Finally the area became a suburb where squares and terraces were erected by Thomas Cubitt and lesser men, who agglomerated a network of small streets between the major roads.

Industry. – An ordnance factory in Charles II reign, the Vauxhall Plate Glass Works 1670-1780, the Coade Stone Factory in late 18C (the site now of County Hall), Doultons, lead shot foundries (a shot tower stood at the centre of the 1951 Festival), candle, vinegar, basket, brush factories, boatyards, breweries and distillers, multiplied as the population increased and labour became available. In addition there were specialist workshops and potteries such as the one producing Lambeth delft. The war devastated acres of Victorian streets, slums, the Lambeth Walk, factories, enabling the authorities to rebuild on a vast scale and earlier in 1950, the then LCC under Herbert Morrison, to clear the debris from the riverside for the 1951 Festival of Britain and future arts centre.

■ SOUTH BANK ARTS CENTRE★★

All the buildings on the South Bank are connected by elevated walkways. Access for cars is from the rear; by train and underground, direct from Waterloo Station.

The Royal Festival Hall★. – The hall was the only permanent building erected that bright summer of the 1951 Festival of Britain, the occasion being seized to build a new concert auditorium for London, since the Queen's Hall had been gutted by incendiaries and the Albert Hall's acoustics were still doubled by an echo.

The building was planned by Sir Leslie Martin and Sir Robert Matthew, LCC architects, who worked, it was said, from the inside. Design began with the hall: firstly its acoustics; then visibility of the stage, which will hold a choir of 250, and the seating comfort of 3 000 auditors. The architects continued aesthetically as satisfactorily in the design of foyers, staircases, concourses, bars and restaurants, managing the space to avoid crowding, afford views of the river and inner perspectives of the building itself; finally the whole edifice was successfully insulated against sound from the neighbouring Waterloo Station. In 1954 an organ was installed. In 1962-5 the river frontage was enlarged, redesigned to include the main entrance, and faced with Portland stone.

Queen Elizabeth Hall and Purcell Room. – In 1967 the opening of the Queen Elizabeth Hall and Purcell Room, a second concert hall seating 1 100 and recital room (370), began the second phase of building. The exterior is in unfaced concrete, but the interior, acoustically, is again superb.

Hayward Gallery. – The gallery, which houses temporary exhibitions of painting and sculpture under the auspices of the Arts Council, was opened in 1968 and also belongs to the second building phase. The building, a terrace-like structure of unfaced concrete, in fact "works" successfully inside to provide, on two levels, five large gallery spaces, often subdivided, and three open air sculpture courts, beside viewpoints over the river.

National Film Theatre. – The NFT which opened in 1951, was rebuilt in 1957 and enlarged in 1970 so that it now comprises two cinemas (seating 466 and 165).

National Theatre★. – The theatre opens the third phase in the South Bank scheme, both by its position downstream from Waterloo Bridge and, more importantly, by its design. The architect, **Denys Lasdun,** has incorporated three theatres – a conventional proscenium type, the Lyttelton seating 900, an upper amphitheatre with places for 1 100, the Olivier, and a studio theatre, the Cottesloe (capacity 200) – workshops and ample public amenities, within a construction in which the external height is cut by strata-like terraces which parallel the course of the river at the building's foot.

The Old Vic. – The cradle of the National Theatre and, until 1976, its home, was built in 1818 as the Coburg. In 1880 it was taken by Emma Cons (d 1912), a pioneer of social reform and run as the Royal Victoria Music Hall and Coffee Tavern with a varied programme of concerts, temperance meetings and penny lectures, the last proving so popular that in 1889 the Morley Memorial College for Working Men and Women was founded within the theatre *(see below)*. Under Lilian Baylis (d 1937), who succeeded her aunt, the theatre, now known as the Old Vic, became a centre for music, opera and drama, especially Shakespeare, with a company, in which virtually every British actor of note played at some time. The stage was difficult and draughty; the seats in the pit and the gods were hard and one had to beware of pillars, but prices were low — 4d in the gallery, 5s in the stalls — and the acting was wonderful. In 1940 the Vic was bombed and the company moved to the New Theatre. It returned after the war and, after many vicissitudes, moved in 1976 as the National Theatre Company into the new National Theatre *(see p 139)*.

Shell Centre. — *York Rd*. The Shell Centre, built between 1957-1962, is the largest of Shell's three buildings beside the Thames, a ten storey, U-shaped concrete pile, which includes a 26 story tower, 351ft high. As one of the biggest office blocks in the kingdom it has 43 acres of floor space, 7 000 windows, 88 lifts, 12 escalators, 240 telephone lines and 4 500 extensions, besides a swimming pool, cinema, rifle range, shops...

County Hall★. — *Belvedere Rd. Open to visitors by appointment only and to those attending Council Meetings: every third Tuesday except during holidays.*

County Hall is the headquarters of the Greater London Council (GLC) and the Inner London Education Authority which together with 32 London borough councils plus the historic City of London, constitute the capital's two tier system of local government *(p 20)*.

The hall, a colonnaded arc 700ft in diameter along the river front and still, amidst all the new constructions, one of London's most distinctive buildings, was designed in 1908 by a 29 year old architect, Ralph Knott. The stone pile with Renaissance inspired, steeply pitched dark tile roof with a multitude of dormers, only completed in 1922, has since been trebled in size but always in compatible style. In addition to the formal council chamber and reception rooms, the latter overlooking the river, there is a reference library of some 90 000 volumes and documents on London.

The South Bank Lion. — The lion, 13ft long, 12ft high, carved out of Coade stone, gazes speculatively from a plinth at the foot of Westminster Bridge. Painted red, it was the mascot in 19C of the Lion Brewery until poised at the bridgefoot in 1952.

St Thomas's Hospital. — The familiar length of red and white buildings with the small square tower remains in outward appearance much as it was built in 1868-71. Behind, on Lambeth Palace and Westminster Bridge Rd, new blocks and a complex of well proportioned white ceramic tile and glass buildings of 7-14 storeys contain the St Thomas's of the 70s, treatment centres, clinics, medical school...

From 13C infirmary to 20C teaching hospital. — The hospital, at first dedicated to St Thomas Becket, originated in an infirmary set up early in 13C by the Augustinian canons of St Mary Overie Church, possibly immediately after the great fire of Southwark of 1212. By 1228 priory quarters were too small and a hospital was built opposite on a site which eventually extended in three quadrangles the length of St Thomas St. In the 16C, although St Thomas's was caring for the sick, the orphaned and the indigent, as a conventual establishment, it was forfeited to Henry VIII and closed, only to be rescued in 1552 by the City which purchased it for £647 4s. The story since is one of expansion, removal in the 19C to Lambeth, research and development, the foundation of the Nightingale Fund Training School for Nurses, of ten aerial attacks between September 1940 and July 1944 and keeping at least one operating theatre continuously open...

Westminster Bridge Rd. — The road which was developed in 1750 when the bridge was built, has a distinctive landmark in the gleaming white spire encircled by red brick bands of Christchurch, built in 1874 with funds from the USA. Further along is **Morley College**, (no 61), erected in 1920 when the college removed from the Old Vic, and rebuilt in 1958 to designs by Edward Maufe, with interior murals by John Piper and Edward Bawden. It has a strong musical tradition.

Southwark, which extends south from the Thames 7½ miles to Crystal Palace, includes the Borough and Walworth, Bermondsey, Rotherhithe, Camberwell and Peckham, and Dulwich. Its history, layer upon layer, peels away to the Middle Ages and even Roman times, in documents and on the spot, for buildings and roads have been rebuilt on ancient sites. Its men — native born and adopted — have been diverse: Shakespeare, Ben Jonson, Christopher Marlowe, Burbage, Alleyn, Fletcher, Massinger, Lily Langtry, Chaucer, Blake, Browning, Dickens, Ruskin, Goldsmith, Spurgeon, William Booth, Astley Cooper, Faraday, Desenfans, Bourgeois, Livesey, Passmore Edwards, Thomas Guy, John Harvard...

The Roman invasion to the Dissolution of the Monasteries.

— The construction by the Romans of a bridge, and the convergence at the bridgehead of roads from the south of England, attracted settlers to the fishing village already established on one of the few sites relatively free of flooding on the low-lying marshlands of the Thames' south bank. By Anglo-Saxon times the bridge had become a defence against ship-borne invaders and the village, the *sud werk* or south work, against attacking land forces: Olaf of Norway's rescue of Ethelred from the Danes is commemorated locally in Tooley St (a corruption of St Olave's St), the Conqueror fired Southwark before he took London by encirclement.

In the *Domesday Book,* Southwark was described as having a strand where ships could tie up, a street, a herring fishery and a minster or priory. In 1540, at the Dissolution, the priory reverted to the crown, Henry acquired from Archbishop Cranmer the Great Liberty Manor, granted to Canterbury in the 12C (which extended from the Old Kent Rd to the High St) and for good measure, Bermondsey Abbey (f 1082) among whose tenants were the Bishops of Winchester and the Knights Templar whose 100 acres by the 15C, had become the famous Paris Garden. The bishops had erected a veritable palace which they named **Winchester House** and the notorious prison known as the Clink. Also along the main bank were local stews (brothels) whose prosperous occupants were known as "Winchester geese."

There were also two hospitals, St Thomas's, originally at the priory gate and subsequently across the road, and the Lock or Leper Hospital in Kent St (Old Kent Rd) beyond the Bar or bounds of the mediaeval town (closed 1760).

The people of Walworth, Newington, Camberwell, grew and sold produce at the market first held on London Bridge, later in the High St and finally on the present site; Southwark people were also fishermen and boatmen ferrying passengers and goods across the river. Industries developed such as plaster and mortar making (pollution from the lime burners was being complained of to the king in 1283), weaving, brewing (by refugees from the Low Countries) glassmaking and leather tanning (note the Bermondsey street names: Leathermarket, Tanner, Morocco and the windows in Christchurch, *p 145*). For entertainment there were the midsummer Southwark Fair, the occasional frost fairs when the Thames froze over, brothels and taverns. Not all inns, however, were licentious, many prospered as staging posts for the regular coaches to the ports and the south, and as hostelries for travellers awaiting the morning opening of the bridge to enter the City.

The Dissolution to the 20C.

— Henry rapidly sold off the monastery estates. The City already had interests in Southwark and these it increased but it never acquired jurisdiction over the Clink prison or Paris Garden which is why theatres were built in this single area. The reign of the **Rose** (1587), the **Swan** (1596), the **Globe** (1599) and the **Hope** (1613) was brief however: those that had not already reverted or become bull and bear baiting rings were closed finally under the Commonwealth.

The stews or brothels, particularly along the river bank, descended from early public bath houses, were so notorious by the 12C that a code of conduct was drawn up for them under Henry II. Beneath their signs, the Boar's Head, Cross Keys, Swan, Saracen's Head, they continued until they became so infamous that they had to be closed, of all people, by Henry VIII. They re-opened, of course, but with the closure of the theatres, finally disappeared.

In 18 and 19C, City merchants and businessmen began to build out-of-town houses in Camberwell and Dulwich. The area closer to the river, largely owned by the City and known as the Borough of Southwark which time has shortened to the **Borough,** became heavily industrialised, particularly following the building of the bridges, the 19C expansion of the docks and the coming of the railway. The introduction of the 1d workmen's return to London Bridge brought dense urbanisation to the fields where Robert Browning had once walked and a village after which a butterfly, when seen for the first time in England, was named the Camberwell Beauty.

By the end of the 19C the last of the prisons had been demolished: the Clink, instituted for miscreants within the liberty, in 1780, the Marshalsea on the last of its three sites and where Dickens' father had been locked up for debt, in 1842, King's Bench in 1880 and Horsemonger Lane Jail, also a place of public execution, in 1879.

Southwark, in 19C, became increasingly the area of Livery Company almshouses and charities and, in the 20C, of two pioneer ventures — **Clubland,** an educational and social youth centre founded by the Methodist, James Butterworth in the 1920s *(no 56 Camberwell Road — the Chapel designed by Edward Maufe, was the first church to break away from the Gothic tradition — visit on application to the caretaker)* and the **Peckham Experiment** *(St Mary's Rd, Camberwell)* which from 1935-1945 was conducted as a social and recreational centre, concerned with preventive as well as curative medicine for an all-income, cross-section of the community.

In 1939-1945 came widespread devastation. Southwark is, therefore, now after extensive rebuilding, an amalgam of the very old and the new, each area with its particular characteristic even to street furniture such as the Dulwich finger posts and the bollards made from sawn off cannon with a cannon ball in the mouth, inscribed Wardens of St. Saviour's 1827, and, further along, Clink 1812.

■ SOUTHWARK CATHEDRAL★★ (St Saviour and St Mary Overie)

The history of the site records a progress from Roman villa to nunnery (AD 606), priory of Augustinian canons (1106) to parish Church of St Saviour (1540) and, finally, Cathedral (1905). The name, according to Stow derived from the nunnery being endowed with "the profits of a cross-ferry" from which the church came to be known as "over the river" or St Mary Overie. The first sight of the present building which lies below the level of London Bridge and Borough High St, is of a solid square central tower, 14C below, early 15C above, with paired lancets surmounted by a chequer pattern and pinnacles.

Interior. – *(Enter through the southwest door).* Immediately behind you is the Gothic arcading of the church rebuilt after a fire in 1206, for in addition to the succession of "owners" who altered, embellished, restored or let the church fall into ruin, it suffered disastrous fires. In the far corner, at the end of the north aisle, are the ceiling **bosses** from the 15C wooden roof, rescued when this collapsed in 1838: the pelican, heraldic sunflowers and roses, malice, gluttony, falsehood, Judas being swallowed by the devil... At the end of the nave (Norman fragments in the north wall), re-erected in neo-Gothic style in 1890-97 to marry the 13C chancel which remained, are a collection of **memorials** and **tombs**, vivid in colour and carving and some pithy in their epitaphs: John Gower (1330-1408), poet and friend of Chaucer, with "small forked beard, on his head a chaplet of four roses, a collar of essex gold about his neck" lies, pillowed on his own works, beneath a canopy of red, green and gold. The north transept, with 13C Purbeck marble shafts set against 12C base walls, includes the allegorical Austin monument of 1633 showing a standing figure, Agriculture, between girls in large sun hats, fallen asleep in the harvest field, also the reclining figure, with gaunt face framed by a full wig, of the quack doctor, Lionel Lockyer (1672)...

From beneath the great brass candelabrum of 1680, suspended between the massive 13C piers which support the central tower, there is an uninterrupted view of the intimately proportioned, 13C chancel in true Early English style. The **reredos** appears in sumptuous Gothic glory, framed by the virtually unadorned arches to the chancel aisles, triforium and clerestory. The screen, which was presented by Bishop Fox in 1520, remained empty until 1905 when statues were carved to people the niches; the lower register was gilded in the thirties. Funeral pavement stones commemorate the burial in the church of Edmund (d 1607), brother of William Shakespeare, and the Jacobean dramatists, John Fletcher (d 1625) and Philip Massinger (d 1640).

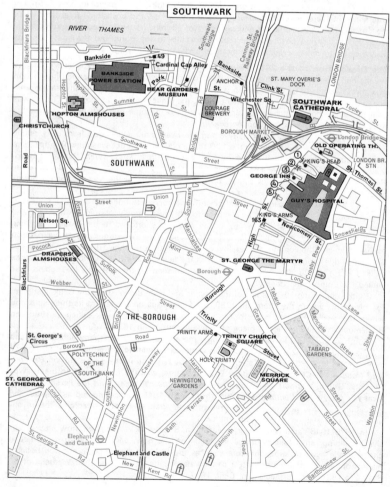

Adjoining the asymmetrical, stilted arch which opens the north chancel aisle is the **Harvard Chapel,** dedicated to John Harvard who was born in Borough High St and baptised in the church in 1607 (emigrated 1638). Mementoes include the American made window, a tablet to the Pilgrim Trust and a carved scallop shell, the pilgrim emblem.

The wall monument with the colourful three-quarter figure is to John Trehearne (d 1618), "Gentleman porter to James I" (note the epitaph). Beyond, against the wall, is a rare figure of a knight, possibly a Templar, meticulously carved in oak about 1275. To the right is the free standing monument to Richard Humble and his wives in full 17C finery. The retro-choir, 13C and square ended, is divided into four equal aisles by elementarily shaped piers; sparsely adorned, it is easy to imagine its having served as tribunal, prison, billet, sty and bakery.

(After photograph, Jarrold's, Norwich)

Alderman Humble and wives, 1616.

The south chancel aisle (tessellated paving from the Roman villa) leads past the free standing tomb of Lancelot Andrewes (d 1626), Bishop of Westminster, member of the commission which produced the Authorised Version, a figure in shallow ruff and ample deep blue robes, beneath a modern canopy, gilded and crested. In the south transept — 14 and early 15C principally, with early Perpendicular tracery (renewed) in the three light windows, the large window ornately 19C — are, on the right, a miniature recumbent effigy of William Emerson (d 1575), high above, a colourful half figure in gown and ruff, John Bingham (d 1625), saddler to Queen Elizabeth and James I, and to the left, the red painted arms and hat of Cardinal Beaufort, 15C Bishop of Westminster. Note the exquisite Jacobean communion table with turned legs, in rare groups of four in front, three behind.

Against the wall of the south aisle is the memorial to Shakespeare — a 1911 alabaster figure, reclining beneath a modern Shakespearean window.

Westwards from Southwark Cathedral

Clink St. — Behind the cathedral and market, gaunt 19C warehouses overshadow docks and cobbled alleys which lead down to the river, past the old west wall and rose window of the bishop's Winchester House banqueting hall beneath which, and also below the high tide water level, lay the Clink prison from which the expression to be "in Clink" derived.

Bankside. — The Anchor Tavern *(no 1 Bankside just west of Cannon St Rlwy Bridge)* was erected in 1770-75 on the site of earlier inns and is associated in its history not only with the river and the prison (truncheons, manacles etc in one bar) but also with Shakespeare and Dr Johnson and Boswell, through the Thrales who at one time owned it. More importantly Henry Thrale also owned the brewery in Park Street of which Johnson remarked, as executor, "We are not here to sell a parcel of boilers and vats but the potentiality of growing rich beyond the dreams of avarice". The brewery has a bronze plaque of Shakespeare and contemporary Southwark on its Park St wall, to mark the probable site of the **Globe Theatre** (1599-1613).

Bear Gardens Museum. — *Bear Garden Alley. Open Tuesdays to Fridays, May to September, 11am to 6pm (weekends 12 to 5pm); October to April, 12 to 3pm (weekends to 4pm); 20p.*

The museum, which is in a converted 18C warehouse on the site of the 16C bear baiting ring and later Hope Playhouse, possesses a remarkable, small collection on the Bankside Elizabethan theatre and **wooden O's,** the Globe, the Hope, the Swan and the first, the Rose (1587), also the bear and bull baiting rings and a diorama of Southwark at the time of one of the great Frost Fairs on the frozen Thames. *Additional temporary exhibitions.*

Two 18C private houses stand on either side of Cardinal Cap Alley. The first, no 49 Bankside, an attractive small house decorated on the coping with pinecones, was built on the site of the Cardinal's Hat, a 16C stew. It bears a plaque which solemnly declares that it was where "in 1502 Catherine Infanta of Aragon and Castile and afterwards first Queen of Henry VIII, took shelter on her first landing in London" and also that it was where Christopher Wren lived during the building of the cathedral — all of which would appear unlikely as the house, although the oldest on Bankside, was built 50 years after the Great Fire. The houses, beyond the alley, now used as the Lodgings of the Provost of Southwark Cathedral, slightly larger and more stylised, are some 30 years later. There is a unique **view★★** at this point across the river, of three 17C City buildings rising one behind the other: St Benet's, the College of Arms, St Paul's.

The **Bankside Power Station,** a massive landmark among its peers with its single 320ft chimney, was designed by Giles Gilbert Scott (completed: 1964). Present capacity is 300 000 k/w — in 1891 when a station first started operating on Bankside, 330 k/w supplied the City's entire needs! *(Visits only by written appointment.)*

The Hopton Almshouses. — *Hopton St.* A group of two storey brick and tile cottages, the main wing pedimented, were built round three sides of a garden in 1752 and remain to this day bright with paint and still very rural.

South, down Borough High Street

The Borough, kernel not only of Southwark but of London south of the Thames, rings with historic street and inn names though many of the old buildings have now gone.

St Thomas's Old Operating Theatre. — *St Thomas St. Open Mondays, Wednesdays, Fridays 12.30 to 4pm and by appt — Tel 407 3662 Ext. 34; 20p.*

The entrance to the awesome early 19C operating theatre is through the tower door of St Thomas's Parish Church (now Southwark Cathedral chapterhouse — *not open*), formerly at the centre of the buildings of Old St Thomas's Hospital. This extended back from the High St in four quadrangles. St Thomas St itself was lined from halfway along by officials' houses of which the late 18C terrace remains (the wide gateway served as a hospital side entrance).

The church attic was already in use as a herb garret when, in 1821, the hospital committee decided to convert it into a women's operating theatre since it adjoined the Dorcas women's ward in one of the hospital's two front blocks. The theatre (rediscovered in 1956) is semicircular, about 40ft across with a 14ft amphitheatre ringed by 5 rows of "standings" for students. At the centre was the operating table, a sturdy wooden structure with upraised headpiece, and below, on the floor, a wooden box of sawdust which could "be kicked by the surgeon's foot to any place where most blood was running". In the corner was a small washbasin about the size of a large soup plate, in which surgeons washed their hands after — sometimes even before — operating. The theatre was last used in 1862 and is the only one of the period to be preserved in London. The hospital *(qv)* moved to its present site, near Westminster Bridge in 1871.

Guy's Hospital. — The vast, 1 000 bed unit with one of London's tallest towers among its new buildings, retains the iron railings, gateway and square forecourt of its foundation construction of 1722. The court is flanked by the original tile roofed brick wings which lead back to the slightly later, Palladian style, centre range with a stone frontispiece decorated with allegorical figures by Bacon. In the court stands a bronze statue by Scheemakers of Thomas Guy (1644-1724), son of a Southwark lighterman and coal dealer, who began as a bookseller (Bibles), gambled successfully on the South Sea Bubble and other enterprises and then, like his 20C successor at Guy's, Lord Nuffield, who also rose from humble stock to be a very rich man, became a munificent patron of medical institutions. In the chapel (centre of the right wing) is a full size memorial in high relief by John Bacon of Guy, portrayed before the 18C hospital into which a stretcher case is being borne. In the quads to the rear are a statue of Lord Nuffield and a mid 18C alcove from old London Bridge.

The Yards and the Inns of Southwark. — A series of narrow streets and yards off Borough High St just after St Thomas St, mark the entrances to the old inns which were the overnight stop of people arriving too late at night to cross the bridge into the capital. These inns were also the starting point for coach services to the southern counties and the ports. **King's Head Yard** ①: the King's Head, known as the Pope's Head before the Reformation, now a 19C building, sports a robust, somewhat supercilious, coloured effigy of Henry VIII. **White Hart Yard** ②: the pub (no longer in existence) was the headquarters of Jack Cade in 1450 and where Mr. Pickwick first met Sam Weller. **George Inn Yard** ③: the **George Inn★**, when rebuilt in 1676 after a fire, had galleries on three sides — only part of the south range remains but this still possesses two upper galleries outside and panelled rooms inside. Shakespeare is played in the cobbled yard in summer and open fires and traditional fare warm customers in winter. Note the Act of Parliament clock constructed in 1797 when a tax of 5s made people sell their timepieces and rely on clocks in public places — the act was repealed within the year.

Talbot Yard ④: recalled by Chaucer in the Prologue: "In Southwark at the Tabbard as I lay, At night was come into that hostelrie Wel nyne and twenty in a compagnye of sondrye folk... and pilgrims were they alle That toward Canterbury wolden ryde".

Queen's Head Yard ⑤: site of the Queen's Head (demolished: 1900) sold by John Harvard before he set out for America; Newcomen St: the King's Arms dating from 1890 takes its name from the brightly painted lion and unicorn supporting the arms of George II (not George III as inscribed), a massive emblem which originally decorated the south gatehouse of old London Bridge. A plaque at no 163 indicates the final site of **Marshalsea Prison** (1376 to 1811), the notorious penitentiary of which only one high wall remains.

St George the Martyr. — The stone spire and square tower of the 1736 church on a site dating back to 12C mark the end of the first section of the High St. Dickens features the church in *Little Dorrit*.

Trinity Street (east of Borough High Street) marked by a contemporary pub, the Trinity Arms, leads into two complete, early 19C, squares. The first, **Trinity Church Sq★** is an unbroken quadrilateral of three storey houses, punctuated on the ground floor with round arched doorways, and united above by a narrow white course and coping. At the centre, in the garden, are a statue and a church. The statue, more than lifesize, is believed to have been brought in 1822 from Westminster Hall where it had stood in a niche for 450 years so making it the oldest statue in London: it is known as **King Alfred**. The church with a portico of colossal, fluted columns and a small openwork tower, built in 1824 and bombed, has been transformed (1975) by the Henry Wood Rehearsal Hall Trust into a studio for use by major orchestras, principally the LSO and LPO. The adjoining and equally complete **Merrick Square★** of more modest houses, is named after the merchant who left the property in 1661 to the corporation of Trinity House.

ST GEORGE'S CATHEDRAL, ELEPHANT and CASTLE

St George's Roman Catholic Cathedral. – *Lambeth Road.* St George's, one of the first major Roman Catholic churches to be built in England after the Reformation was opened in 1848. It was designed by **A W Pugin** (1812-52), the impassioned advocate of the Gothic Revival (of the late 13C and early 14C English architectural style), who ended his days in the Bedlam hospital opposite, now the Imperial War Museum. The cathedral, destroyed by incendiary bombs during the War, was rebuilt to the design of Romilly Bernard Craze, and reopened in 1958.

Pugin's vision was never realised, so the stock brick exterior is characterised by a massive stump, the foundation of what was to have been a soaring spire.

Interior. – The new cathedral with an added clerestory is much lighter than the old: fluted columns of white Painswick stone support high pointed arches; plain glass lights the aisles, the only elaborate windows being those at the east and west ends which form jewelled pendants with rich red and deep blue glass. The new building's sole ornate feature is the high altar with its carved and gilded reredos. Statues are modern in uncoloured stone, memorials few but including the canopied figure of Cardinal Manning.

St George's Circus. – The circus now a forlorn roundabout, was laid out in 1769 by act of parliament as London's first designed traffic junction with the obelisk to Brass Crosby *(qv)* marking the central island. Five, now six, roads converged at the centre of St George's Fields, long an open area crossed by rough roads where rebels had assembled (the Gordon Rioters), cattle grazed, a windmill turned, preachers roused crowds. In the vicinity are the **Drapers' Almshouses** (1820) two storey cottages with neo-Gothic windows and Nelson Sq where post war municipal housing adjoins a 1799 terrace. In Blackfriars Rd (no 27) stands **Christchurch**, the South London Industrial Mission, rebuilt in brick in a shady garden, which contains inside *(ring)* modern windows illustrating all the local trades including that of the Mrs Mops who in delighted return keep the church clean and polished.

Elephant and Castle. – The crossroads where the Roman Stane Street from Sussex was joined on its way to London Bridge by Watling Street from Kent and roads from villages where Lambeth is now, remained unnamed until the middle of 18C, when the corner smithy became a tavern and took as its sign the elephant and castle of the Cutlers' Co which, like so many other City companies, has associations with the area. Roads proliferated with the construction of bridges over the Thames in the 18 and 19C until congestion at the junction became notorious. Aerial devastation produced a new opportunity and in the 1950-60s, the 40 acre site was entirely redesigned and rebuilt.

CAMBERWELL and PECKHAM

The area offers an assortment of interests and buildings of 18, 19 and recent 20C. Grouped geographically they include:

Cambridge House *(131 Camberwell Rd)*, early 19C houses, now the University Settlement; South London Antiques Centres, 159-161 Camberwell Rd filled with lesser antiques, frippery and commemorative 19C china – jubilee mugs etc; **King's College** and **Maudsley Hospitals** on either side of Denmark Hill and beyond, in Champion Park, behind the bronze statues of the General and his wife, Evelina, the **William Booth Memorial Salvation Army Training College** (1932).

Camberwell Grove off Camberwell Church St, is a wide avenue, closely planted, rising and lined by late 18, early 19C, Georgian town houses and terraces, Victorian cottages and villas. At the avenue's opening is the Mary Datchelor Girls' School, founded from monies left in 1726 in charity by Mary Datchelor *(qv)* who had been bequeathed a City coffee-house by her father. In 1863 the coffeehouse was sold for £30 000 and the school established in Camberwell which since late 19C has been endowed by the Clothworkers' City Co. Near the avenue's top are Grove Chapel (1819) and opposite a small crescent of attractive stuccoed houses of 1830.

St Giles *(Peckham Rd)*, neo-Gothic with a towering spire, is remarkable for its gargoyles of Gladstone and other contemporary statesmen and inside, brasses dating from 1497 (Mighell Skinner) 1532... Camberwell School of Arts and Crafts and the South London Art Gallery, Peckham Rd, combine massive elongated new buildings with the old school (1903), all red brick gables and the even older gallery (1890), where caryatids guard the entrance.

Georgian Terraces *(nos 29, 30-34, ie both sides)*: the northerly of the two ranges, once known as Camberwell House was at one time a school attended by Thomas Hood; the south asymmetrical terrace, overlooking Lucas Gardens, is preceded by a cobbled forecourt furnished with a contemporary gas lamp, iron gateway etc...

Nunhead Green *(southeast)* is marked by the rebuilt tavern which claims a licence dating back to Henry VIII's reign and the attractive white stucco, **Beeston's Gift Almshouses,** erected in 1834 by the Girdlers' Co on land left them in the 16C by Cuthbert Beeston.

Asylum Rd *(north side, leading to the Old Kent Rd)* contains near its top end, a 20C church, an 18C house and 19C almshouses.

St John's *(Meeting House Lane)*, designed by David Bush in 1964, has a high, asymmetrical, brick end wall and an interior where roof lines, curving organ pipes, lead the eye to the bronze Christ, rescued from the bombed parish church and now high on the brick wall behind the altar; colour comes from the ground level window, a glowing abstract of blues, greens, yellows and from a joyous *Mother and Child* by Ron Hinton (1966). The 18C **house** is of yellow stone with a great circular bow window. Just beyond, lying back from the road round three sides of a forecourt, is a long, two storey, brick range with a central, pedimented portico, the Licensed Victuallers Benevolent Institution of 1827 (now Caroline Gardens).

The Strand was an ancient track, midway between the highway west out of the City to Oxford in the north and London's main thoroughfare, the Thames; it was a street of great mansions and law students' hostels or inns from Plantagenet to Hanoverian times, the south side being especially favoured by provincial bishops for their town houses purchased, after the Dissolution, by the nobility. Between the big houses and down the lanes were hundreds of small houses, ale houses, bordels, coffeehouses – the Grecian, now the Devereux public house, was a favourite of Addison, Twinings (no 216) the tea men, opened in 1706 as Tom's Coffee House. There were also shops and from 1609 an arcade known as the **New Exchange**, patronised by James I and his Queen, Charles I and later Pepys who recounts how he bought gloves, linen, lace, garters, stockings and even books there – 76 of the 150 shops were milliners and mercers (demolished: 1737). In the late Victorian – Edwardian era, the Strand was known for its hotels – the Cecil with 1 000 bedrooms (now Shell Mex), the Metropole, Victoria, the Grand, besides those of today – also its restaurants, theatres and its gaiety – a popular 19C music hall song was *Let's all go down the Strand.*

Along the commercial thoroughfare of today built and rebuilt in 19 and 20C, only the churches remain from the mediaeval period and street names or rebuildings of the palaces and mansions: Essex St and Devereux Ct after the Elizabethan favourite, Robert Devereux's Essex House (owned later by another favourite, Robert Dudley, Earl of Leicester); Arundel St after the great house of the Howards, Hungerford Lane after 15C house of a notorious family who demolished it, opened a market to pay off gambling debts and even built the footbridge in 1845 to attract customers before ultimately selling out for **Charing Cross Railway Stn** to be built on the site. Finally on either side of the station are Villiers and Buckingham Sts after George Villiers, presented in 1624 by James I with York House, onetime palace of the archbishops. Northumberland Avenue is built on the site of the famous Northumberland House.

St Clement Danes★. – St Clement's, designed by **Wren** in 1682, with the open spire in three diminishing pillared stages, crowned by a small dome and turret added by **James Gibbs** in 1719, was burnt out in 1941 and rebuilt as the RAF church in 1955-8. To the Wren design of panelling and galleries, a tunnel vault with an enriched coffered plaster decoration massed to surround a Stuart coat of arms, have been added airforce mementoes including 800 squadron and unit badges carved as slate keys and inlaid in the pavement, floor memorials of the badges of the Commonwealth air forces and the Polish squadrons. There are also a USAAF and other shrines and Memorial Books with 125 000 names. The grand pulpit is the original Grinling Gibbons one put together splinter by splinter after the war.

Tradition has it that boats with oranges and lemons came up the Thames to land fruit for sale in Clare Market (on the site of Kingsway – Drury Lane) and paid a tithe in kind to the church; association is disputed *(p 54)*, but a carillon rings out the **nursery rhyme** at 9am, noon, 3 and 6pm on weekdays.

Samuel Johnson was a regular worshipper, hence the bronze statue overlooking Fleet St.

St Mary-le-Strand. – The second church on an island site is a Baroque miniature. It was designed by **James Gibbs** in 1714-17 with a semicircular, columned, west porch and columns above supporting a pediment. The tower immediately behind the porch, is in four tiers, the centre two columned beneath a final turret (compare with the later St Clement Danes and St Martin-in-the-Fields).

Inside the decoration is concentrated in the plasterwork roofing.

King's College. – The college, founded in 1829 and since 1898 a part of London University, was housed from its earliest days in the east extension of Somerset House, built in accordance with Chambers' designs until recently when the Strand front was renewed in an unrelated, modern style. The courtyard, long and narrow is distinguished at the end by the colonnaded pavilion which completes the Somerset House river front.

Roman Bath. – *5 Strand Lane. Open Mondays to Saturdays: 10am to 12.30pm; 5p, NT.*

The bath, fed by a nearby spring is long and rounded at one end, is possibly Tudor, more likely 17C but is certainly not Roman. Dutch 17C tiles, the traditional delft and a tulip design, panel areas of the walls.

Somerset House★. – The present building, foretaste in size of future ministries, was erected enduringly in Portland stone in 1777-90 to the designs of **Sir William Chambers**; it housed the Navy and Navy Pay Offices, the, then small, Tax and Excise offices and three learned societies; the Royal Academy, which Chambers was instrumental in founding and of which he was treasurer, the Antiquaries and the Royal Society.

Somerset House : river front.

The 18C building stands on the site of the palace begun by Protector Somerset in 1547 and still incomplete when he was executed in 1553. In that time it became the duke's obsession to build supremely: to acquire additional land he demolished the 13C Mary-le-

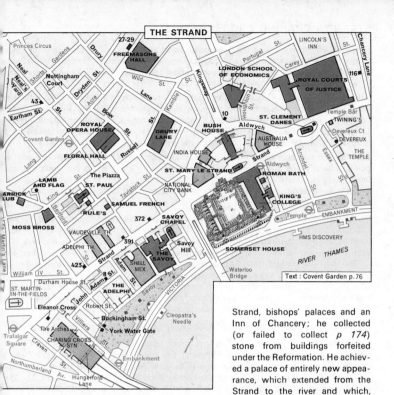

Text : Covent Garden p. 76

Strand, bishops' palaces and an Inn of Chancery; he collected (or failed to collect *p 174*) stone from buildings forfeited under the Reformation. He achieved a palace of entirely new appearance, which extended from the Strand to the river and which, on his execution, passed to the

own and was given by each Stuart to his queen, Anne of Denmark (when it was known s Denmark House), Henrietta Maria, who returned to it at the Restoration and Catherine f Braganza.

he building. — The narrow Strand façade, inspired by Inigo Jones' Palladian riverside allery designed for Henrietta Maria, has a triple gateway and giant columns beneath a balus-ade decorated with statues and a massive statuary group by Bacon.

Inside is a vast courtyard nearly 120 yds long by just over 100 across: Chambers' gift y in design on a more domestic scale and he treated the courtyard as a square of ter-ace houses. The Strand block, in which the societies were accommodated (the names are till over the doors) and which contains the so-called **Fine Rooms,** notable for their pro-ortions and plasterwork, has two short advanced wings and is the most elaborate. A conti-uous balustrade, punctuated by vases (supplied by Mrs Coade at 6 gns each!) unites the onts.

The riverside front, which is 800ft long including the later extensions, stands on a ontinuous line of massive arches which would, in 18C, have been at the river's edge.

Located in Somerset House today are the Board of Inland Revenue and the **Probate egistry** *(access to the index free; examination and copies of wills available on payment — Mondays to Fridays 10am to 4.30 pm).*

he Savoy. — The Savoy is now a precinct including a chapel, a **theatre** built by Richard 'Oyly Carte in 1881 to stage the Gilbert and Sullivan operas (of which 13 appeared etween 1875 and 1896) and a **hotel,** also built by D'Oyly Carte in 1889.

The name dates from 1246, when Henry III granted the manor beside the Thames to is queen's uncle, Peter of Savoy. On the acres extending from the Temple to the Adelphi e built a palace which by 14C had passed to the Dukes of Lancaster, and as "the fairest anor in England" became, until his death, the "lodging" of King John of France, captur-d by the Black Prince at Poitiers (1356). The last owner, was John of Gaunt who, how-ver, was forced to flee to Ely Place in 1381 when the palace was sacked by Wat Tyler's entish rebels. The manor was annexed in 1399 by Henry IV.

he Queen's Chapel of the Savoy (Chapel of the Royal Victorian Order). — *Savoy Hill. Open Tuesday to Friday 11.30am to 3.30pm; closed August and September.*

The chapel, largely rebuilt after the war, dates back to a bequest by Henry VII for the onstruction of a hospital for 100 "pouer, needie people" and the erection of a dependent lace of worship in 1510-16. The hospital was dissolved in 1702 but the chapel and burial ard survived to be made into the Chapel of the Royal Victorian Order in 1937.

Savoy Hill is famous as the site of the BBC's first studios and offices: 1923-32 (plaque n the Embankment façade of no 2 Savoy Place).

he Adelphi. — The riverfront retains the name although the massively ungraceful stone nd brick block with cumbersome angle statues could scarcely be more remote from the Royal Adelphi Terrace erected by Robert Adam in 1768-72 (demolished 1937). The Adam rothers — *adelphi:* Latinised form of Greek for brothers — purchased the site on a 99 year ease and transformed the area by the construction along the foreshore of a towering mbankment arcade, the Adelphi Arches, superimposed by a terrace of eleven houses. The ow was framed by John, now John Adam St, Robert and Adam Sts, the end houses in the latter, which overlooked the river, pedimented and decorated to form advanced wing to the terrace. It was the first and possibly finest of Thameside concepts but it prove exhorbitantly costly and a failure financially; now only a few houses remain to give an ide of what the quarter must once have been like.

John Adam St: no 8 was built for the Royal Society of Arts (f 1754) in 1772-4 by Ada with a pillared porch surmounted by giant fluted columns framing a Venetian window note the cornice inscription: "Arts and Commerce promoted". (From the Strand, just we of New South Wales House, steps down to Durham House St are overlooked by th delightful RSA rear façade surmounted at the crest by a slender water carrier).

Adam St: the east side has a run of houses beginning with no 10, Adam House, neat an compact with a rounded corner and curved ironwork; 9 and 8 are the street's standar with attractive, pilastered doors; no 7, in the axis of John Adam St, is a typical example o Adam in full decorative style with his favourite acanthus leaf motif on pilasters, cornice an ironwork *(illustration p 25)*.

Buckingham St. — 17 and 18C brick houses with pilastered, hooded and corbelle doorways still line both sides (nos 12, 17, 18, 20 date from 1670s). Pepys lived at no 1 from 1679-88. At the bottom, where in 1626 was the river's edge, stands the **York Wate Gate**, a triple arch of rusticated stone decorated with the Villiers arms and a scallop shel

Beneath the viaduct from Charing Cross Station to Hungerford Railway Bridge an connecting Villiers and Craven Sts (Benjamin Franklin lived at no 40) are Hungerford Lan where there is a Saturday coin, medal, stamp and Victoriana, market, The Arches, wher there are military and police paraphernalia and coin shops and, between the two, th **Players Theatre Club** *(members only)* in an old music hall.

The Strand's north side opens with Chancery Lane and the Royal Courts of Justice.

Chancery Lane. — *(Map p 99)*. The lane which takes its name from the grant of land b Henry III to his Lord Chancellor, Bishop of Chichester in 1227 (hence Rolls Passage Bishop's Ct etc) is now commercial as well as legal. At the lane's top end are the Paten Office (25 Southampton Bldgs) and the **London Silver Vaults** *(basement of no 53, Chan cery House; open Mondays to Fridays, 9am to 5.30pm, Saturdays to 12.30pm)* where i fifty rooms, each entered through a strongroom door, there is a gleaming array of Georgian Victorian and more modern silverware with prices as various.

The Public Record Office. — *Open Mondays to Fridays 1 to 4pm. Mornings by appt only.*

The office, established in 1838, is housed in a 19C neo-Gothic building which extend to Fetter Lane. On display in the corridor are old chests including those of the Pyx from Westminster Abbey, and the Million Bank with multiple locks; in the museum are *Domes day* (also a printed copy, with translation, in which one may check whether places were i existence in 1086), letters from English kings and queens dating back to Richard II, from Mazarin, Bismarck, Louis XVI and Marie Antoinette... There are accounts (and tally sticks *p 168*), a drawing illustrating the murder of Darnley, wills — Shakespeare, Jane Austen Emma Hamilton — logs and despatches, Nelson's and Wellington's; there are Guy Faw kes' confessions... seals... treaties...

The three 16/17C effigies in terracotta (by Torrigiano) and alabaster are from the forme Chapel of the Rolls (successor to a 13C chapel for Jewish converts).

Royal Courts of Justice. — The Law Courts date from 1874-82 when the Perpendicula design of G E Street was constructed to replace the ranges erected around the courts original seat in Westminster Hall. The centrepiece inside is the Great Hall, a vaulted arcade 230ft long, 82ft high, decorated with foliated doorways, blind arcades, diapering and a seated statue of the architect. The early courtrooms and the majority still — there are more than 20 — depend from the hall which is marked outside by a needle spire, counterpoint t the long arched façade, the heavy tower and polygonal west end.

Aldwych. — The sweeping semicircle was laid out in 1905 as part of the Kingsway improvement plan. The huge half moon island on the Strand is occupied by massive buildings — Australia House, India House (reliefs), the National City Bank and, in the centre, the 1925-35 **Bush House**, base of the BBC External Services.

The Registry of births, deaths and marriages. — *St Catherine's House, 10 Kingsway Public Search Rooms open Monday to Friday 8.30am to 4.30pm.*

Registration has been compulsory since 1837 and there are now some 250 millior entries; nearly 4 000 people a week use the search rooms.

London School of Economics. — *Houghton St.* The school which numbers 3 000 full-time students and 400 part-time students (40% postgraduates), was founded in 1895 under the auspices of Sydney Webb and is now part of London University. The British Library of Political and Economic Science, which contains 650 000 volumes and 1 500 00C other items, including pamphlets and tracts, is also housed in the building.

The north side of the Strand backing on to Covent Garden, continues with the narrow front of the Strand Palace Hotel (no 372), Stanley Gibbons stamp shop (391), the Vaude-ville and Adelphi Theatres and the brick and terracotta Civil Service Stores (423-7) — compare the building with New South Wales House opposite by Lasdun.

Charing Cross. — Where the Strand met the road from Westminster and the road north, there developed the village of Charing (from Anglo-Saxon *ceirring*: a bend) where in 1290 Edward I placed the last of the 12 **Eleanor Crosses** marking the funeral cortege of his queen to Westminster. The original Cross, octagonal and of solid appearance in marble and Caen stone which stood where the statue of Charles I is now, was destroyed by the Puritans; the present one outside the station dates from 1860.

SYON PARK ★★ (Brentford, Hounslow) ————————————

Open Good Friday, Easter Saturday, Sunday and Monday; third week in May to end of July, Mondays to Fridays 1 to 5pm; August and September, Sundays to Thursdays 1 to 5pm; holiday Mondays 11am to 5pm; 40p.

The colonnaded east front of Syon House is visible across the river from Kew Gardens, the Northumberland Lion with outstretched tail silhouetted against the sky; a second beast, also from the model by Michelangelo, crowns the main, Lion Gate and graceful Adam screen on the London Rd (A 315). Nothing adorns the castellated main front, which therefore gives no hint of the rich ornamentation within.

The house's history. — On the walls inside are portraits of the men and women who built up the house and their royal patrons, by Gainsborough, Reynolds, van Dyck, Mytens, Lely and, often most penetratingly, by unknown artists of the English 16C school. Two men were principally responsible for the construction: the Lord Protector, Duke of Somerset, brother of Henry's queen, Jane Seymour, in the 16C and Hugh Percy, 1st Duke of Northumberland in the 18C. Somerset was given the former monastery site in 1547 by his nephew Edward VI and erected a Tudor mansion in the plan of a hollow square, dined his monarch there in 1550, laid out gardens, including the first physic (botanical) garden in England... but in 1552 he was charged with conspiracy and executed. For the next two centuries Syon was a political storm centre as the owners intrigued, conspired and often died brutally: John Dudley was beheaded (1553) for promoting his daughter-in-law, Lady Jane Grey, as queen; Percys, Earls of Northumberland, were executed for supporting Mary Queen of Scots (1572), were found dead in the Tower (1585) and imprisoned for association with the Gunpowder Plot... With the marriage in 1682 of Elizabeth Percy to Charles, 6th Duke of Somerset, Syon returned to a descendant of its first owner, who also held office under the crown. By the 18C, the house and grounds, in the opinion of the new heirs, the Duke and Duchess of Northumberland, were in urgent need of remodelling: they commissioned **Robert Adam** and **Capability Brown** to produce designs.

The interior. — Adam is at his most formal in the high, wide Hall which has a black and white marble pavement, an apse at the north end framing a statue of the *Apollo Belvedere,* another opposite, upraised and screened by Doric columns, before which is the bronze figure of the *Dying Gladiator.* The ceiling reflects the pavement design.

The Ante-Room. — The ante-room, by contrast, gleams darkly with heavy gilding, reds, blues, yellows, in the patterned scagliola floor, and green marble and scagliola pillars, which line the walls on three sides and stand forward from the fourth to "square" the room. Gilded statues gaze down from the entablature.

State Dining Room. — The long apartment with column screened apses at either end was the first to be remodelled by Adam: deep red-purple niches with copies of antique statues along the left wall are reflected in pier mirrors, frieze, cornice, ceiling, decorated half domes, beautiful doorcases and doors, afforded a perfect setting for the banquets given by the duke and duchess to the fashionable world of the late 18C.

Red Drawing Room. — Scarlet Spitalfields silk, blooming with pale gold roses, on the walls and at the windows, a carpet, signed and dated 1769, woven at Moorfields, door pilasters with ivory panels covered with ormolu, gilded ceiling studded with Cipriani painted medallions, provide great richness — but the room is, in fact, dominated by its Stuart portraits: Charles I (Lely), his queen, Henrietta Maria (van Dyck); his sister Elizabeth of Bohemia (van Honthorst); his elder brother who pre-deceased him, Prince Henry (van Somer); his daughter, Princess Mary of Orange (Hanneman), Henrietta, Duchess of Orleans (Mignard), Princess Elizabeth (Lely), his sons, Charles II and his wife Catherine of Braganza (Huysmans) and James II as Duke of York (Lely).

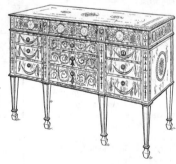

The Long Gallery. — The long gallery of the Tudor house was transformed by Adam into a ladies' withdrawing room (far enough away from the dining room not to hear any masculine after dinner ribaldry!). It is 136ft long, 14ft wide and has a crossline decoration on the ceiling, grouped pilasters, wall niches, pier mirrors, so arranged as to disguise the length. Much of the furniture was designed, as throughout the house, by Adam, notably the veneered chest of drawers made by Chippendale.

The Print Room. — The furniture in this small room includes two remarkable walnut, marquetry inlaid cabinets of the late 17C; the walls are again hung with family portraits.

(By permission of the Duke of Northumberland)

Adam commode.

■ SYON PARK GARDENS★

Open 1 March to 30 September 10am to 6pm; winter 10am to 5pm or dusk when earlier; closed 25, 26 December; 45p. Restaurants, bar, cafeteria and car park. Garden Centre.

The gardens, which extend to the river, were originally landscaped by Capability Brown, and remain admired for their shrubs and trees, and vast **rose garden** *(separate entrance).*

Great Conservatory. — The conservatory, a beautiful semicircular building of white painted gun metal and Bath stone, with a central cupola and end pavilions was designed by Charles Fowler in 1820-27. Inside are cacti and small birds flying free.

The World of Motoring. — *Entrance from inside the gardens; 30p. Exhibits, bookshop.*

London Transport Collection. – *Separate entrance; 25p.*

The exhibition contains examples of buses from the horse-drawn era to the immediate past, trams and early locomotives. Around the sides of the hall are a selection of the posters for which London Transport is famous among graphic connoisseurs; old tickets uniforms...

South of Syon Park

Isleworth Parish Church of All Saints. – The church beside the river on the south outskirts of Syon Park, has a square crenellated west tower of ragstone, dating back to 15C and containing two 18C monuments, one to a church benefactor. The church was bombed and on the site since 1970, has stood a well proportioned modern vessel of brick, wood and plain glass, with only small brasses rescued from the fire.

The London Apprentice. – The pub on the river dates back centuries, the present building some 200 years with plasterwork and panelling in different bars. The name is said to be after the 16/19C apprentices who rowed up the river on their annual holiday and made the inn their own for a day.

Osterley, Ham, Hampton Court, the other great houses on London's periphery are described on pp 124, 85 and 92. A selection of those a little further out to north, east, south and west is indicated on the map on pp 182-183 together with times of opening and charges (summer 1977).

TATE GALLERY ★★★ (Millbank, Westminster)

Open daily 10am to 6pm (Sunday from 2pm); closed 1 January, Good Friday, 24, 25, 26 December; for special exhibitions: see the press.

In 1977-78 the latest extension to the gallery should be complete and the museum fully open with space to exhibit the greater part of the 6 500 pictures and sculptures that go to make up its two collections: The **British School** from 16 to mid 19C and **Modern Art** from 1850 to the present. Meanwhile the British School on the left, has been rehung but not to its full extent and Modern Art, on the right is being progressively rehung. Special exhibitions, always a feature of the Tate, are mounted in the long gallery in line with the entrance.

The opening of the extension will be celebrated by two successive exhibitions, 1850-*c* 1950, 1950-1977, to display the museum's Modern Art acquisitions in full.

Foundation to 1977 extension. – The Tate buys canvases before the paint is dry, controversial sculptures, because it is a place to see the evolution and range of style, the contribution to a school of contemporary greater and lesser artists.

The gallery developed because within 50 years of the purchase of the Angerstein collection and the founding of the National Gallery in 1824, the nation had acquired a large number of pictures – notably through the Chantrey bequest, for the purchase of works by living artists as well as earlier masters, two major collections (the Vernon and Sheepshanks) and the Turner bequest of 282 oil paintings and 19 000 water colours (1856). These pictures were shuffled between National Gallery, the V & A and Marlborough House until, in 1891 Henry Tate, sugar broker, munificent benefactor and collector of modern art, offered his collection to the nation and £80 000 for a building, if the government would provide the site. The government offered the emplacement of the former Millbank Prison.

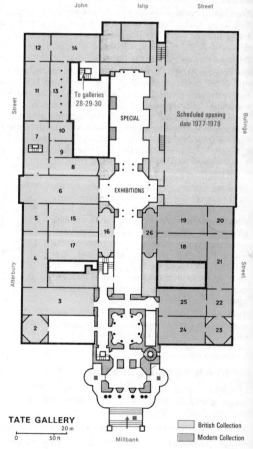

TATE GALLERY

British Collection
Modern Collection

In 1897 the museum opened as the Gallery of Modern British Art – "modern" being translated as post 1790! As Tate (d 1899) and the Duveens, father and son, continued to sup-
ly funds for extensions, there came the bequest by Sir Hugh Lane (drowned in the *Lusi-
ania* in 1915) of 39 modern foreign paintings "to found a collection of Modern Conti-
ental Art in London", supported in 1923 by the creation of a fund by Samuel Courtauld
or the purchase of modern French paintings. As a result the gallery acquired, over the
ears, a great number of Impressionist and Post Impressionist canvases.

In 1967 the pictures were reorganised into the **British Collection** of works by artists
orn before 1850 working in Britain and the **Modern Collection** of painting and sculpture
y artists of all nationalities, including British artists, born in or after 1850.

GALLERY	SUBJECT, PAINTERS AND PARTICULAR PICTURES
3	**Early portraits (16-17C):** Mytens, Johnson, Lely, Kneller: *Man in a Black Cap* (Bettes), *The Cholmondeley Sisters, Saltonstall Family* (Des Granges), *Endymion Porter* (Dobson).
2	**Hogarth:** portraits of archbishops, children, his servants, and *Self-portrait with his dog, Punch;* also first English stage scenes: *Beggar's Opera;* (no engravings).
4	**18C – first half:** animal paintings – Stubbs; landscapes, Wilson, Samuel Scott, Woot-ton, Seymour, Cozens, Girtin *(The White House, Chelsea).*
17	**Portraits** – Reynolds (3 Self-portraits including *"as a deaf man"*), Romney, Zoffany, Gainsborough (*Giovanni Bacelli,* Artist's daughter and landscapes); Wright of Derby *Experiment with an air pump;* Benjamin West.
15	Closed for redecoration, to be rehung with works by Blake.
16	Painters of the Sublime, the Exotic and the Horrid: Fuseli.
5	**18-19C, the Sublime and the Picturesque** – Melodramatic landscapes: theatrical high drama by Fuseli; portraits by Lawrence: *Kemble as Hamlet.*
6, 7	**Turner.**
11	Turner; James Ward: *Gordale Scar.*
8	**Constable:** *Flatford Mill, A Country Lane, Study of Clouds.*
9	**British Landscape 1800-50:** Cotman *The Drop Gate,* G R Lewis *Harvest Scene.*
10	Blake (to be rehung with British landscape 1800-50).
12	Martin, Danby (landscapes), and Dadd.
14	**Victorian and Edwardian** – everything from moral interior scenes to romantic and finally very cool portraits: Watts, William Morris; Tissot *(Ball on Shipboard),* Whistler *(Harmony in Grey and Green, Old Battersea Bridge)* Sargent *(Lord Ribblesdale, Study of Mme Gantreau).*
28	**Pre-Raphaelites:** Holman Hunt *(Strayed Sheep),* Ford Maddox Brown *(The Last of England),* Millais *(Ophelia),* Henry Wallis *(Chatterton).*
13	**20C British** (provisional arrangement): Steer, Sickert, John, Gilman, Gertler, Spencer Gore, Victor Pasmore, Duncan Grant, Matthew Smith, John Piper, Paul Nash (to be rehung with Victorian and Edwardian paintings).

Galleries on the right of the entrance are showing Impressionism and Post Impressionism
and the styles up to Pop Art through half a dozen and single examples many of which ap-
pear in rotation. Among the artists always represented are Monet, Degas, Renoir, Van
Gogh, the Douanier Rousseau, Cézanne, Matisse, Picasso, Braque, Modigliani, Chagall;
Klee, Max Ernst and Dali; also Giacometti, Mondrian, Ben Nicholson, Sutherland, Francis
Bacon, Jackson Pollock, David Hockney.

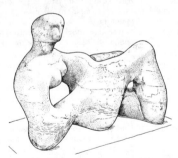

Henry Moore: Recumbent Figure 1938.

*Henry Moore's sculptures are to be seen in Ottawa and Toronto, Perth, Australia,
Buffalo, Boston, Columbia University, the Lincoln Center and Museum of Modern Art
in New York, in Brussels, the Hague, at UNESCO and Beaubourg in Paris besides in
Manchester and Leeds, St Matthew's Northampton, Dartington Hall, Oxford and
Cambridge and in London in Battersea Park – Three Draped Stone Figures, on
Millbank –Locking Piece and at Westminster –Knife Edge. Perhaps most spectacular
of all, however are the bronze King and Queen, overlooking Glenkilin Kircudbright-
shire and high on the Yorkshire Moors.*

*The Tate, in addition to stone and marble carvings, also possesses many of the
bronzes and series of the small and fascinating preliminary maquettes.*

The THAMES ★★

Regular steamer services began on the Thames in 1816 and by mid-century were transporting several million. Passengers were families and friends out for an evening, a day or weekend, often to the estuary and seaside towns of Herne Bay, Margate, Ramsgate. In the week, the boats were crowded with workers crossing into the docks, boatyards, to the arsenal and south bank factories. Fares were a penny from one pier to the next.

Pleasure boat services

There are regular services from Easter to September from Westminster down river (20 min intervals) to the Tower (20 mins) and Greenwich (50 mins) and up river (½ hr intervals) to Putney (30 mins) Kew (90 mins), Richmond (150 mins) and Hampton Court (225 mins; midday boats only).

Boats may be boarded at any of the piers and down river also at Charing Cross.

London's Bridges. — Twenty-eight bridges span the tideway from Teddington Lock to the Tower; one is a footbridge, 9 are rail bridges, 18 road bridges. The most singular is Tower Bridge; the oldest and the newest, London Bridge.

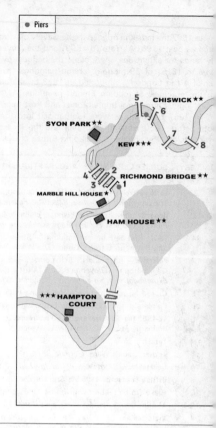

NAME	DATE	ARCHITECT	HISTORY	CHARACTERISTICS
Richmond ★★	1774	James Paine	Toll bridge until mid 19C; painted by Turner.	Classical, stone, very handsome with 5 arches and parapet (widened 1937)
Richmond Rlwy	1848	Joseph Locke	Richmond-Staines-Windsor line.	Iron and concrete. Typical early railway style.
Twickenham	1933	Maxwell Ayrton		Concrete. 3 wide spans.
Richmond Footbridge	1894			Double footbridge. Forms the crest line of the 3 gate weir.
Kew (King Edward VII)	1903	Wolfe Barry and Brereton	Replaced an 18C bridge.	Stone. 3 spans with attractive solid outline.
Kew Rlwy	1869	W R Galbraith	Opened as part of the S W Rlwy.	Lattice girder. 5 arches.
Chiswick	1933	Baker		Concrete. 150ft wide centre span.
Barnes Rlwy	1849	Locke		Iron. Unique humpback outline.
Hammersmith	1884-1887	Joseph Bazalgette	Replaced the first Thames suspension bridge (1827).	Suspension. Lines ruined by typically Victorian pavilions.
Putney	1884	Bazalgette	Replaced a wooden toll bridge of 1729.	Cornish granite. The boat race starts just upriver.
Fulham Rlwy	1889	William Jacomb	Originally part of the District Rlwy.	Iron girder trellis. Footpaths parallels rail bridge.
Wandsworth	1938	E P Wheeler	Replaced a 19C bridge.	Concrete; flat, low lying, 3 spans.
Battersea Rlwy	1863		Still the only bridge to carry a railway line directly connecting north and south England.	Concrete
Battersea	1890	Bazalgette	The ferry was replaced in 1771 by a wooden bridge lit by oil lamps in 1799, gas in 1824. Subject of Whistler *Nocturne* painting.	Iron. Flat, decoratively painted but now spiked by emasculated sodium lamp standards. Note the tollmen's huts still at either end.
Albert	1873	R W Ordish	Opened by Prince Albert.	Suspension cantilever. A cat's cradle, nattily painted in 3 colours.
Chelsea	1934	Forest and Wheeler	Replaced an 1858 suspension bridge.	Suspension. Clean lined; typical of interwar bridges.
Victoria Rlwy	1859		Symbolised the immense importance of 19C railways.	Originally 900ft long × 132ft wide to accommodate 10 tracks to Victoria Stn; since widened.
Vauxhall	1900	Maurice Fitzmaurice	Replaced an earlier iron bridge.	Iron and stone; high iron parapet with figures, Engineering, Science etc. against the piers.
Lambeth	1932	G Topham Forest	The horse ferry was only replaced by a bridge in 1862.	Steel; spanking scarlet and black parapet.

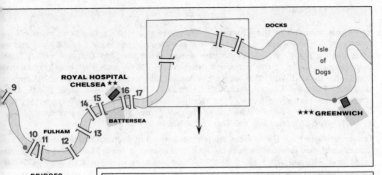

BRIDGES

1. Richmond
2. Richmond Rlwy
3. Twickenham
4. Richmond Footbridge
5. Kew
6. Kew Rlwy
7. Chiswick
8. Barnes Rlwy
9. Hammersmith
10. Putney
11. Fulham Rlwy
12. Wandsworth
13. Battersea Rlwy
14. Battersea
15. Albert
16. Chelsea
17. Victoria Rlwy
18. Vauxhall
19. Lambeth
20. Westminster
21. Hungerford
22. Waterloo
23. Blackfriars
24. Blackfriars Rlwy
25. Southwark
26. Cannon Street Rlwy
27. London
28. Tower

H M SHIPS

A Discovery
B Wellington
C Chrysanthemum
D President
E Belfast

NAME	DATE	ARCHITECT	HISTORY	CHARACTERISTICS
Westminster★	1862	Thomas Page	Successor to the stone bridge of 1750, the first to be built after London Bridge and where Wordsworth composed his sonnet (1807).	Stone. Flat with lanky piers, square arches.
Charing Cross Rlwy or Hungerford	1862		Replaced Brunel's suspension bridge (1845- subsequently incorporated in Clifton S. Br)	Gracelessly functional (parallel footbridge).
Waterloo	1945	G G Scott	Replaced Rennie's 19C bridge.	Concrete; sleek and white, with 5 low spanning arches.
Blackfriars	1899	James Cubitt	Replaced an 18C structure.	Iron and stone. River bank footpath.
Blackfriars Rlwy	1886		Opened as part of the Dover line.	Iron; high parapet, coats of arms at either end, typify 19C rlwy prosperity.
Southwark	1919	Ernest George	Replaced Rennie's 1815-1819 bridge.	Iron; 3 arches. Referred to as the Cast Iron Bridge in Dickens' *Little Dorrit*.
Cannon Street Rlwy	1866	J W Barry J Hawkshaw		One vast structure with the black brick train shed, crowned with twin pavilions.
London Bridge★★	1973	Harold King	see p 154.	Concrete. 3 low arches balanced on slender piles.
Tower Bridge★★	1894	Barry and Brunel	see p 154.	Iron drawbridge. *(See cover illustration.)*

"Every drop of the Thames is liquid history"

The Thames provides work, has influenced the capital's size, the country's wealth. Throughout its 215 miles (from Thames Head 3 miles from Cirencester, to the Nore) it is not scenically spectacular although the upper reaches near its source in the Cotswolds are extremely pleasant; it has mirrored ships of every type from men o'war to tugs, from the *Great Eastern*, Millwall (1856) to state barges and rowing shells; in its tidal waters it reflects the Houses of Parliament, the South Bank Centre, the **Embankment**★ (1864-70) spiked by Cleopatra's Needle (erected in 1877) and the RAF, eagle crowned, memorial, offices, wharves, pubs, parks, power stations, bridges, City and other churches, St Paul's, houses... the ebb and flow of London life.

If you take a boat up or downstream you will also see the bridges, HM Ships *(p 154)* moored along the Embankment and most spectacularly the Tower, Greenwich, Lambeth Palace, Syon Park, Hampton Court, as our forefathers saw them as they travelled London's main highway by leisured state barge or more modest craft.

153

The THAMES★★

HM Ships moored in the Thames. — Discovery★ in which Captain Scott made his firs expedition to the Antarctic in 1907, is now a museum *(open daily 1 to 4.30pm)* and se cadet training ship; the First World War sloops, *Wellington* and *Chrysanthemum,* head quarters respectively of the London division of the RNVR and RNR and beyond ther *President,* a Second World War frigate, the floating Livery Hall of the Honourable Compan of Master Mariners. The cruiser, *Belfast,* (1939, 11 500 tons) saw service with Arcti convoys, took part in the Battle of the North Cape and D-Day *(access by river ferry fror Tower Pier or from Symon's Wharf, Vine Lane off Tooley St S E 1; 11am to 6pm (4.30pr winter) except Christmas Eve and Day; £1; children 20p).*

Tower Bridge★★. — The familiar, stone clad Gothic towers, steel lattice-work footbridg(*(closed)* and road drawbridge, was the joint undertaking in 1886-94 of Isambard Kingdom Brunel and Sir John Wolfe Barry. The 1 100 ton bascules were operated until 1972-6 b 4 steam hydraulic engines (one now in the Science Museum) and in the first year opene(the bridge more than 6 000 times — now only 250 times a year. In 1952 a bus failing t(notice the lights and signals, was caught on the bridge as it opened but successfull("leaped" the gap of several feet to safety.

London Bridge★★. — London Bridge was the only crossing over the lower Thames unti 1750 when Westminster was constructed. The Romans probably built the first bridge o(the single gravel spit which exists in the clay; the Saxons certainly erected a wooder structure which had to be repeatedly rebuilt against the ravages of floodwater, ice and fire In 1176-1209 a stone bridge was constructed, 905ft long 40ft wide with 19 pointec arches rising from slender piles on boat shaped wood and rubble piers. These blocked the river bed so that the water poured down as through sluices, and many, including Pepys refused to shoot the bridge in the river boats which were the principal transport of the day equally they enabled ice to form and the river to freeze, when great Frost Fairs would b(held, most famously in 1683-4. On the bridge itself were houses, shops, a chapel — Pete(the Bridgemaster had been chaplain to St Mary Colechurch (disappeared) — also a draw bridge at the seventh arch from the south and gatehouses which as part of the City defence were closed at night and which were where traitors' heads were exposed — Jack Cade (1450), Thomas More (1535).

In 1831, following an act of 1823, John Rennie constructed a robust granite bridge o(5 wide spans, 60yds upstream. It endured 150 years before being replaced in 1973 by the present, sleek crossing — Rennie's bridge was sold for £1 million and is now in Arizona

Woolwich Free Ferry. — The ferry operated by 3 roll-on roll-off vessels each capable of carrying 1 000 passengers and 200 tons of vehicles on the 5 minute crossing, dates back to 14C and is the last regular service of hundreds which once plied the stream.

Tunnels. — The most famous of the river tunnels was the Thames Tunnel constructed by Marc Isambard Brunel from 1825-43 during which time it caved in twice, was abandoned and at length, on completion, celebrated by an underground banquet and the award of a knighthood to the engineer. In 1865 it was sold to what is now London Transport to carry the Metropolitan, Rotherhithe-Wapping line; five other tunnels connect other LT lines.

In addition there are also in use two pedestrian passages, Greenwich-Isle of Dogs, built in 1902, and the Woolwich Foot Tunnel of 1912 for when bad weather stops the ferry, and five road tunnels: Blackwall, a pedestrian and road tunnel dating back to 1897 and its 1963 parallel (southbound traffic), Rotherhithe of 1908 and the Dartford Road Tunnel, an 18C project realised in 1963 and doubled in 1977.

River flow control. — Teddington Lock, where some 1 200 million gallons pour daily over the weir, was built in 1912 as part of the system of 50 locks and 140 weirs devised to control the water level in the upper reaches. It marks the boundary between the non-tidal and tidal Thames — high tide is 1½ hours later than at London Bridge — and is approximately 94 miles from the Tongue (opposite Margate) which is the seaward limit of the jurisdiction of the Port of London Authority. Above Teddington the river is controlled by the Thames Water Authority.

Construction of the **Woolwich Reach Flood Barrier** was undertaken in 1972-80 for 3 reasons: central London is sinking on its bed of clay and Britain itself tilting — Scotland and NW are rising, SE is dipping by about a foot a century; tide levels are rising — by 2ft at London Bridge in the last 100 years; and surge tides. The barrier is of a rising section, gate type, with each gate, on pivots between concrete piers housing the operating machinery; the four main hollow steel plated gates each 200ft across × 66ft high and weighing 3 300 tons, and side gates, will rest invisibly in concrete cells on the river bed except when raised against floodwaters.

Shipping and the docks. — London grew to importance as a port and developed and remained for centuries the great centre of world trade. Ships were built downstream; traders, unable to sail beneath London Bridge and equally unable to approach the wharves on shore across the mudflats, moored in midstream and depended on the fleet of some 3 500 lighters and other craft for all their handling. There were thousands of boats of every size on the river as all the old engravings show; there were also thieves: River Pirates, Night Plunderers, Scuffle Hunters and Mudlarks. The 19C saw the construction of the first commercial dock, the West India, soon followed by others until by the end of the century there were 5 systems extending over 3 000 acres with 36 miles of quays and 665 acres of dock basins. In 1909, the enterprise, in urgent need of modernisation, was taken over by the newly instituted Port of London Authority which remains the controlling authority although the docks, which prospered throughout the first half of this century, served stalwartly despite bombing and fire raids (December 1940) during the war, have now transferred to Tilbury.

Open March to October 9.30am (2pm Sundays) to 5pm; rest of the year 9.30am to 4pm and closed Sundays, 80p (20p November to February); Jewel House: closes 5pm March to October; 4pm rest of the year; 30p (10p November to February). Guided tours: ½ hour, exteriors only excepting St Peter's. Restaurant outside the entrance. Weekdays are slightly less crowded than weekends, winter is by far the best time.

Queues for the Jewel House vary, always go there first, the earlier the better.

The realm of the Tower. — William I constructed the Tower to ensure that he remained "the Conqueror". The fortress, first of wood (1067) then of stone (c 1077-1097), was intended primarily to deter Londoners from revolt; additionally its vantage point beside the river, gave immediate sighting should any hostile force approach up the Thames. Norman, Plantagenet and Tudor successors showed their approbation by extending the work until it occupied 18 acres; they built first one and then a second fortified perimeter, excavated moats, built a second chapel, barracks, transferred the royal residence to new (now demolished) palatial buildings. The last king in residence was James I.

From 1300 to 1810 the Tower housed the Royal Mint, and briefly, the Royal Observatory; because of its defences, it served for centuries as an arsenal for small arms and early on, for the same reason, it became the Royal Jewel House. For a while it was used as a bank by City merchants until, in 1640, Charles I "borrowed" the commoners' deposits amounting in all to £130 000. From the 13C until 1834 it stabled the Royal Menagerie (in the now disappeared Lion Tower).

The Royal Armoury was first displayed in the White Tower by Henry VIII and the collection increased under Charles I when suits and accoutrements from Greenwich, Westminster and Hampton Court were redistributed between Windsor and the Tower to make the latter one of the world's greatest collections.

The Tower from the beginning served as a prison both for the many such as the 600 Jews accused of adulterating the coin of the realm in 1282, and the individuals captured in battle or suspected of intrigue. Among the latter were David, King of the Scots (1346), King John of France (1356-60, captured at Poitiers), Richard II (1399), Charles, Duke of Orleans (1415-27, captured at Agincourt), Henry VI (1465-71), the Duke of Clarence, drowned in a butt of malmsey (1477), the Little Princes (Edward V and Richard of York, 1483-5), Perkin Warbeck (1499), Thomas More (1534-5), Anne Boleyn (1536), Thomas Cromwell (1540), Protector Somerset (1552), Lady Jane Grey (1554), Robert Devereux, Earl of Essex (1601), Sir Walter Raleigh (1603-15), Guy Fawkes (1605), James, Duke of Monmouth (1685) and, this century, Roger Casement and Rudolf Hess.

Jewel House. — *(30p).* British orders of chivalry and decorations for valour (robes and insignia), the coronation robe, maces and 16 silver state trumpets provide the ground floor introduction to the scene.

The Crown Jewels★★★. — The jewels date from the Restoration, all the earlier regalia with the exception of the 14/15C ampulla or vessel in the form of an eagle and the anointing spoon believed to have been made for King John's coronation in 1199, having been sold or melted down by Cromwell.

The Crowns: St Edward's made for the coronation of Charles II and weighing nearly 5 lbs is now worn only at a monarch's coronation. The name, not the form, derives from the veneration felt by later kings for the Confessor: **Imperial State,** made for the coronation of Queen Victoria in 1838, is worn on state occasions such as the Opening of Parliament. The ruby is the one said to have been given to the Black Prince by Pedro the Cruel after the Battle of Najena 1367 and to have been worn by Henry V at Agincourt; the diamond incorporated centuries later, is the second largest of the Stars of Africa cut from the **Cullinan diamond** (mined 1905, presented to Edward VII in 1907); there are 2 998 other jewels in the crown; **Queen Elizabeth,** the Queen Mother's Crown made for the coronation of 1937, incorporates the **Koh-i-Noor** diamond, the 14C stone which was presented by the East India Co to Queen Victoria. Queen Victoria's small crown will be familiar to every stamp collector.

Orbs and Sceptres. — The **Royal Sceptre** contains the **Star of Africa,** at 530 carats the biggest diamond in the world. **Swords of State** and staffs lie beside equally beautifully worked bracelets, armills, spurs and plate, including Queen Elizabeth's salt, ewers and vast dishes. The display fascinates every time by its purity and brilliance, the timeless craftsmanship, mass of gleaming gold, chased, modelled, its symbolism and history.

Chapel of St Peter ad Vincula. — *Admission only in guided parties.*

The chapel, consecrated on the feast of St Peter in Chains in 12C, rebuilt in 13 and 16C, is chiefly known as the burial place of "two dukes between the queens, to wit, the Duke of Somerset and the Duke of Northumberland, between Queen Anne and Queen Catherine, all four beheaded", to who Stow might have added Lady Jane Grey, Guilford Dudley, her husband, Monmouth and hundreds more.

Tower Green. — The lawn was the burial ground, the square the site of the scaffold (A). Of the seven most famous victims all were beheaded with an axe except Anne Boleyn, who was executed by the sword. Although the bodies of those executed on the green and many of those on Tower Hill were buried in the Tower, the heads were placed on pikes and displayed for all to see at the southern gateway to London Bridge. A new block was made for each victim.

Middle Tower. — The 13C tower (rebuilt 18C) stood between 2nd and 3rd drawbridges and was originally preceded by a causeway (which included the 1st drawbridge) and the Lion Tower (demolished). The moat, now the setting for occasional performances of the *Yeomen of the Guard,* was drained and grassed over in 19C.

The TOWER of LONDON ★★★

Byward Tower. – 13C, the main gate – the portcullis and lifting machinery can be seen on 1st floor. Wall paintings include English Leopards and French *fleurs-de-lys*.

Bell Tower. – Elizabeth, while confined in the adjoining Lieutenant's Lodgings (now the Queen's House – *not open*) walked for exercise along the ramparts.

Traitor's Gate and St Thomas's Tower. – The gateway served as the main entrance to the Tower when the Thames was London's principal thoroughfare; only later, when the river was used as a less vulnerable and more secret means of access than the road, did it acquire its chilling name. The Tower contains an oratory named after Thomas Becket.

Bloody Tower. – The Garden Tower, as it was formerly called, although, according to legend, the place where the Little Princes were murdered in 1485 *(see also the White Tower)* only acquired its lurid name in 16C, probably after the suicide of Henry Percy, 8th Earl of Northumberland. The longest, most famous "resident" was **Sir Walter Raleigh** who occupied the years from 1603-1615 writing a *History of the World* for Prince Henry (a copy with his watch is in the sitting room). Above are the bedroom, with a four poster and the small pointed hat of the portraits, and the ramparts and brief Raleigh Walk.

Wakefield Tower. – The tower in the Middle Ages, as well as a defence, served as a major junction between the palace and the river from which passengers would alight and crossing by way of St Thomas's and the bridge (19C reconstruction), arrive in the large vaulted chamber on the first floor of the Wakefield. This was adjoined by a small oratory – where Henry VI was discovered murdered in 1471 – and the palace Great Hall – where Anne Boleyn stood trial (demolished 17C). Part of the same defence are the 13C embrasured wall extending north to the Cold Harbour Gate (B – *now only visible as excavations*) and the east wall and perimeter towers. These replaced the Roman City Wall (still partly visible), incorporated originally in his stronghold by William I.

Beauchamp Tower★. – The 13C tower now faced with Tudor brickwork, has served since 14C as a place of confinement and is even named after an early prisoner, Thomas Beauchamp, 3rd Earl of Warwick (1397-99 freed). In the main chamber are dozens of carved graffiti

White Tower or Keep★★★. – The White Tower, one of the earliest fortifications on such a scale in western Europe, was begun by William I in 1077 and completed 20 years later by William Rufus. The 100ft high walls of Kentish and Caen stone, erected in an uneven quadrilateral, are marked at the corners by three square and one circular tower. Two walls divide the interior into a large west gallery and two unequal, east chambers on every floor.

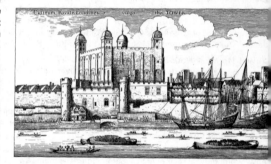

(After Hollar's engraving)

The Tower in 17 C.

In 1241 Henry III had first the royal apartments and then the exterior entirely white washed from which time only it became known as the White Tower. In 18C when repairs were being undertaken, and the windows on all but the south side enlarged, children's bones, thought to be those of the Little Princes, were discovered beneath an old staircase.

1st floor: Sporting and Tournament Galleries. – Crossbows, swords and firearms, light and beautifully balanced as birds on the wing or heavy and angular, display weapon makers' craftsmanship and also the jewellers' art, for many are beautifully enriched with gold and silver mounts, chasing and incrustations. Of all the collection the prize is a brace of **pistols** with mountings of silver gilt made by Peter Monlong, a Huguenot who emigrated to London and by 1695 when the pistols were made, was Gentleman Armourer to the King. The Armour for the Tournament and for the Tilt – German, Italian and English – appears massive and weighty, made with incredible skill.

2nd floor: St John's Chapel★★. – The small stone chapel, 55½ft long rising through two floors remains much as in 1080 when it was completed. An inner line of great round columns with simply carved capitals, bear circular Norman arches which enfold the apse in an ambulatory and are echoed above in a second tier beneath the tunnel vault.

Mediaeval monarchs passed the night in vigil in St John's before riding from the Tower to their coronation; some also lay in state there – Henry VI in 1471 – while Mary Tudor was betrothed there by proxy to Philip II in 1553.

Mediaeval and 16C Galleries. – The armour of the trooper and his officer in the field from 13-16C – chain mail, back and breast plates, helmets and arms and a case from 1500-1600, show the rapid evolution in design before armour was superseded. As a contrast there are contemporary chased and gilded suits of parade armour for man and horse.

3rd floor: Greenwich Royal Armour Gallery. – The great Council Chamber, which this top floor originally was, is filled with the presence of Henry VIII, four of whose suits stand in brave array: one of 1520 for the king aged 29, which weighs 94 lbs (a modern tin helmet weighs 2½ lbs, a light flack jacket 10 lbs, a heavy one 16 lbs), one of 1540 of greater girth, a tournament armour for the king and his horse. All came from Greenwich as did

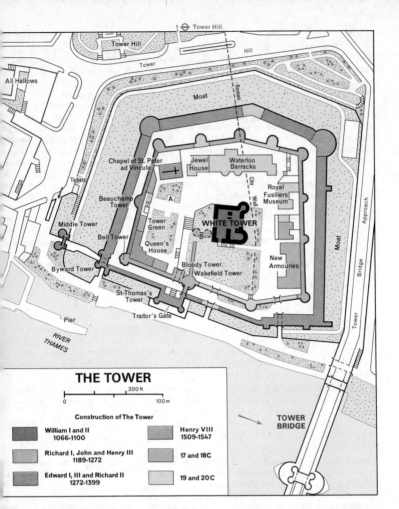

THE TOWER

```
|————————————| 200 ft
0                    100 m
```

Construction of The Tower

William I and II 1066-1100	Henry VIII 1509-1547
Richard I, John and Henry III 1189-1272	17 and 18C
Edward I, III and Richard II 1272-1399	19 and 20C

TOWER BRIDGE

those of Robert Dudley (1588) and Worcester (note the weight, without reinforcements, 110 lbs). Also displayed are a boy's ¾ armour and a helmet and cuirass, probably made for Charles I as a boy (1610), and ornate mid 17C suits.

Basement. — The area, the ground floor in fact, has been an arsenal since 18C and today houses in arrangement on the walls, helmets (English and captured foreign examples by the hundred), cuirasses, muskets, lances, halberds, "secrets" for fur hats... There are also 16, 17, 18C mortars and cannon, guns raised from the *Mary Rose* (1545) and a case of instruments of torture in use in 16/17C when the basement was a prison.

Waterloo Barracks, Royal Fusiliers' Museum, New Armouries. — The barracks and museum *(5p)*, which goes back to the formation of the regiment in 1685, were both built in 1845. The New Armouries, a late 17C brick building, contains study collections and an exhibition of Oriental armour and arms including an Indian 18C suit for an elephant.

Ceremony and Pageantry. — The **Yeoman Warders,** originally a detachment of the Royal Bodyguard founded by Henry VII on Bosworth Field (1485) is now made up of regular ex-servicemen. They wear Tudor uniform, embroidered with the sovereign's monogram (blue for every day, scarlet for ceremony) and may be seen on daily parade at 11am in the Inner Ward. The **Ceremony of the Keys** *(admission on written application only)*, the ceremonial closing of the Main Gates, is enacted nightly at 10pm. The 31 boundary stones of the Tower Liberty are beaten every third year at Rogationtide by the choirboys of St Peter's, armed with long white wands, the Governor and Warders in procession (1978, 1981...).

Royal Salutes are fired by the HAC from 4 guns on the wharf: 62 guns for the Sovereign's birthday, accession, coronation; 41 for the State Opening of Parliament, birth of a royal infant... The **Ravens** about which legend has it that if they die out the Tower will fall, now number six. In olden days ravens acted as London's scavengers.

TOWER HAMLETS (The City and Tower Hamlets)

Tower Hamlets, the East End, source of London's commercial prosperity from the 16 to the mid 20C with its shipping, wharves, docks, provider of fresh produce to the City through Spitalfields Market, of calico and silk (16/18C), of clothes and shoes and furniture, has always been, except for those who work or have lived there, a world apart, beyond the City wall. The Romans built a signal station at Wapping; in *Domesday* the odd manor is recorded; by the 12C the population, grouped in small communities, had grown to 800 and the area east as far as the Lea and north to Hackney Downs had been given into the charge of the constable and named Tower Hamlets (a name revived under the 1965 Act).

TOWER HAMLETS

In 1598 Stow was describing the riverside, east from St Katharine, as a "continual street... or filthy strait passage, with alleys of small tenements or cottages, inhabited by sailors, victuallers almost to Radcliffe and Radcliffe itself hath been also increased in building eastward (to) Limehouse". The overcrowding became ever worse, intensified by the arrival of English craftsmen — woodworkers, boat-builders, masons, spinners and weavers and 10 000 ex-slaves who fled to the waterside to work as dockers. In 16C Dutch traders and craftsmen began to settle — leatherworkers, nail and locksmiths — followed within the century, by the line of refugees which continues to this day: Dutch and French Huguenots (13 000 French arrived in 1687), the Irish, Jews, Chinese, W Indians, Indians, Pakistanis... Houses, in 16/19C, were used as workshops and factories as well as dwellings with families selling out and moving on as soon as they had the wherewithal to leave the terrifying conditions starkly described by Mayhew in his *Survey of the London Poor*, 1850.

100 years later the area is transformed: the docks, which were bombed and set ablaze on so many nights during the war, are nearly deserted; the population once 600 000, now numbers less than 200 000; the housing is now 95% authority owned; cottage industry is virtually extinct. Only a few landmarks remain and the traditional, famous names: Whitechapel, Mile End, Commercial St (where the first university settlement, Toynbee Hall, was instituted in 1884), Stepney (where Dr Barnardo founded his first home for abandoned children in 1874), Sidney St, Middlesex St (Petticoat Lane with its Sunday market), Wapping, Limehouse, the Isle of Dogs, that tongue of land which may or may not have got its name as the place where "the Queen" or "her dad", as locals describe Elizabeth I and Henry VIII, kept their hounds when in residence at Greenwich.

Tower Hill, Trinity Square *(Map pp 9-12, S/YZ)*

Tower Hill. — The hill was from earliest times and is still a place of free speech and a rallying point from which marchers set out, nowadays, usually to Westminster. For three centuries from 1455, 75 years after Wat Tyler and the Kentish rebels summarily executed the Lord Chancellor and others outside the Tower, a permanent scaffold and gallows stood on the site (last execution: Lord Lovat in 1747).

Royal Mint. — *Tower Hill.* The Mint, of which the Chancellor of the Exchequer is Master Worker and Warden, was installed in the Classical stone building in 1811 and transferred to new and larger premises in Llantrisant, near Cardiff, in 1968.

The first mint in London was under the Romans; by 11C there were 70 in various parts of the country which, by 14C, had been reduced to 2 and under Henry VIII devolved into one which, in mid 16C, was placed in the Tower.

Trinity Square Gardens. — The gardens enclose, from west to east: the **scaffold site** (railed enclosure), the **Mercantile Marine Memorials** of 1914-18 and 1939-45 Wars by Edwin Lutyens and Edward Maufe respectively, a 50ft section of the **Wall**, the upper part mediaeval, the base principally Roman, and a monumental Roman inscription (original in the BM) to the procurator who saved London from Roman vengeance after the City had been sacked by Boadicea in 61AD.

Trinity House. — The late 18C, elegant two storey building relieved by plain Ionic pillars (rebuilt after the war), is the seat of the Corporation of Trinity House (1514). Note the particularly fine weathervane.

The flat topped tower building in stone is the former headquarters of the PLA.

All Hallows-by-the-Tower. — *Page 51.*

Whitechapel High St and Rd, Mile End and Bow Rds, Stepney

Whitechapel Art Gallery. — *80 High St, by Aldate East underground. Open Tuesdays to Sundays 11am to 6pm. Temporary, modern exhibitions, see press.*

The gallery of 1901, surmounted by twin angle turrets, is decorated, like the adjoining Passmore Edwards library, with contemporary arts and crafts reliefs.

A few doors on (no 90) is **Bloom's Kosher Restaurant**, famous for its salt beef sandwiches.

Great Synagogue. — *Adler St.* The synagogue of 1958, incorporating an advisory centre, library and after-care association, acts as the Jewish centre of Tower Hamlets today, replacing the Great Synagogue of Duke's Place, Aldgate opened in 1722, which was totally destroyed in the war. Ten local synagogues closed between 1968-75, reflecting the community's decline in numbers from 125 000 in 1900, to 12 000 today.

Nathan Mayer Rothschild *(qv)* is buried in the now disused cemetery in Brady St.

Whitechapel Bell Foundry. — *34 High St.* The foundry, whose records go back to 1570 and which may be 150 years older, has been on its present site since 1738. It has cast, and after the 1666 Fire and last war, recast Bow Bells, St Clement Dane's, Big Ben...

The London Hospital. — *Whitechapel Rd.* The "London" has been extending and modernising its building around the 18C entrance ever since it opened in 1757.

It was conceived by a young surgeon, John Harrison, and six others in a tavern in Cheapside in 1740 and began as the London Infirmary in a house near Bunhill Fields. It soon removed to occupy first one then five houses with 68 beds in Prestcot St (by the Mint) and when that was insufficient moved again to Whitechapel which afforded 161 beds. Two centuries later the number is 1350.

Trinity Almshouses. — *Mile End Rd.* The almshouses, built by the Corporation of Trinity House in 1635 for "28 decay'd Masters and Comanders of ships", form a terrace of basement and ground floor cottages around three sides of a tree planted quadrangle.

Queen Mary College. – *Mile End Rd.* The college, incorporated in London University in 1905, originated in the mid 19C as the Philosophical Institute. A grand building and library (costing £20 000 in all) failed to arouse continued interest and the Drapers' Company took over and reconceived the institution as a **People's Palace** where education would be combined under one roof with gymnastics, swimming, music... The educational side prospered, merged with the adult education Bromley and Bow Institute to form the East London College and become part of the university; it took its present name in 1934 upon receiving a Royal Charter. On the site of the recreational halls stand '50s buildings of glass, brick and concrete as typical of their period as is the terracotta brick and stone institutional building erected in 1885 at the back of a wide forecourt on the main road.

St Mary, Stratford Bow Church. – *Bow Rd.* The church, which dates back to 14C, stands on an island site in the middle of the road, a little west of where Queen Matilda's single arched, "bow" bridge, which gave the area its name, spanned the Lea.

St Dunstan and All Saints. – *Stepney.* The church on an early Christian site and with a dedication to the contemporary 10C mayor, Dunstan the great divine – is now an amalgam of rebuildings dating from 13C with memorials inside as ancient.

St George-in-the-East. – *Cable St (open).* St George's, with a two tier octagonal lantern squarely buttressed and crowned by a balustrade and flat topped sculptured drums, is Hawksmoor's and the East End's most distinctive tower. Consecrated in 1729, it was bombed and fired in 1941 and has been rebuilt with the original 18C exterior surrounding a small modern church inside.

Bethnal Green, Spitalfields, Shoreditch *(Map pp 5-8, H/VX)*

Bethnal Green Museum. – *Cambridge Heath Rd. Open daily 10am to 6pm, Sundays from 2.30pm; closed 1 January, Good Friday, 24, 25, 26 December.*

The museum is known particularly for its displays of costume for the rich and poor on working and wedding days, Spitalfields silk and the earlier figured calico, woven first by Londoners and, from late 17C, by Huguenots arrived from France, also for its dolls' houses (1673 – Edwardian times), toys (including dolls), model theatres and marionettes. There are, in addition, continental furniture and ceramics in the *art nouveau* style and a large group of Rodin's bronze and marble sculptures.

The **building,** the oldest surviving example of the type of prefabricated iron and glass construction utilised by Paxton (now with a brick encasement), was originally erected to contain items from the 1851 Exhibition retained to form the nucleus of the V & A; it was re-erected and opened on the present site in 1872.

St John's Church. – *Cambridge Heath/Bethnal Green corner.* The west tower of the church (1825-8) by Soane, though not high, is an easily distinguished landmark as it rises from a square, clock stage, through a circle of columns to a vaned cupola.

Spitalfields Market. – The fruit, vegetable and flower market takes place in two large hangar like buildings of 1900 and 1935 respectively and in the surrounding streets (8 acres in all) in the early hours of weekday mornings; *all is over by 9am.*

The market was granted a royal charter by Charles II in 1682 and acquired by the City Corporation in 1902.

Christ Church. – *Spitalfields.* Hawksmoor's spire still dominates the area almost as it did when built in 1714-30, although now more starkly having been rebuilt in 19C without the original dormers on each face, corner crockets and stone finial. It rises above a Classical west portico through an echoing interplay of ascending circular bays and arches, dramatically cut by the horizontal lines of entablature, cornice... At the east end a Venetian window is framed by paired niches beneath a pediment. The crypt is used for the recovery of alcoholics in vagrancy. *The church is closed.*

Note the doorways of the mid 18C merchants' and weavers' houses in Fournier St.

Geffrye Museum★. – *Kingsland Rd, Shoreditch. Open Tuesdays to Saturdays and holiday Mondays 10am to 5pm, Sundays from 2pm; closed Mondays, Good Friday, 25, 26 December. The museum, under ILEA, caters especially for school parties; advance booking essential.*

The **almshouses** and chapel were erected around three sides of an open court and the plane trees planted in 1712-19 by the Ironmongers' Co with a bequest left by Sir Robert Geffrye, Lord Mayor. The two storey brick buildings, perfectly proportioned, are decorated only with continuous modillioned eaves and at the centre, marking the chapel, stone trimming, a pediment and niche in which stands the periwigged figure of the founder.

Inside a series of rooms illustrate furniture and furnishings from Tudor times to 1930s; there is also a reconstruction of a Georgian street, including shopfronts and a woodworker's shop with bench and tools and, at the back, his family kitchen.

St Leonard's Parish Church. – *Shoreditch High St.* The mid 18C church with 192ft spire is on the site of an earlier church within whose precincts were buried: **James Burbage** (d 1597) a joiner by trade and the head of Lord Leicester's players who in 1576 built in Shoreditch the first English playhouse, **The Theatre;** Cuthbert Burbage (d 1635), his son who in 1599 built the **Globe; Richard Burbage** (d 1619), also his son, the first actor to play Richard III and Hamlet; William Somers (d 1560) court jester to Henry VIII; Richard Tarlton (d 1588), one of Queen Elizabeth's players; Gabriel Spencer (d 1598), a player at the Rose Theatre; William Sly (d 1608) and Richard Cowley (d 1619), players at the Globe.

To the north, Holy Trinity, Trinity Rd (1849), has been known since Grimaldi's day as the Clowns' Church and holds an annual service for circus folk.

159

The Riverside: St Katharine Dock, Poplar, Limehouse

St Katharine Dock★. — The present development is the third on the site. The first was the **Hospital of St Katharine by the Tower** founded in 1148 by Queen Matilda, first of an unbroken succession of royal patrons. The mediaeval community which traded from its own wharves developed into a hospital, travellers' shelter, and refugee settlement, being outside the City walls where no immigrant might live. The first to seek shelter were the English forced to quit Calais in 1558, closely followed by Flemings, Huguenots... until by 18C the overcrowded community town numbered nearly 3 000. In 19C the site was sold and the nucleus of the community moved to Regent's Park from where it returned to the East End in 1920s and after being bombed out is now in Butcher Row in new buildings.

St Katharine Dock, Ivory House.

The St Katharine site was developed in 1828 by **Thomas Telford** with a series of basins surrounded by warehouses covering in all some 25 acres. The dock was the nearest to the City and for 100 years it prospered exceedingly.

After the war, when it was bombed, the dock was abandoned until 1968 when it was reorganised to provide moorings for private yachts, the warehouses were transformed into bars and restaurants and, most notably, Telford's Italianate building, renamed Ivory House, converted into executive flats above a shopping arcade. Also overlooking the basins are the 1960s **World Trade Centre** (including the PLA offices) and a large striated brown hotel with before it a leaping bronze fountain by David Wynne of a *Girl with a Dolphin* (1973).

Wapping Wall and High St. — Wapping was the landing for generations of watermen, the setting for Dickens' novels along the densely populated waterfront cut by alleys, steps, stages and docks; Execution Dock was where condemned pirates and thieves — Captain Kidd in 1701 — were left for the tide to wash over them three times. Today docks and streets are largely deserted and landmarks are few: **Wapping Pierhead,** a parallel terrace of 18C houses leading down to the river; the modern building of the **Metropolitan Special Constabulary** (Thames Division) or River Police, established in 1798, which patrols the 54 miles of waterway in 33 boats; the early 16C **Prospect of Whitby.**

Three local churches especially are interesting: **St Paul Shadwell,** (Highway), known in 17/18C as the Church of the Sea Captains among who was Captain Cook, **St Matthias,** (Poplar High St), built in 1776 by the East India Co with 7 mighty masts and a stone column inside to support the roof and **St Anne's,** Limehouse, Hawksmoor's first East End church, 1712-24 with a characteristically distinctive square tower.

TWICKENHAM (Richmond upon Thames) ──────────────

Twickenham, which in the 20C, on occasions, echoes to the cheers of English and French rugby fans (Stadium, Rugby Rd), in the 19C, saw Louis-Philippe, cousin of Louis XVI and future King of France (1830-1848), three of his five sons, several descendants and a number of sympathisers, living in as many as nine houses in the immediate vicinity. Of these four remain: Bushy House, now the residence of the Director of the National Physical Laboratory (Teddington); Morgan House, Ham Common, now part of the Cassel Hospital, York House and Orleans House.

York House. — *Richmond Rd. The house (council offices) is closed; the gardens open.*

The Yorke family lived on and worked a farm on the site in the 15 and 16C; successors, who from 1700 altered and rebuilt the house, retained the name including, in 19C, members of the exiled French royal family and this century, an Indian merchant prince.

The three storey brick house has a terrace at the rear overlooking the large walled garden which leads to a rose garden, formal garden and to woodlands beside the Thames.

Sion Rd. — The road by York House leading to the river, is joined halfway down, at the rounded Waterman's Lodge, by Ferry Rd, a close of "two down, two up" cottages. Beyond is **Sion Row**, a terrace of 12, three storey houses built in 1721, in ordered lines with a uniform cornice, three lights and off centre entrances, personalized by individual doorways. At the end, parallel to the river, *(passenger ferry in summer, Saturdays only, to Ham House)* is a straggling line of houses of all periods: a pub, all corners and balconies, the Ferry House, four floors of white stucco with a slate roof, and finally, behind a wall, Riverside House, a rambling two storeys beneath broad eaves, built in 1810.

Orleans House Gallery. — *Open Tuesday to Saturday, 1 to 5.30pm (October to March to 4.30pm); Sundays, Easter and holiday Mondays 2 to 5.30pm. Temporary exhibitions.*

Orleans House itself was demolished in 1926, only the **Octagon,** added in 1720, ten years after the house was first built, still remaining. This wing by James Gibbs has a brick exterior, and splendid plasterwork, including fireplace, figures and ceiling.

Marble Hill House★. – *Open 10am to 5pm (4pm November to January); closed on Fridays, 24, 25 December.*

Marble Hill House was built in the mid 1720s by Henrietta Howard, with monies settled on her by her royal lover, the future George II.

She acquired a parcel of land beside the river; plans were sketched by the Architect to the Prince of Wales, Colen Campbell. It was 1731, however, before Henrietta, now Countess of Suffolk and Mistress of the Robes, could "often visit Marble Hill" and several years more before she took up residence there with her second husband, George Berkeley. She was an active hostess and received politicians, lawyers, and men of letters, including Alexander Pope and Horace Walpole. The most famous of later residents was another royal mistress, Mrs. Fitzherbert, who lived there briefly, in 1795.

The gardens, now disappeared but in the 18C considered integral to the houses design, were, from 1824, the preoccupation of **Alexander Pope,** a near neighbour at Crossdeep, in a house of which nothing remains and gardens of which only a grotto survives.

The House. – The Palladian style, stucco, house is three storeys high with the centre advanced beneath a pediment and an insignificant, 18C, entrance.

From the small hall, the square mahogany staircase leads directly to the Great Room, a 24ft cube splendidly rich in white and gold with carved decoration and copies of van Dyck paintings upon the walls. Lady Suffolk's bedchamber *(left),* divided by Ionic pillars and pilasters to form a bed alcove, is completed, like the other rooms, by a rich cornice and ceiling decoration. Though the actual furniture and furnishings were dispersed, an almost exact reconstruction is being successfully achieved from a detailed inventory made on her ladyship's death in 1767.

Close by is the long and beautiful, contemporary, Montpelier Row.

Strawberry Hill★. – *Twickenham (St Mary's College, Waldegrave Rd). Conducted tours Wednesday and Saturday afternoons on prior application – Tel 01-892 0015.*

"A little plaything... the prettiest bauble you ever saw". – Horace Walpole, Cambridge and Grand Tour graduate, MP with few prospects although the son of the former PM, man about town, historian, antiquarian, diarist, and letter-writer extraordinary, was truly delighted when in May 1747 he acquired a 50 year old cottage at Strawberry Hill on the outskirts of Twickenham.

The great houses in the vicinity were Classical: Marble Hill, York, Orleans, Ham... Walpole announced that as "Grecian columns and all their beautiful ornaments look ridiculous when crowded into a closet or a cheesecake house... I am going to build a little Gothic structure at Strawberry Hill". The result with battlements, cloister, round tower, turret and gallery, made it so different that though by no means the first building to include Gothic features, it became the chief influence in 18/19C **Gothic Revival.**

The interior was even more remarkable. Under *The Committee of Taste,* established by Walpole with two friends, rooms were transformed or newly planned to incorporate Gothic gems from every source: chimneypieces were modelled on tombs – that in the Round Room on the tomb of Edward the Confessor, in the Holbein room after that of Archbishop Warham at Canterbury; ceilings, in the Round Room on a window in old St Paul's, in the Long Gallery, on the fan vaulting in the Henry VII Chapel, in the Tribune on the chapter-house at York. In each case the design is reproduced more or less exactly but probably in inferior material – *papier maché* for the fan vaulting! – and the original context totally disregarded. Against the grand opera setting, Walpole displayed his collection – it was an age of collectors: Sir Hans Sloane, Angerstein, the Ist Marquess of Hertford, Walpole's cousin, with who he corresponded, and who was acquiring the nucleus of the future Wallace Collection. But where the Hertfords were perfectionists, Walpole was indiscriminate, with the result that his "profusion of rarities" ranged from a Holbein portrait of Catherine of Aragon to Cardinal Wolsey's hat, from a missal with miniatures by Raphaël to a brass padlock in the shape of a hand.

Walpole died in 1797. By 1841, by way of a great niece, Strawberry Hill had come into the possession of the 7th Earl of Waldegrave and his wife, Frances, and the collection been auctioned at a sale which lasted 32 days, was attended by 50 000 and realised £33 468.

In 1855, Frances Waldegrave, remarried and a prominant political hostess, decided to reinstate the house. Restoration, refurbishing, made "Strawberry", in Lady Waldegrave's own words "more like a fairy place than ever". When it proved not large enough, an extension was added. How much the countess spent is not known as each time her reckoning approached £100 000, she put away the books, feeling, it is said that she had made a mistake in the addition. There are four, never completed, account books! Under her aegis Strawberry Hill in the 1860s and '70s became a meeting place for those in politics, letters, the arts and society. When she died in July 1879 the house dimmed into obscurity only to be rescued in 1923 when the Vincentian Community established St Mary's College in new buildings in the grounds.

Interior. – The main door, adjoining a small cloister, leads into the hall and staircase described by Walpole as "the most particular and chief beauty of the castle" with its rose "paper painted in perspective to represent Gothic fretwork", staircase balustrade after Rouen Cathedral, "adorned with antelopes (our supporters) bearing shields" and star spangled vault. The light, as in many parts of the house, is filtered to Gothick obscurity through painted Flemish glass.

Above are the Blue, or breakfast room, the library, where books are ranged behind ogee arches and the ceiling is in Tudor style and the Long Gallery. The Waldegrave wing, opens with the anteroom to the great gallery which served the beautiful Lady Waldegrave, whose portrait hangs at one end, as banqueting hall or resplendent ballroom beneath glittering chandeliers.

Open daily 10am (Sundays 2.30pm) to 5.50pm; closed Fridays, 1 January, Good Friday, 24, 25, 26 December. Restaurant, photography permitted.

Origin. – The 1851 Exhibition was the parent of the V & A as of the neighbouring Kensington museums *(qv)*. The collections which derived from purchases of contemporary works manufactured for the Exhibition (and displayed from 1852 in Marlborough House) and items of all periods accumulated by the Government School of Design at Somerset House, have, since 1909, been exhibited in the idiosyncratic building by Aston Webb of brick, terracotta and stone with a tall pierced central tower, crowned by a figure of Prince Albert. Gifts and bequests from its earliest days and subsequently purchases, have transformed the originally disparate agglomeration of items to the present collection with its vast brief of "the fine and applied arts of all countries, all styles, all periods".

The museum's treasures are displayed in **primary galleries** where a wide variety of arts afford an idea of a period or a civilisation, and in single **subject galleries,** such as the ceramic rooms, where, for example, the development of individual factories may be studied in detail. In all there are some 7 miles of galleries. The guide-index and plan below are designed to help you pinpoint what interests you in the maze-like interior.

FLOOR	ROOM	SUBJECT
		BRITISH GALLERIES
		Furniture, silver, embroidery, porcelain, glass: 1500-1750
Upper ground floor (Exhibition Rd door and stairs)	52	Tudor panelling, chests and plasterwork. Henry VII bust by **Torrigiano;** Queen Elizabeth's virginals; gold salts (Vyvyan; 1592) and plate; clocks; knives; German stonewares. **Sizergh Castle Rm** (Westmorland) 1575: four poster, chairs; **Gt Bed of Ware.**
	53	English embroidery 1540-1640.
	54	Oxburgh hangings (Mary Queen of Scots *c* 1570); early English delftware; **Bromley-by-Bow Rm** (James I hunting lodge, 1606), plaster ceiling, carved wood chimneypiece. **Grinling Gibbons'** reliefs *(Crucifixion, Stoning of St Stephen),* carved limewood cravat; gold, silver plate, lead glass crystal.
	55	Portrait **miniatures:** Holbein, Hilliard *(Young Man leaning against a Tree),* Oliver, Cooper; silver toilet services.
	56	Salt glazed stoneware by Dwight; tin glazed (Lambeth, Bristol delft) ware. **Clifford's Inn Rm** (*c* 1687); state bed; Queen Anne walnut furniture; gold plate, Huguenot silver; locks; Chinoiserie, japanned furniture.
	57	**Henrietta Place Rm** (*c* 1725) by James Gibbs – plasterwork, early Georgian furniture. Silver (by Paul de Lamerie also Walpole Salver); 1720-35 walnut bureaux, chair; Spitalfields silks (17/18C).
	57A	18/19C portrait miniatures; embroideries.
	58	Tapestries (1725); mirrored cabinet (John Channon), gilded furniture; **Hatton Garden Rm** (*c* 1730), small scale Palladian; mahogany;early kneehole desk. **Norfolk House Music Rm** (1756): splendid gold and white rococo room. **George St Rm** (Westminster, *c* 1755). Gilded mid 18C furniture by Matthias Lock; Worcester porcelain.
		British furniture 1750-1900
Upper 1st floor	126	**Chippendale** organ case, mahogany cabinets, bureaux, chest of drawers (brass mounts); clocks; Chelsea-Chinese musicians.
	125	Chinoiserie bed (*c* 1755); John Ellicott clock; japanned and chinoiserie furniture, 18C Chinese wallpaper. English porcelain figures (mid 18C Chelsea, Bow, Derby, Staffs); Beilby and other glass; stone and tin glazewares; Poplar and Spitalfields textiles. **Wotton-under-Edge Rm:** provincial rococo. **Croome Court Library** (1760s) "Sett of large mahogany bookcases from a drawing of Mr. Adams"; **Glass Drawing Rm,** Northumberland House (1770s) by Adam.
	123	**Lee Priory Rm** (Canterbury, 1785), Gothic revival; silver Newdigate and Sprimont centre-pieces 1743, 1747; late Chelsea porcelain, Wedgwood Etruria; 18C bookbindings.
	122	David Garrick's Chippendale furniture; neo-Classical, Regency furniture; 18C French wallpaper; Lawrence portraits.
	121	Regency furniture (Henry Holland's chairs for Carlton House); gold plate; engraved and cut glass; Swansea, Derby, Wedgwood Worcester porcelain; Rhinoceros – Rockingham vase, 1826; glass.
	120	Regency – Victorian transition: japanned *papier maché* and Gothic. (Pugin) furniture; pieces from 1851 Exhibition; Derby, Coalport... porcelain; tiles.
	119	William Morris and followers: furniture, stained glass, tiles.
	118	**Birmingham House Rm** (1877); late Gothic revival; Egyptian revival (1870-80s); inlaid furniture; models, bronzes; art pottery; glass; tile panels.
		Related ceramic study galleries
2nd floor	139	Pottery (17-19C), **18C porcelain** (Chelsea, etc), enamels, waxes; Schreiber collection.
	140	**18/19C porcelain** (Derby, Lowestoft, Swansea, Coalport, Staffs).
	137	Lead glaze, delft (17-20C), salt and stonewares; tiles.
	141	Tiles – mediaeval and later stamped, inlaid, painted.
Upper 1st floor	131	Glass including stemmed wine glasses.

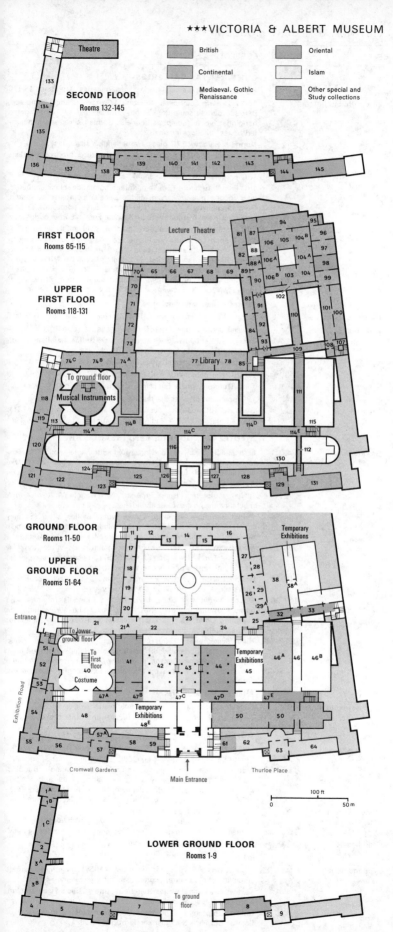

FLOOR	ROOM	SUBJECT
		CONTINENTAL GALLERIES
		Furniture, silver, porcelain, glass, embroideries, sculpture: 16-18C
Lower ground floor	1 A, B, C	16-17C north European furniture; German amber altarpiece; Baroque portrait sculpture (Bernini), Italian mid 17C embroidered hangings; ivories, sculptors' models; German silver, silver mounted boxes; Limoges enamels.
	2	Northern Baroque 17C glass, Netherlandish silver, lace.
	3	17C French and Flemish cabinets and furniture; bronzes; **Northern French manorhouse room;** baroque sculpture.
	4	18C porcelain (Meissen, French); continental glass.
	5	18C French furniture (Boulle parquetry commode, black cupboard, later rococo pieces, carved, gilded panels) compared to Dutch, German, Italian; Vincennes and early Sèvres porcelain; Tiepolo drawings, floral marquetry; neo-Classical French corner cupboards.
	6	18C vestments, guns, sculpture, bronzes, goldsmiths' work.
	7	18C French commode, secretaire, bed; **Mme de Sérilly's boudoir** (Marie-Antoinette's music stand and work-table); Taskin harpsichord, Riesener jewel casket; 18C Italian **Cabinet of Mirrors;** Houdon busts *(Voltaire);* **Italian oval room** (*c* 1780); 5 lapis lazuli columns illustrating 5 orders of architecture (once Marie-Antoinette's), *Mme de Pompadour* by Boucher; mirrors; porcelain.
		Related ceramic study galleries
Upper 1st floor	127-8	French 16-19C earthenware; **18-19C porcelain;** painted enamels.
2nd floor	138	**Limoges painted enamels;** 16C Italian enamels (also 142).
	134-5	Tin glazed earthenware; Spanish pottery; **Italian Maiolica;** Dutch delftware; Spanish, French, Italian, Dutch tiles.
	136	German and continental stone, tin, lead glazed ware.
	137	English and continental earthenware 13-20C; tiles.
	141	Tiles: Dutch, German, English, Swiss, Italian, Spanish; stoves.
	142	18C porcelain other than French; painted enamels.
1st floor	112	Glass BC 15C-AD 20C : vessels, Venetian chandelier... (also 131).
	111	Stained glass; 116-7 — English and continental mediaeval to 19C.
		MEDIAEVAL, GOTHIC, RENAISSANCE ART
Ground floor	43	**Early Middle Ages:** ivory carvings, gold and enamel work (Gloucester candlestick), small bronzes, Limoges and other *champlevé* enamels; church furnishings; glass: Byzantine, Roman, Egyptian.
	23	**Gothic:** 14-15C: English embroidery, stained glass.
	22	Italian sculpture: Pisano *Prophet;* N. Pisano, *Wooden Angel;* reliefs, ivories, *maiolica,* embroideries.
	24-5	French sculpture: angel in painted wood, ivories, silver (Studley bowl); English metalwork, enamelling, alabasters; Flemish tapestry; Spanish metalwork, Valencian altarpiece of St George.
	26-29	**Renaissance:** 16C Northern Europe: embroidery, silver **(Burghley nef),** metalwork (Marquart clock, 1597); decorated altarpieces; German plate; lead and stone wares; stained glass.
	16-12	**Italy:** maiolica, chests, glass, mss but most importantly sculpture: Donatello *Ascension, Dead Christ,* bronzes.
	17-20	Duccio *Virgin and Child,* Della Robbia roundels (armorial and labours of the months), Rossellino busts and *Virgin with the Laughing Child;* **15, 16C small bronzes;** Venetian glass; maiolica; Paduan fireplace, Piedmontese altarpiece.
	21A-21	**High Renaissance:** 1500-1600; Italian, French stained glass; Spanish, Italian metalwork; **small bronzes** (Cellini and others); Giovanni Bologna *Samson and the Philistine,* Bernini *Neptune and Triton;* wax models by Michelangelo, Bologna; German gilt bronze altarpiece.
		Related small sculptures
Upper ground floor	62	English alabasters; English and continental ivories 10-19C.
	63-4	Terracotta figures; small Italian (Riccio) and other bronzes.
		ORIENTAL ART
		China, Korea, Japan
Ground floor	44	Chinese painted pottery (jar, 2000 BC; T'ang horses, camels),
	47D, E	bronze vessels; jade carvings (horse's head, buffalo); Buddhist sculpture; porcelain (early white, celadons, blue and white); *cloisonné* enamels; Coromandel lacquer screen; embroidery (dragon robes) imperial thrones; Japanese screens; lacquerware.
Lower ground floor	8	Bronze vessels; Japanese *netsuke.*
1st floor	98	Woven fabrics, court robes (Carpets: 97 *on application*).
Upper 1st	129-30	Chinese jade, hardstone and ivory carvings; snuff bottles; glass.
2nd floor	143-5	Pottery, porcelain, painted enamels.
		India
Ground floor	41	Mughal arts, 16-19C: jade wine cup (1657); paintings; carpets (Fremlin — floor centre); cotton paintings, jewellery.
	47A	Textiles; Bali and Javanese betel nut cutters; **Tipu's Tiger,** Tibetan, Burmese, Nepalese Buddhas.
	47B	Indian sculpture and bronzes; God Siva dancing in a circle of flames; Burmese Buddhist shrine of gilt wood.

FLOOR	ROOM	SUBJECT

ISLAM

Ground floor	42	Persian tiles, pottery (lustreware, Kufik decoration); stucco figures; damascened brassware (ewer) and bronze (lamp); Syrian enamelled gilt glass; Persian and Turkish carpets, textiles Ardabil Carpet (1540; 30 million knots).
	47B	Persian, Mesopotamian pottery; Egyptian crystal ewer.
Lower ground floor	9	Persian and Mamluk 12-18C bronzes, brass, tinned copper (also 88); painted lacquer; carved wooden ladles; oil paintings.
2nd floor	133	Ceramics: Persian, Turkish, Egyptian plates, dishes, tiles.
1st floor	97	Carpets *(on application)*.

SUBJECT GALLERIES

JEWELLERY, GOLD, SILVER AND METALWORK (also Period Rooms)

1st floor	93	English and continental snuffboxes, watches etc.
	92-1	Rings from Classical times to 1970s; jewels: **Armada** (*c* 1558) Canning (late 16C); Russian imperial jewels; Cory Diamonds (19C).
	65-7	English domestic silver, late 14C-1970 (spoons 1300-1597) Pusey Horn (15C) Frewen Cup (17C).
	68-9	Continental domestic silver.
	81	Pewter and lead; cutlery; cut steelwork.
	82	17, 18C European brass and copper; Sheffield plate.
	89	European mediaeval *champlevé* and *cloisonné* enamels; bronzes (including crucifix figures).
	83, 84	Ecclesiastical silver; monumental brasses.
	88A, 90	Arms, armour (Europe, Near East): techniques of ornament (also 88).

IRONWORK

| 1st floor | 113-115 | Wrought iron: gates, signs, weathervanes, locks, firebacks. |

MUSICAL INSTRUMENTS

| Mezzanine | 40 | Early keyboard instruments (spinets, virginals, harpsichords) lutes, recorders etc. Recordings in the "juke box". |

COSTUME

| Ground floor | 40 | European fashions 1600-1947; fans 107 (1st floor). |

TEXTILES (also Period Rooms)

1st floor	109	Embroidery; 17, 18C coverlets (also 23, stairs to 126).
	102	Patchwork quilts.
	96-99 100-1	Textile study rooms: embroidery, silks and woven and printed fabrics; peasant embroidery, lace (96).

TAPESTRIES AND CARPETS

Ground floor	38	Mediaeval hangings: French (Arras, Tournai) 15C hunting scenes; Trojan war; pastorals *(millefleurs)* Flemish, 16C Brussels.
	48	**Raphaël Cartoons.**
Staircase	25	Spanish carpets.
Ground floor	32, 33	European carpets; Sheldon tapestry maps; Oriental carpets.
1st floor	94	16-20C tapestries shown in rotation.
	97	Persian, Turkey, Caucasian, Central Asian, Chinese, European carpets *(open on application)*.

ARCHITECTURE

| Ground floor | 48E | House and shop fronts; Sir Paul Pindar's house (*c* 1600). |
| | 46 | Cast courts: mediaeval to 17C features — Trajan's column, Santiago cathedral door, Ghiberti's *Paradise Door* (Baptistry, Florence), Donatello, Michelangelo sculptures *(David)*. |

Related larger sculptures: English and Continental 17-19C

| Ground floor | 50 | Nicholas Stone, Roubiliac (*Handel* from Vauxhall Gdns), Cibber (*Raving* and *Melancholy Madness* from outside Bedlam), Flaxman, Chantrey, Stevens; Santa Chiara Chapel... |

PAINTINGS (also Raphaël Cartoons, 48 and Period Rooms)

1st floor	103	**Constable:** oils including *Dedham Mill, Salisbury Cathedral*; studies *(Haywain)*, oil sketches.
	106	Watercolours: British school, mid 18C to today, with examples of 20C foreign artists (shown in rotation).
	105	Rembrandt, Tintoretto *(Self-portrait)*, French mid 19C, Degas.
	104	British oils: Wilson, Gainsborough, Reynolds, Turner, Crome.
	87	Foreign oils: Italian, Netherlandish and German 15-19C.

PRINTS AND DRAWINGS, LIBRARY, THEATRE

1st floor	70-73	Half a million items displayed in rotation from mediaeval mss to locksmiths' designs, Japanese wood blocks etc etc.
	74B	Art of the Book: printing, binding, illustration...
1st floor	77-8	The **National Art Library:** reference collection of 300 000 publications on architecture, sculpture topography, theatre, fashion, heraldry, printing, binding, mss, autographs.
2nd floor	132	Stage design from 18C; playbills, costume design prints.

Open Mondays to Saturdays 10am to 5pm, Sundays from 2pm; closed Good Friday, 24, 25, 26 December, 1 January. Major alterations to the house and rearrangement are in progress.

The collectors. – The gathering of one of the world's finer collections of 18C French art was the lifework of the 4th Marquess of Hertford (1800-70) who lived most of his life in Paris at his small château, Bagatelle, in the Bois de Boulogne *(see Guide: Paris)*. He transformed the family art collection founded by his great grandfather in 18C with portraits by Ramsay and Reynolds, increased by the 2nd Marquess (Romney, Reynolds, Hoppner) and enlarged further by the 3rd Marquess (Thackeray's Marquis of Steyne), who purchased 17C Dutch and 18C English paintings, 18C French furniture and Sèvres porcelain. Richard Wallace, the 4th Marquess' natural son (1818-90), benefactor, founder of the Hertford British Hospital in Paris (also provider of the drinking fountains still known by his name – one in the forecourt), extended especially the armoury, the majolica ware, 15, 16C Limoges enamels (plaques after Dürer of the Passion, portraits), and the mediaeval and Renaissance bronzes and goldsmiths' work. He it was who brought the collection to England which his widow subsequently left to the nation (opened as a museum, 1900).

Boulle commode.

The 4th Marquess' taste was all-embracing save, as he declared, "I only like pleasing paintings". He collected old masters, tapestries, oriental armour, Sèvres porcelain and the finest French furniture of the 17 and 18C; more originally he also bought extensively the light 18C French painters, Watteau, Boucher and Fragonard and his contemporaries, both French (Prud'hon, Delacroix, Géricault, Corot...) and English (Gainsborough, Lawrence, Bonington, Turner).

NB: *the gallery numbering and chronological sequence therefore, is counter clockwise. The gallery numbers on the first floor correspond with those below as follows: I becomes XII, II XIII... V and VI become XVI, VII XVII... the publications' room XIX, IX XX etc.*

The collection. – French 17 and 18C furniture from the workshops of the master cabinet makers **Boulle** (1642-1732), **Cressent** (1685-1768) and **Riesener** (1734-1806), also a large number of 18C French clocks are to be seen throughout the house. Very broadly the arrangement is:

- Major pictures of all schools and very fine furniture: first floor in the long gallery – Gallery XVI
- French 18C pictures, porcelain, furniture, 17C painting and the gold boxes: landing and first floor, left, and oval room – XX, XXI, XXII, XVIII, XVII
- Flemish and Dutch pictures (interiors, landscapes): first floor, far right – XIII, XIV, XV
- Armour, European and Oriental: ground floor, back of the house and far left – V, VI, VII, VIII
- The Boningtons: ground floor sharp left – IX and corridor
- Early Italian paintings and works of art: ground floor, left – X
- The miniatures: ground floor, the bow room overlooking the courtyard – XI
- Mediaeval and Renaissance works of art – the majolica and small bronzes: ground floor, far right – III, IV
- The Canalettos and Guardis (also very fine Sèvres porcelain): first floor, right – XII
- Bronzes after Giovanni di Bologna etc. – 1st floor, Conservatory.

GROUND FLOOR

George Street

Manchester Street

Spanish Place

Courtyard

Wallace Fountain

Manchester Square

The superb wrought iron and bronze staircase balustrade, chased and gilt, was made *c* 1735 for the Palais Mazarin (now the Bibliothèque Nationale); it was sold for scrap-iron a century later, rescued by the 4th Marquess and adapted to the present staircase by Wallace. Note the interlaced Ls, the royal emblem sunflowers.

GOLD MINIATURE BOXES

18C and principally French, the 89 boxes are in multicoloured gold, hardstone, mounted with Sèvres porcelain, jewelled, enamelled, painted, incorporating tortoiseshell, oriental lacquer, miniatures, square, oblong, oval, round, with oblique corners, shell-shaped... and quite exquisite – Galleries XVII and IX.

PAINTINGS

ARTIST	TITLES and GALLERIES
Boucher	*Mme de Pompadour, Judgment of Paris:* XIX, staircase, XVIII
Bronzino	*Eleonora di Toledo:* III
Canaletto	Venice: XII
Philippe de Champaigne	*Adoration of the Shepherds, Portrait of an Ecclesiatic; Annunciation:* IV; XVI
Foppa	*The Young Cicero reading:* X
Fragonard	*The Swing, a Boy as Pierrot, Souvenir:* XVIII
Gainsborough	*Mrs Robinson — Perdita, Miss Haverfield* (a small girl in a large hat): XVI
Greuze	*Mlle Sophie Arnould:* XX
Guardi	Venice: XII
Frans Hals	*Laughing Cavalier:* XVI
Holbein	Self-portrait (miniature): XI
Hoppner	*George IV as Prince of Wales:* I
Lancret	*La Belle Grecque:* XVIII
Lawrence	*George IV, Countess of Blessington:* Entrance, I
Murillo	Religious paintings: XI, XVI
Nattier	Portraits and small scenes: XX, XVIII
Rembrandt	*Titus, the artist's son,* Self-portrait, two groups: XVI
Reynolds	*Mrs Carnac, Nelly O'Brien, Perdita,* two children's portraits: *The Strawberry Girl, Miss Jane Bowles:* XVI
Rigaud	*Mary Queen of Scots:* IV
Salvator Rosa	*Landscape with Apollo and the Sybil:* XVI
Rubens	*Landscape with a Rainbow, Holy Family:* XVI, XIII
Titian	*Perseus and Andromeda:* XVI
Van Dyck	Full length portraits: *Philippe Le Roy* and his wife: XVI
Velasquez	*A Lady with a Fan* also court pictures: XVI
Vigée-Le Brun	*The Comte d'Espignac* (boy in a red coat): XX
Watteau	The pastorals: *Halt during the Chase; Fête in a Park; The Music Party, The Music Lesson, A Lady at her Toilet;* XVI, XVIII

FURNITURE

MAKER	ARTICLES and GALLERIES
Boulle (1642-1732)	Cabinet, wardrobe, pedestal clock and other fine pieces; wardrobes (pair); toilet mirror: XXI, I and X, XXII
Cressent (1685-1768)	Chest of drawers, veneered with gilt bronze dragon mounts; writing table; gilt bronze clock case, cabinet: XVI, I, XII
Riesener (1734-1806)	3 drop front secretaires (made for Marie-Antoinette); 2 chests of drawers; King Stanislaus' roll-top desk with inlay work and bronze mounts; chased and gilt corner cupboards (for Marie-Antoinette); mahogany cylinder top desk; table mounted with Sèvres plaques; oval secretaire; chest of drawers: XVIII, XVI, XIV, IX, XXII, I

It is interesting to compare the furniture in Hertford House with that at Osterley and Syon Parks.

WANDSWORTH (Wandsworth)

Surprisingly to many, reminders of the locality's mediaeval history, its 17 and 18C associations and its 19C development are still apparent.

Wandsworth began as a Surrey village straggling along the banks of the **Wandle,** a river which rises west of Croydon, is only 10 miles long and in addition to the "fishful qualities" noted by Izaak Walton, neither dries up in summer nor freezes in winter. As early as 1602 its waters were harnessed to work corn and iron mills. Potters, calico bleachers, fullers, launderers, printers, coppersmiths, all of whom needed a constant water supply, swelled the population and were joined in late 17C by silk weavers and felt hat makers, many of whom where Huguenot and whose presence is recalled in **Huguenot Place** (Trinity Rd/Wandsworth Common Northside) the Huguenot Burial Ground (St Anselm's RC Church), which formerly served English and French Protestants and contains stones dating from 1697 and, in the road off the west side of Streatham Common, **Factory Gardens.** The factories referred to were silk weaving mills and felt hat making shops, the latter a Huguenot specialty and, specialty of specialties, cardinals' red hats! It was said that a cardinal caught in a shower could only be certain of not getting a red face if his hat had come from Wandsworth.

All Saints Parish Church, on an ancient site, is 18C with 19C additions, St Ann's (St Ann's Hill), the Pepperpot Church, 1820's and the Friends' Meeting House, 1778, in place of a 1697 building (burial ground).

The "1723 House", Wandsworth Plain, is a terrace of six fine, three storey, brick houses with short flights of steps up to Corinthian pilastered front doors, a central pediment and wall sundial. Armoury Way, at the back, recalls Tudor times when every parish had its armoury.

Wandsworth Prison, Heathfield Rd, has, a contemporary opinion commented in 1851, "nothing to recommend it to the eye".

■ PALACE OF WESTMINSTER★★★

Open 10am to 5pm Saturdays; holiday Mondays and following Tuesdays; Mondays, Tuesdays, Thursdays in August, Thursdays in September. Tours start: Norman Porch (2).
Westminster Hall: during the Recess, weekdays 10am to 4pm (5pm Saturdays); during the Session, Mondays to Thursdays 10am to 1.30pm (5pm Saturdays) provided neither House is sitting on those days. Closed when either House is sitting and on Sundays, 25, 26 December and Good Friday.

Princely palace to Mother of Parliaments. — "King William I built much at his palace, for" according to Stow, he found the residence of Edward the Confessor "far inferior to the building of princely palaces in France". Agrandised and embellished but unlike the Tower, never strongly fortified, William's palace continued for centuries, never actually being demolished but gradually disappearing beneath frequent rebuildings caused by fires of which the most devastating were those of 1298, 1512 and finally, 1834. Of that early period there remain Westminster Hall, St Stephen's Crypt, the later (1526-9) two storey St Stephen's cloister and the Jewel Tower. Hemming in the palace on all sides were houses for members of the court, knights and burgesses, who, as representatives of local communities or commons began from 1332, to meet apart as the House of Commons.

Parliament's opening ceremony, as now, was before the monarch, but then in a richly ornamented hall known as the Painted Chamber from where the estates would adjourn — the Lords to the White Hall, the Commons remaining or to the Chapterhouse or even the monks' refectory. After the fire of 1512 Henry VIII did not rebuild the old palace and, until he confiscated Wolsey's York House in 1529, had no royal residence at Westminster. Among the buildings to survive was St Stephen's, the king's domestic chapel, which was granted by Edward VI in 1547 to the Commons as their chamber. It was while they were in St Stephen's that King Charles came to arrest and impeach Hampden, Pym and three others (1642) and it was there that they continued to sit until 19C. The Lords, so nearly blown up in the **Gunpowder Plot** of 1605 continued to meet in the White Hall until the night of 16 October 1834 when cartloads of notched tally sticks (old Exchequer forms of account), were put into the underground furnace which overheated... In hours what had come to be known as the Houses of Parliament had been burnt almost to the ground.

The buildings. — **Charles Barry** and **Augustus Pugin** together won the competition of 1835 for a new design, stipulated as being either Elizabethan or Gothic in style: Barry was a Gothicist by necessity, Pugin by innermost fervour. Barry's ground plan was outstanding in its apparent simplicity: the two chambers were to be on a single, processional axis — the throne, woolsack, bars of the two chambers and Speaker's chair all in line. At the centre would be a large common lobby to which the public would have access through St Stephen's Hall; libraries and dining rooms, in parallel to the main axis, would overlook the river. The centre would be distinguished by a lantern and slender spire (above the lobby), the ends by a new clock tower and tower above the royal entrance. This plan, executed in Yorkshire limestone (badly quarried and in constant need of repair), is equally remarkable in its exterior for the interplay of symmetry and asymmetry: the towers balance but are totally unlike, the St Stephen's turrets are not a pair; in contrast the long waterfront is entirely regular with Gothic pinnacles and windows extending from end to end with mediaeval tracery, carving, niches and figures, individually designed by Pugin in the Perpendicular tradition. The foundation stone was laid in 1840, the Victoria Tower completed by 1860; there were 1 000 rooms, 100 staircases, 2 miles of corridors spread over 8 acres; construction had united the work of hundreds of painters, sculptors, craftsmen; Barry was knighted, Pugin died in Bedlam, both in 1852.

(After photograph, Kardorama, London)

Palace of Westminster.

INTERIOR

Royal entrance and staircase (1). – The route through the Victoria Tower, where the sovereign is met by high officers of state on the Opening of Parliament, proceeds up a flight of stairs, lined on state occasions by the Household Cavalry, to the **Norman Porch** (2). This is square in shape, Perpendicular in style with gilded vaulting.

The Robing Room★. – The room where the sovereign assumes the Imperial State Crown and crimson parliamentary robe, presents, with the Lords' Chamber, Pugin's most remarkable concentration of decorative invention – every inch of wall space and panelled ceiling is ornamented with sovereigns' badges, patterned and gilded, coloured, carved, is hung with flocked paper and pictures, frescoed after the legend of King Arthur...

The Royal Gallery. – The gallery, the sovereign's 110ft processional way, is decorated by frescoes by Maclise, gilt bronze statues of monarchs from Alfred to Queen Anne and portraits of every sovereign and their escort from George I. In the **Prince's Chamber**, which follows, are the Tudor monarchs and their wives – all six of Henry VIII.

House of Lords★★. – The "magnificent and gravely gorgeous" chamber is the summit of Pugin's achievement; a symphony of design and

PALACE OF WESTMINSTER

workmanship in encrusted gold, gilding and scarlet. The throne and steps beneath a niched and finialed Gothic canopy mounted on a wide screen, all in gold, occupies one end of the chamber. The ceiling is divided by ribs and gold patterning above the red buttoned leather benches (the one with arms is for the bishops – said to prevent those who have dined too well from rolling off) and the woolsack (" most uncomfortable"). The cross benches lie between the clerk's table and the bar of the house behind which the Commons stand when summoned by Black Rod to hear the speech from the throne. Looking down from between windows are bronze statues of 18 of the barons who witnessed King John's assent to *Magna Carta*.

Central Lobby★. – The 75ft high, octagonal lobby through which everyone passes, is where one waits for one's MP. If parliament is in session one spots faces, if the house is in recess one notices the Perpendicular arches encircling windows and entrances decorated with English sovereigns, the life size 19C statesmen, the mosaics over the doorways, the gilded and patterned roof ribs, the chandelier, all by Pugin.

Corridor (3) **and Commons Lobby.** – The lobby, destroyed in the 1941 air raid, has been reconstructed to incorporate stones from the old fabric in a newly named **Churchill Arch** which is flanked by his statue in bronze by Oscar Nemon and that of Lloyd George.

House of Commons★. – The benches are in the traditional green hide beneath an unadorned Gothic timber structure. There is seating for 437 members out of the 635 elected. At the end is the canopied Speaker's chair with before it those of the Clerks and the table of the house with the bronze mounted despatch boxes and the mace. Red stripes on either side of the green carpet mark the limit to which a member may advance when addressing the house – the distance between the stripes is reputedly that of two drawn swords. The government sits on the Speaker's right, the PM opposite the despatch box. When a division is called, members leave for the tellers' lobbies past the Speakers' right for Aye and through the far end to No – the Lords divide similarly but vote "Content" or "Not Content"

Libraries. – The libraries, overlooking the river, are oases of silence, the Lords' again the more remarkable for Pugin's decoration. Note in the Lords' Library, the warrant signed by Cromwell and the council for Charles I's execution.

The Terrace. – The terrace is one of London's most special places for tea.

WESTMINSTER★★★

St Stephen's Hall. — The long narrow hall *(public entrance)* was reconstructed by Barry to look like the 14C chapel with ribbed vaulting springing from clustered piers and at the end two superimposed arches, the uppermost filled with a mosaic of St Stephen between King Stephen and Edward the Confessor. Note the brasses on the floor delimiting the old Commons chamber (60 × 30ft; *see also the Derby relief p 178*).

Westminster Hall★★. — The hall, scene throughout the Middle Ages of royal Christmas feasts, of joustings, ceremonial and congregation, was added to his father's palace by William Rufus in 1097. It was repaired by Thomas Becket, flooded in 13C "when men did row wherries in (its) midst", and re-roofed by command of Richard II in 1394. The king, however, before rebuilding was complete in 1401, was arraigned there before parliament and deposed. Sir Thomas More (1535), Somerset (1551), Northumberland (1553), Essex (1601), Guy Fawkes (1606) and Charles I all later stood trial in the hall. This century it has been where monarchs and Churchill have lain in state.

When peripatetic courts following the king were decided to be no longer practical, the Great Hall, already a place of pleadings and trial, was appointed the permanent seat of justice with the floor space divided between courts of Common Pleas, Chancery and King's Bench, bookstalls and shops.

The interior. — The master mason, Henry Yevele and carpenter, Hugh Herland, commanded in 1394 to re-roof the 240 × 70ft hall, rebuilt the upper walls and erected what is probably the finest timber roof of all time, a superb **hammerbeam★★★**. It weighs more than 660 tons, which is the reason for the exterior buttresses, and rises to 90ft at the crest; it depends on projecting hammerbeams 21ft long × 3ft 3ins × 2ft 1in thick, held on curving wooden braces resting on carved stone corbels. The beams, which support vertical posts on which the superstructure rests, are carved with great flying angels.

Nine light Perpendicular windows occupy the north and south ends, the latter set back in 19C by Barry to effect a dramatic junction up wide flights of steps with St Stephen's Porch. Flanking the arch are six 14C statues of early English kings.

St Stephen's Crypt (Chapel of St Mary). — The domestic chapel built by Edward I between 1292-7 was on two levels, the upper being reserved for the royal family. After St Stephen's had been granted to the Commons, the lower chapel was used for secular purposes until the 19C when the mediaeval foundation was redecorated as a chapel.

EXTERIOR *(Map p 177)*

The Clock Tower – Big Ben★. — The 316ft tower, erected close to the site of the old palace clock tower which had existed from 1288-1707 and at one time had the staple or wool market at its foot, was completed by 1858-9 with clock and bell. The name Big Ben, probably after Sir Benjamin Hall, First Commissioner of Works and a man of vast girth, applied originally only to the bell which after recasting at the Whitechapel Foundry weighs 13 tons 10 cwts 3 qtrs 15 lbs, measures 9ft in diameter and 7ft in height and early on developed a 4ft crack. The clock mechanism (electrically wound) weighs about 5 tons. The dials of cast iron tracery are glazed with pot opal glass and are 23ft in diameter; the minute spaces 1ft sq; the figures 2ft long. The minute hands of copper are 14ft long, weigh 2 cwts, and each travel 25 miles a year. Big Ben was first broadcast on New Year's Eve 1923. The light above the clock remains lit while the Commons is sitting. A Jubilee fountain of heraldic beasts, sculpted in iron, was opened by the Queen in May 1977.

Victoria Tower★. — *Open on application in writing to the Clerk of the Records.*
The tower, the taller of the two at 336ft, was designed as the archive for parliamentary documents — previously kept in the Jewel Tower and therefore saved from the 1834 fire. Among the 3 million papers are master copies of acts from 1497, journals of the House of Lords from 1510, the Commons from 1547, records of the Gunpowder Plot, Charles I's attempted arrest of Hampden, Patents of Nobility, the Articles of Union of 1706...

Victoria Tower Gardens. — In the gardens stand a cast of the great bronze group by Rodin the *Burghers of Calais* (who ransomed themselves to Edward III in 1347), a slim statue of Emmeline Pankhurst, the suffragette, and her daughter, Christabel.

Smith Square. — The square now synonymous, according to mood, with politics or music, began to develop in 1713 with the erection at the centre of **St John's** by **Thomas Archer**. The tall, Baroque church, rising by colossal columns and open pediments and balanced by four ornate corner towers, is said to have been compared by the queen to an up-turned footstool and is known to many as the Queen Anne Footstool. It was badly bombed but has been restored with giant Corinthian pillars beneath a deep cornice, Venetian windows and a very large 18C chandelier, to serve as a concert hall.

In the square's southeast and southwest corners respectively are Transport House, where the Labour Party has its headquarters and the Conservative Central Office.

The four streets which enter the square midway along each side, the square itself and the streets to the north, include among inevitable rebuildings, many of the original Georgian houses, most notably nos 6-9 Smith Sq, Lord North Street entirely except its northern end and the south end of Cowley St (occasional date stones 1722, 1726).

Jewel Tower. — *Open 10.30am to 4pm; closed Sundays, 1 January, 24, 25, 26 December.*
The L shaped tower with a corner staircase turret, dates from 1365 when it was built with a moat surrounding it as the king's personal jewel house and treasury — there is a brick vaulted strongroom on the first floor with a later iron door (1612). When Westminster ceased to be a royal palace, the tower, with windows renewed in 1718, became the archive for parliamentary papers *(see above)* and subsequently the weights and measures office — Standards of Weight and Length are displayed in the top chamber. In the vaulted lower chamber are the tower's rediscovered ancient wooden foundations.

■ WESTMINSTER ABBEY★★★

Open daily 8am to 6pm (7.30pm on Sundays; 8pm on Wednesdays from March to November); choir, transepts and Royal Chapels (50p) Mondays to Fridays 9.20am to 4.45pm (5.45 Saturdays but closed between 2.45 and 3.45) open, also 6 to 8pm Wednesdays (March to November); Chapterhouse (10p) 10.30am to 6.30pm (4pm October to March); Museum (11p). Closed 25 December.

Monastery Church to Royal Peculiar. — The Westminster Abbey in which **William I,** the first king ever to be so, was crowned on Christmas Day 1066, had been built by Edward the Confessor in the Norman style; only with the Plantagenet Henry III's rebuilding in 13C did it acquire the Gothic appearance so familiar today. **Sebert,** 6C King of the East Saxons is credited with building the first church and monastery, or abbey, on Thorney Island, a thicket covered triangle formed by the twin outflows, some 700yds apart, of the Tyburn into the Thames. **Edward the Confessor** "built it of new", intending to make the church his sepulchre and indeed died and was buried in it within a week of the dedication on 28 December 1065. He also built the parish church of St Margaret's outside the precincts and a royal palace. The now important centre soon became known as Westminster: the minster in the west, as opposed to the rival cathedral in the east, St Paul's.

In 1220, inspired by the Gothic style of Amiens and Reims, came **Henry III's** rebuilding, beginning with the Lady Chapel to provide a noble shrine for the Confessor who had been canonised in 1163. When the Lady Chapel was complete, construction continued west over the existing building which was demolished as the new construction replaced the old: by late 13C, the east end, transepts, choir, the first bay of the nave and the chapterhouse were complete; progress then halted and it took another two centuries to finish the nave.

When **Henry VII** came to construct his chapel, Gothic, in its Perpendicular form, was still the ecclesiastical style and he produced the jewel of the age (1503-19). Later additions, notably the west towers (1722-45) by Wren and Hawksmoor, and repairs by Scott and others have kept to the Gothic spirit: heavenward vaulting, soaring windows between slender, buttressed, walls, flying buttresses, gabled transepts with traceried rose windows surmounting doors with enriched covings, and, at the east end, the long chancel culminating in the Henry VII chapel, more delicate, more finely niched and pinnacled than any other part.

Dissolution in 1540 resulted in the forfeiture of abbey property, the confiscation of the treasure, but not, as elsewhere, in the destruction of the fabric. It disbanded the 600 year old Benedictine house of some 50 monks, dismissed those supervising the widespread properties and serving on missions abroad and the abbot, a man of temporal as well as spiritual power with his own lavish household. In their place in 1560, in a charter granted by Elizabeth I, were established the Collegiate Church of St Peter with a royally appointed dean and chapter of 12 prebendaries (canons) and in that of 12/13C monastic school, the College of St Peter, known by tradition as Westminster Abbey or The Abbey, and Westminster School.

Although the detail in the vaulting and mediaeval carving is inexhaustible, the abbey should be viewed as built, as the setting for state occasions when it is brilliant with colour, resounds to the music of coronations and royal weddings (since the marriage in 1923 of the future George VI and Queen Elizabeth). It is no longer a royal mausoleum.

The abbey dimensions are: west door to east window inside, 511ft 6in of which the nave is 166ft, Henry VII's Chapel, 104ft 6ins; the nave, including the aisles, is 72ft wide and 102ft high; the height outside to the topmost pinnacles of the west towers is 225ft, the lantern 151ft. The fabric is Caen and Reigate stone.

INTERIOR

Nave and transepts. — The soaring vaulting remains in the beauty of its conception; the carving on screens and arches, in spandrels and covings is delicate, often beautiful, sometimes humorous; the ancient tombs in Henry VII's, St Edward's and the surrounding ambulatory chapels (broadly beyond the high altar), making no pretence of portraying the living, are dignified, and, on occasion, revealing in expression (a few are derived from death masks). The 18 and 19C surfeit of monuments in the transepts and aisles has become a byeword even though sculpted by the great names of the day — Roubiliac, the Bacons, Flaxman, Le Sueur, Westmacott, Chantrey.

It is at the dean's discretion who is buried in the abbey and to who memorials may be erected — situations not synonymous since 18C when the custom developed after several of like calling had been interred, of commemorating others of equal standing: the most famous result is **Poets' Corner★** where Chaucer (1), who as Clerk of Works was associated with the palace and abbey, and the statues of Dryden (2) and Ben Jonson (3), court poets, have been joined by Shakespeare (4) (a "preposterous monument" in Horace Walpole's opinion), Milton (5), Blake (6) (bust by Epstein, 1957, against the pillar), Burns (7), Longfellow (8), so that by 18C, Addison (9) was commenting "In the poetical quarter I found there were poets who had no monuments and monuments which had no poets". Plaques and stones are now more the order of the day — Auden, Hardy, Gerard Manley Hopkins (10) were added in 1975-6. Of all the pavement stones, however, the most famous will always be that in the nave, surrounded by Flanders Poppies, to the **Unknown Warrior** (11).

The nave west end, north aisle and north transept are chiefly filled with politicians, philanthropists and commanders. Note against the first south pier the famous **painting of Richard II** (12) and in the north aisle, low down, the small stone which covered the upright figure of the playwright "O rare Ben Johnson" (13) (misspelt!). The choirscreen, a 13C structure of stone, lierne vaulted in the arch between the nave and the choir, was richly redesigned in 19C with gabled niches.

Choir and Sanctuary. — In the choir, re-embellished in mid 19C — the eye is led immediately to the gilded blaze of 19C high altar screen and the altar before it. This area, the **Sanctuary,** is approached by a low flight of steps marked on the left by a gilded and blackwood 17C pulpit and is laid with a 13C Italian pavement of porphyry and mosaic. It is where the crowning is performed in the **coronation** ceremony and the sovereign receives the peers' homage. To the right hangs a 16C tapestry and on it a large 15C altarpiece of rare beauty. Beyond is an ancient 13C sedilia painted with full length royal figures (Henry III, Edward I and a bishop). On the left are three tombs, each a recumbent figure on a chest beneath a gabled canopy — Aveline of Lancaster (14; d 1274) a great heiress and a great beauty, Aymer de Valence, Earl of Pembroke (15; d 1324), cousin to Edward I and, Edmund Crouchback (16; d 1296), youngest son of Henry III, husband of Aveline.

North ambulatory chapels. — The chantry chapel of Abbot Islip is known for its rebus — an eye and a slip or branch of a tree clasped by a hand, also a man slipping from a tree; the **Chapel of Our Lady of the Pew,** in the thickness of the wall, contains a modern alabaster Madonna and Child *(p 175)*; St John the Baptist's and St Paul's Chapels, mediaeval tombs in decorated recesses or beneath ornate canopies with highly coloured effigies and elaborate gilded wall memorials with helms at the crest.

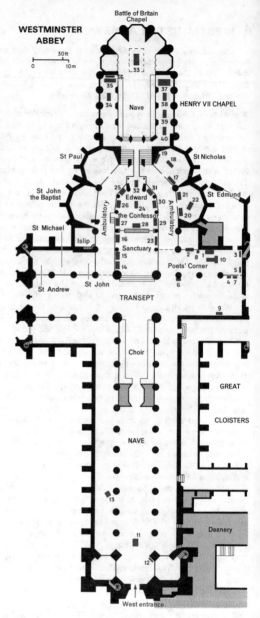

WESTMINSTER ABBEY

30ft
0   10m

Battle of Britain Chapel

Nave

HENRY VII CHAPEL

St Paul
St Nicholas

St John the Baptist

Edward the Confessor

Ambulatory   Ambulatory
St Edmund

St Michael

Islip
St Andrew
Sanctuary
Poets' Corner

St John
TRANSEPT

Choir
GREAT
CLOISTERS

NAVE
Deanery

West entrance

From the ambulatory note the small gilded kings and queens on Crouchback's tomb (16).

South ambulatory chapels. — St Nicholas' chapel contains the tomb of Philippa, Duchess of York (17; d 1431) with wimple and veil about her expressive head, the vault of the Percys (18) and the tomb of Anne, Duchess of Somerset (19; d 1587), widow of the Protector. In St Edmund's Chapel are the tombs of William de Valence (20; d 1296), halfbrother of Henry III, the figure remarkably carved with clothes and accoutrements powdered with crests, and the marble effigy of John of Eltham (21; d 1337), 2nd son of Edward II. In the centre, on a low altar tomb, is the abbey's finest **brass:** Eleanor Duchess of Gloucester (22; d 1399) in widow's gown beneath a triple canopy.

Note, in the ambulatory Sebert's tomb (23) and the sedilia painting of the Confessor.

Chapel of Edward the Confessor★★. — The chapel, with the Confessor's shrine (24) at the centre, ringed by the tombs of five kings and three queens, is also known as the Chapel of the Kings. The shrine itself is in two parts, the lower, prepared by Henry III, is of Purbeck marble, the upper is a stepped wooden construction made after the original had been looted at the Dissolution. On either side are **Queen Eleanor of Castile** (25; d 1290), she of the crosses, slender and serene, in gilded bronze by the master goldsmith **William Torel; Henry III** (26; d 1272), in gilded effigy, builder of the chapel who spent more than all the money he possessed in constructing the abbey; **Edward I,** Longshanks (27; d 1307), the first king to be crowned in the present abbey (1272) and who, as the Hammer of the Scots, brought the Scottish regalia and the Stone of Scone south in 1297.

Coronation Chair and Screen (28). — The carved stone screen, which closes the west end of the chapel was completed in 1441. At the centre stands the Coronation Chair made of oak and once brightly painted and gilded with, below the seat, the **Stone of Scone.** For coronations the chair is brought round the screen to the sanctuary.

On the chapel's south side are **Richard II** (29) who married **Anne of Bohemia** in the abbey in 1382 and raised her tomb there in 1394. In the centre is the gilt bronze figure of Edward III (30; d 1377) on an altar tomb of Purbeck marble, surrounded in niches at the base, by bronze representations of his children, of whom 6 remain (towards the ambulatory) including the Black Prince. Beyond, carved in white marble once painted and gilded, lies his queen, **Philippa of Hainault** (31; d 1369) who interceded for the Burghers of Calais. Finally, at the end on a Purbeck marble tomb, is the oak figure, once silverplated, of the young Henry V (32; d 1422) and, above the king's beautifully carved chantry chapel (in which Catherine of Valois is now buried).

Henry VII Chapel★★★. – The fan-vaulted roof is superb, the banners of the Knights Grand Cross of the Order of the Bath still and brilliant, the stall pinnacles surprising with their crowning helmets and coifs, the stalls patterned with the heraldic plates of former occupants and their esquires and witty with inventive 16/18C misericords. (The chapel was first used for the knights' installations in 1725 when George I reconstituted the order.) The great double gates at the entrance are made with wooden frames in which are mounted pierced bronze panels of the royal emblems of Henry

(After photograph, Jarrold's, Norwich)

The Coronation Chair.

Tudor and his antecedents: the roses of Lancaster and York, the leopards of England, *fleur-de-lys* of France, the falcon of Edward IV, father of Elizabeth, Henry's queen. At the east end is the high, railed tomb, of the founder, Henry VII and Elizabeth of York (33).

Circling the chapel are fan-vaulted aisles, blocked with tombs including, on the north side, **Queen Elizabeth I** (34) in white marble, ruffed, austere, the only colour the regalia, lions and the overhead canopy; beneath is the coffin of Mary Tudor without any monument. At the east end are memorials to two young daughters of James I, Princess Sophia and Princess Mary (35) and in a small sarcophagus, the bones found in the Tower in 1674 and presumed to be those of the Little Princes (36).

The 1947 Battle of Britain Chapel with a many faceted, brightly coloured memorial window, records the badges of the 68 Fighter Squadrons which took part.

In the south aisle are buried, without sculptured memorials, in a royal vault (37), Charles II, William III and Mary, Queen Anne and her consort, George of Denmark. Three grand tombs occupy the centre, all effigies upon tomb chests: Lady Margaret Beaufort (38; d 1509), mother of Henry Tudor, in widow's hood and mantle, her wrinkled hands raised in prayer, her face serene in old age, **Torrigiano's** masterpiece in gilt bronze; **Mary Queen of Scots** (39) in white marble, like Elizabeth but beneath a much grander canopy and with a crowned Scottish lion in colour at her feet; and Margaret Douglas, Countess of Lennox (40; d 1578) niece of Henry VIII, mother of Darnley and grandmother of James I – a beautiful woman carved in alabaster.

Chapterhouse★★. – The chamber (1248-53), used at one time as a royal treasury, is octagonal, 60ft in diameter, with vaulting springing from a slim central pier of attached Purbeck marble columns, encircled by two shaft rings. At each of the eight angles the lierned ribs descend onto a single marble column which reaches to the floor; marble shafts reappear at the windows and bearing the trefoiled blind arcade which circles the house and once provided seating for the monks in conclave; the arcade walls are still figured with the original paintings. The windows show the development, which was not followed in the body of the church as it would have spoilt the architectural unity, to the massive glazing characteristic of the mid Gothic style; each bay rises nearly 40ft to quatrefoils and cusped circles. The floor tiles, are original.

Chapterhouse as parlement. – The King's Great Council met under Henry III in the chapterhouse in 1257 confirming that it was intended from the first to accommodate secular assemblies as well as the 60-80 monks of St Peter's. Under Edward I it became the Parlement House of the Commons and continued after the Dissolution, when the hall passed into the direct ownership of the Crown. By 19C it had become an archive for state papers: the floor had been boarded over, a second storey inserted. In 1865 the building's condition necessitated complete reconstruction and a century later, after wartime destruction, reglazing, enabling a return to be made to clear glass, decorated with the coats of arms of sovereigns and abbots and the devices of the two mediaeval master masons, Henry de Reyns who designed Henry III's abbey and Henry Yevele, who built the nave (southwest and southeast windows).

Chapel of the Pyx. – *Open on application at the Chapterhouse.*

The chamber built between 1065-1090 as a monastery chapel and retaining the only stone altar in its original position, was converted into the monastery treasury in 13/14C. At the Dissolution it passed to the Crown and was used as the strongroom in which gold and silver coins were tried against the standard specimens kept there in a box or pyx.

Museum. – *Open April to September daily 9.30am to 6pm; October to March, Mondays to Saturdays 9.30am to 4pm; closed Good Friday, 25 December; 11p.*

The museum in the low Norman undercroft with two of the several pillars in its 110ft length still decorated with 11C carving, contains a number of unique wax and wood funeral effigies. Edward III and Catherine of Valois – both full length, are of wood, the king with a slight droop at the corner of the mouth resulting from a stroke, is thought to be after a death mask. Of the 11 wax effigies, the contemporary figure of **Charles II** in his Garter robes is unforgettable though not carried at his near clandestine funeral. Among the women are Catherine, Duchess of Buckingham, natural daughter of James II and wife of John Sheffield, builder of Buckingham House, who had her effigy made during her lifetime and Frances, Duchess of Richmond and Lennox who was the model for Britannia on the old penny piece. (She is in the beautiful robes she wore at the coronation of Queen Anne and accompanied by her pet parrot – the oldest extant stuffed bird!). **Nelson**, of who it was said by a contemporary "it is as if he was standing there", was purchased by the abbey in 1806 in an attempt to attract the crowds away from his tomb in St Paul's!

Jericho and Jerusalem Chambers. – *(Not open).* Both are in the former abbot's, now the dean's, lodgings. The Jericho Parlour has linenfold panelled walls of early 16C and is 150 years older than the Jerusalem Chamber where Henry IV died in 1413 (H IV PtII 4 v).

The Bells. – There are 12 bells which ring out on great occasions and some 25 days of festival and commemoration including 25, 26, 28 December, 1 January, Easter and Whit Sundays and the Queen's official birthday, generally between noon and 1pm.

Dean's Yard. – From the Sanctuary, opposite the red granite column with a crowning statue erected in memory of Old Westminsters who died in the Crimean War and Indian Mutiny, a gateway designed by Sir Gilbert Scott leads through to Dean's Yard, once the heart of the abbey precinct. Around the central lawn and trees stand the 20C Abbey Choir School, and **Church House** completed in 1940 with a long four storey façade and inside the Hoare Memorial Hall where the Commons met during the war, and the large, circular, Convocation Hall. On the east side are auxiliary buildings of the abbey, some late mediaeval and much altered, others Georgian, and the end of Westminster School. This extends back around Little Dean's Yard to include the Palladian, College, the mid 17C brick Ashburnham House, incorporating part of the 12/16C Prior's Lodging and School (the Great Hall), part of the late 11C monastic dormitory and until 1884 the school's only classroom. (Rebuilt and once more emblazoned with the arms of former headmasters and pupils.) College hall, formerly the abbots' state dining hall, is now the refectory for the 470 boys.

Sanctuary. – The right of sanctuary, extended in the monastery's time over a considerable area, became so abused by vagabonds, thieves and murderers, and the quarter so overbuilt with squalid houses, that it was first restricted and finally abolished in all but name, under James I. The column stands on the site of the gatehouse (demolished: 1776) in which **Sir Walter Raleigh** spent the last night before his execution and **Richard Lovelace** penned the poem with the line "stone walls do not a prison make..." Close by, on the opposite side of what is now Gt Smith St stood the almonry where **Caxton** first set up his press in 1476 using as his imprint, William Caxton, in the Abbey of Westminster.

Facilities. – At the west entrance the **Abbey Bookshop** has an extensive range of books. There is a large **brass rubbing centre** in the cloisters.

ENVIRONS *(Map p 177)*

St Margaret's★. – The church was erected within the shadow of the abbey originally by Edward the Confessor to serve local parishioners. In mid 14C the establishment of the wool staple, or market, at Westminster (close to the site of Big Ben) increased local prosperity and the now dilapidated church was rebuilt and yet a third time in 1488-1523. Scarcely completed by the Reformation, it was saved from becoming building stone for Protector Somerset's palace in the Strand by parishioners who "with bows and arrows, staves and clubs and other such offensive weapons... so terrified the workmen that they ran away in great amazement". In mid 19C Sir Gilbert Scott undertook a radical renewal-restoration to give the church much of its present late Perpendicular appearance.

Inside all thought of the august surroundings vanishes and one is in a parish church with a rich assemblage of Tudor monuments: sympathetic old Blanche Parry, Chief Gentlewoman of Queen Elizabeth's privie chamber, the behatted wife and cloaked figure of Thomas Arnway (d 1603) who left money to be loaned to the young to set them up in business, a Yeoman of the Guard (d 1577 at 94), Richard Montpesson, kneeling by the altar steps... There are no monuments to Caxton, buried in the old churchyard, nor to Walter Raleigh executed in Old Palace Yard on 29 October 1618 and buried beneath the high altar, although he is commemorated in the west window, presented in late 19C by citizens of the USA. The east window is unique: it was made in Flanders in 1501 at the command of Ferdinand and Isabella of Spain to celebrate the marriage of their daughter, Catherine, to Prince Arthur; but by the time it arrived Arthur was dead, the widowed princess affianced to the future Henry VIII. The window was despatched outside London and only retrieved in 1758 when the House of Commons purchased it for 400 guineas and presented it to the church. The carved limewood reredos of 1753 is based on Titian's *Supper at Emmaus.*

St Margaret's is the House of Commons' church not only through the Palace of Westminster lying within the parish but by a tradition inaugurated on Palm Sunday 1614 when the Commons met for the first time for corporate communion and, being mostly Puritains, preferred the church to the abbey.

A **Garden of Remembrance** flowers in November each year in the churchyard.

■ WESTMINSTER ROMAN CATHOLIC CATHEDRAL★

Open daily 7am to 8pm; Good Friday, Easter Saturday from 9am; Easter Sunday 7.30am; 25, 26 December 7am to 4.30pm. Campanile (view of Westminster and the Thames) lift, 15p.

Italian Byzantine in 20C Victoria. – The land was in disuse in 1884 when Cardinal Manning purchased it as the site for a new cathedral. It had been a derelict marsh centuries before when the Benedictines of Westminster Abbey had originally taken it over to establish a local produce market and fairground; following the Reformation it was occupied by a maze, public garden, bullring, house of correction and finally a prison which during the Commonwealth held 1 500 Scots taken prisoner at the Battle of Worcester, 1651, pending their deportation.

Cardinal Manning and his successor, Cardinal Vaughan, determined on early Christian inspiration for the architecture of the new cathedral in that age of neo-Gothicism, perhaps in part, because as a second building in Westminster, they had no wish to emulate the style in which the great abbey had been achieved centuries before.

The architect, **J F Bentley** travelled widely in Italy before producing in 1894, Byzantine-Italian plans which promptly began to be executed (1895) and by 1903 had been completed so far as the fabric was concerned. Within the seven years 12½ million bricks had been laid and there had arisen a building 360ft long × 156ft wide, distinguished by a domed campanile 273ft high.

The interior. – The initial impression is of vastness and fine proportions – the nave, the widest in England, is roofed with three domes. The decoration has still to be completed and unpointed bare brick walls, awaiting mosaics, rise above the lower surfaces and piers, faced with coloured marble and granite. The eye follows the successively raised levels of the nave, chancel and apse. The altar, beneath its baldacchino with yellow marble columns, is dominated by a suspended crucifix. On the main piers are the 14 Stations of the Cross, distinctive low reliefs over beautifully incised lettering by Eric Gill (sculptor and type face designer, one of whose founts has been used in this volume).

The second chapel off the north aisle contains the body of the English martyr, John Southworth, hanged, drawn and quartered at Tyburn in 1654. By the south transept are an early 15C statue of the Virgin and Child, carved by the Nottingham school in alabaster which originally stood in the abbey (replica now there), was removed for five centuries to France and returned in 1955, also a bronze of St Teresa of Lisieux by Giacomo Manzu and a chi-rho, executed in flat headed nails, by David Partridge.

The cathedral is known for its music.

ENVIRONS *(Map pp 5-8, EY)*

Victoria St. – The street is now almost totally 20C, with point blocks and towers of steel, brown glass, stone, marble facing and concrete; all angles and canted corners but, for the pedestrian below, half a mile of covered way before shop windows. International oil and chemical companies, Westminster City Hall, **New Scotland Yard,** government ministries, flank the diagonal, cut last century through Georgian Westminster to link Parliament and Victoria Railway Station (1862).

Punctuating the street on its south side are Ashley Place piazza before the cathedral, Artillery Row leading to Vincent Sq *(see below)* and Strutton Ground (market) which continues as the ancient Horseferry Rd to Lambeth Bridge.

The file of new buildings along the north side of Victoria St is marked at its west end by the Victoria Palace Theatre of 1910 and nearby period pub and, halfway along, by the garden in front of **Caxton Hall,** a building of 1878 which one finds for the event occurring inside, not to look at in itself. Further back are St James's Park Underground Station and London Transport headquarters by Charles Holden (1927-9) with decorative statuary groups by Jacob Epstein and reliefs by Eric Gill, Henry Moore and others.

Vincent Sq. – The vast square was laid out in 1810 on part of the former Tothill Fields in order that its centre might provide playing fields for Westminster School. Along the length of the northeast side are **Westminster Technical College** (1893 with post-war extensions) and the high square brick building of the **Royal Horticultural Society** (f 1804), with at the back the New Agricultural Hall (1923-8), famous for its individual flower shows held almost continuously throughout the year *(open to non-members).*

Greycoat School. – *Greycoat Place.* The grey uniform of this Westminster Charity school, founded in 1698, can be seen on the small wooden figures in niches contrasting puritanically with the brilliantly coloured royal coat of arms set between them on the pedimented stucco. Greencoat Place, nearby, housed a green liveried school (1633).

Queen Anne's Gate★. – *(Map p 135).* The street dates from when the queen was on the throne and is decorated with a statue of her as a very young woman. It is as built with substantial 2½ bayed, three storeyed, terrace houses of now darkened brick on either side. The sash windows are square beneath continuous eaves and wide courses, the pilastered doorways, in several instances, protected by flat hoods richly carved and decorated with angle and centre pendants. The street's hall-mark is the satyrs' white masks set in place of tablet stones above the ground and first floor windows of every house. No 15, at the southeast corner, avoids the right angle with a canted wall, and around a second corner, between blocked windows, provides the background for Queen Anne.

Beyond Cockpit Steps, leading down in the days of Whitehall Palace to the pit and now to Birdcage Walk, is Old Queen St, incomplete but with several 18C houses still – note the rounded hood on corbels at no 28.

History. — The square was laid out by Nash in 1820 as part of a proposed north-south communication between Bloomsbury and Westminster. It was placed on the open space at the meeting of the Strand and King St, later Whitehall, an age old site on the edge of the village of Charing which had been marked in 1290 by the last of the Eleanor Crosses (destroyed by the Puritans in 1647) and since 1675 by the statue of Charles I. It was overlooked from the southeast by the early 17C Northumberland House, mediaeval and magnificent with a lion over the gateway *(p 149)*, and from the north by St Martin-in-the-Fields and the Royal Mews, soon replaced by the National and National Portrait Galleries. Of Nash's proposed connecting roads Pall Mall East was built, St Martin's Lane was straightened at the north end and Charing Cross Rd, laid (1880s). The square, begun in 1829, was only completed in 1840s when Charles Barry levelled it and constructed the north terrace as a frontispiece to the National Gallery and the column itself was erected. The remodelled clover-leaf fountains appear to greatest advantage at night when floodlit.

The monuments: Nelson, a small man in life, is here three times lifesize in a sculpture 17ft 4½ ins tall. The monument including the pedestal decorated with bronze reliefs cast from French cannon, fluted granite column, bronze capital and the admiral, stands 185ft overall. The lions by **Landseer** (20ft long, 11ft high) were mounted in 1867, twenty five years after the column was erected. Against the north terrace wall are Imperial Standards of Length and busts of 20C admirals, on the south corner plinths, two 19C generals (also to the south two lamps from or after those on the *Victory* — the east one on a police observation post). The northwest pedestal is empty, the northeast one occupied by an equestrian figure of George IV, commissioned by the king for Marble Arch. The bronze never made the arch and only reached the square in 1843!

Charles I.

Charles I was cast by **Hubert Le Sueur** in Covent Garden in 1633 (date and signature on left forefoot) where it stood until discovered in St Paul's crypt by Cromwell's men in 1655. It was sold "for the rate of old brass, by the pound rate" to a brazier who made a fortune from "relics" in theory made from the statue which actually he kept intact. Eventually it was purchased for £1 600 by Charles II and set up overlooking the execution site (wreath-laying 30 January (11am) by Royal Stuart Society). Before and behind the National Gallery are **James II** by Grinling Gibbons, **George Washington** after Houdon (marble in Richmond, Virginia) and Henry Irving. On the island is Nurse **Edith Cavell.**

The buildings: St Martin-in-the-Fields★. — The church is known in dis-associated ways: for its spire, as the church where actors' memorial services are often held and, since the 30s, as an open door for the unemployed and down-and-out.

Gibbs, in 1722-6, designed the present church which is at least the third on the site, one being mentioned in 1222 and a rebuilding recorded in 1544. The steeple, towering in 18C above the surrounding slums, rises by 5 stages to a pillared, octagonal lantern and concave obelisk spire. Before the west front, he set an outstanding Corinthian portico, crowned by a triangular pediment bearing the royal arms — Buckingham Palace stands within the parish. Inside the interior is dark beneath a barrel vault supported on tall columns which carry the arches and support galleries to north, south and west. In the former churchyard are buried Nell Gwynn (d 1687), George Farquhar the playwright (d 1707), J F Roubiliac (d 1762) and Thomas Chippendale (d 1779).

London Coliseum. — *St Martin's Lane.* The theatre was built in 1904 by Sir Oswald Stoll to rival Drury Lane. Retained marble pillars, terracotta front, electrically lit globe winking against the night sky, combined with an interior refurbishing have transformed it, since 1968, into the home of the former Sadler's Wells now the **English National Opera.**

Post Office. — *St Martin's Pl.* The 1960s building with a very long counter — and long queues for first day covers — is open 24 hours a day, 7 days a week (*poste restante* etc).

Admiralty Arch *(qv)* **and Spring Gardens.** — The 17C pleasure garden frequented by Pepys, became the site of the first LCC office and is now a court with modern statuary.

Canada House. — The house, which occupies the square's west side is a Classical building of golden Bath stone erected in 1824-7 by Sir Robert Smirke jointly for the Royal College of Physicians *(qv)* and the former Union Club.

Traditions. — The square is associated with political rallies especially; about 50 000 can mass around the column at a time.

Since the war each year the Norwegian nation has sent a **Christmas Tree** which stands in the square from about mid December and at night is lit up. The first lighting is performed by the ambassador accompanied by Norwegians in national costume who open the carol singing which continues nightly around the tree and a crib until Christmas.

On New Year's Eve revellers congregate at midnight to hear the chimes of Big Ben.

Palace of Whitehall. — Henry's confiscation of Wolsey's London palace in 1529 was a matter of convenience as well as concupiscence. The property dated back to mid 13C when it had passed by bequest to the See of York; in 1514 Wolsey made it his personally, rebuilding, enlarging and enriching it, adding to the grounds until they occupied 23 acres. Henry VIII continued building and increased the royal precinct until it extended from the modern Trafalgar Sq to Westminster Hall, from the river to St James's Park.

Always respected by the early owners of Whitehall was Scotland, a parcel of land until 16C the site of a Scottish royal palace but later built over and the streets named Little, Great **Scotland Yard** etc. The newly formed Metropolitan Police, given an office there in 1829, became known by their address and retained it even when they moved in 1890s further along the Embankment and later, in 1967, to Victoria St.

Tudors and Stuarts continued after Henry to live in and alter Whitehall Palace but William and Mary disliked it and bought Kensington and, after a disastrous fire in 1698, did nothing to restore it. Today there remain Tudor walls and windows in a quad off Downing St (visible behind the Treasury), the end of Queen Mary's Terrace, (a riverside quay and steps built by Wren for the queen in 1691; south end of Horseguards Av) **Henry VIII's Wine Cellar** *(open Saturday afternoons March to September on written application to the Dept of Environment; entrance through Ministry of Defence)* and the Banqueting House.

Banqueting House★★. – *Open Tuesdays to Saturdays, holiday Mondays, 10am to 5pm, Sundays 2 to 5pm, closed 1 January, Good Friday, 24, 25, 26 December; 10p.*

The hall, the third on the site, has been called a memorial to the Stuarts: it was built on the order of James I in 1619; Charles I commissioned the sumptuous ceiling paintings from Rubens in 1629 and stepped onto the scaffold in Whitehall through one of its windows on 30 January 1649; Charles II received the Lords and Commons in the hall on the evening of his restoration on 29 May 1660; after James II's flight in 1689, William and Mary received within it the formal offer of the crown.

Banqueting houses served many purposes: they were the setting for court ceremonial and revelry – the reception of royalty and embassies, state banquets, the distribution of Royal Maundy, touching for the King's Evil, for dancing, music-making and courtly masques.

Inigo Jones, King's Surveyor and famous masque designer, constructed for James I at the centre of the Tudor palace, a Palladian inspired, building. Although the exterior has been refaced in Portland stone (1829 by Soane) and a new north entrance and staircase were added by Wyatt in 1809 (lead bust of Charles I over the door, and bronze of James I by **Le Sueur** inside) and although the interior was put to multifarious uses from 18/20C, it now looks as splendid as in 17C.

Exterior. – The building stands two storeys high above a rusticated basement with an open balustrade at the crest. Note the details: windows alternately pedimented and, above, straight hooded; framing pilasters, advanced centre; balconies, cornice and ornamented frieze.

Interior. – Inside it is empty – a gilded space awaiting players. It has the distinction of being a double cube – 110ft × 55ft × 55ft – circled by a delicate balcony, supported on gilded corbels; above, richly decorated beams quarter the ceiling decorated with Rubens flamboyant **paintings** in praise of James I. (The lower walls in Stuart times would have been hung with Mortlake and other tapestries.) Today it is used for occasional functions when, beneath the chandeliers, it still serves superbly.

WHITEHALL

Text: Westminster p. 168

WHITEHALL - TRAFALGAR SQUARE★★

The government offices which line Whitehall are from the north:

Old Admiralty★ — The Old Admiralty of 1722-6 was, in Horace Walpole's phrase "deservedly veiled by **Mr. Adam's** handsome screen" in 1759-61, a single storey, blind porticoed wall with angle pavilions and a central arch crowned by a low balustrade between winged seahorses. (In 1890s vast terracotta brick additions were made to the rear.)

Horse Guards★. — *The guard is ceremonially mounted daily at 11am (10am Sundays) in the forecourt by the Queen's Life Guard (the detachment can also be seen riding from and to Knightsbridge). For Trooping the Colour: p 30.*

The low 18C stonefaced edifice designed symmetrically by **William Kent** around three sides of a shallow forecourt, is pierced by a central arch and marked above, like its mid 17C predecessor on the same site, by a clock tower. The building, without adornment, is completed by the statue like presence of the Household Cavalry sentries, the Life Guards in scarlet tunics and white plumed helmets, the Blues and the Royals, in blue with red plumes. On the parade where the Colour is Trooped are two memorials, the **Guards'** (1926) and **Cadiz**, a joyous fantasy of 1812, incorporating an original French mortar supported on the back of a winged and scaly Welsh (or Chinese?) dragon!

Scottish Office (Dover House), **Welsh Office** (Gwydyr House). — The 18C houses, both named after 19C owners are, in the latter case, open to the street, the only ornament a Venetian window above a tripartite door and in the former, a tall screen with an advanced porch designed by Henry Holland for the then owner, Frederick, Duke of York, in 1787.

Old Treasury. — Treasuries have stood on the site since 16C. The present one of 1845 by Barry, utilising the columns from the building by his predecessor, Soane, was the first of the phase of government building which has continued to 20C. The current style is exemplified in the monolithic **Ministry of Defence** opposite. The small, jaunty, bronze before the MoD, is of Sir Walter Raleigh, beheaded nearby.

Downing St. — No 10 has been the residence of the PM since 1731 when Sir Robert Walpole accepted it *ex-officio* from George II. The "four or five very large and well built houses, fit for persons of honour and quality, each having a pleasant prospect of St James's Park", were erected in 1680s by Sir George Downing, diplomat, courtier and general opportunist of the Commonwealth and Restoration. The speculation was successful. The row was rebuilt in 1720s. No 10 contains the **Cabinet Room** and staircase, on which hang portraits of each successive resident, and outside, since 1732, bootscrapers — a domestic reminder of the condition of even main thoroughfares in 18C London.

The Cenotaph. — The slim white monument by Lutyens (1919), is without any effigy; the horizontal lines are very shallowly arced, the vertical converge 1 000ft up in the sky; flags stir in the wind on either side. Whether in the weekday rush of traffic, solitary at night, the focal point on Remembrance Sunday, it says all.

Home Office, Foreign and Commonwealth Offices and Treasury. — The two Victorian-Italian palazzo style buildings of 1868-73 and 1898-1912 are best known for the Treasury door on St George St, from which the chancellor goes to the House on Budget Day and the Home Office balcony overlooking the Cenotaph from which members of the Royal Family observe the Remembrance Sunday service.

Parliament Square. — The square and Parliament St, laid out in 1750 when the first Westminster Bridge was being built, was most recently redesigned in 1951. The bronze statues are of **Churchill** by Ivor Roberts Jones, **Smuts** by Jacob Epstein, **Palmerston,** Derby — note the pedestal reliefs: the old Commons in 1833 — **Disraeli, Peel, Canning** and **Lincoln. Boadicea** can be seen by the bridge heroically riding her chariot.

Oliver Cromwell, one of London's most telling statues, by Hamo Thornycroft, stands before Westminster Hall and **Richard Lionheart,** in Old Palace Yard.

Middlesex Guildhall. — The hall, which has been described as *art nouveau* Gothic, stands richly embossed with figures beneath an extraordinarily turreted tower.

██ WOOLWICH (Greenwich) _____

Woolwich. — The fishing village was transformed firstly by the Tudor monarchs into the most important naval dockyards in the country (*Great Harry* was built there in 1512 in Henry VIII's time) and secondly in 1716-7, when the gun casting works were transferred from Moorfields and it became the **Royal Arsenal** (maximum extent 1914-18: 1 200 acres, 80 000 men and women; closed 1963 except for research).

Royal Artillery Museums. — The town is now the base of the RA which occupies, besides barracks, the 720ft long, arcaded former **Royal Military Academy** (f 1741; amalgamated with Sandhurst 1964). **R A Museum** — history of the regiment: *open Mondays to Fridays 10am to noon, 2 to 4.30pm.*

The **Rotunda Museum,** up the hill, contains 18/20C "hardwear" :*open daily 10am to 12.45pm (noon on Saturdays) 2 to 5pm (winter 4pm); closed 1 January, Good Friday, 25, 26 December.*

This most elegant of small museums began as a campaign tent designed by John Nash in 1814 for the somewhat premature celebrations, held in St James's Park, by the allied sovereigns of the defeat of Napoleon. In 1819 the Prince Regent ordered the tent's reerection at Woolwich "to house military curiosities".

Thamesmead. — The architecture of the town, 11 miles from Charing Cross on 1 500 acres of marshland with a 3 mile river frontage and an estimated population of 50 000 by the year 2000, has been described as "persistant — sharp and invigorating".

The ZOO ★★★ (Regent's Park, Westminster)

Open: every day except Christmas Day; March to October 9am, November to February 10am to 6pm (7pm Sundays and holiday Mondays), or sunset if earlier; adults £1.40, children 70p; aquarium 20p, children 10p; children's zoo free.

Noah's Ark. – The Zoological Society of London and the Zoo developed from the aim proposed to an audience of scientists by Sir Stamford Raffles in 1826 of founding a society for "the advancement of Zoology and Animal Physiology and the introduction of new and curious subjects of the Animal Kingdom". The first part has been so far achieved that conservation of species in the wild state and even their re-introduction where extinct, is now a major objective. Landmarks along the way have been the contribution by members and the zoo's staff to systematic anatomy, the establishment in 1962 and 1964 of the Wellcome Institute of Comparative Physiology and the Nuffield Institute of Comparative Medicine, to study reproductive physiology (including human fertility), biochemistry and disease which affect diet, health and husbandry.

The second part of Sir Stamford's phrase has resulted, since 1828 when the society opened on a 5 acre site in Regent's Park with a small collection of animals looked after by a keeper in a top hat, bottle green coat and striped waistcoat, in today's collection of over 6 000 animals of 1 162 species on a 36 acre corner of the park, cared for by a staff, including research workers, of more than one hundred. A large proportion of the animals are now bred in Regent's Park and at Whipsnade.

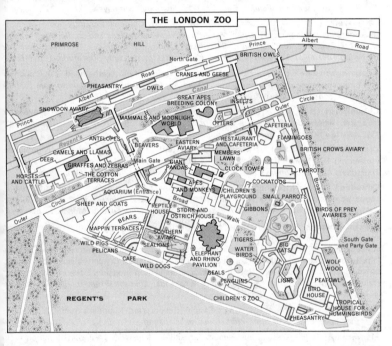

Housing. – The gardens were originally laid out by **Decimus Burton** who also designed several buildings of which there remain the Ravens' Cage on the Members' Lawn, the Clock Tower and the Giraffe House. Houses for all animals from tropical climates were kept heated and closed until the turn of the century when Carl Hagenbeck at the Hamburg Zoo revolutionised current practice by providing paddocks for tropical animals and surrounding enclosures not with bars but moats and ditches; the first effect in London was the construction in 1914 of the Mappin Terraces and, in imaginative extension, the founding on 480 acres of derelict Bedfordshire farmland, of Whipsnade (1931).

Since 1930s the Zoo has been the setting of often highly innovative architecture: the Great Apes Breeding Colony (1933) and the Penguin Pool (1934) with intersecting spiral ramps, both by Lubetkin (the pool, the first example of such use of pre-stressed concrete is now a scheduled building). In the last twenty years there have been the Cotton Terraces (1963), which in new pavilions and Burton's altered Giraffe House, house giraffes and zebras, camels and llamas, horses and cattle, antelope and deer (Père David herd); the distinctively roofed Elephant and Rhino Pavilion by Casson (1965); the 150ft by 80ft high Snowdon Aviary (1965), which in summer contains as many as 150 birds in natural surroundings and through which the visitor passes on an elevated walkway, and the Charles Clore Pavilion for Small Mammals (1967) with its **Moonlight World**, where one sees animals only active at night.

In 1972 there arose the Michael Sobell Pavilions for Apes and Monkeys (Guy and other gorillas; also the giant pandas Ching-Ching and Chia-Chia) and in 1976, the New Lion Terraces, a series of tree and greenery planted enclosures from which the big cats survey lesser mortals.

London Zoo and Whipsnade (p 184) are complementary and together house one of the world's most comprehensive collections of wild animals.

IDEAS FOR AN EXCURSION

Ascott House★★ (AC). – Wing, SW of Leighton Buzzard. Anthony de Rothschild collection of paintings, French and Chippendale furniture, Oriental porcelain. *Open April to September Wednesdays, Saturdays, holiday Mondays, July and August, Sundays also, 2 to 6pm; garden 40p; house 50p. NT.*

Audley End★ (BC). – Saffron Walden. Jacobean mansion with additional Adam decoration; wooded park by Capability Brown. *Open daily April to September 10am to 5.30pm, October to March Sundays 11am to 3.30pm; 50p. D of E.*

Ayot St Lawrence: Lullingstone Silk Farm, Ayot House (AC). – Raw silk from the silkworm egg to the reeled hank. *Open April to September, Mondays to Fridays 10am to 1pm, 2 to 6pm, Sundays 2 to 6pm; 50p.* **Shaw's Corner.** – GBS' home 1906-1950. *Open April to November, Wednesday to Sunday and holiday Mondays 11am to 1pm, 2 to 6pm or sunset if earlier; closed Good Friday; 50p. NT.*

Bekonscot Model Village (AC). – Warwick Rd, Beaconsfield. Houses, stone churches, castle, rlwy, shops, cricket green, race course extending over an area of 40 000sq ft. *Open daily 10am to 6pm (4pm in winter); closed Christmas holiday; 30p, children 15p.*

Bluebell Rlwy and Museum (BD). – Sheffield Park Station, Uckfield. Vintage steam engines etc. *Trains to Horsted Keynes (60p rtn) daily June to September, March to May, October, November weekends; December to February, Sundays.*

Chartwell★ (BD). – Westerham. Sir Winston and Lady Churchill's country home; mementoes; gardens (yellow roses). *Open March to November (gardens and studio, April to mid-October) Tuesdays to Thursdays, Saturdays, Sundays and holiday Mondays (but not following Tuesdays) 2 to 6pm or sunset if earlier; 80p, garden only 30p, studio 10p. NT.*

Chessington Zoo★ (AD). – On A 243 between Surbiton and Leatherhead. 1 000 animals and birds, miniature rlwy, summer circus. *Open April to September 9.30am to 5pm (weekends and school holidays 6pm); 65p, children 35p.*

Chislehurst (BD). – Prehistoric chalk caves. *Open Easter to October daily (November to Easter, weekends only) 11am to 5.30pm; "ordinary" 35 minute tour – 30p; "long" 1½ hour Sundays only 3pm tour – 40p.*

Claydon House★ (AC). – Middle Claydon, NW of Aylesbury. Florence Nightingale museum in 18C house; rococo state rooms. *Open April to October, weekends, Tuesdays to Thursdays, holiday Mondays (but not following Tuesdays), 2 to 6pm; 60p.*

Cliveden★ (AC). – Maidenhead. 19C house surrounded by formal, rose, water gdns; herbaceous borders. *Open: house April to October Wednesdays, weekends, 2.30 to 5.30pm; gardens March to November. Wednesdays to Sundays and holiday Mondays; 80p. NT.*

Crystal Palace★ (BD). – National Sports Centre, Penge. Centre with excellent indoor and outdoor facilities (Olympic indoor pool, squash, badminton, tennis, skiing, fencing, athletics, hockey, cricket etc; 17 000 seat stadium); *membership obligatory to play, visitors 20p.* In the park, site of the re-erected 1851 Great Exhibition Crystal Palace until it burnt down in 1936, the endearing, brightly coloured, exhibition monsters (lake in SW corner), children's zoo *(open Easter to September weekends, holidays 11am to 6pm, term time weekdays 1.30 to 5.30pm),* boating.

Eton College★★ (AD). – 15C King's Chapel, School Yard (founder's statue: Henry VI); grounds; *open daily 2 to 5pm, chapel also at evensong.*

Flamstead (AC). – West of Harpenden. Attractive village with 14 and 15C church with Perpendicular screen and wall paintings.

Forty Hall (BC). – Forty Hill, Enfield. 17C mansion in its own park; furniture; local museum. *Open Easter to September 10am to 8pm (weekends, holiday Mondays to 6pm), October to Easter 10am to 5pm; closed Mondays.*

Greensted-juxta-Ongar (BC). – St Andrew's Anglo Saxon church of 850 AD, only surviving example of a split oak trunk construction; 17C shingled spire.

Greys Court★ (AC). – Rotherfield Greys, Henley-on-Thames. 16C house with 18C furniture and plasterwork; gardens, mediaeval ruins, Tudor donkey water wheel; Carlisle Collection of miniature rooms. *Open April to September: house Mondays, Wednesdays, Fridays; gardens Mondays to Saturdays 2.15 to 6pm; closed Good Friday; gardens 50p, house 10p, Carlisle Collection 20p. NT.*

Guildford (AD). – Cathedral of the Holy Spirit, Stag Hill: 1936-1961 by Sir Edward Maufe in simplified Gothic style in local brick; contemporary work by artists and craftsmen. *Open June to August 9am to 7pm (September to May to 5pm).* – University of Surrey, Stag Hill, 1966. – Yvonne Arnaud Theatre, by the River Wey, 1965. – **Loseley House** (west of Guildford), an Elizabethan mansion of stone from Waverley Abbey, including panelling from Nonsuch Palace; plasterwork; grounds and Loseley Park Farm. *Open June to September Wednesdays to Saturdays and holiday Mondays, 2 to 5pm; 45p.*

Harrow (AC). – Buildings 19C; old school (f 1571), speech room, chapel and war memorial, *open by appt only (Tel 01-422 1455).* **Kodak Museum**, Headstone Drive, Wealdstone, *open Monday to Friday 9.30am to 4.30pm by appt only (Tel 01-427 4380; ext 76).*

Hatfield House★★ (BC). – Splendid Jacobean mansion and surviving Tudor palace wing surrounded by gardens and parkland; famous portraits and relics of Queen Elizabeth. *Open late March to September daily including holiday Mondays (otherwise closed Mondays) 12 noon to 5pm, Sundays 2 to 5.30pm; 80p.*

Hever Castle★ (BD). – Edenbridge. Late 13 and 15C moated castle (birthplace of Anne Boleyn) in extensive grounds; formal Italian garden, fountains, statuary. *Open April to September, Wednesdays, Sundays, holiday Mondays, gardens to 7pm, castle 2 to 5.30pm; gardens 30p, castle 50p (extra days with extra rooms, Tuesdays, Fridays: £1).*

Hughenden Manor★ (AC). – High Wycombe. Rebuilt by Disraeli in 1847 as his country seat; Victorian furniture, letters, portraits etc. *Open February to November, Wednesdays to Fridays 2 to 6pm, weekends and holiday Mondays 12.30 to 6pm; closed Good Friday; 50p. NT.*

Hunting Lodge (BC). – Epping Forest, Ranger's Rd, Chingford. Queen Elizabeth's lodge, a Tudor timber framed building; forestry museum. *Open Wednesdays to Sundays and holiday Mondays 2 to 6pm (or dusk if earlier); closed 25, 26 December; 10p.*

Ightham Mote★ (BD). – Ivy Hatch. 600 year old moated manorhouse. *Open Fridays April to October 2 to 5pm, November to March till dusk; 35p.*

Kent and E Sussex Light Rlwy (BD). – Tenterden. *Open June to August, Wednesdays, Saturdays, Sundays; April, May, September, October, weekends; March, November, December, Sundays only; open holiday Mondays.* – Ellen Terry Museum, Smallhythe Place. *Open March to October daily except Tuesdays and Fridays, 2 to 6pm or dusk if earlier. NT.*

Knebworth House★ (AC). – Off M1, south of Stevenage. Tudor mansion remodelled in 1843 by Sir Edward Bulwer Lytton, statesman and novelist. Park: deer, bird gdn; adventure playground. *Open daily April to September; closed Mondays except holiday Mondays, October Sundays only; 11.30am to 5.30pm; house 35p, park 40p.*

Knole★★ (BD). – Sevenoaks. Vast 15C house with Jacobean interior; 17, 18C furniture, paintings; beautiful wooded park. *Open March to November, Wednesdays to Saturdays, holiday Mondays 10am to noon, 2 to 5pm (3.30pm March and November), Sundays 2 to 5pm (3.30pm November); 70p. NT. Connoisseurs' day Fridays (not Good Friday), extra rooms £1. Garden 1st Wednesday in month, May to September 20p. (NB: many rooms have no electric lighting – choose a bright day.)*

Leeds Castle★ (BD). – Near Maidstone. The "castle of the mediaeval queens of England"; water and woodland gardens. *Open April to September, Tuesdays to Thursdays, Sundays, holiday Mondays, 1 to 5.30pm; grounds 60p plus 60p for castle.*

Lullingstone Roman Villa (BD). – Off A 225 south of Dartford. Excavated villa with painted walls and extensive mosaics (under cover). *Open March, April, October weekdays 9.30am to 5.30pm, Sundays from 2pm, April from 9.30am; May to September weekdays and Sundays 9.30am to 7pm; November to February 9.30am to 4pm; Sundays from 2pm; 30p. D of E.* – Eynsford Castle; 12C ruin: *same times as villa; 10p.* 13C parish church.

Luton Hoo★★ (AC). – Exit 10 off M1, A6, and Park St. Wernher collection of pictures (Dutch, Italian), tapestries, English china (Bow, Chelsea, Worcester), mediaeval ivories, jewels (Fabergé, Renaissance), small bronzes, silver; mementoes of Russian Imperial Family; park by Capability Brown. *Open: house mid April to September, Monday, Wednesday, Thursday, Saturday 11am to 6pm. Sundays 2pm; 50p; gardens mid April to mid July Wednesdays, Thursdays 11am to 6pm, Sundays 2pm, mid July to September as house; 20p.*

Mapledurham House★ (AD). – NW of Reading off A 4074. Elizabethan house beside the Thames; moulded plaster ceilings, oak staircases, 16, 17, 18C paintings. *Open weekends and holiday Mondays 2.30 to 5.30pm from Easter Sunday to September; 60p. Access also by river from Caversham Bridge, Reading, leaving 2.15pm.*

Moor Park Mansion (AC). – Rickmansworth. 18C reconstruction of Palladian style house incorporating 17C house of James, Duke of Monmouth. *Open Mondays 9.30am to 4.30pm except holiday Mondays; 12 ½ p. (Guided tours in summer 1st Saturday in month).*

Nyman's Gardens (BD). – Handcross, south of Crawley. Walled gardens, rare trees, shrubs, bulbs. *Open April to October, Tuesdays to Thursdays 2 to 7pm or sunset if earlier, Sundays and holiday Mondays from 11am; 40p. NT.*

Penshurst Place★ (BD). – Tonbridge. Great hall of 1340, crypt (armoury). Birthplace of Sir Philip Sidney; state rooms, picture gallery; toy museum. Tudor gdns, orchards, park. *Open daily except Mondays and Fridays, April to September 2pm to 6pm, holiday Mondays 11.30am to 6pm; 75p.*

Petworth House★★ (AD). – Petworth junction A 272 and 283. Late 17C mansion (19C alterations) in park by Capability Brown. Important collection of paintings; Grinling Gibbons carvings. *Open daily except Monday and Friday April to mid October; open holiday Mondays 2 to 6pm; 70p. N.T. Connoisseurs' day, Tuesdays 2 to 6pm; 90p. No dogs. Park open daily.*

Polesden Lacey★★ (AD). – Near Dorking. Regency villa with Edwardian alterations: pictures, tapestries, furniture; famous gardens – roses, herbaceous plants, clipped hedges, beech walks. *Open: house, March, November, weekends only; April to October, Tuesdays (not following holiday Mondays), Wednesdays, Thursdays, weekends and holiday Mondays, 2 to 6pm or sunset if earlier; garden all year daily 11am to sunset; house 70p; gdn 20p. NT.*

Royal Tunbridge Wells (BD). – The Pantiles: arcaded parade of Beau Nash and 17C dandies.

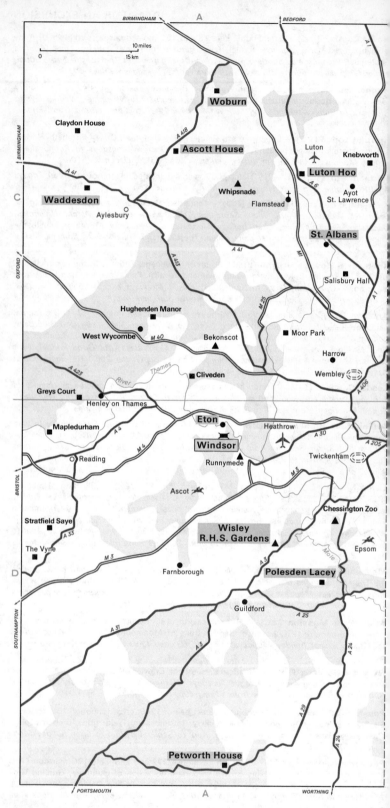

Runnymede (AD). – Northwest of Staines, off A 308. Watermeadow (188 acres) where King John signed *Magna Carta* in 1215 (museum); also President Kennedy memorial (1965).

St Albans★★ (AC). – Cathedral, 11C and every century since; warmly majestic in brick, flint and stone in parkland setting; vast asymmetrically arched nave, wall paintings. *Open daily 7am (Saturdays and Sundays 8am) to 7pm (5pm in winter), Sundays to 6pm.* In the city: old houses, alleys, pubs; Saturday and Wednesday market. **Verulamium:** Roman excavations and museum. *Open daily 10am to 5pm, Sundays 2 to 5.30 (4pm November to March).*

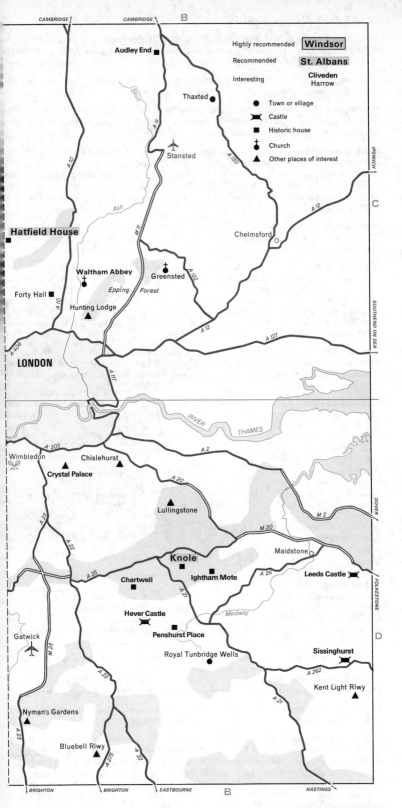

Salisbury Hall (AC). – London Colney. Moated 17C house; staircase, panelling, fireplaces. Charles II, Nell Gwynn, Winston Churchill associations. De Havilland Mosquito aircraft museum; garden. *Open Sundays from Easter to September and from July also Thursdays, 2 to 6pm, holiday Mondays 10.30am to 5.30pm; house 40p, Mosquito museum 20p.*

Sissinghurst Castle★ (BD). – Near Cranbrook. The gardens created by Vita Sackville West and Harold Nicolson – spring, rose, cottage, white and herb, and the "purple border"; Tudor manor house (tower and long library). *Open April to mid October, Mondays to Fridays, noon to 6.30pm; weekends and holiday Mondays from 10am; 70p. NT. No dogs.*

IDEAS FOR AN EXCURSION

Stratfield Saye★ (AD). – South of Reading, off A 33. Carolean house presented to Duke of Wellington 1817; paintings, mementoes (museum); coach house. *Open daily except Fridays, April to September 11am to 5.30pm; 80p.*

Thaxted (BC). – Old wool town, parish church (14C with later 17C additions) and 15C guildhall of three overhanging storeys.

The Vyne (AD). – Near Basingstoke. Diapered early 16C red brick mansion, 17C portico, linenfold panelling, Palladian staircase; grounds. *Open Thursdays, weekends 2 to 6pm, Wednesdays, holiday Mondays also 11am to 1pm; 70p. NT.*

Waddesdon Manor★★ (AC). – Near Aylesbury. 19C manor of Baron Ferdinand de Rothschild; French 17C, 18C furniture; English, Dutch, Flemish, Italian paintings; costume, lace button collections; grounds. *Open April to October, Wednesdays to Sundays 2 to 6pm (grounds: Sundays from 11.30am, holiday Mondays 11am); house and grounds closed Wednesdays after holiday Mondays; house 70p, grounds only 30p. NT. Connoisseurs' day – Fridays £1.*

Waltham Abbey★ (BC). – Waltham Cross. Norman, cathedral scale, pillars and arches; 14, 15C additions and mementoes; attractive abbey gardens. Note the Eleanor Cross in Waltham Cross (main road).

West Wycombe★ (AC). – West of High Wycombe. The village main street retains half-timbered and oversailing, brick and stucco buildings of 15 to 19C *(NT);* West Wycombe House: Palladian house containing fine 18C furniture, paintings, set in landscaped garden and park (farm and forest nature trail). *Open June, Mondays to Fridays, July, August also on Sundays 2.15 to 6pm; 80p, grounds only 30p. NT.* St Lawrence Church: 13C with later additions, paintings, golden ball crowned tower *(view: 10p);* beneath are ¼ mile of caves (18C waxwork scenes etc), *open 2 to 5pm; 50p.*

Whipsnade★ (AC). – Dunstable (M 1 junction 9). Founded 1931 as the country quarters of the London Zoo; over 2 000 animals and birds in beautiful surroundings. *Open every day except Christmas Day, 10am to 7pm or sunset if earlier; £1.25, children 60p, cars extra: £1 (50p in winter).*

Windsor Castle★★★ (AD). – St George's Chapel: *open all the year, except 3 weeks in January, Garter and other ceremonial days, 24, 25 December, 11am (Fridays 1pm, Sundays 2pm in summer, 2.15pm in winter) to 4pm in summer, 3.45 October to April; 30p.* State Apartments when the Queen is not in official residence (see Court Circular in press): *open 10.30am (Sundays 1.30pm) to 5pm early May to mid October, to 3pm mid October to mid March (closed winter Sundays also mid March to early May, most of June and December); 30p.* Old Master Drawings (Holbein, Leonardo), *10p;* Queen Mary's Dolls'

(After photograph, Pitkin Pictorials)

St George's Chapel, Windsor Castle.

House (by Lutyens in 1920s) and exhibition of dolls, *10p – opening times for drawings and Dolls' House as State Apartments.*

Great Park: *open throughout year, sunrise to sunset (Savill Garden near Englefield Green; open March to October 10am to 6pm; 50p);* **Safari Park** (lions, elephants, llamas, dolphins etc) *open daily 10am to dusk; car with 4 passengers £2.50 (holiday Sunday and Mondays £3.00), pedestrians 50p, children 35p; additional charges for some features.*

Wisley, RHS Gardens★★ (AD). – Near Ripley. Superb gardens. *Open all the year, weekdays 10am to 7pm or sunset, Sundays from 2pm; closed 25 December; 60p. No dogs.*

Woburn Abbey and Wild Animal Kingdom★★ (AC). – Northwest of Dunstable on A5. 18C house: French and English furniture, silver, porcelain; Canalettos, Rembrandts, Gainsboroughs, Reynolds...; state apartments. **Park and game reserve;** antiques centre; children's amusements; pub etc. *Abbey open April to October daily from 11.30am to between 5.15 and 5.45pm according to season (Sundays ½ hour later); winter daily 1 to 4.15pm; admission 50p cars, abbey 70p; animal kingdom cars £2.10. Park opens and closes approximately ½ hour earlier throughout.*

Churches, squares, almshouses and pubs have been grouped and galleries also listed together since artists' works, with a few famous exceptions, have not been indexed under the painters' names. Statues are under the subject portrayed. The index is not exhaustive.

Place, street and building names are in roman characters; people, familiar names, historical events, rhymes, etc., in italics *eg* Middlesex St, *Petticoat Lane*, Westminster Abbey, *The Dissolution*, Bank of England, *South Sea Bubble*.

MANUFACTURE FRANÇAISE DES PNEUMATIQUES MICHELIN
© Michelin et Cie, propriétaires-éditeurs, 1977
Société en commandite par actions au capital de 700 millions de francs
R. C. Clermont-Fd B 855 200 507 (55-B-50) - Siège social Clermont-Ferrand (France)
ISBN 2 06 015 430-8

Photocomp. : COUPÉ S.A. - Impression : DÉCHAUX - Printed in France. 6-77-40 - Dépôt légal : 3e trim. 1977.